P9-AFB-799

vol. 2

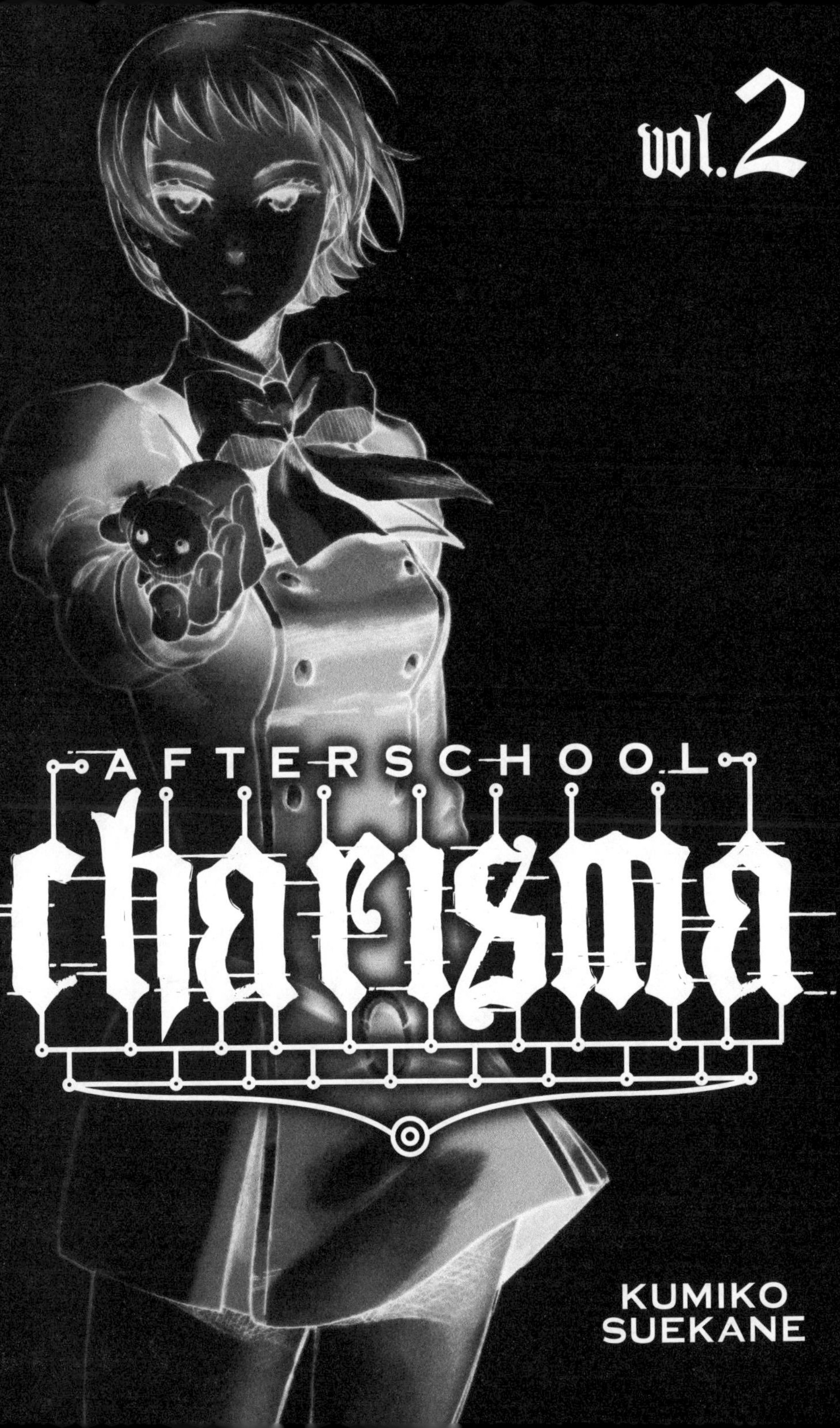
AFTERSCHOOL
charisma

KUMIKO
SUEKANE

afterschool
charisma

c o n t e n t s

CHAPTER seven

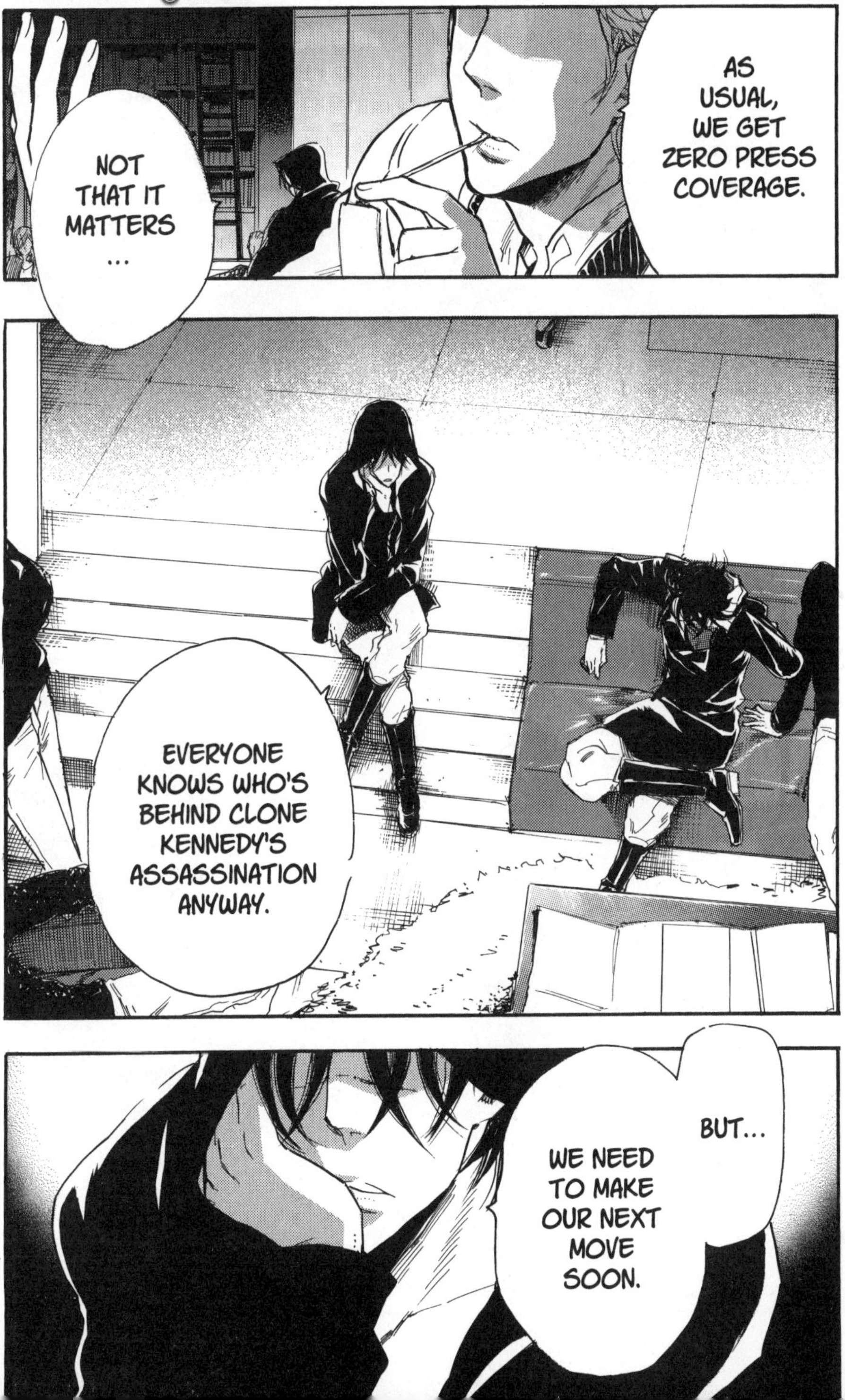
AS USUAL, WE GET ZERO PRESS COVERAGE.
NOT THAT IT MATTERS ...
EVERYONE KNOWS WHO'S BEHIND CLONE KENNEDY'S ASSASSINATION ANYWAY.
BUT...
WE NEED TO MAKE OUR NEXT MOVE SOON.

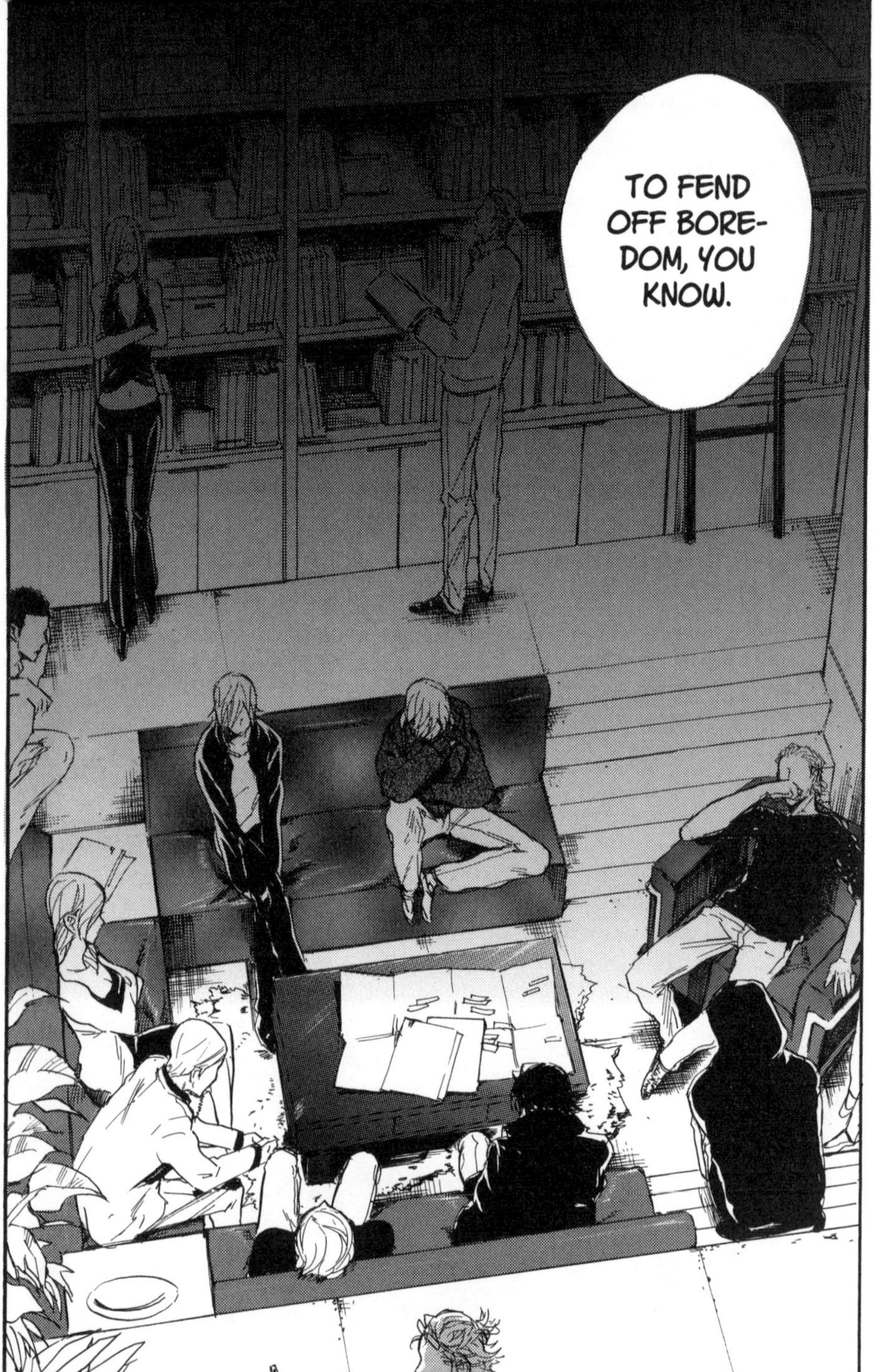
TO FEND OFF BORE-DOM, YOU KNOW.

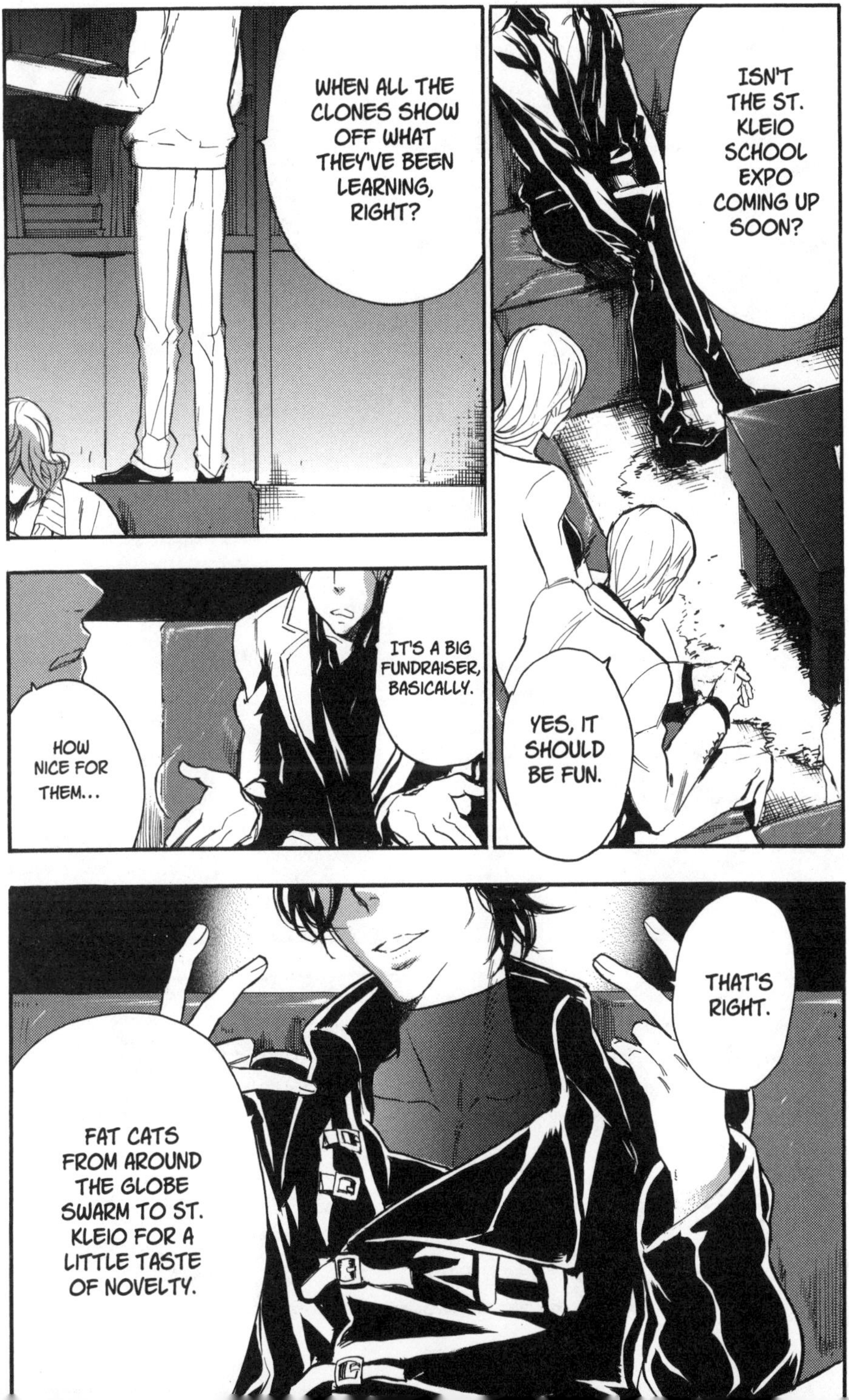
ISN'T THE ST. KLEIO SCHOOL EXPO COMING UP SOON?
YES, IT SHOULD BE FUN.
WHEN ALL THE CLONES SHOW OFF WHAT THEY'VE BEEN LEARNING, RIGHT?
IT'S A BIG FUNDRAISER, BASICALLY.
HOW NICE FOR THEM...
THAT'S RIGHT.
FAT CATS FROM AROUND THE GLOBE SWARM TO ST. KLEIO FOR A LITTLE TASTE OF NOVELTY.

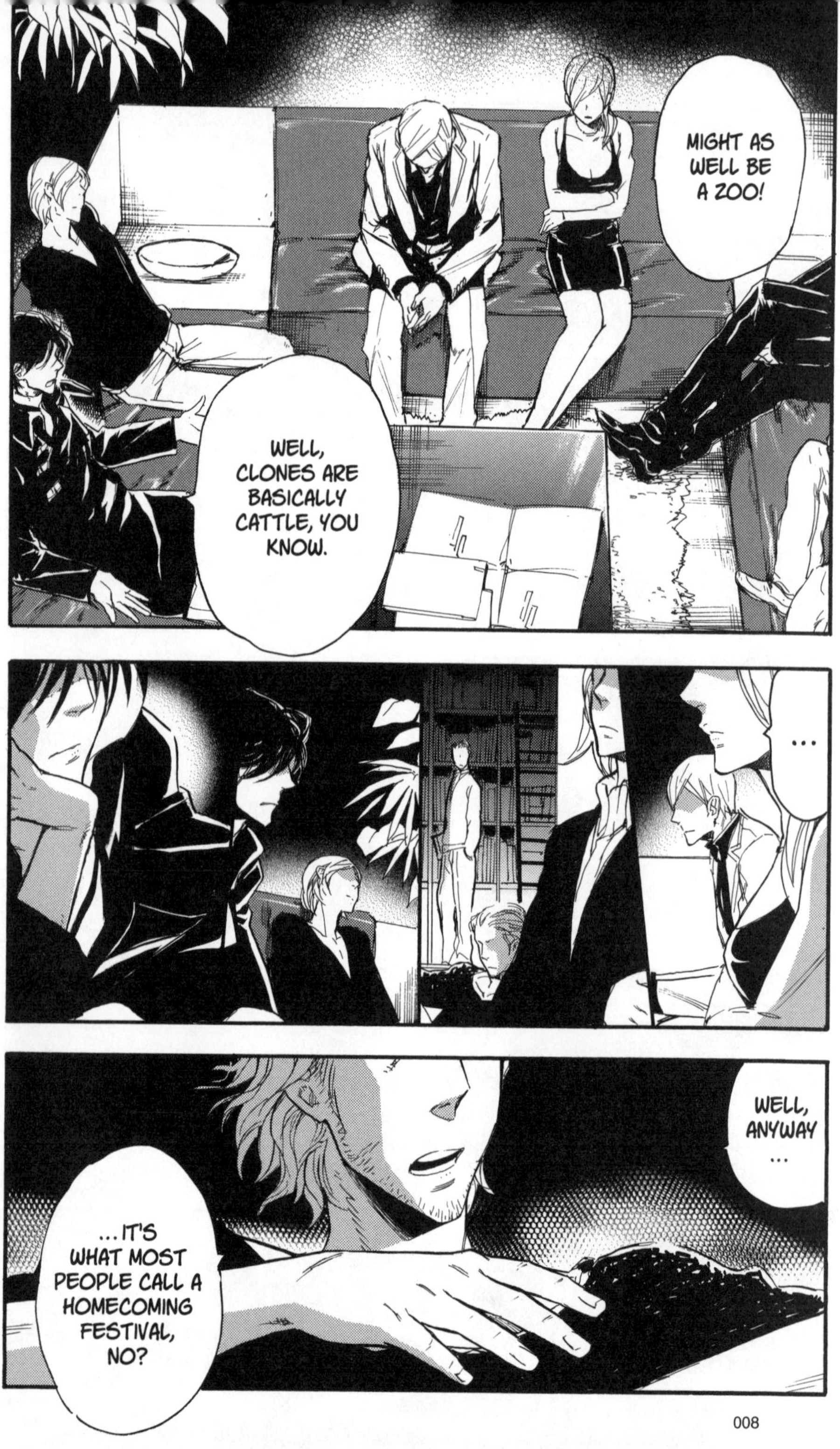
MIGHT AS WELL BE A ZOO!
WELL, CLONES ARE BASICALLY CATTLE, YOU KNOW.
...
WELL, ANYWAY ...
...IT'S WHAT MOST PEOPLE CALL A HOMECOMING FESTIVAL, NO?

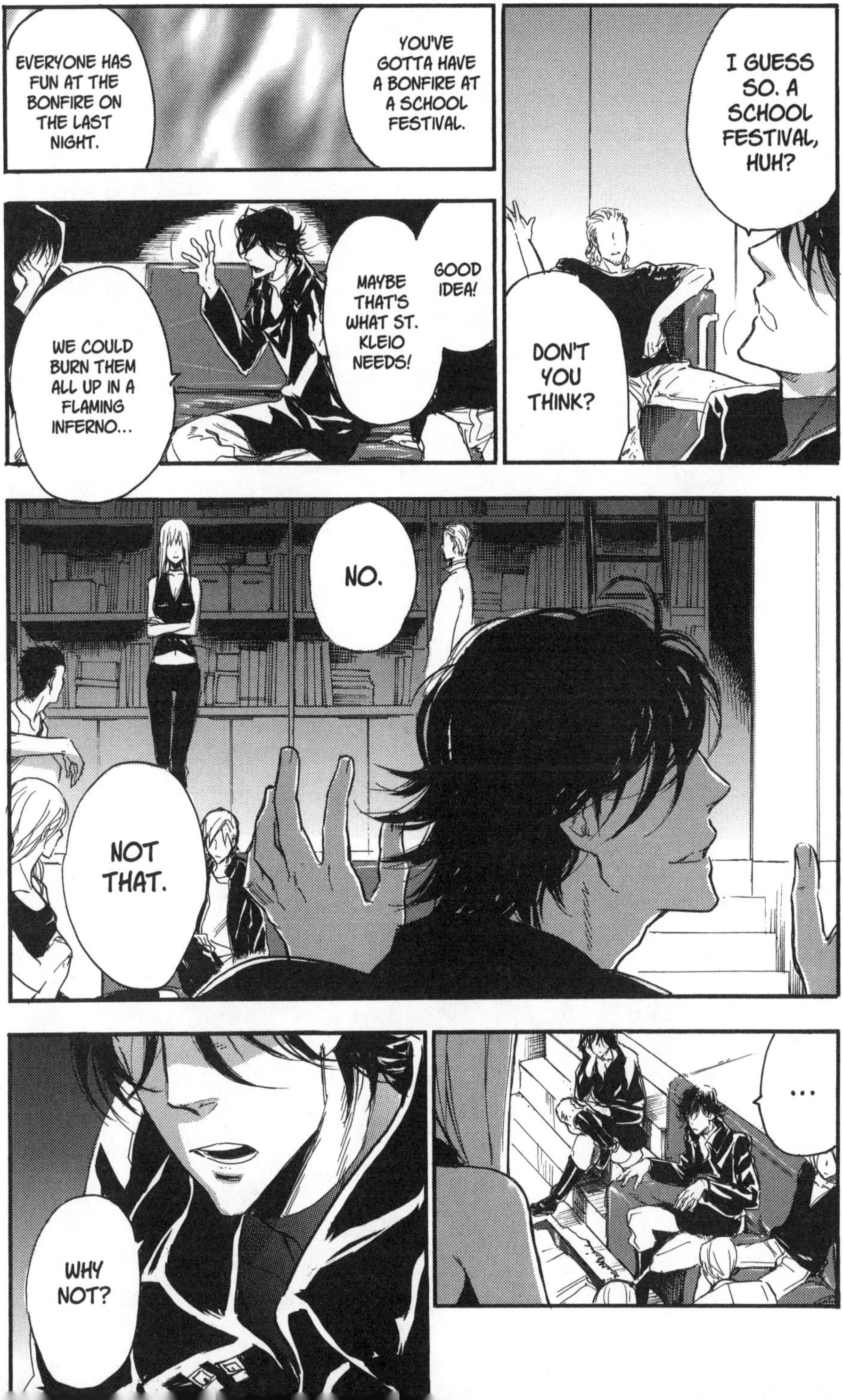
I GUESS SO. A SCHOOL FESTIVAL, HUH?
DON'T YOU THINK?
YOU'VE GOTTA HAVE A BONFIRE AT A SCHOOL FESTIVAL.
EVERYONE HAS FUN AT THE BONFIRE ON THE LAST NIGHT.
GOOD IDEA!
MAYBE THAT'S WHAT ST. KLEIO NEEDS!
WE COULD BURN THEM ALL UP IN A FLAMING INFERNO...
NO.
NOT THAT.
...
WHY NOT?

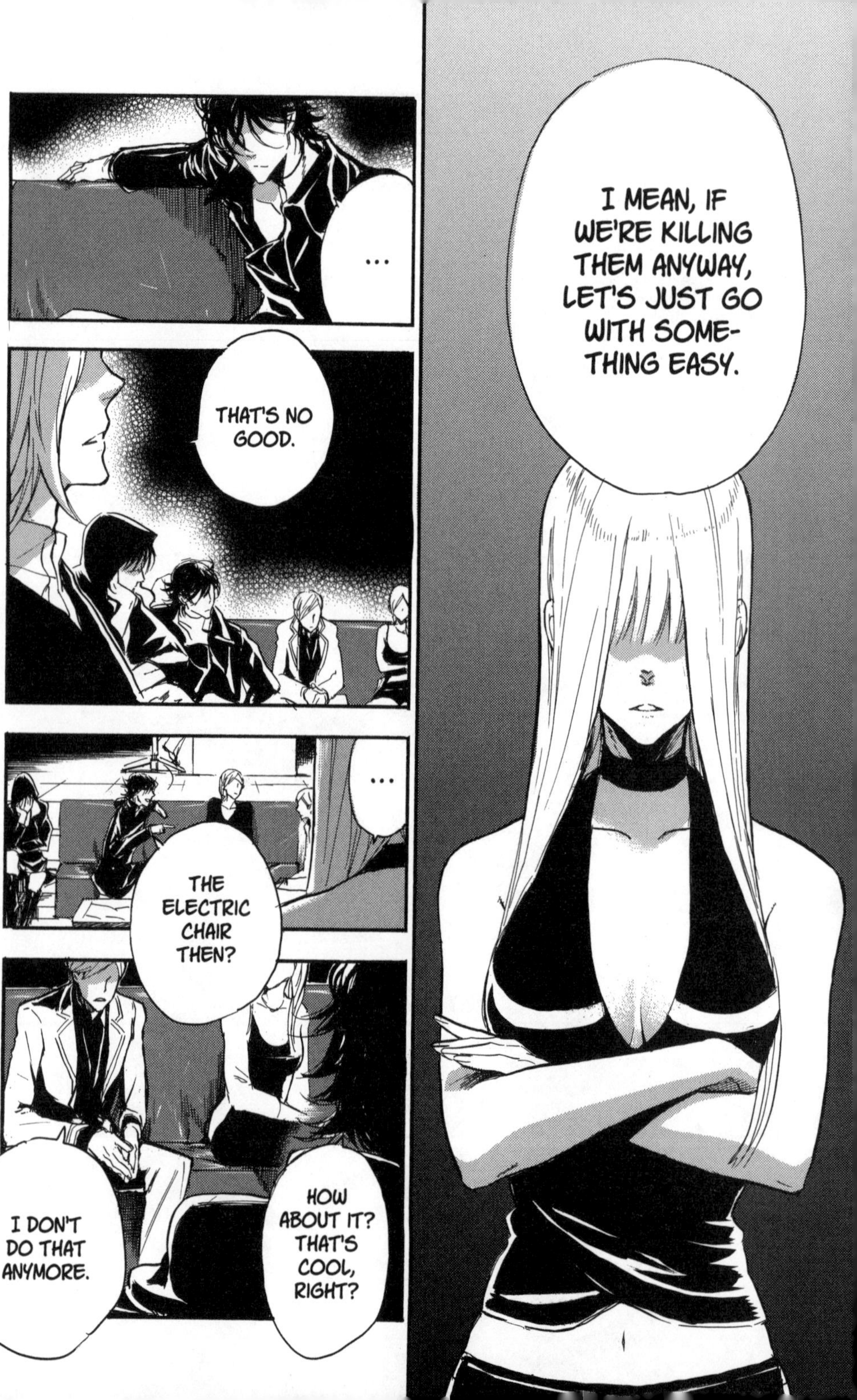
I MEAN, IF WE'RE KILLING THEM ANYWAY, LET'S JUST GO WITH SOME-THING EASY.
...
THAT'S NO GOOD.
...
THE ELECTRIC CHAIR THEN?
HOW ABOUT IT? THAT'S COOL, RIGHT?
I DON'T DO THAT ANYMORE.

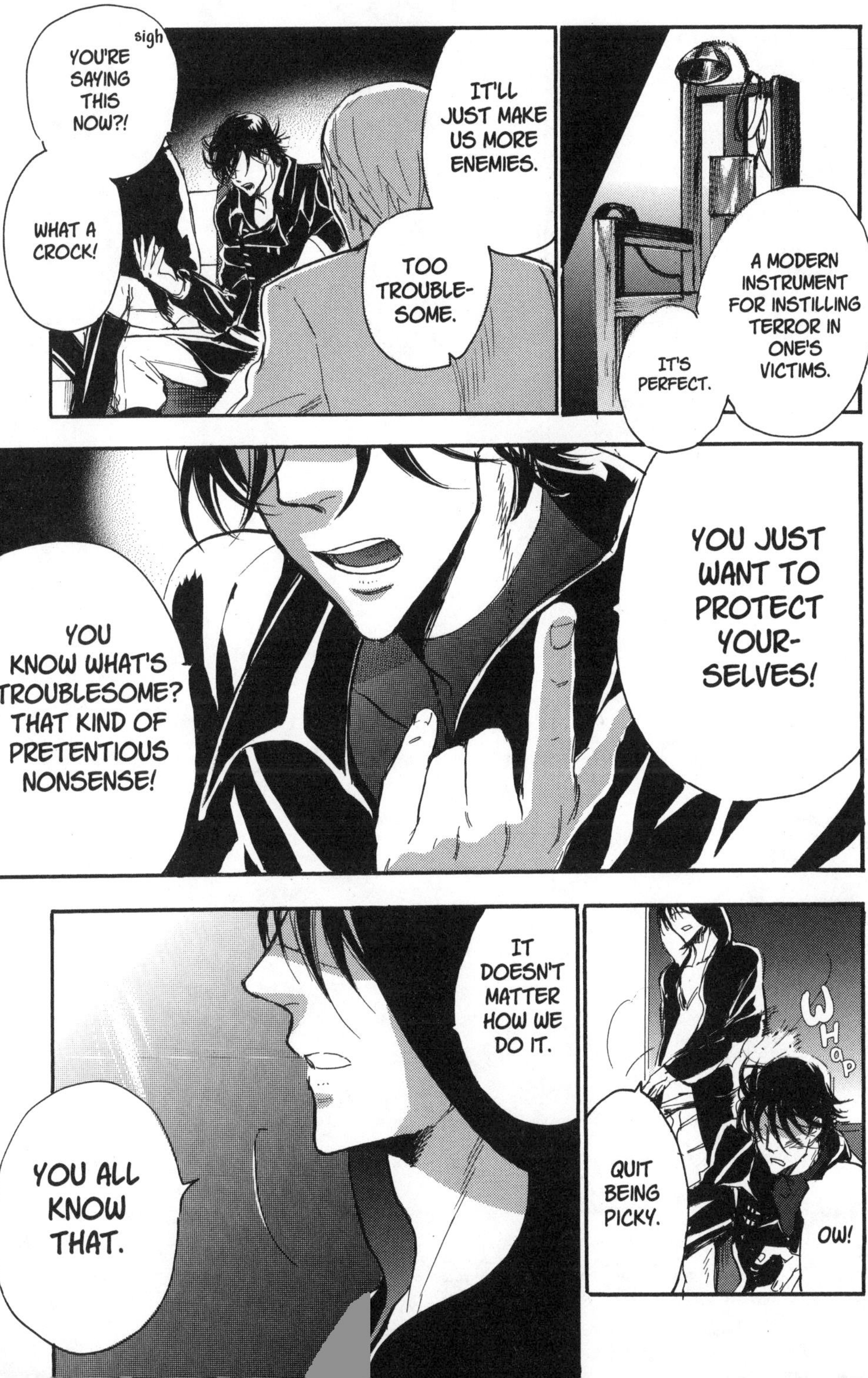
A MODERN INSTRUMENT FOR INSTILLING TERROR IN ONE'S VICTIMS.
IT'S PERFECT.
IT'LL JUST MAKE US MORE ENEMIES.
TOO TROUBLE-SOME.
sigh
YOU'RE SAYING THIS NOW?!
WHAT A CROCK!
YOU JUST WANT TO PROTECT YOUR-SELVES!
YOU KNOW WHAT'S TROUBLESOME? THAT KIND OF PRETENTIOUS NONSENSE!
WHAP
QUIT BEING PICKY.
OW!
IT DOESN'T MATTER HOW WE DO IT.
YOU ALL KNOW THAT.

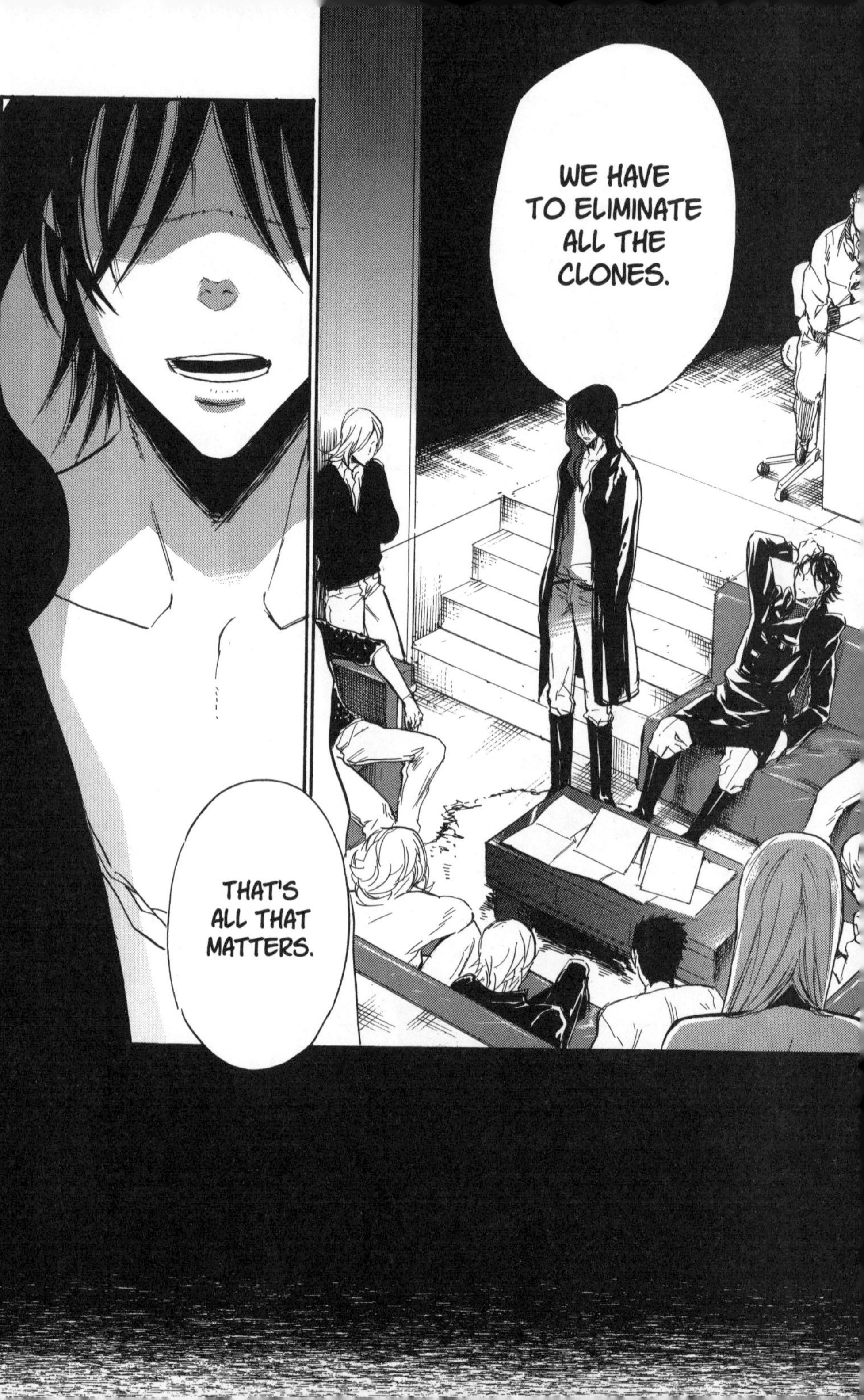
WE HAVE TO ELIMINATE ALL THE CLONES.
THAT'S ALL THAT MATTERS.

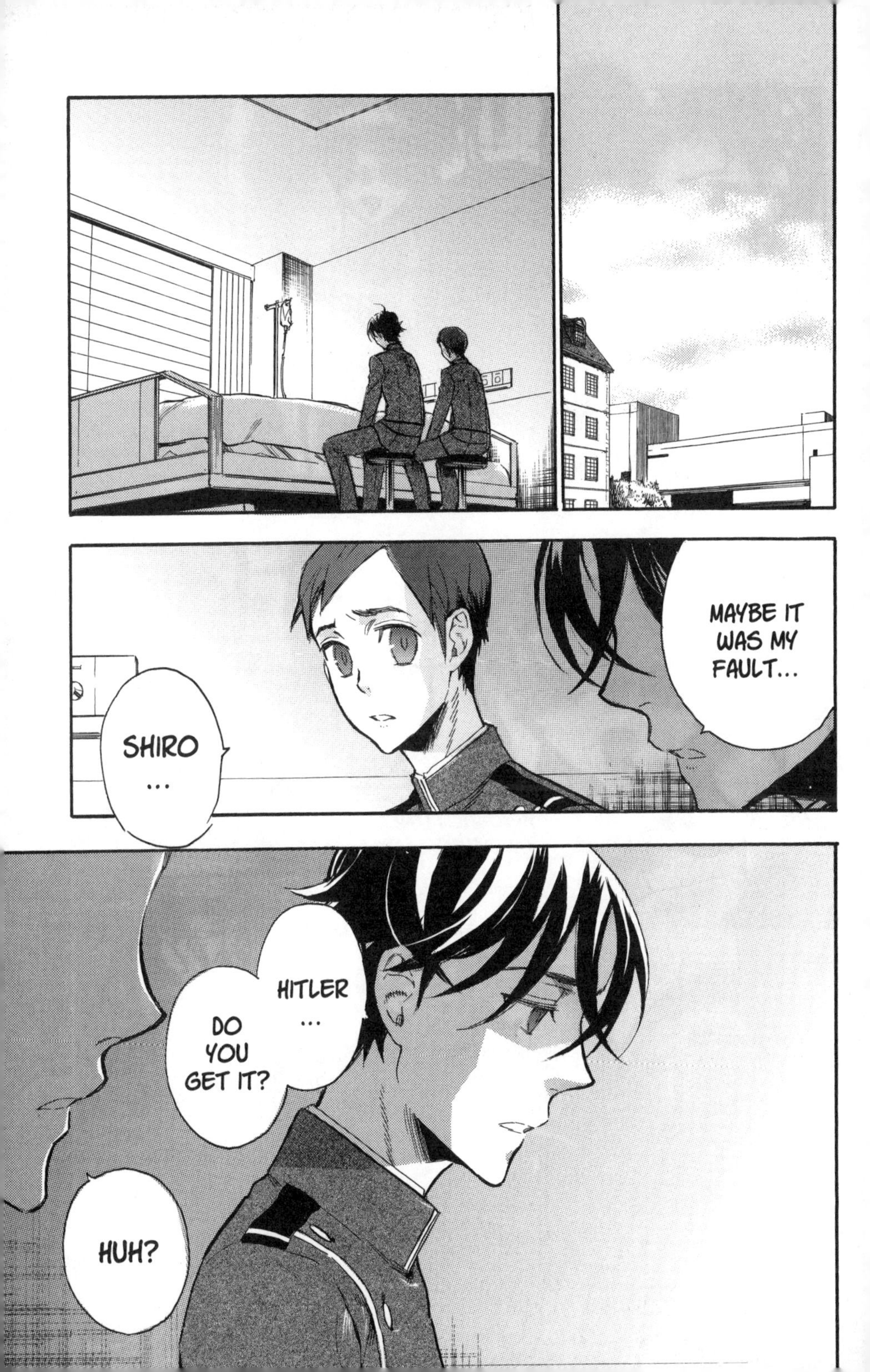
MAYBE IT WAS MY FAULT...
SHIRO ...
HITLER ...
DO YOU GET IT?
HUH?

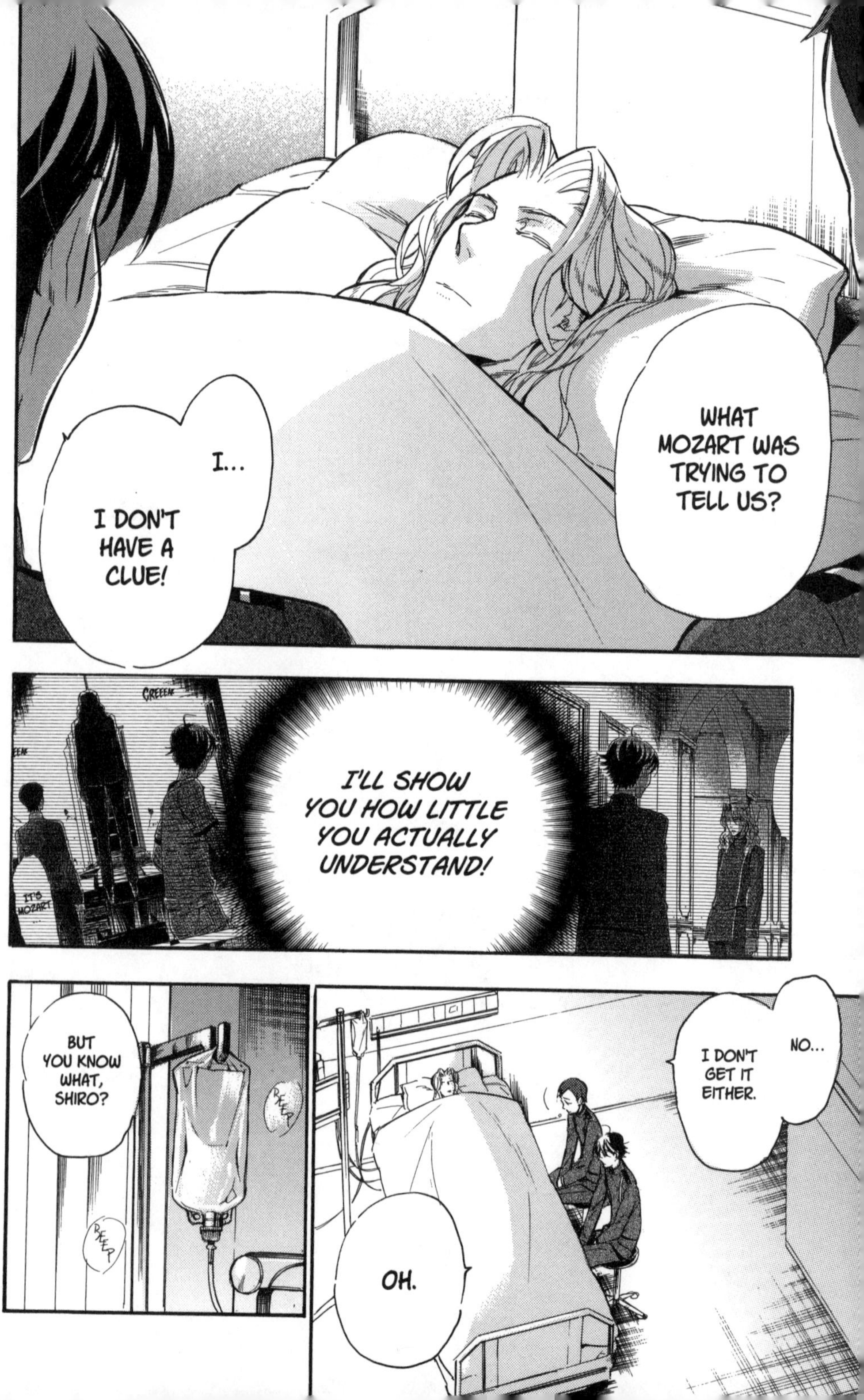
WHAT MOZART WAS TRYING TO TELL US?
I... I DON'T HAVE A CLUE!
I'LL SHOW YOU HOW LITTLE YOU ACTUALLY UNDERSTAND!
GREEEAK
IT'S MOZART...
NO...
I DON'T GET IT EITHER.
OH.
BUT YOU KNOW WHAT, SHIRO?

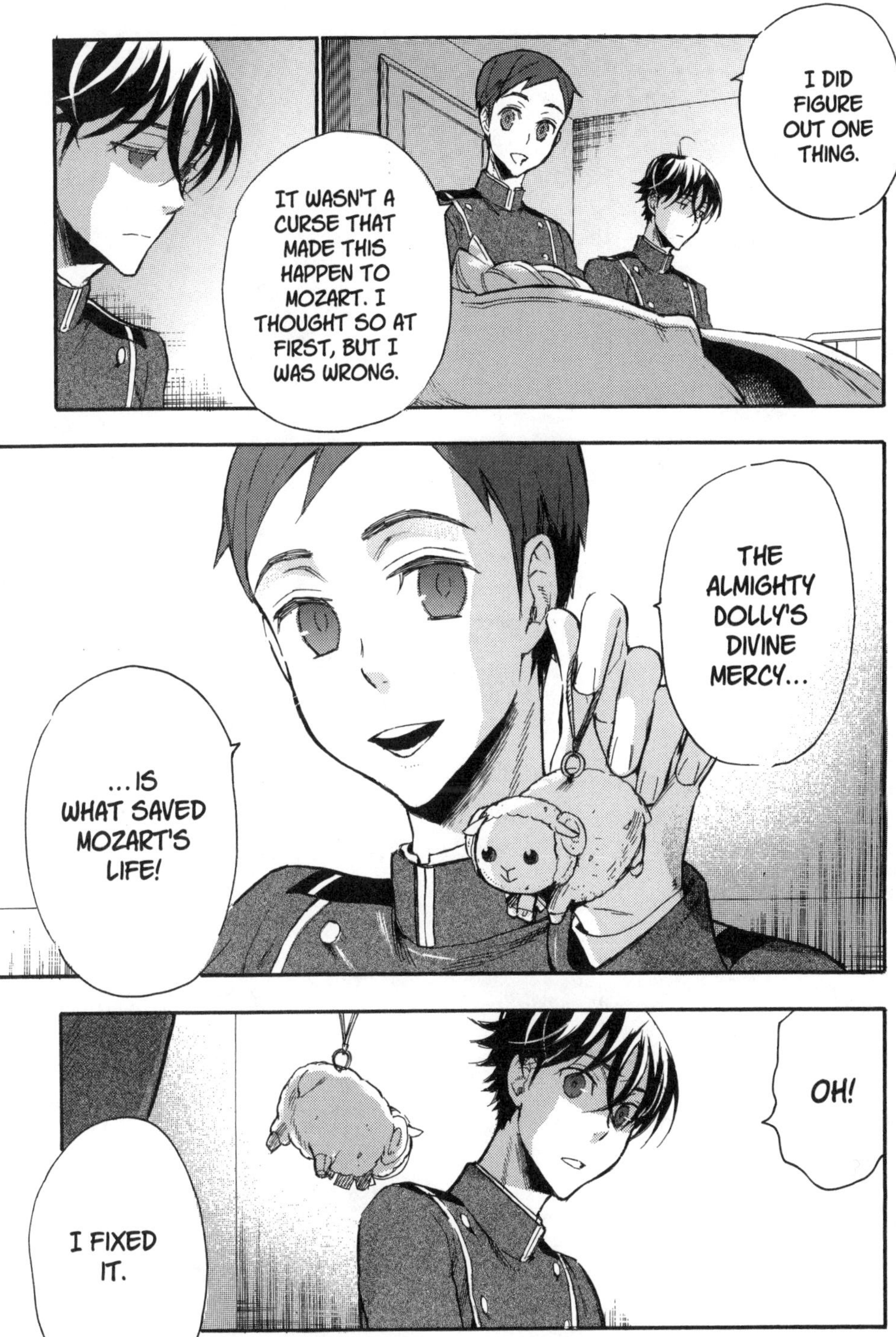
I DID FIGURE OUT ONE THING.
IT WASN'T A CURSE THAT MADE THIS HAPPEN TO MOZART. I THOUGHT SO AT FIRST, BUT I WAS WRONG.
THE ALMIGHTY DOLLY'S DIVINE MERCY...
...IS WHAT SAVED MOZART'S LIFE!
OH!
I FIXED IT.

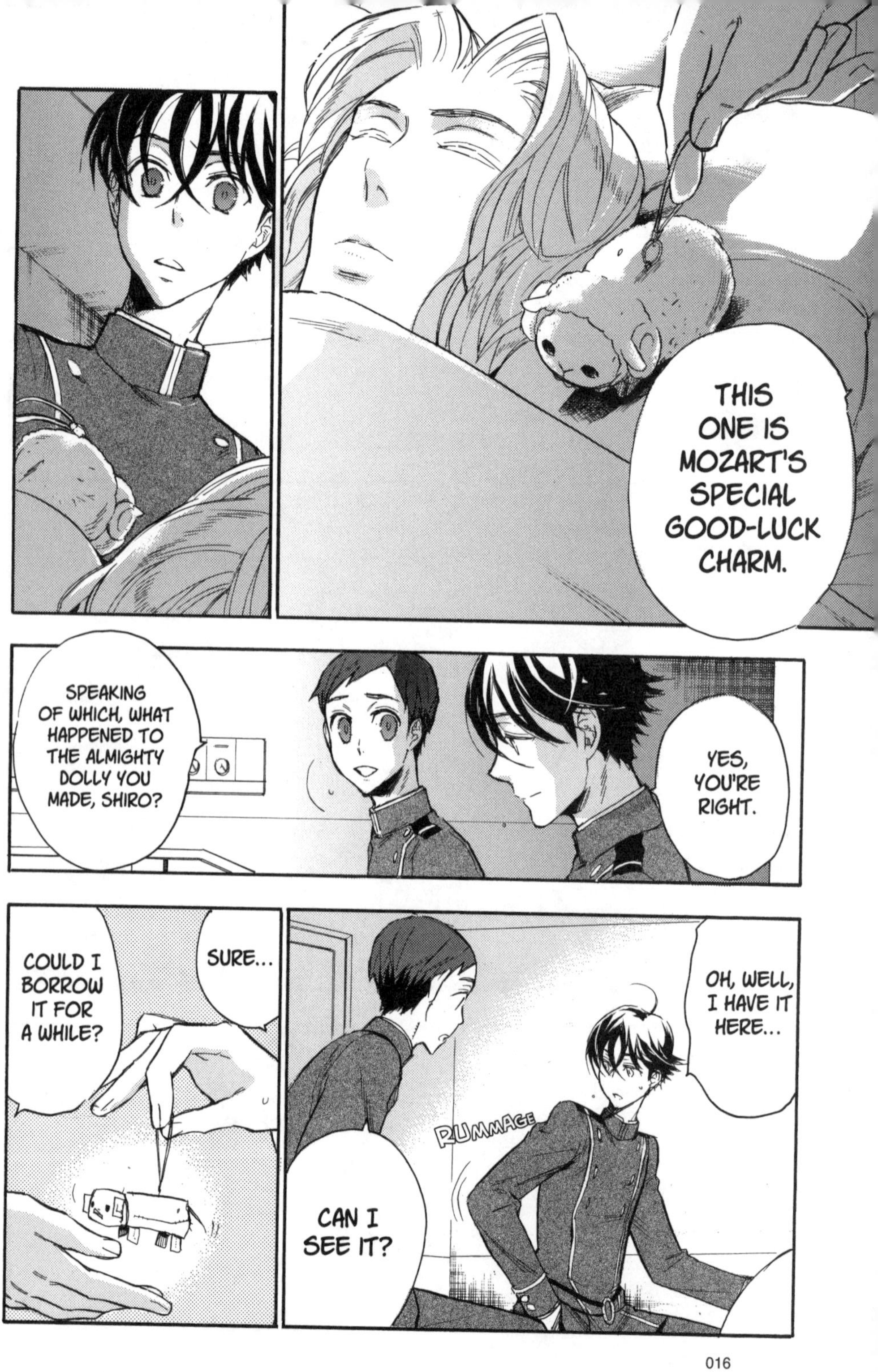
THIS ONE IS MOZART'S SPECIAL GOOD-LUCK CHARM.
YES, YOU'RE RIGHT.
SPEAKING OF WHICH, WHAT HAPPENED TO THE ALMIGHTY DOLLY YOU MADE, SHIRO?
OH, WELL, I HAVE IT HERE...
RUMMAGE
CAN I SEE IT?
SURE...
COULD I BORROW IT FOR A WHILE?

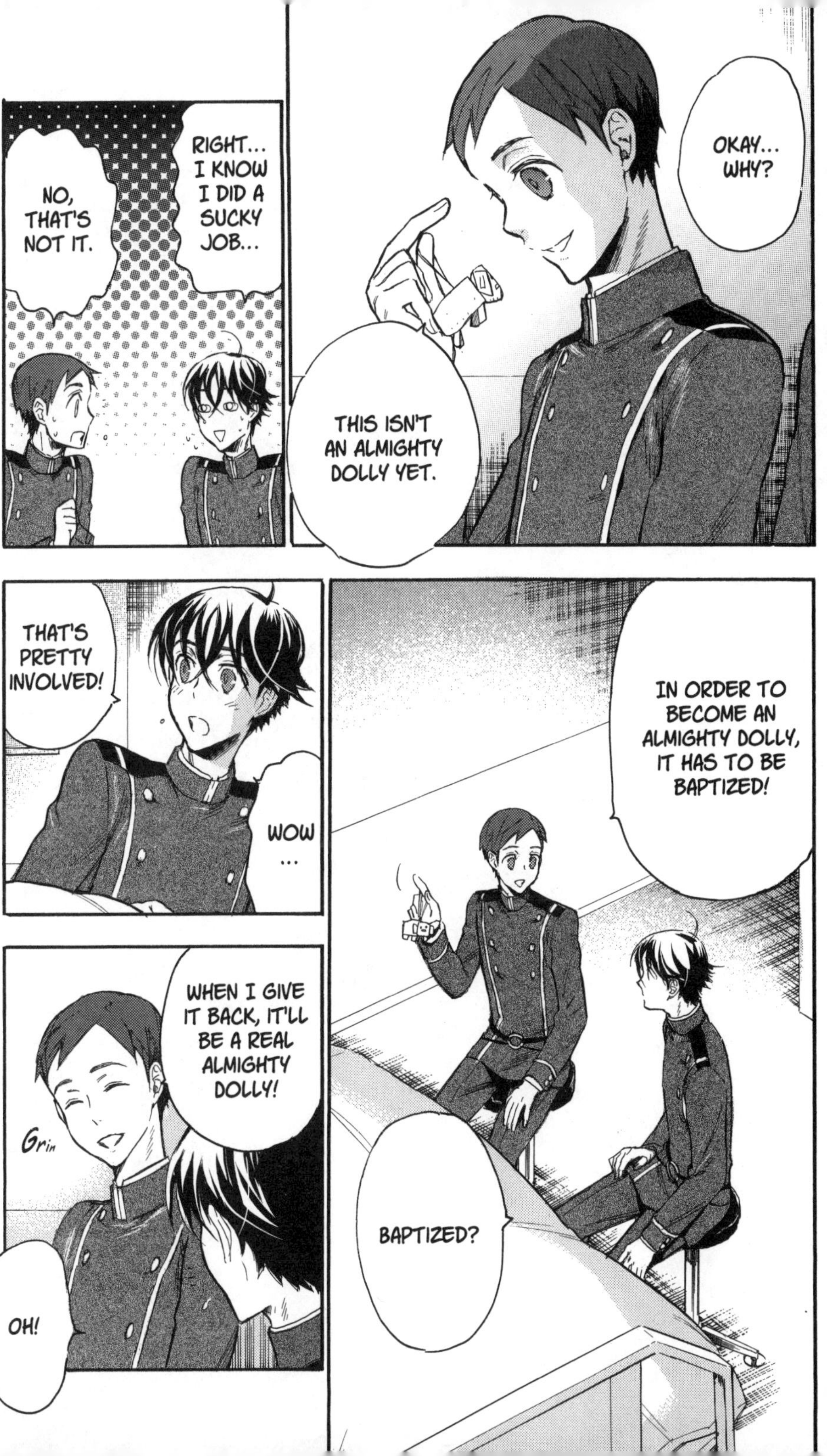
OKAY... WHY?
THIS ISN'T AN ALMIGHTY DOLLY YET.
RIGHT... I KNOW I DID A SUCKY JOB...
NO, THAT'S NOT IT.
IN ORDER TO BECOME AN ALMIGHTY DOLLY, IT HAS TO BE BAPTIZED!
BAPTIZED?
WOW...
THAT'S PRETTY INVOLVED!
WHEN I GIVE IT BACK, IT'LL BE A REAL ALMIGHTY DOLLY!
Grin
OH!

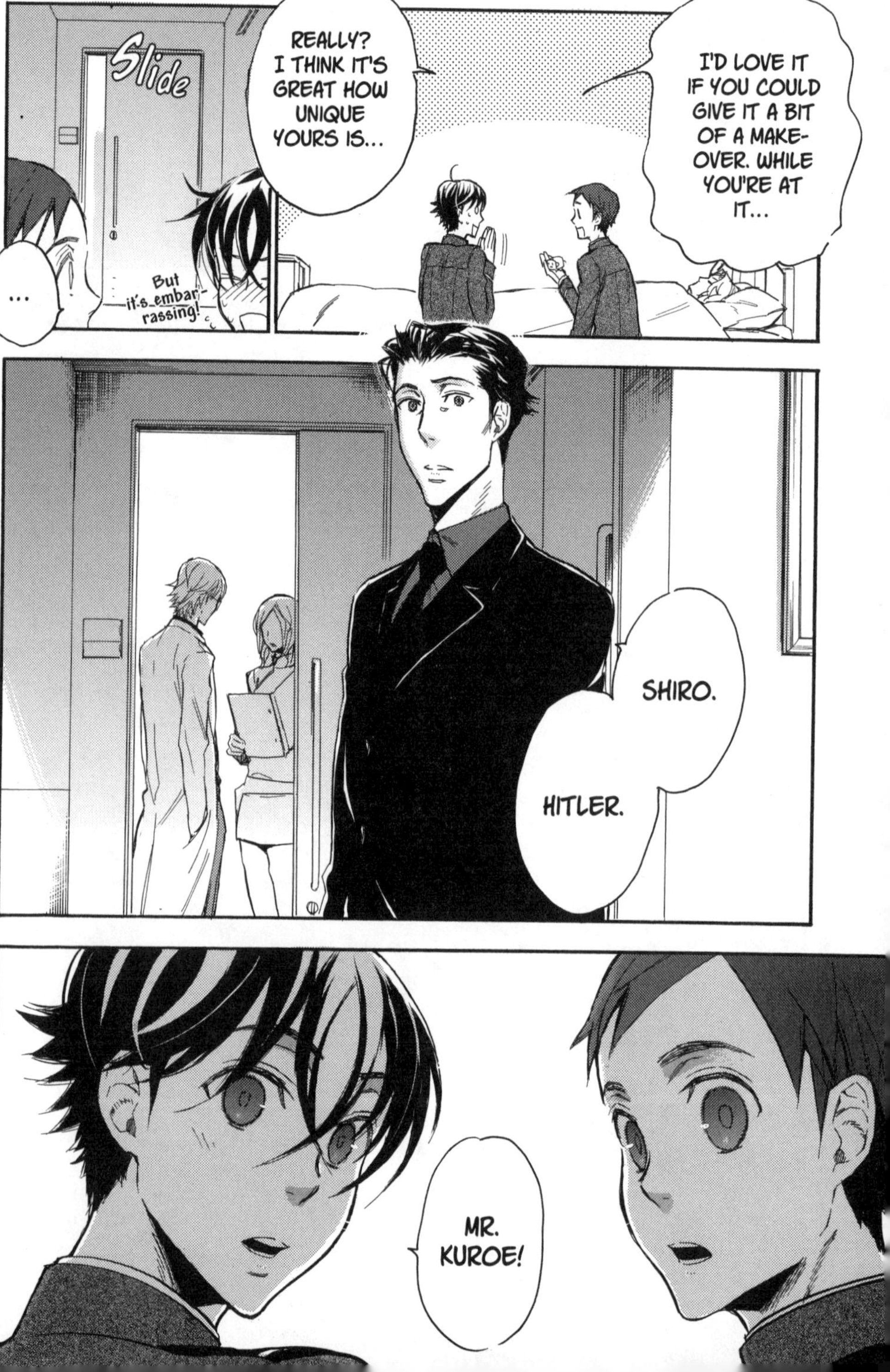
I'D LOVE IT IF YOU COULD GIVE IT A BIT OF A MAKE-OVER. WHILE YOU'RE AT IT...
REALLY? I THINK IT'S GREAT HOW UNIQUE YOURS IS...
Slide
But it's embarrassing!
...
SHIRO.
HITLER.
MR. KUROE!

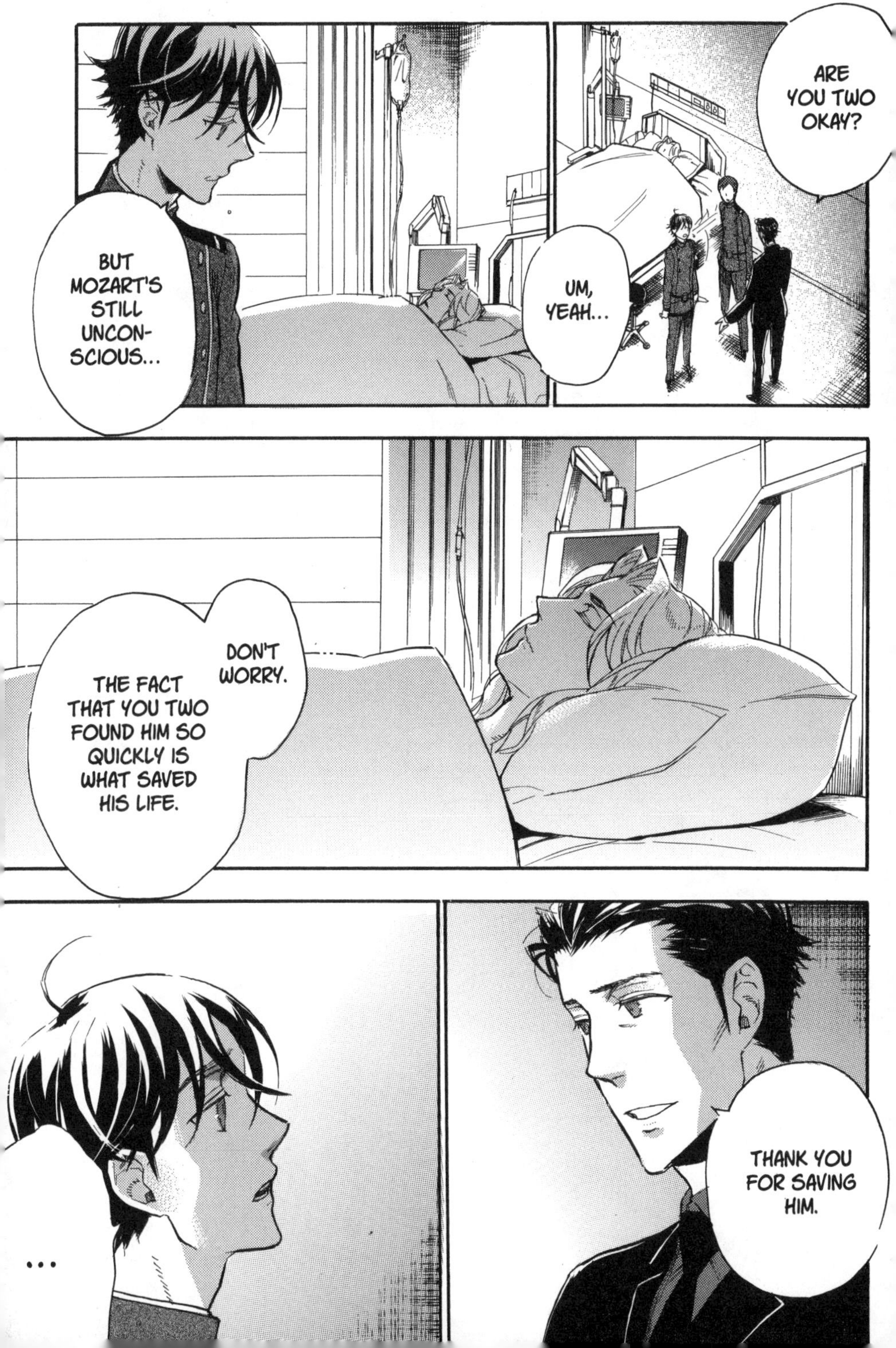
ARE YOU TWO OKAY?
UM, YEAH...
BUT MOZART'S STILL UNCON-SCIOUS...
DON'T WORRY.
THE FACT THAT YOU TWO FOUND HIM SO QUICKLY IS WHAT SAVED HIS LIFE.
THANK YOU FOR SAVING HIM.
...

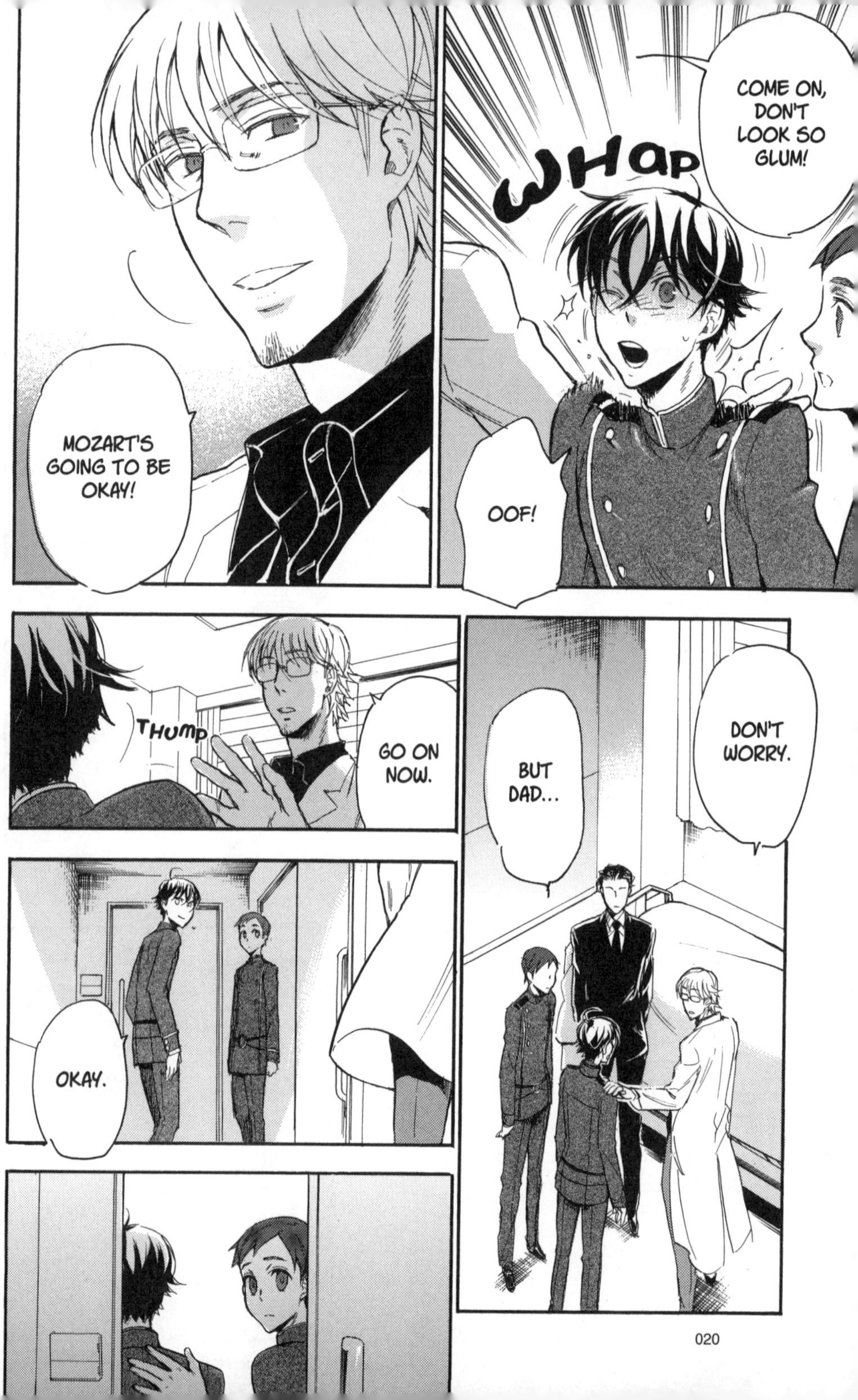
COME ON, DON'T LOOK SO GLUM!
WHAP
OOF!
MOZART'S GOING TO BE OKAY!
DON'T WORRY.
BUT DAD...
GO ON NOW.
THUMP
OKAY.

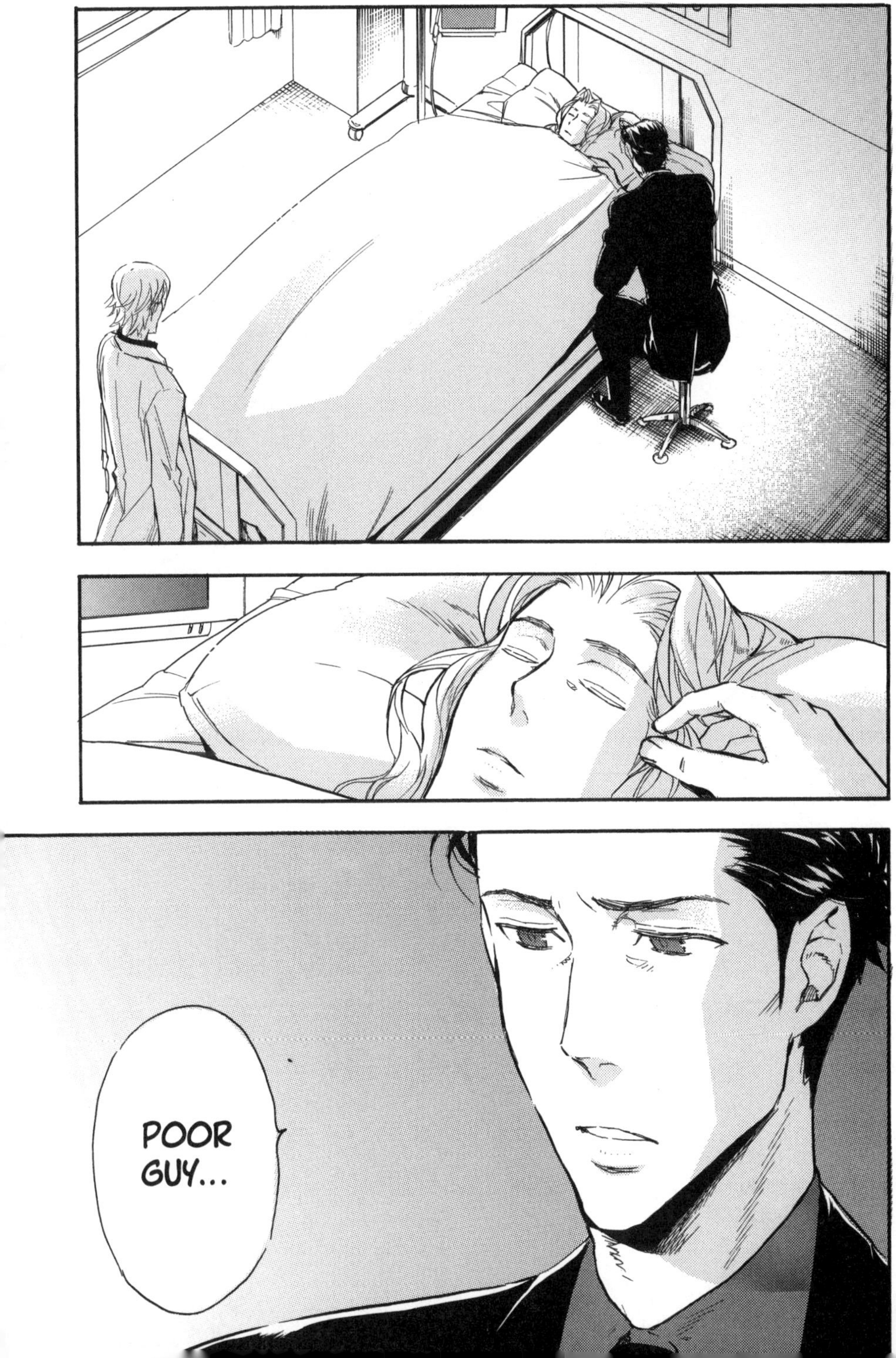
POOR GUY...

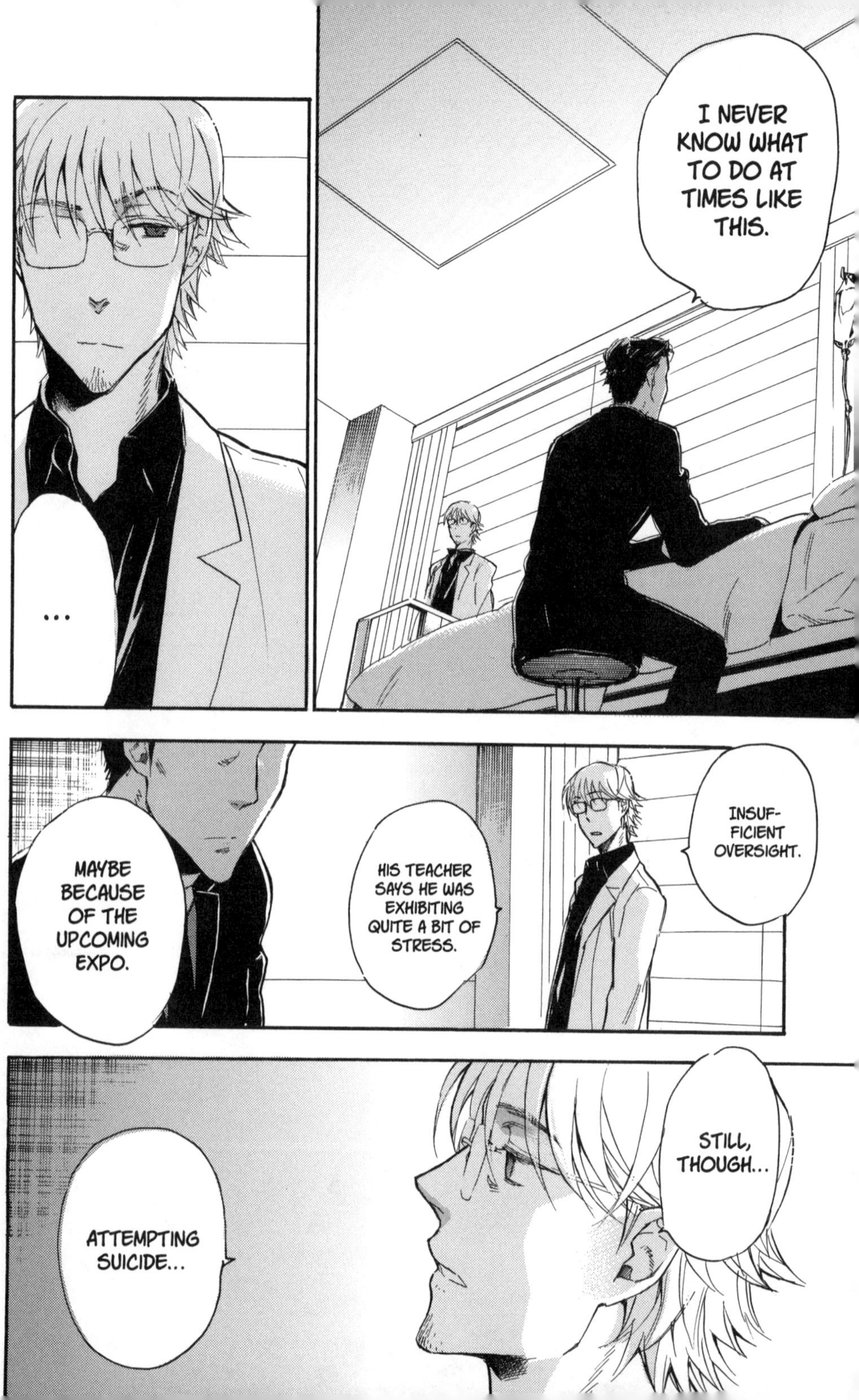
I NEVER KNOW WHAT TO DO AT TIMES LIKE THIS.
...
INSUF-FICIENT OVERSIGHT.
HIS TEACHER SAYS HE WAS EXHIBITING QUITE A BIT OF STRESS.
MAYBE BECAUSE OF THE UPCOMING EXPO.
STILL, THOUGH...
ATTEMPTING SUICIDE...

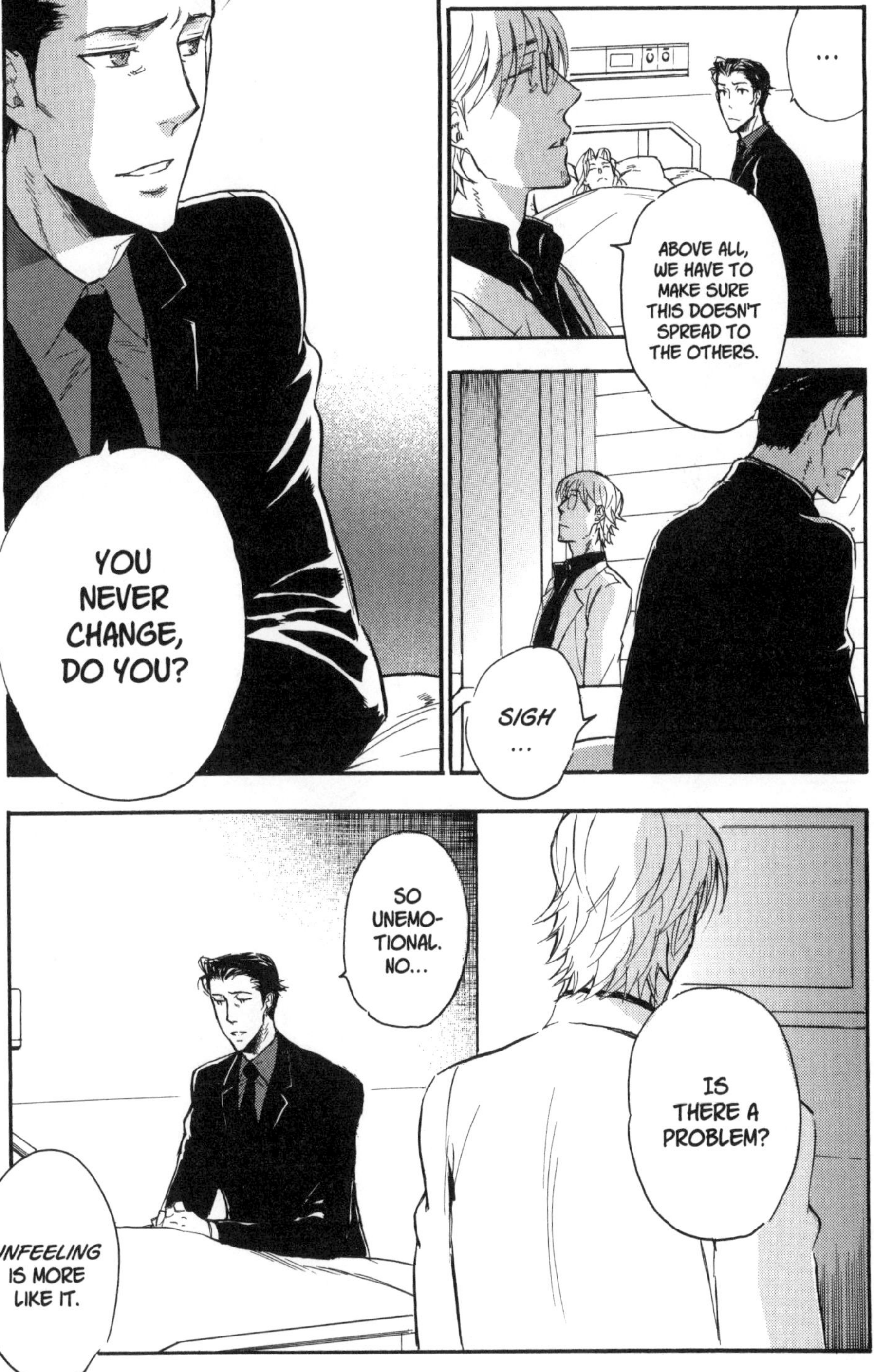
...
ABOVE ALL, WE HAVE TO MAKE SURE THIS DOESN'T SPREAD TO THE OTHERS.
SIGH ...
YOU NEVER CHANGE, DO YOU?
IS THERE A PROBLEM?
SO UNEMO-TIONAL. NO...
UNFEELING IS MORE LIKE IT.

FEELING SORRY FOR HIM WON'T GET US ANYWHERE.

THAT'S NOT THE ISSUE, KAMIYA.

sigh

SO I REALLY HAVEN'T CHANGED?

HMM?

OH PLEASE ...

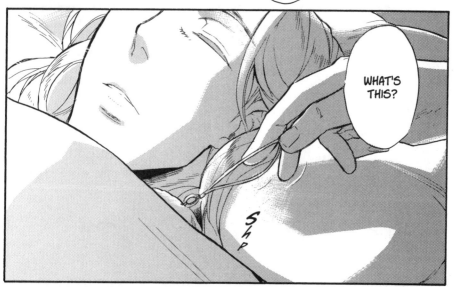

WHAT'S THIS?

smp

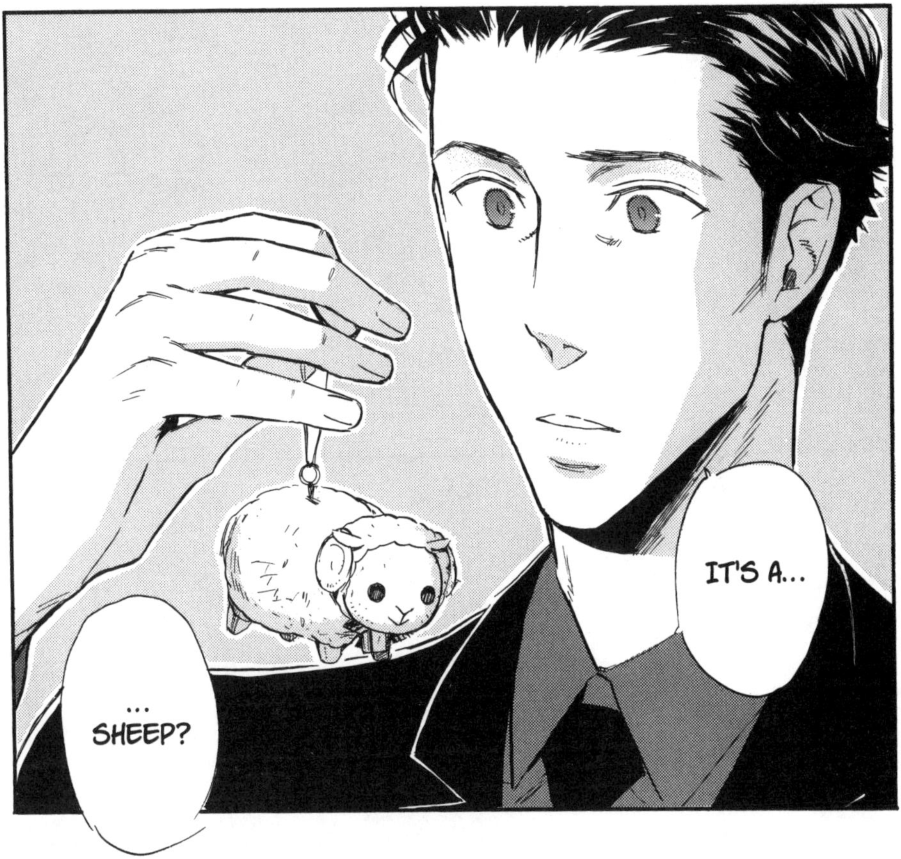
IT'S A...
...SHEEP?

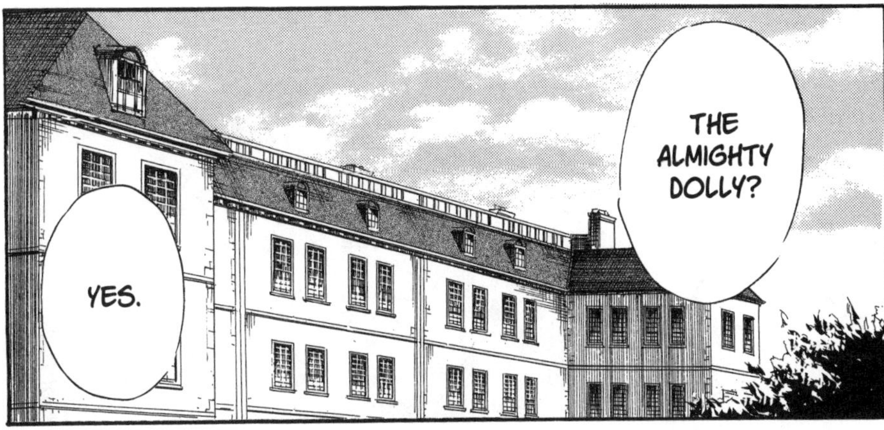
THE ALMIGHTY DOLLY?
YES.

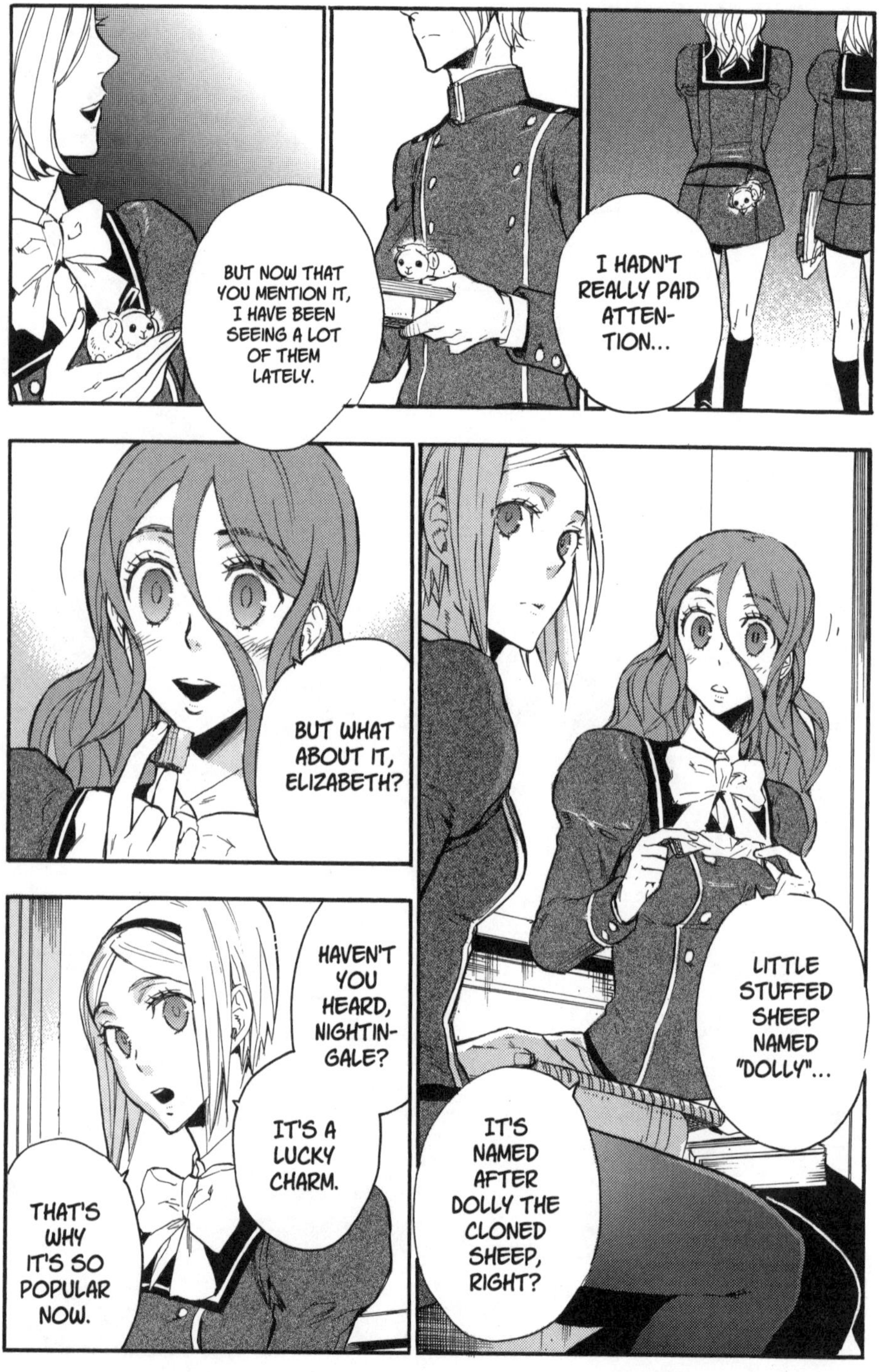
I HADN'T REALLY PAID ATTEN-TION...
BUT NOW THAT YOU MENTION IT, I HAVE BEEN SEEING A LOT OF THEM LATELY.
LITTLE STUFFED SHEEP NAMED "DOLLY"...
IT'S NAMED AFTER DOLLY THE CLONED SHEEP, RIGHT?
BUT WHAT ABOUT IT, ELIZABETH?
HAVEN'T YOU HEARD, NIGHTIN-GALE?
IT'S A LUCKY CHARM.
THAT'S WHY IT'S SO POPULAR NOW.

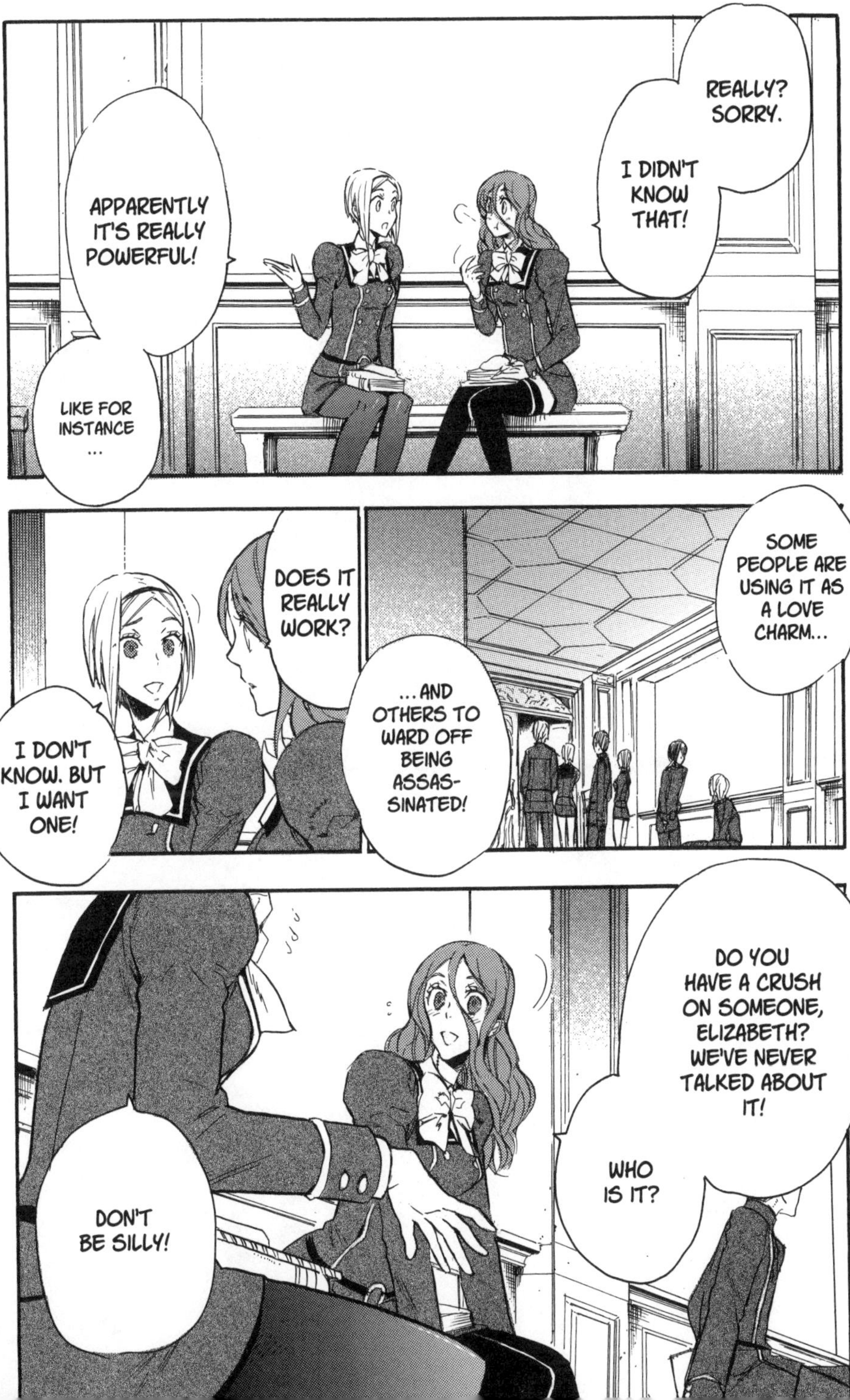
REALLY? SORRY.
I DIDN'T KNOW THAT!
APPARENTLY IT'S REALLY POWERFUL!
LIKE FOR INSTANCE ...
SOME PEOPLE ARE USING IT AS A LOVE CHARM...
...AND OTHERS TO WARD OFF BEING ASSAS-SINATED!
DOES IT REALLY WORK?
I DON'T KNOW. BUT I WANT ONE!
DO YOU HAVE A CRUSH ON SOMEONE, ELIZABETH? WE'VE NEVER TALKED ABOUT IT!
WHO IS IT?
DON'T BE SILLY!

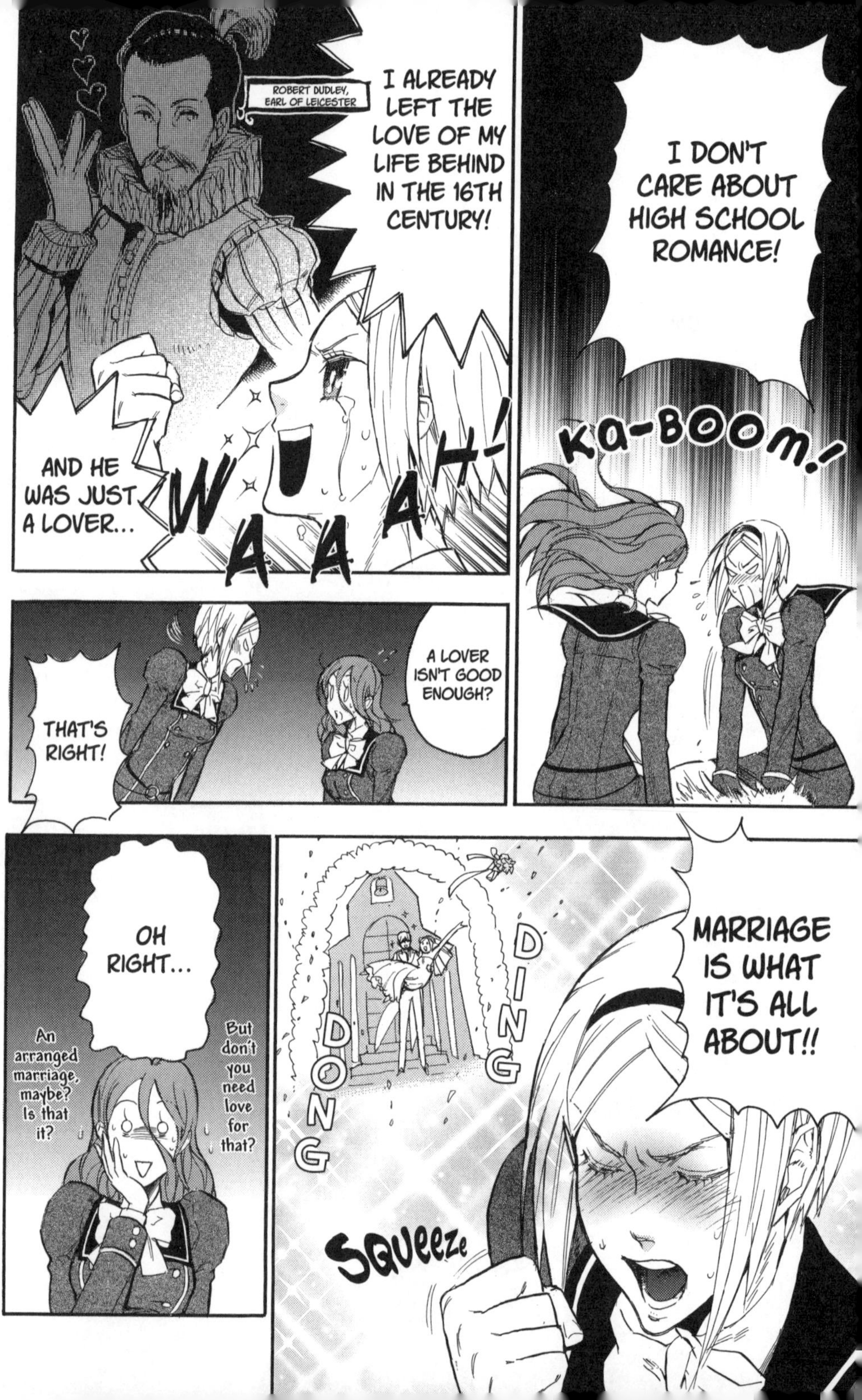
I DON'T CARE ABOUT HIGH SCHOOL ROMANCE!
KA-BOOM!
I ALREADY LEFT THE LOVE OF MY LIFE BEHIND IN THE 16TH CENTURY!
ROBERT DUDLEY, EARL OF LEICESTER
WAAAAH!
AND HE WAS JUST A LOVER...
A LOVER ISN'T GOOD ENOUGH?
THAT'S RIGHT!
MARRIAGE IS WHAT IT'S ALL ABOUT!!
DING
DONG
SQUEEZE
OH RIGHT...
But don't you need love for that?
An arranged marriage, maybe? Is that it?

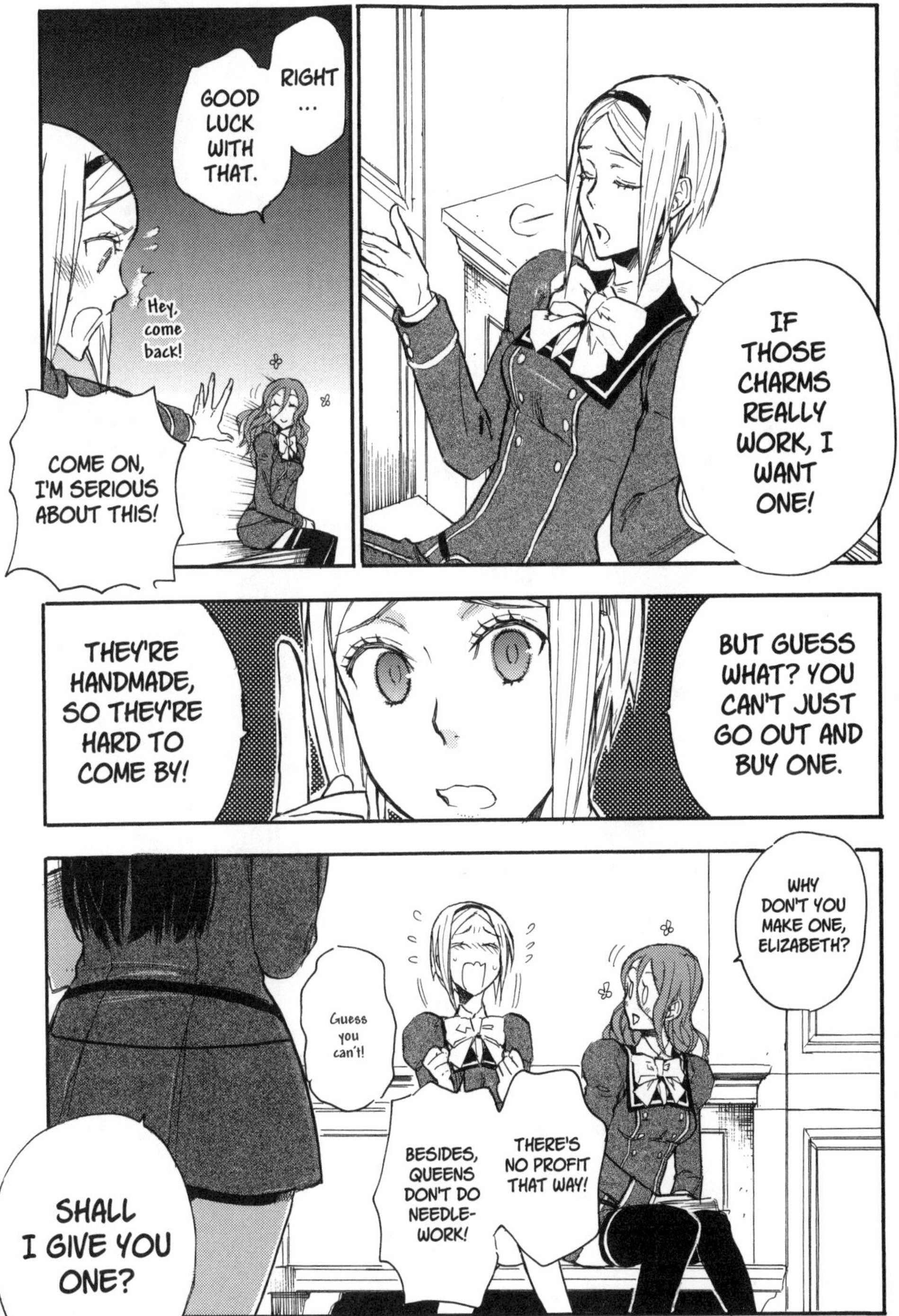
IF THOSE CHARMS REALLY WORK, I WANT ONE!
RIGHT ...
GOOD LUCK WITH THAT.
Hey, come back!
COME ON, I'M SERIOUS ABOUT THIS!
BUT GUESS WHAT? YOU CAN'T JUST GO OUT AND BUY ONE.
THEY'RE HANDMADE, SO THEY'RE HARD TO COME BY!
WHY DON'T YOU MAKE ONE, ELIZABETH?
THERE'S NO PROFIT THAT WAY!
BESIDES, QUEENS DON'T DO NEEDLE-WORK!
Guess you can't!
SHALL I GIVE YOU ONE?

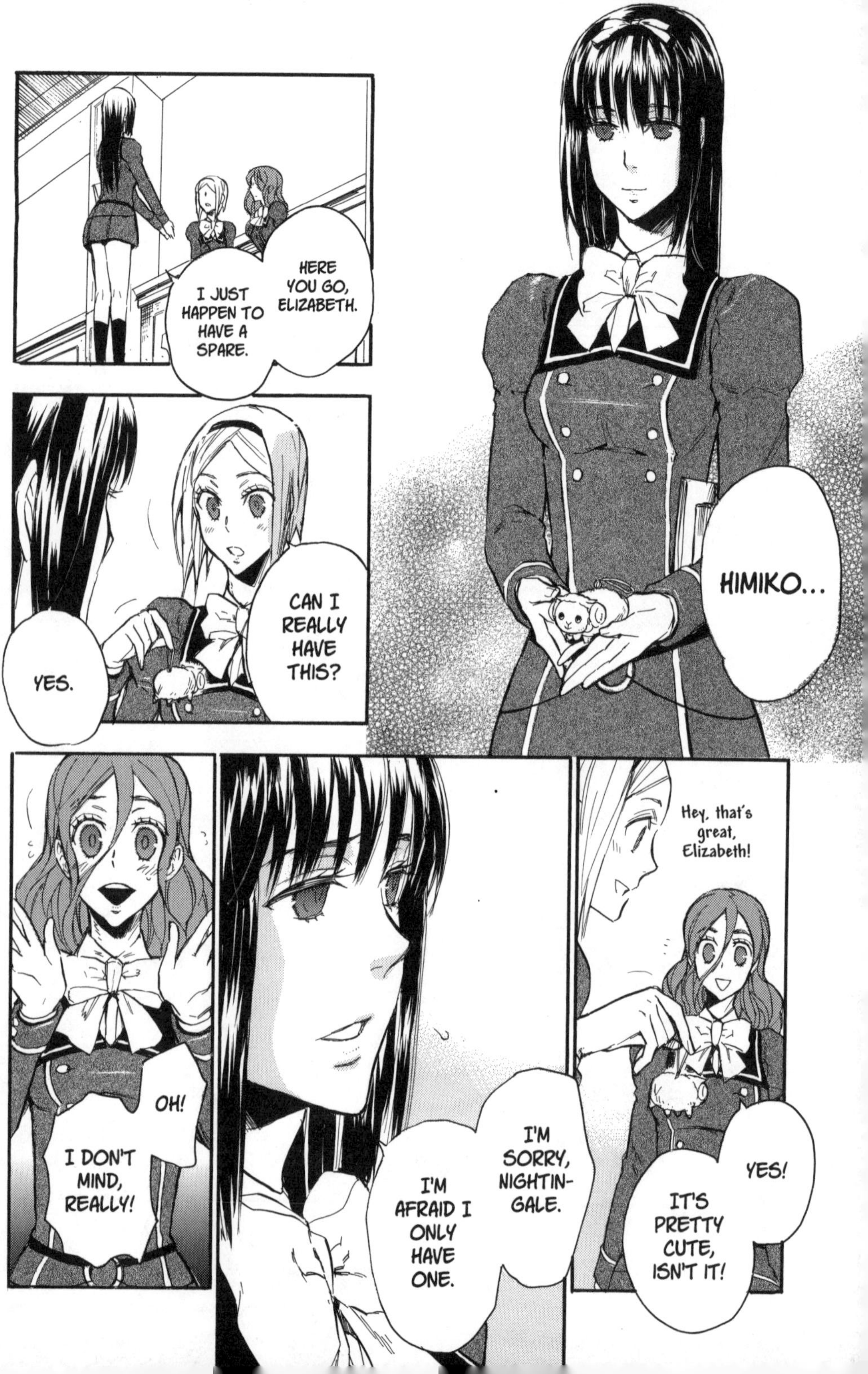
HIMIKO...
HERE YOU GO, ELIZABETH.
I JUST HAPPEN TO HAVE A SPARE.
CAN I REALLY HAVE THIS?
YES.
Hey, that's great, Elizabeth!
YES!
IT'S PRETTY CUTE, ISN'T IT!
I'M SORRY, NIGHTIN-GALE.
I'M AFRAID I ONLY HAVE ONE.
OH!
I DON'T MIND, REALLY!

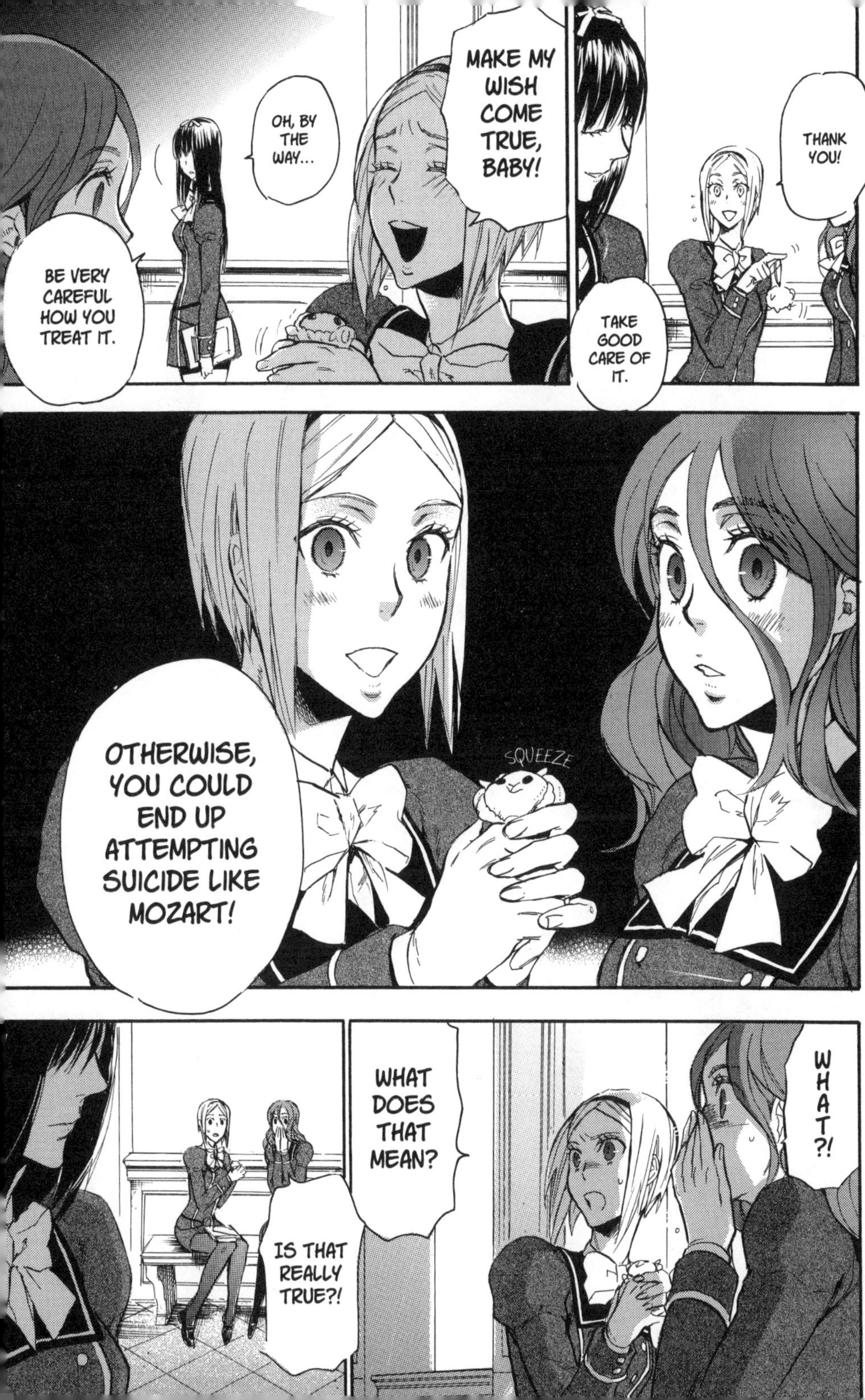
THANK YOU!
TAKE GOOD CARE OF IT.
MAKE MY WISH COME TRUE, BABY!
OH, BY THE WAY...
BE VERY CAREFUL HOW YOU TREAT IT.
OTHERWISE, YOU COULD END UP ATTEMPTING SUICIDE LIKE MOZART!
SQUEEZE
WHAT?!
WHAT DOES THAT MEAN?
IS THAT REALLY TRUE?!

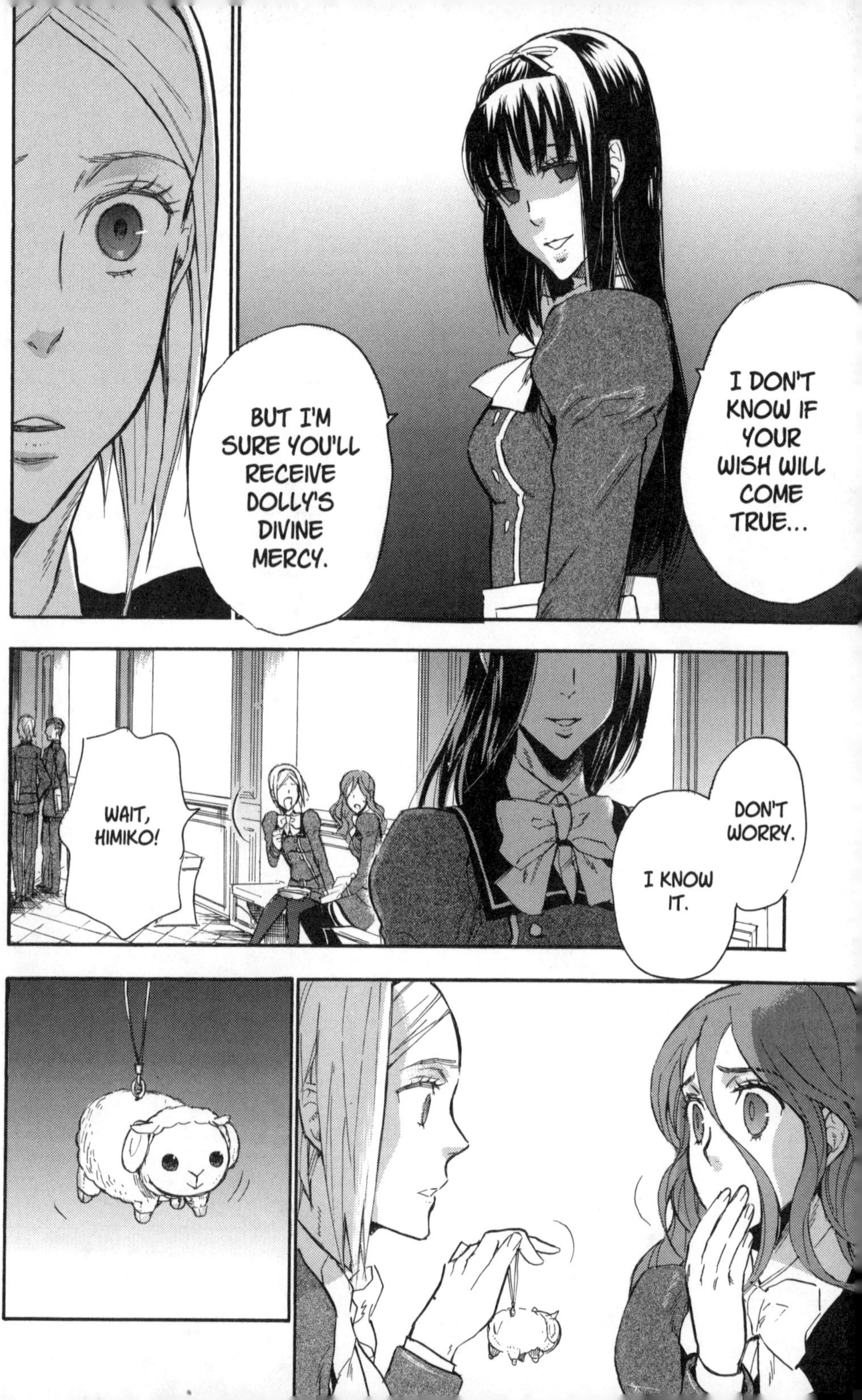
I DON'T KNOW IF YOUR WISH WILL COME TRUE...
BUT I'M SURE YOU'LL RECEIVE DOLLY'S DIVINE MERCY.
DON'T WORRY.
I KNOW IT.
WAIT, HIMIKO!

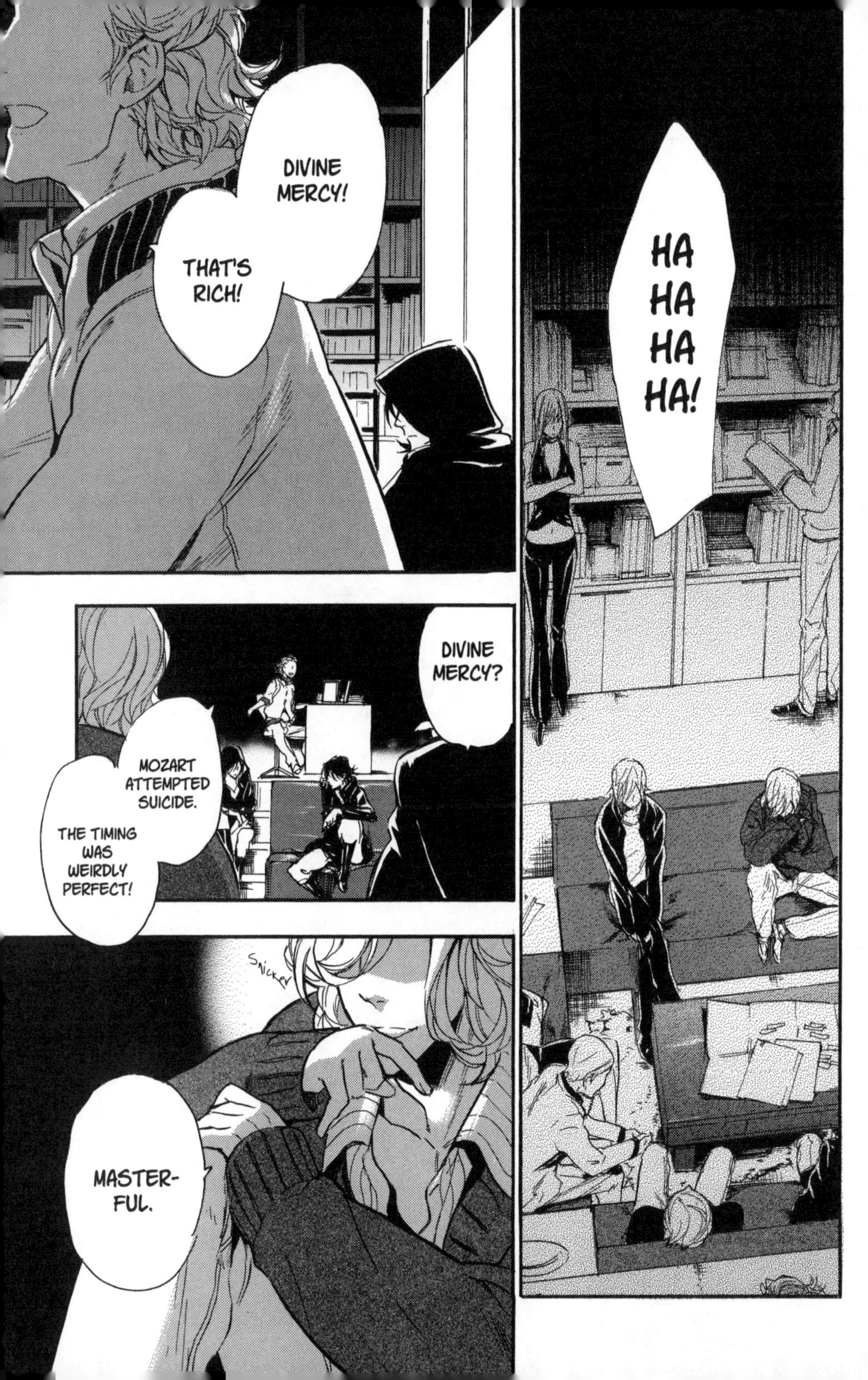

HA HA HA HA!
DIVINE MERCY!
THAT'S RICH!
DIVINE MERCY?
MOZART ATTEMPTED SUICIDE.
THE TIMING WAS WEIRDLY PERFECT!
Snicker
MASTER-FUL.

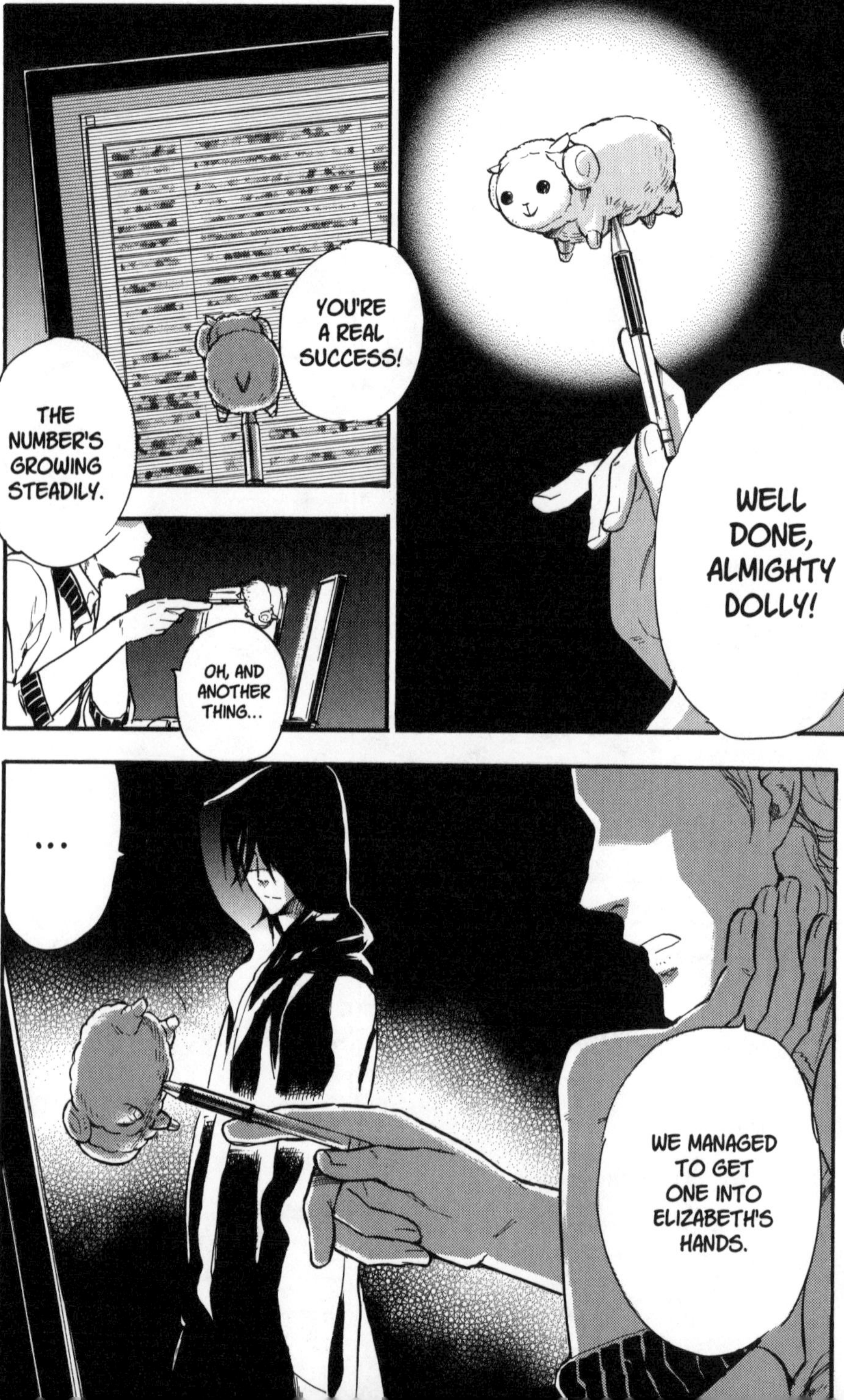
WELL DONE, ALMIGHTY DOLLY!
YOU'RE A REAL SUCCESS!
THE NUMBER'S GROWING STEADILY.
OH, AND ANOTHER THING...
WE MANAGED TO GET ONE INTO ELIZABETH'S HANDS.
...

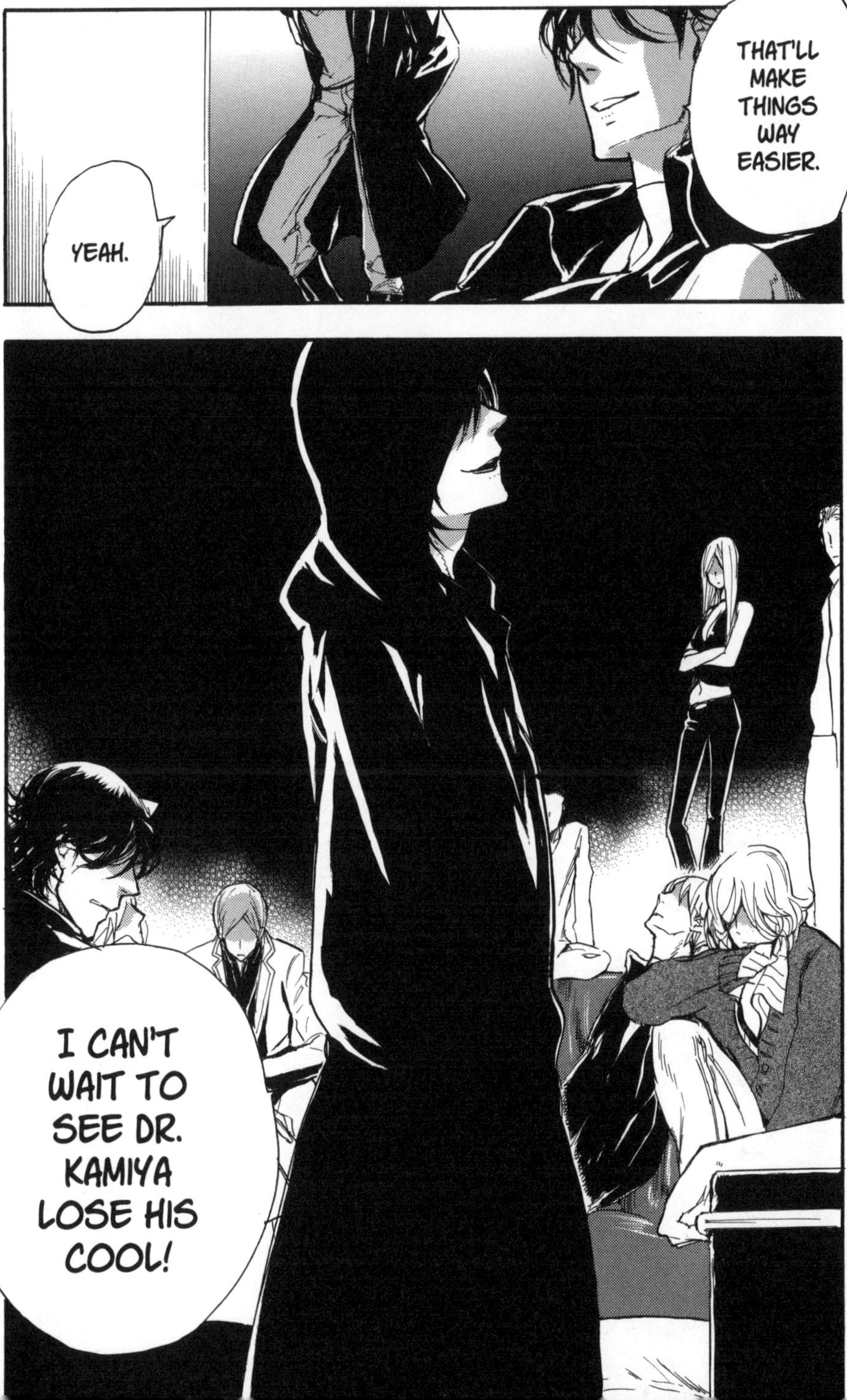
THAT'LL MAKE THINGS WAY EASIER.
YEAH.
I CAN'T WAIT TO SEE DR. KAMIYA LOSE HIS COOL!

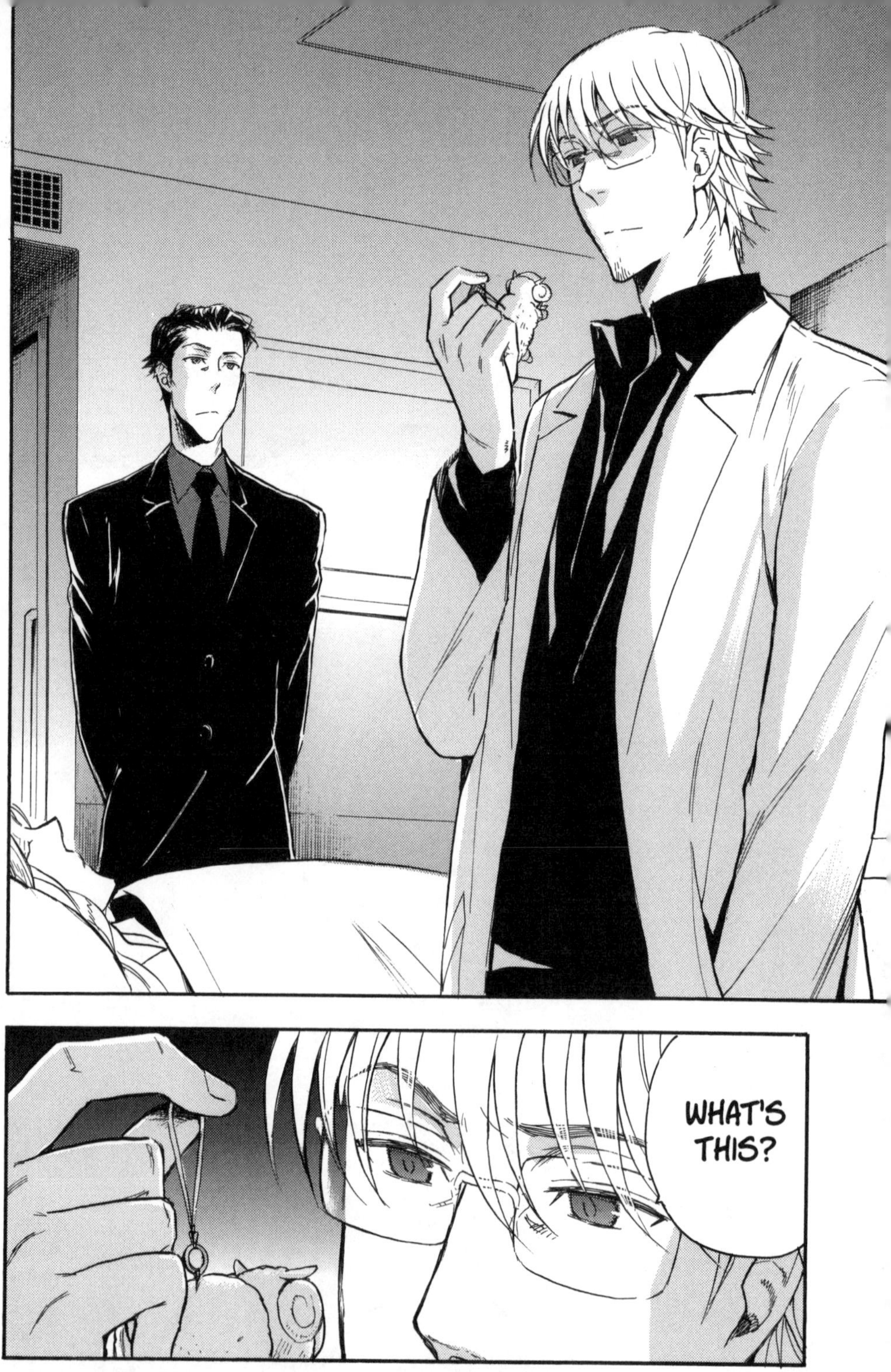
WHAT'S
THIS?

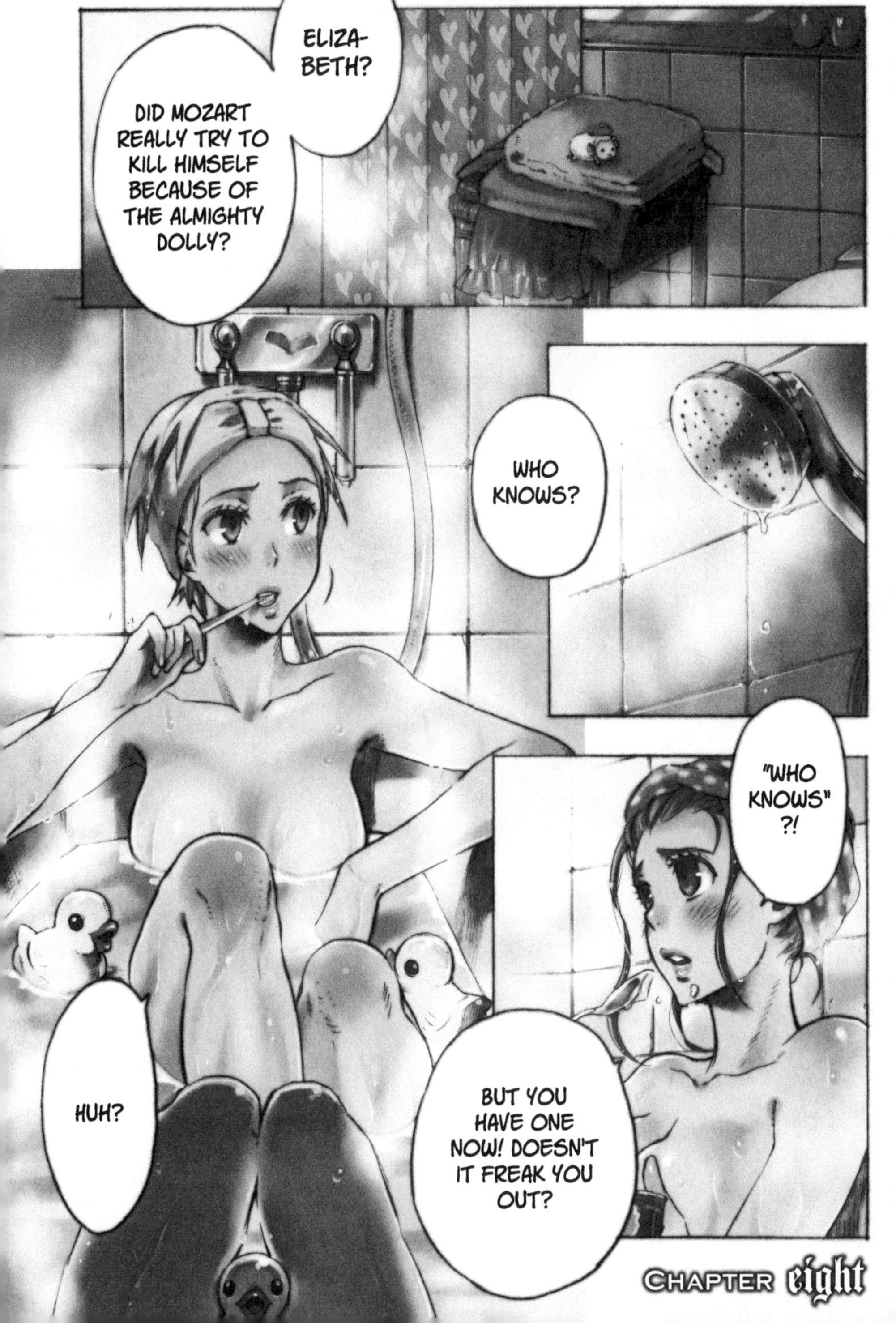
ELIZA-BETH?
DID MOZART REALLY TRY TO KILL HIMSELF BECAUSE OF THE ALMIGHTY DOLLY?
WHO KNOWS?
"WHO KNOWS" ?!
BUT YOU HAVE ONE NOW! DOESN'T IT FREAK YOU OUT?
HUH?
CHAPTER eight

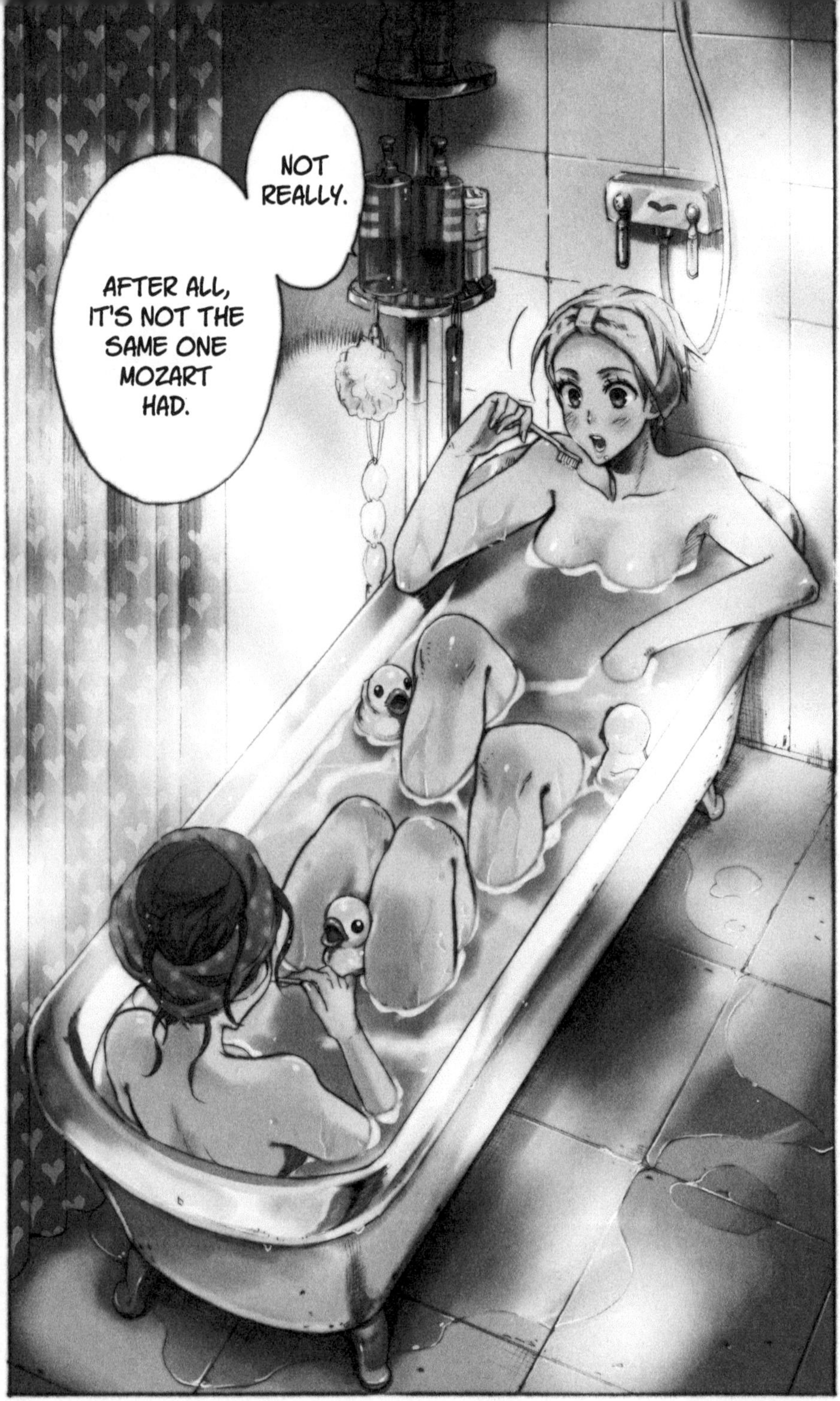
NOT REALLY.
AFTER ALL, IT'S NOT THE SAME ONE MOZART HAD.

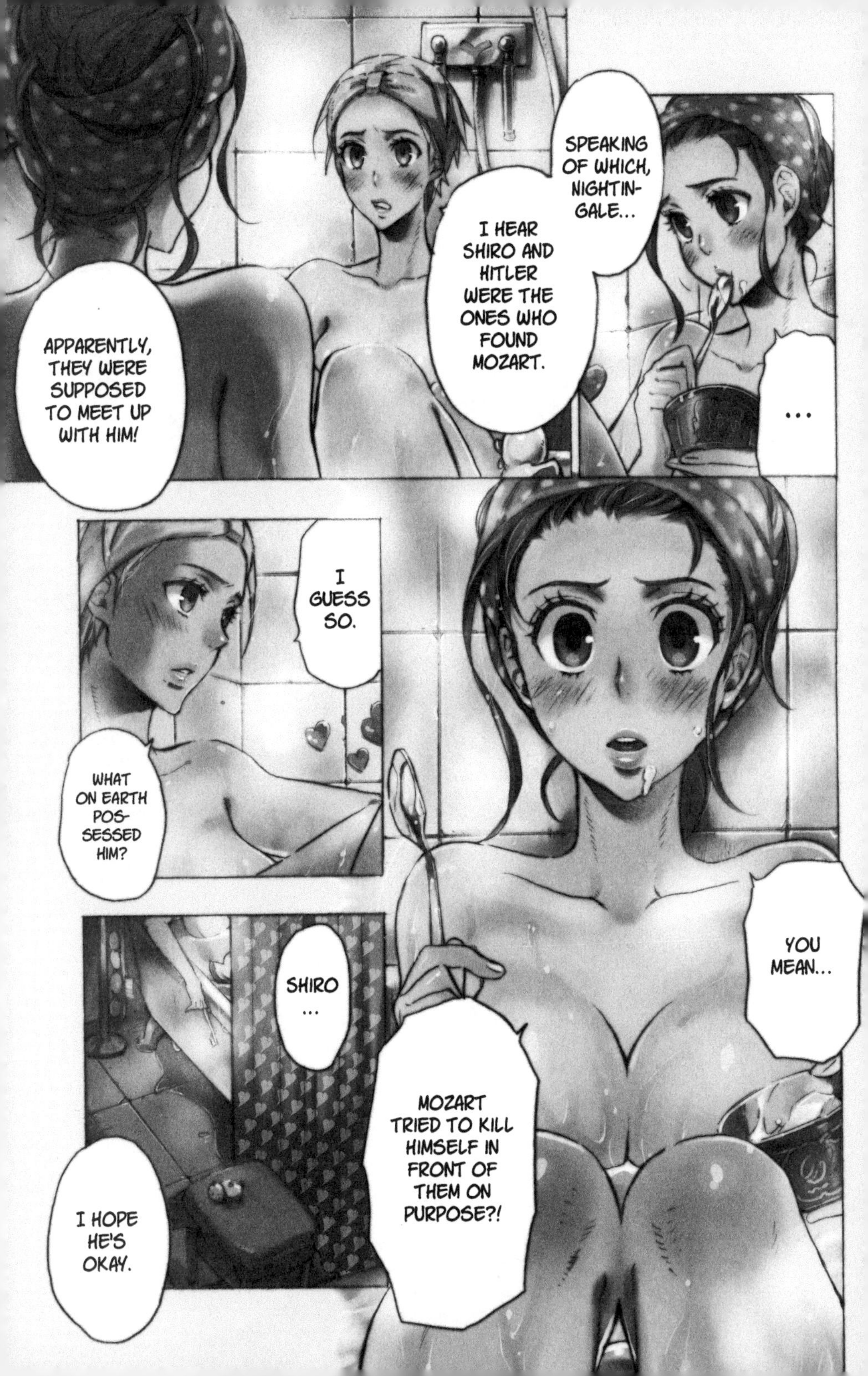
SPEAKING OF WHICH, NIGHTIN-GALE...
I HEAR SHIRO AND HITLER WERE THE ONES WHO FOUND MOZART.
...
APPARENTLY, THEY WERE SUPPOSED TO MEET UP WITH HIM!
YOU MEAN...
MOZART TRIED TO KILL HIMSELF IN FRONT OF THEM ON PURPOSE?!
I GUESS SO.
WHAT ON EARTH POS-SESSED HIM?
SHIRO...
I HOPE HE'S OKAY.

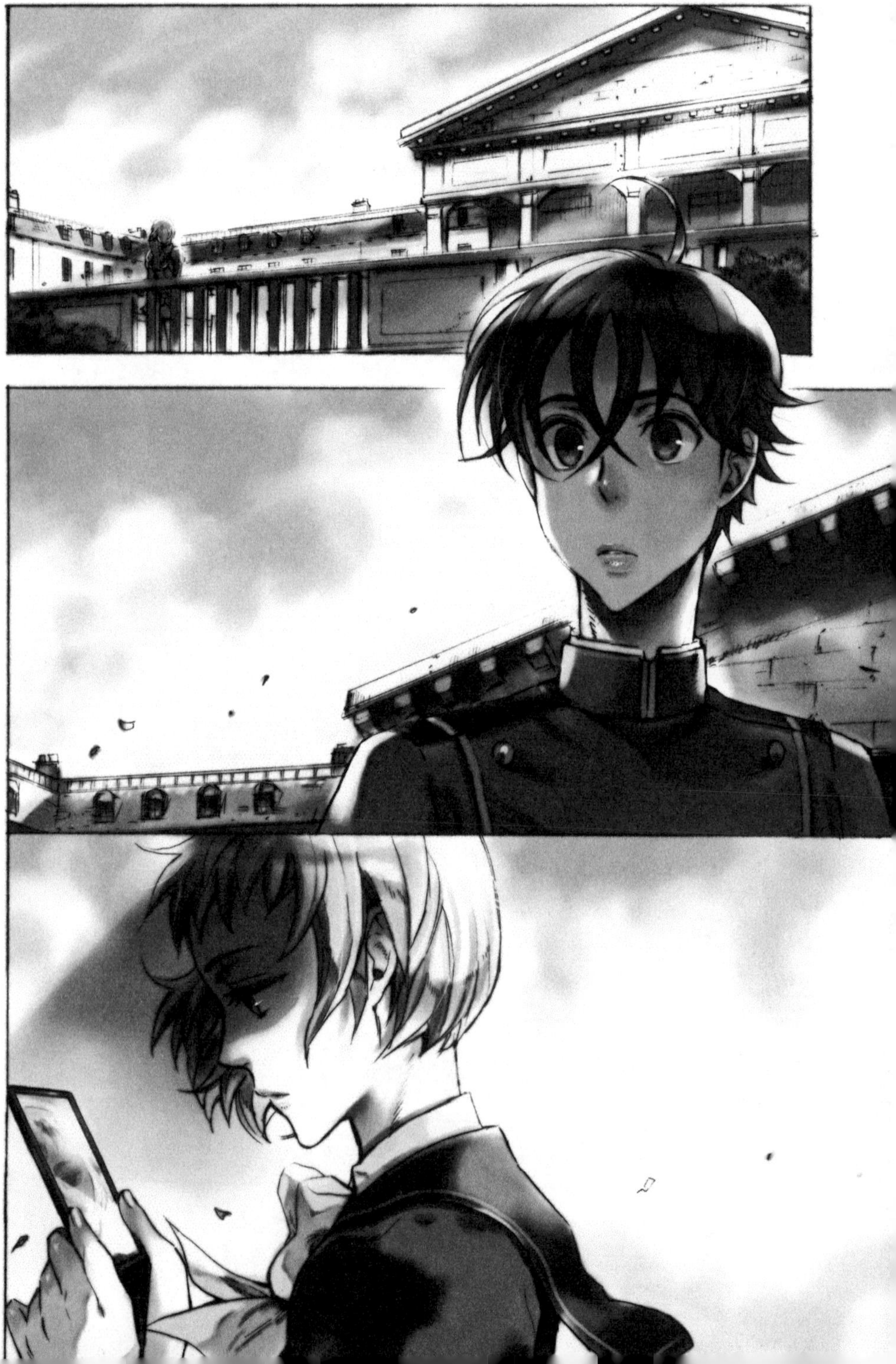

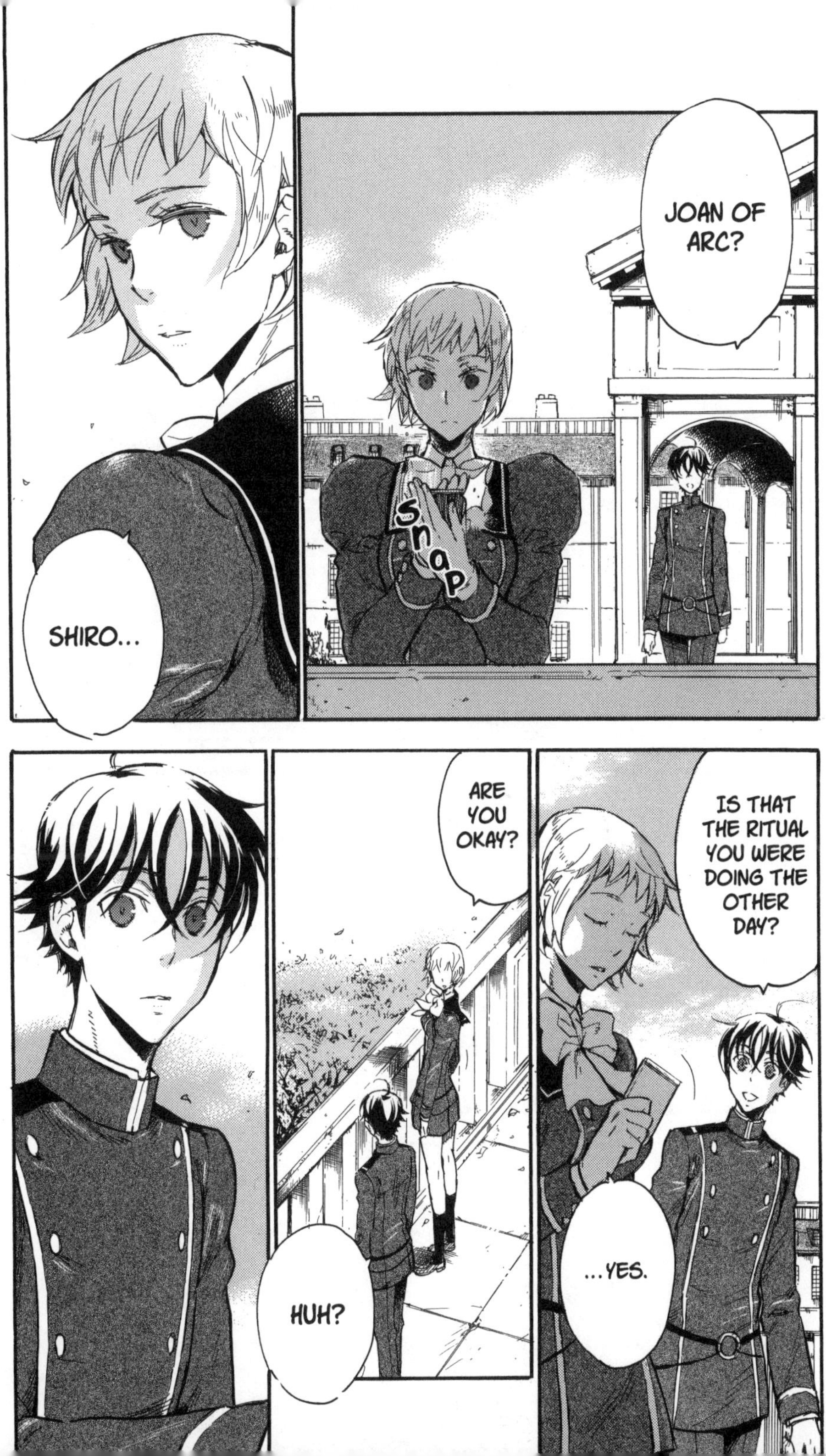
JOAN OF ARC?
SNAP
SHIRO...
IS THAT THE RITUAL YOU WERE DOING THE OTHER DAY?
...YES.
ARE YOU OKAY?
HUH?

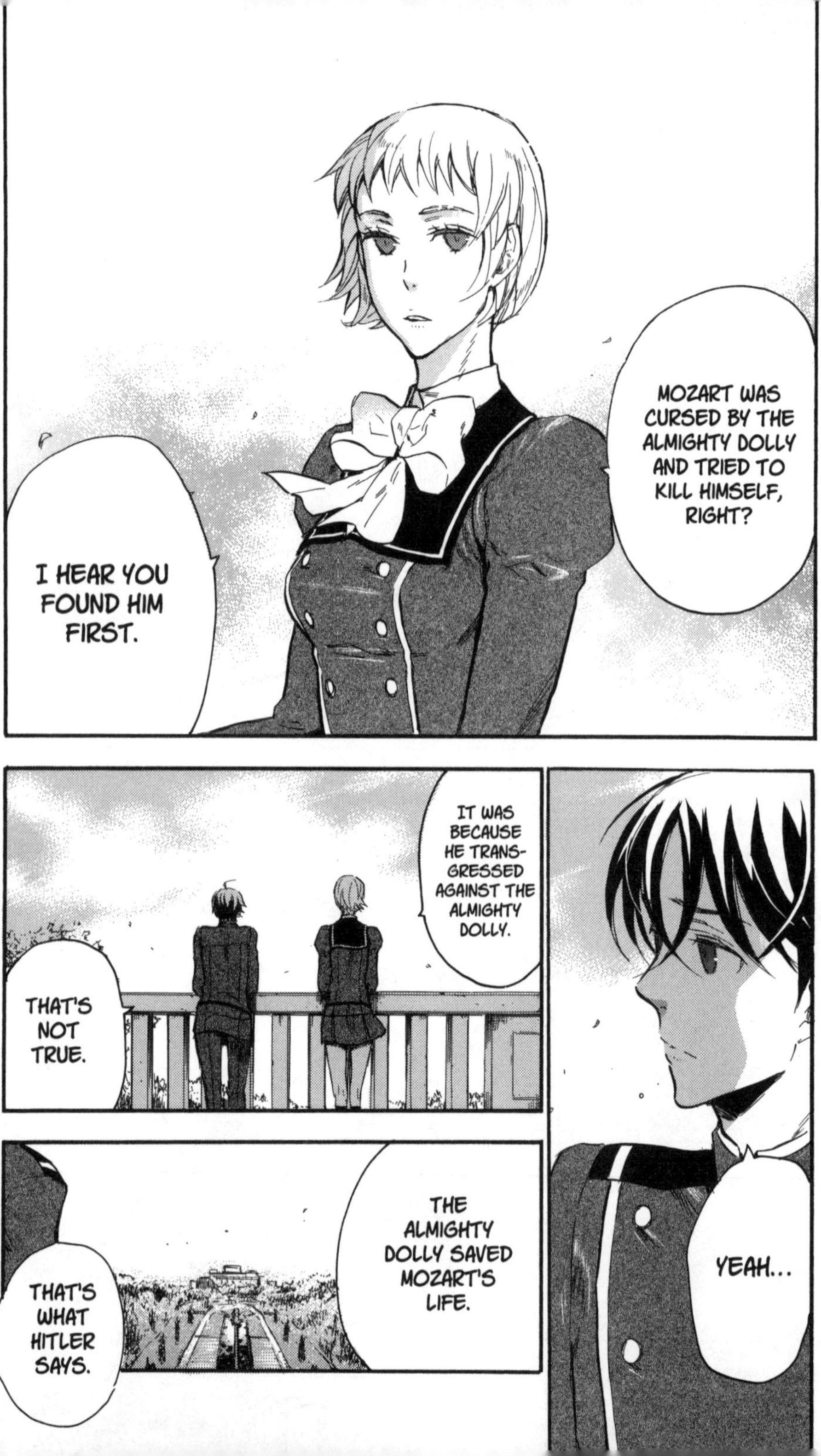
MOZART WAS CURSED BY THE ALMIGHTY DOLLY AND TRIED TO KILL HIMSELF, RIGHT?
I HEAR YOU FOUND HIM FIRST.
YEAH...
IT WAS BECAUSE HE TRANS-GRESSED AGAINST THE ALMIGHTY DOLLY.
THAT'S NOT TRUE.
THE ALMIGHTY DOLLY SAVED MOZART'S LIFE.
THAT'S WHAT HITLER SAYS.

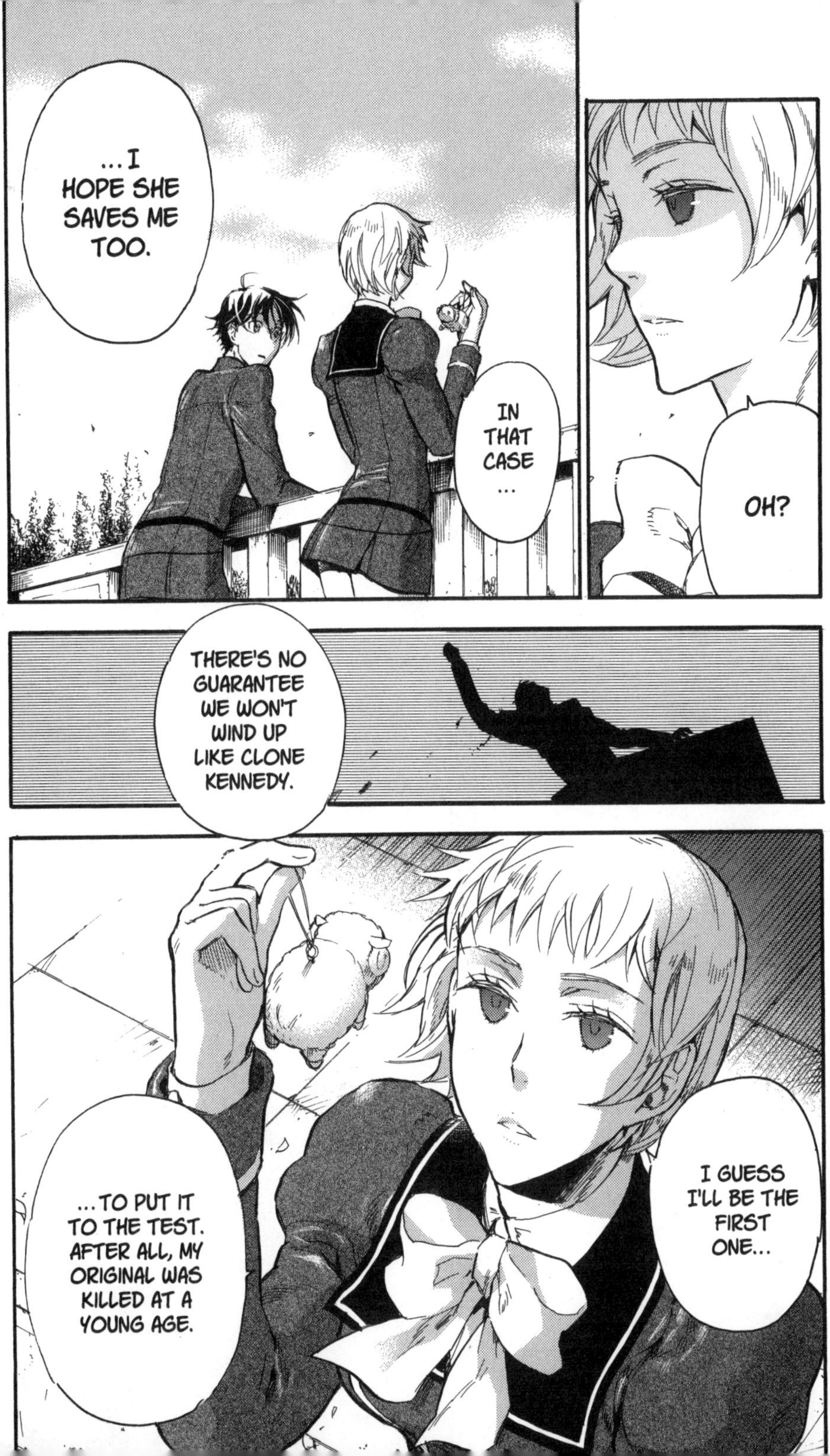
OH?
...I HOPE SHE SAVES ME TOO.
IN THAT CASE...
THERE'S NO GUARANTEE WE WON'T WIND UP LIKE CLONE KENNEDY.
I GUESS I'LL BE THE FIRST ONE...
...TO PUT IT TO THE TEST. AFTER ALL, MY ORIGINAL WAS KILLED AT A YOUNG AGE.

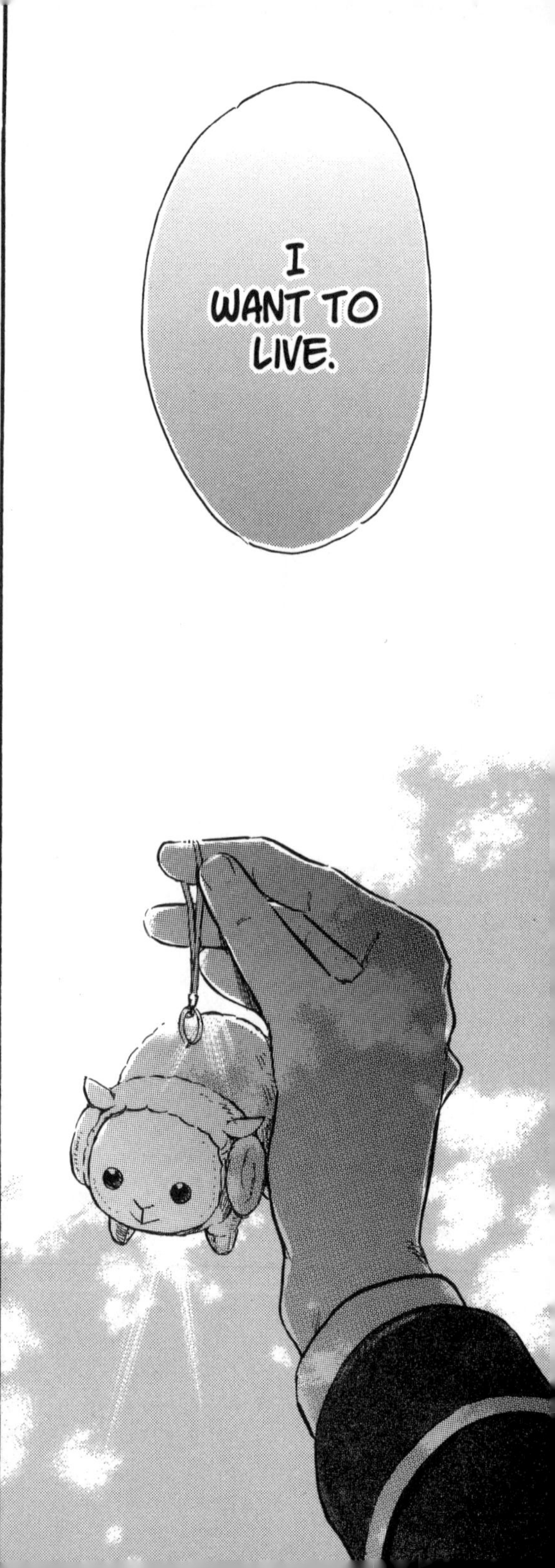
I WANT TO LIVE.

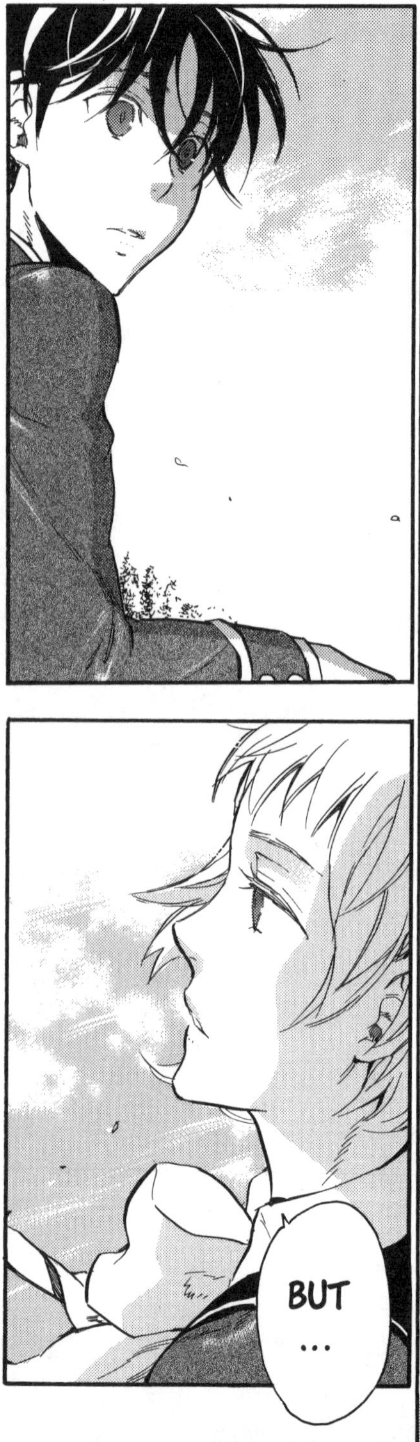
BUT ...

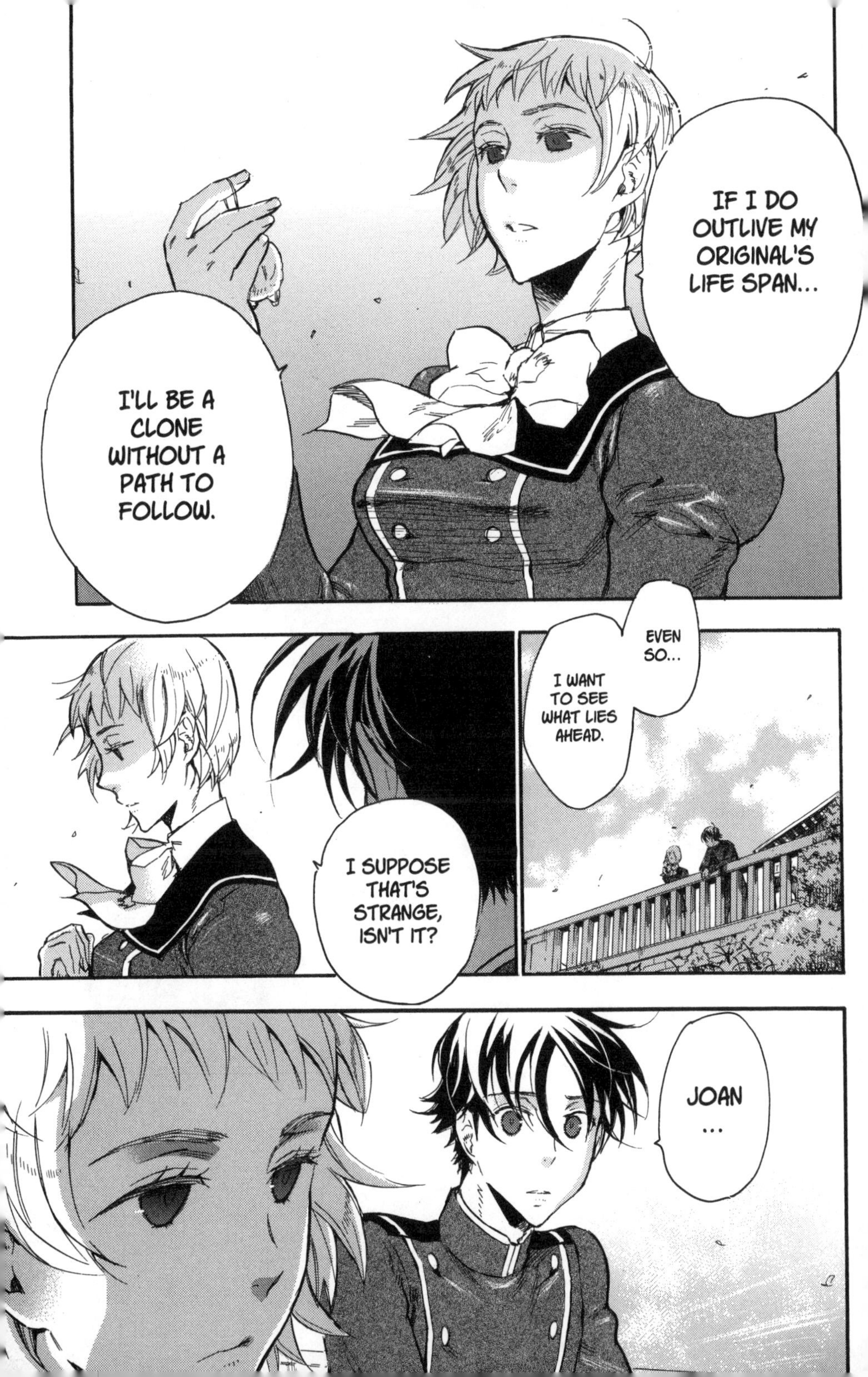
IF I DO OUTLIVE MY ORIGINAL'S LIFE SPAN...
I'LL BE A CLONE WITHOUT A PATH TO FOLLOW.
EVEN SO...
I WANT TO SEE WHAT LIES AHEAD.
I SUPPOSE THAT'S STRANGE, ISN'T IT?
JOAN ...

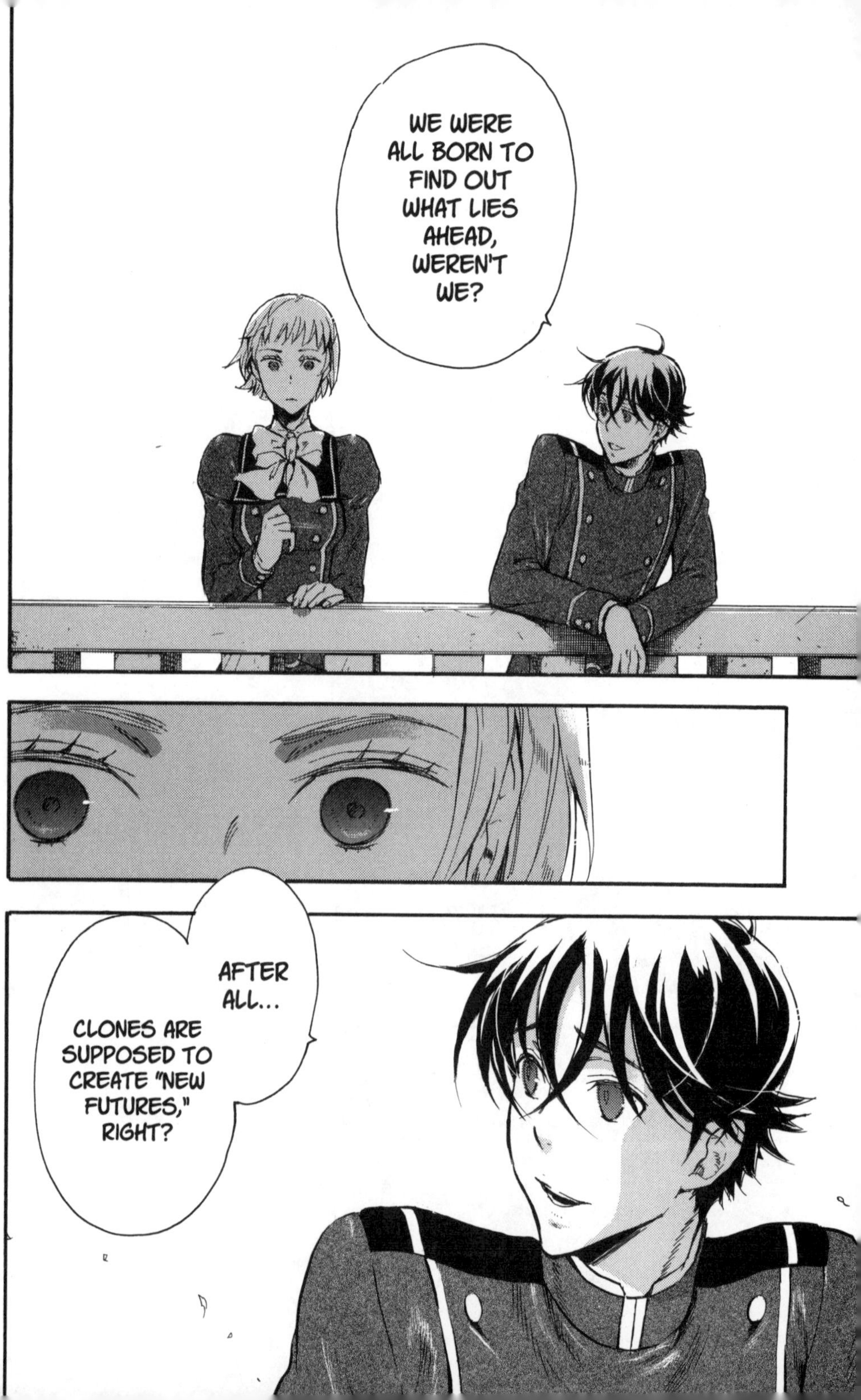
WE WERE ALL BORN TO FIND OUT WHAT LIES AHEAD, WEREN'T WE?
AFTER ALL...
CLONES ARE SUPPOSED TO CREATE "NEW FUTURES," RIGHT?

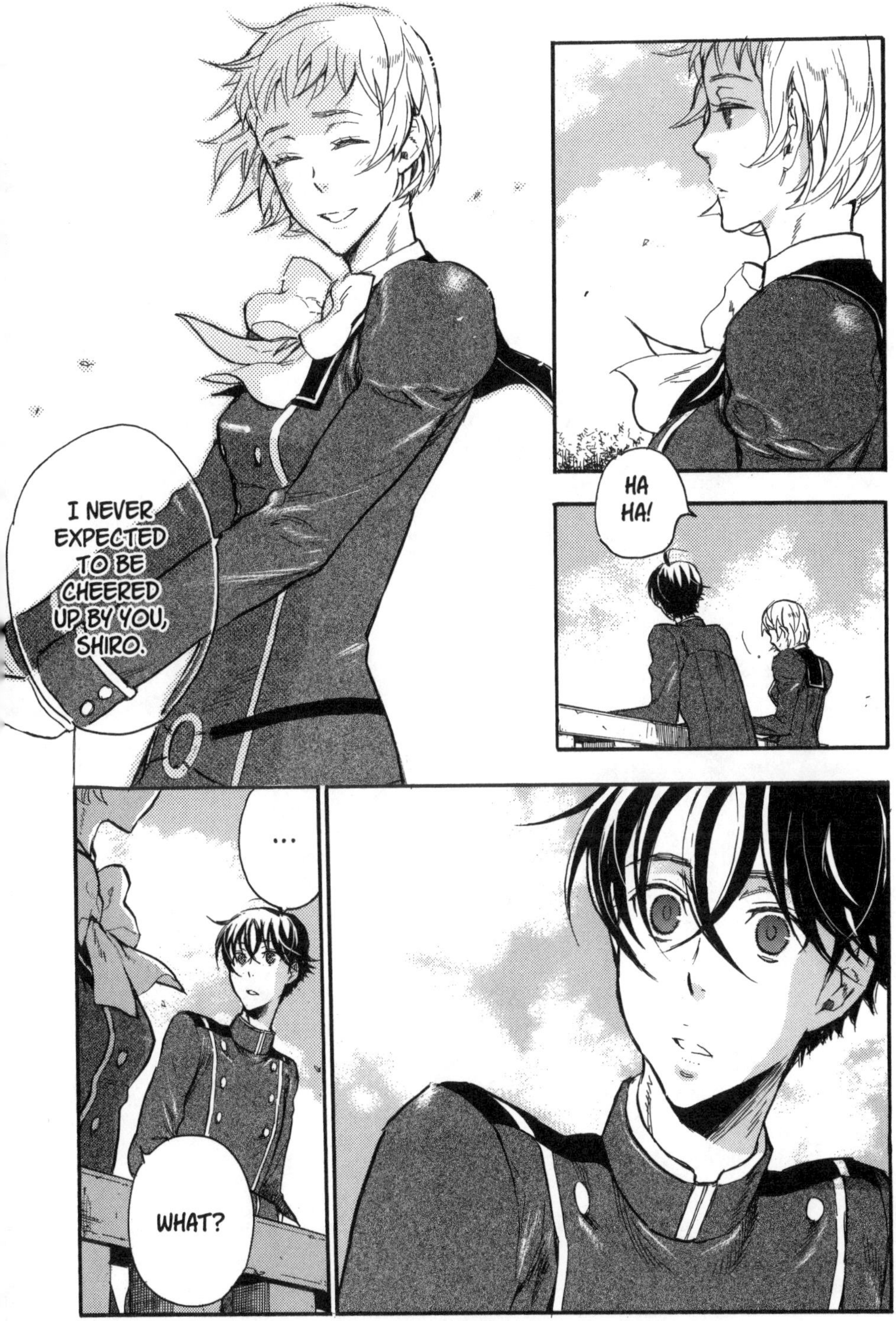
HA HA!
I NEVER EXPECTED TO BE CHEERED UP BY YOU, SHIRO.
...
WHAT?

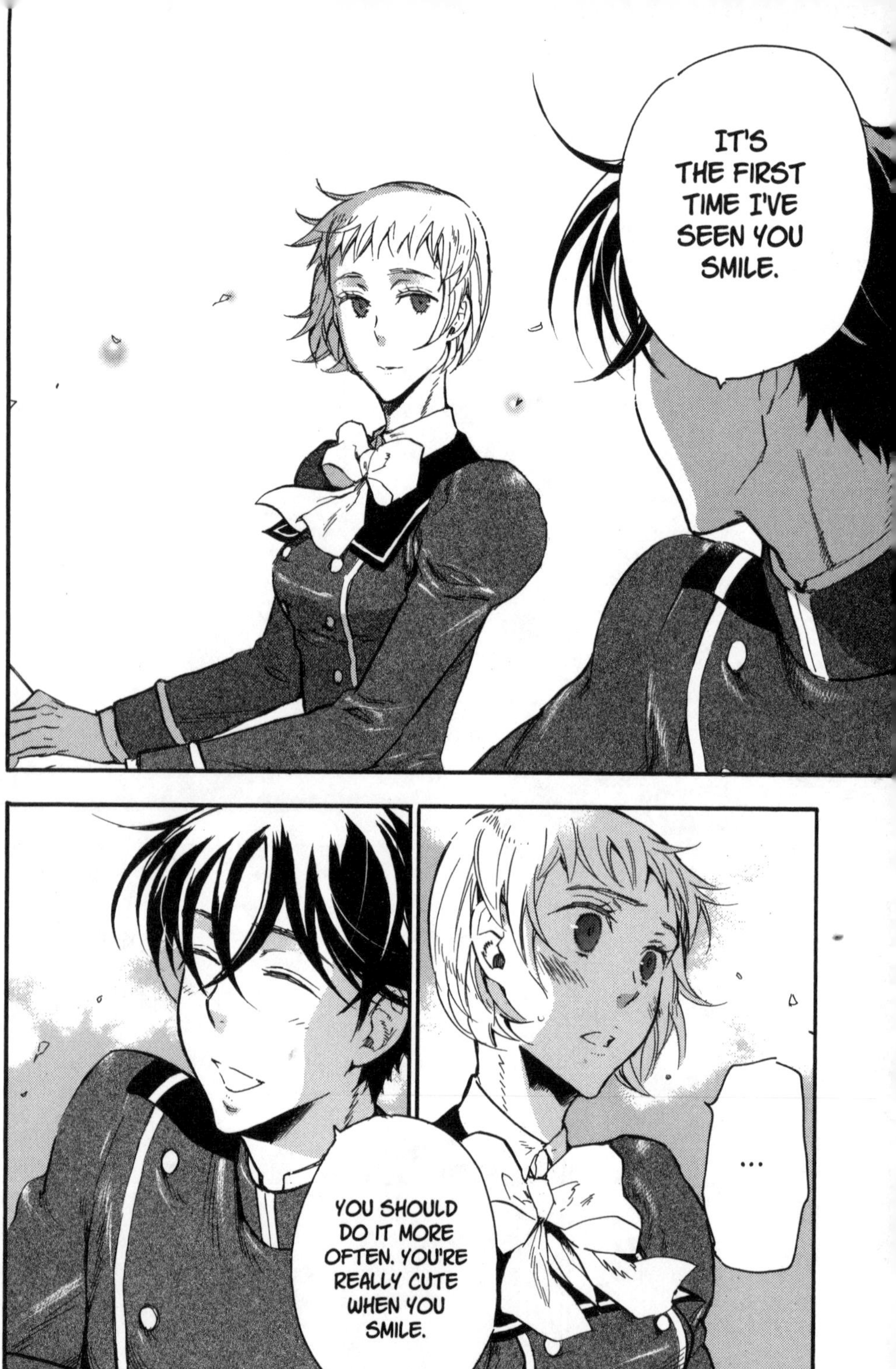
IT'S THE FIRST TIME I'VE SEEN YOU SMILE.
...
YOU SHOULD DO IT MORE OFTEN. YOU'RE REALLY CUTE WHEN YOU SMILE.

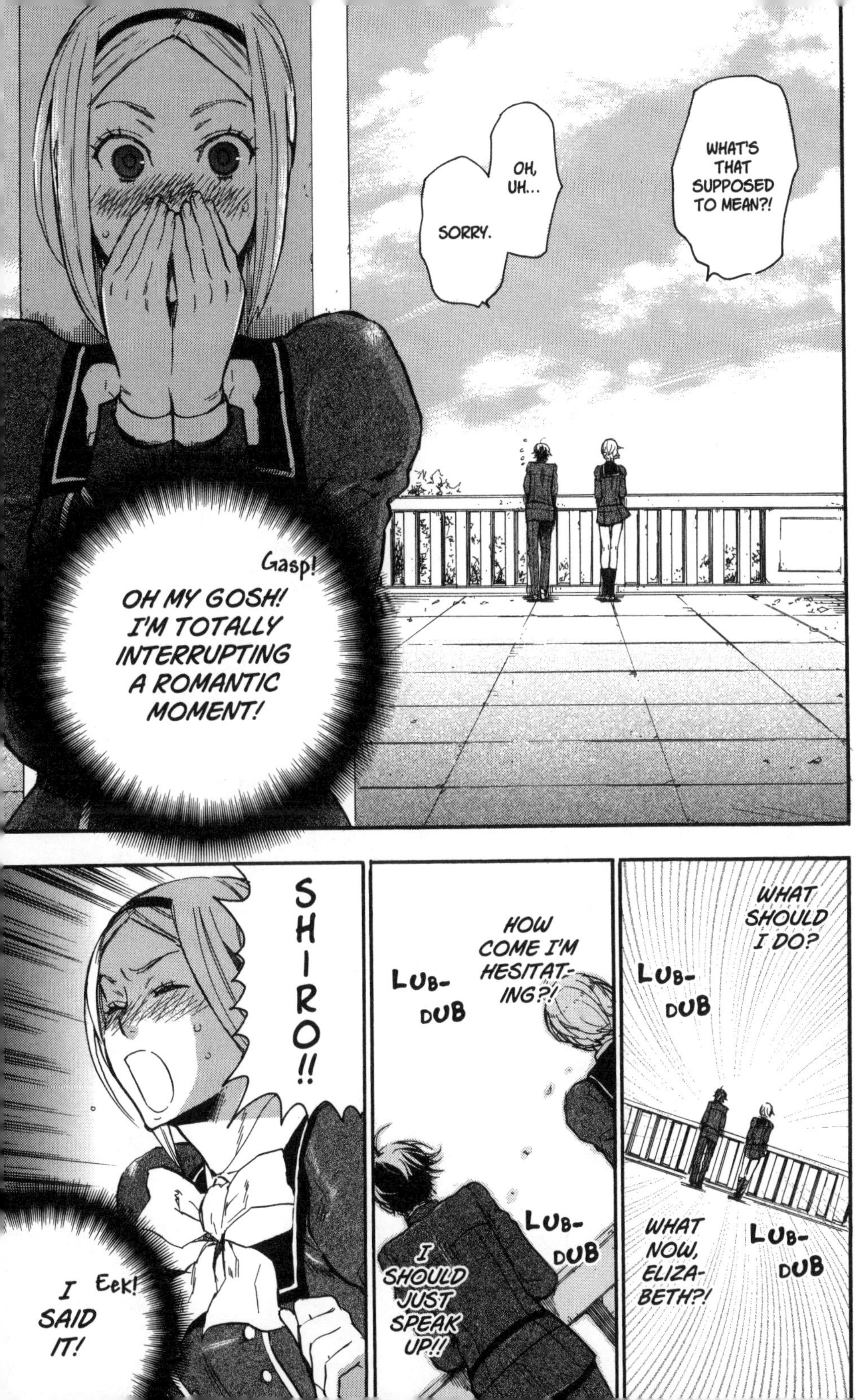
WHAT'S THAT SUPPOSED TO MEAN?!
OH, UH...
SORRY.
Gasp!
OH MY GOSH! I'M TOTALLY INTERRUPTING A ROMANTIC MOMENT!
WHAT SHOULD I DO?
LUB-DUB
LUB-DUB
WHAT NOW, ELIZABETH?!
HOW COME I'M HESITATING?!
LUB-DUB
LUB-DUB
I SHOULD JUST SPEAK UP!!
SHIRO!!
Eek!
I SAID IT!

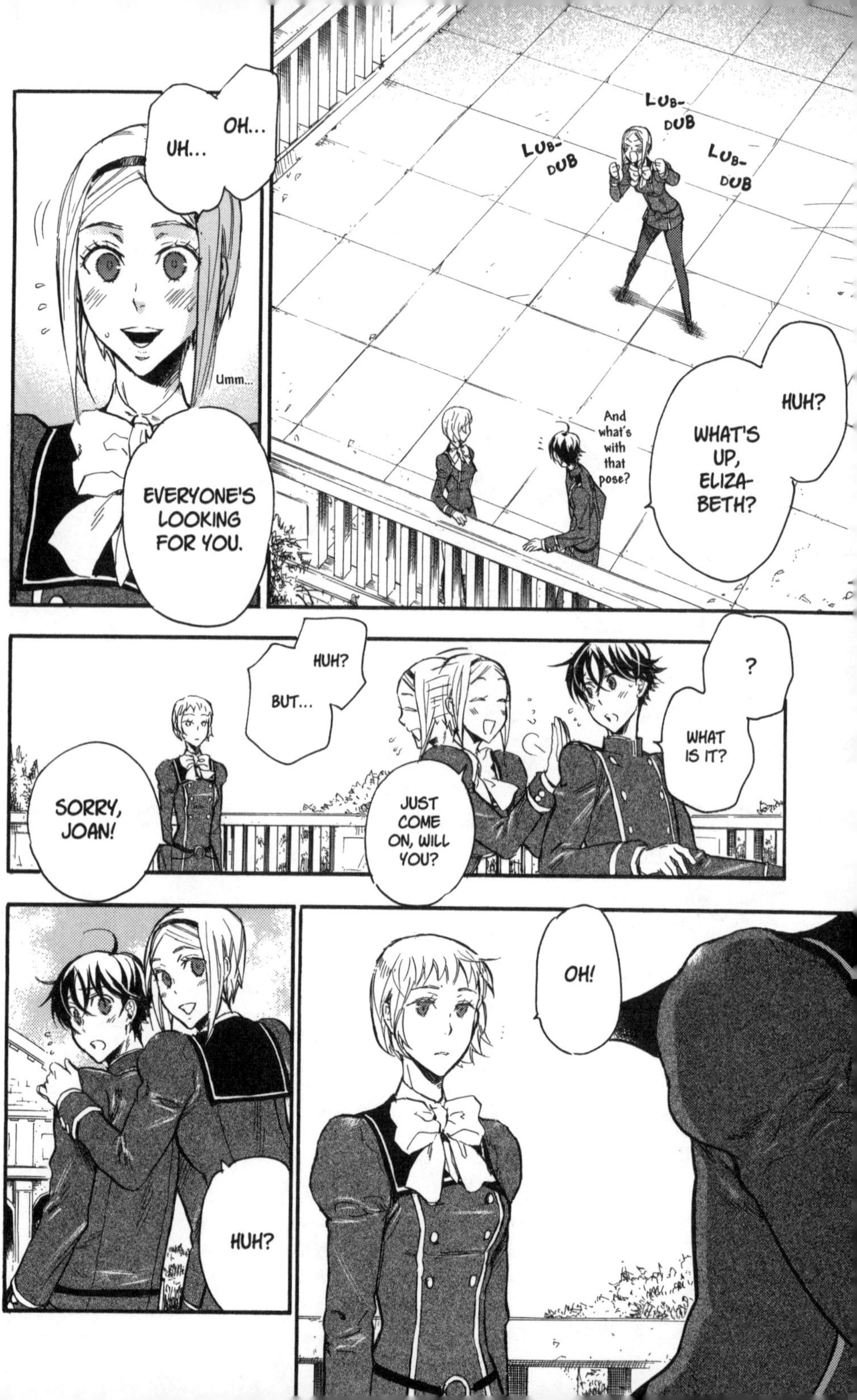
LUB-DUB
LUB-DUB
LUB-DUB
HUH?
WHAT'S UP, ELIZABETH?
And what's with that pose?
OH...
UH...
Umm...
EVERYONE'S LOOKING FOR YOU.
?
WHAT IS IT?
JUST COME ON, WILL YOU?
HUH?
BUT...
SORRY, JOAN!
OH!
HUH?

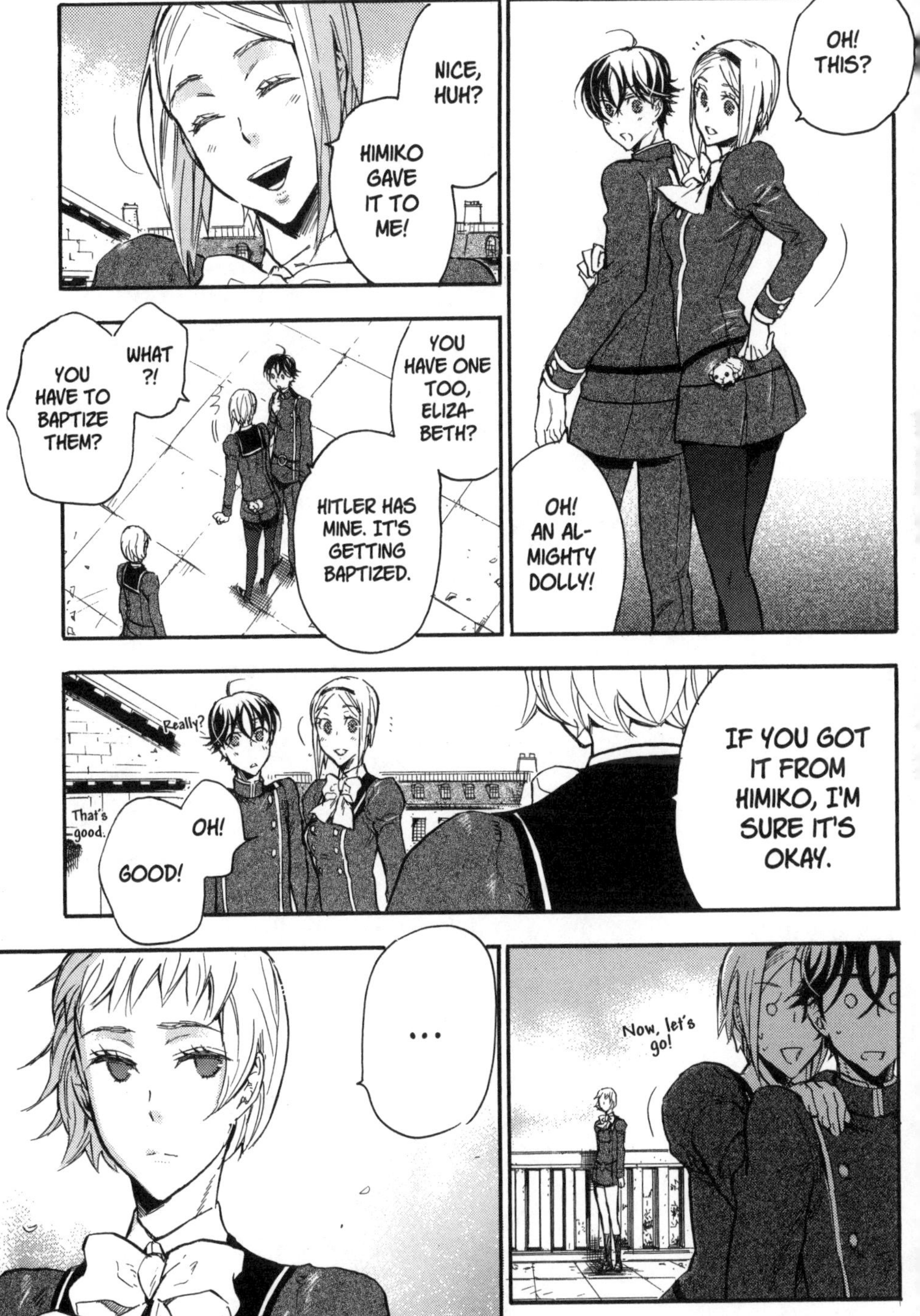
OH! THIS?
OH! AN AL-MIGHTY DOLLY!
NICE, HUH?
HIMIKO GAVE IT TO ME!
YOU HAVE ONE TOO, ELIZA-BETH?
HITLER HAS MINE. IT'S GETTING BAPTIZED.
WHAT?!
YOU HAVE TO BAPTIZE THEM?
IF YOU GOT IT FROM HIMIKO, I'M SURE IT'S OKAY.
Really?
OH! GOOD!
That's good.
Now, let's go!
...

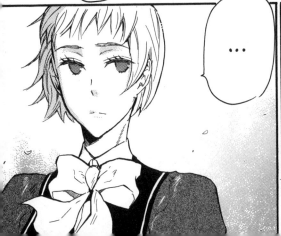

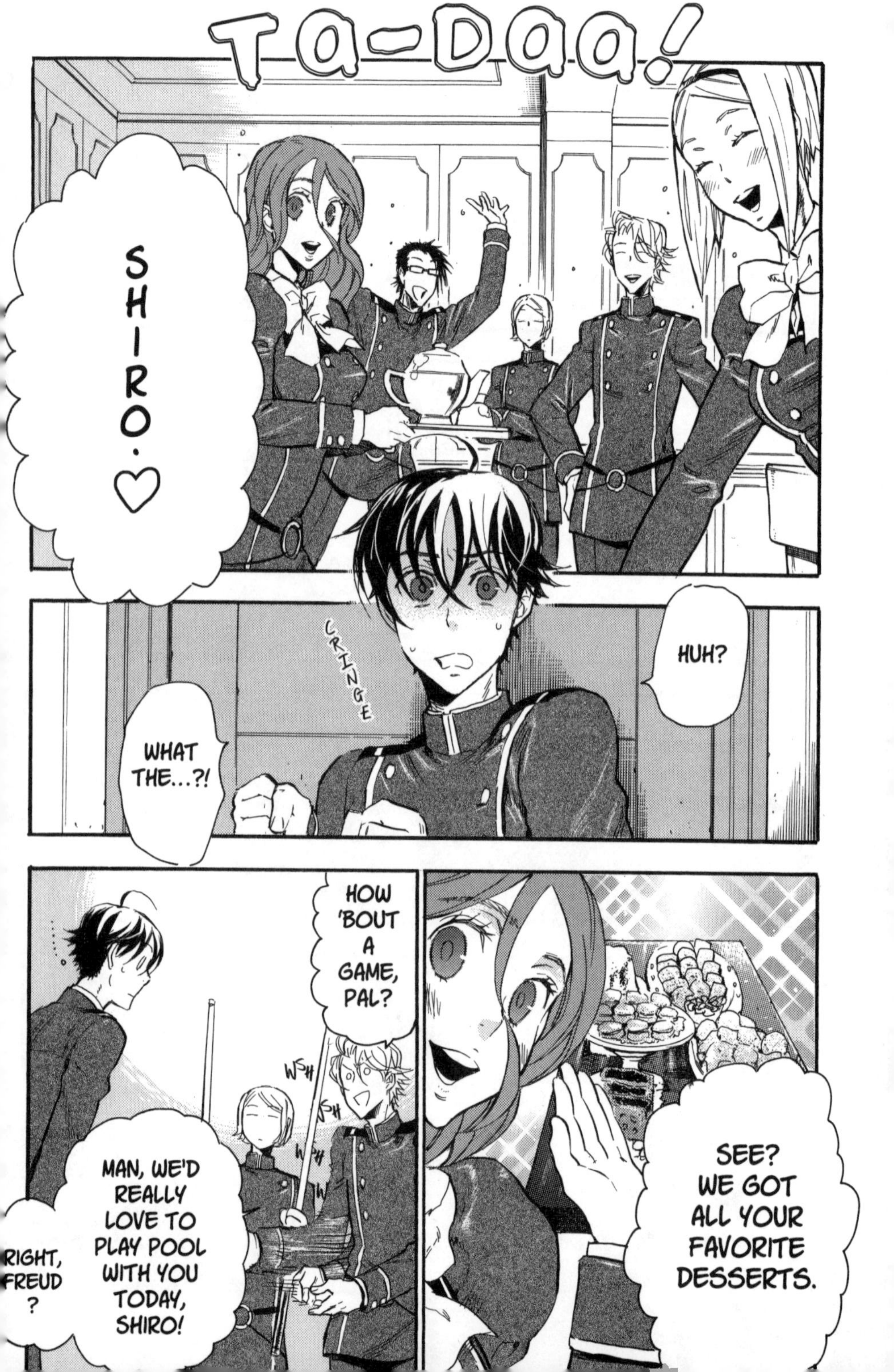
TA-DAA!
SHIRO. ♥
HUH?
CRINGE
WHAT THE...?!
SEE? WE GOT ALL YOUR FAVORITE DESSERTS.
HOW 'BOUT A GAME, PAL?
WSH WSH WSH
MAN, WE'D REALLY LOVE TO PLAY POOL WITH YOU TODAY, SHIRO!
RIGHT, FREUD?

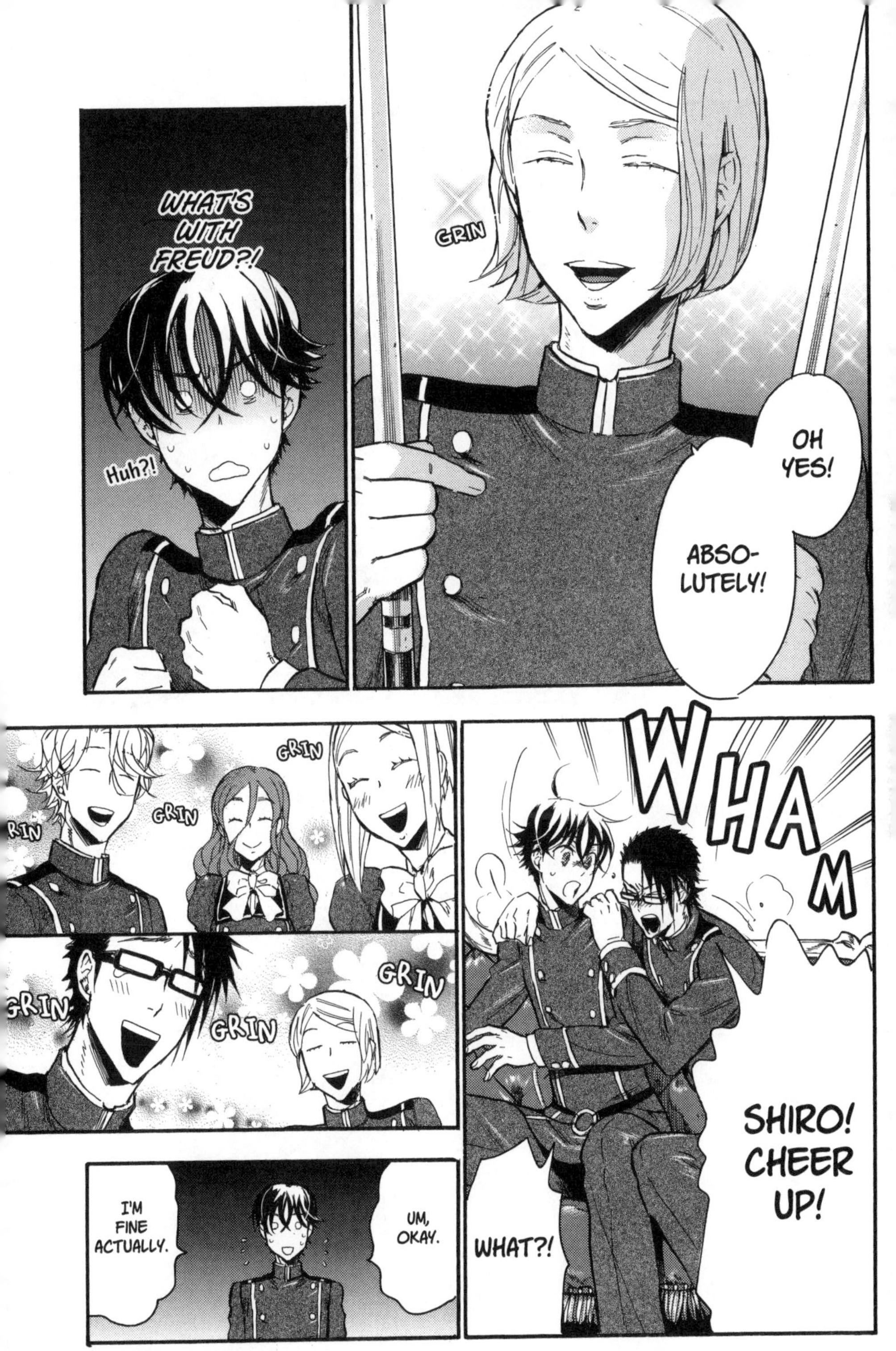
GRIN
OH YES!
ABSO-
LUTELY!
WHAT'S WITH FREUD?!
Huh?!
WHAM
SHIRO! CHEER UP!
WHAT?!
GRIN
GRIN
GRIN
RIN
GRIN
GRIN
GRIN
UM, OKAY.
I'M FINE ACTUALLY.

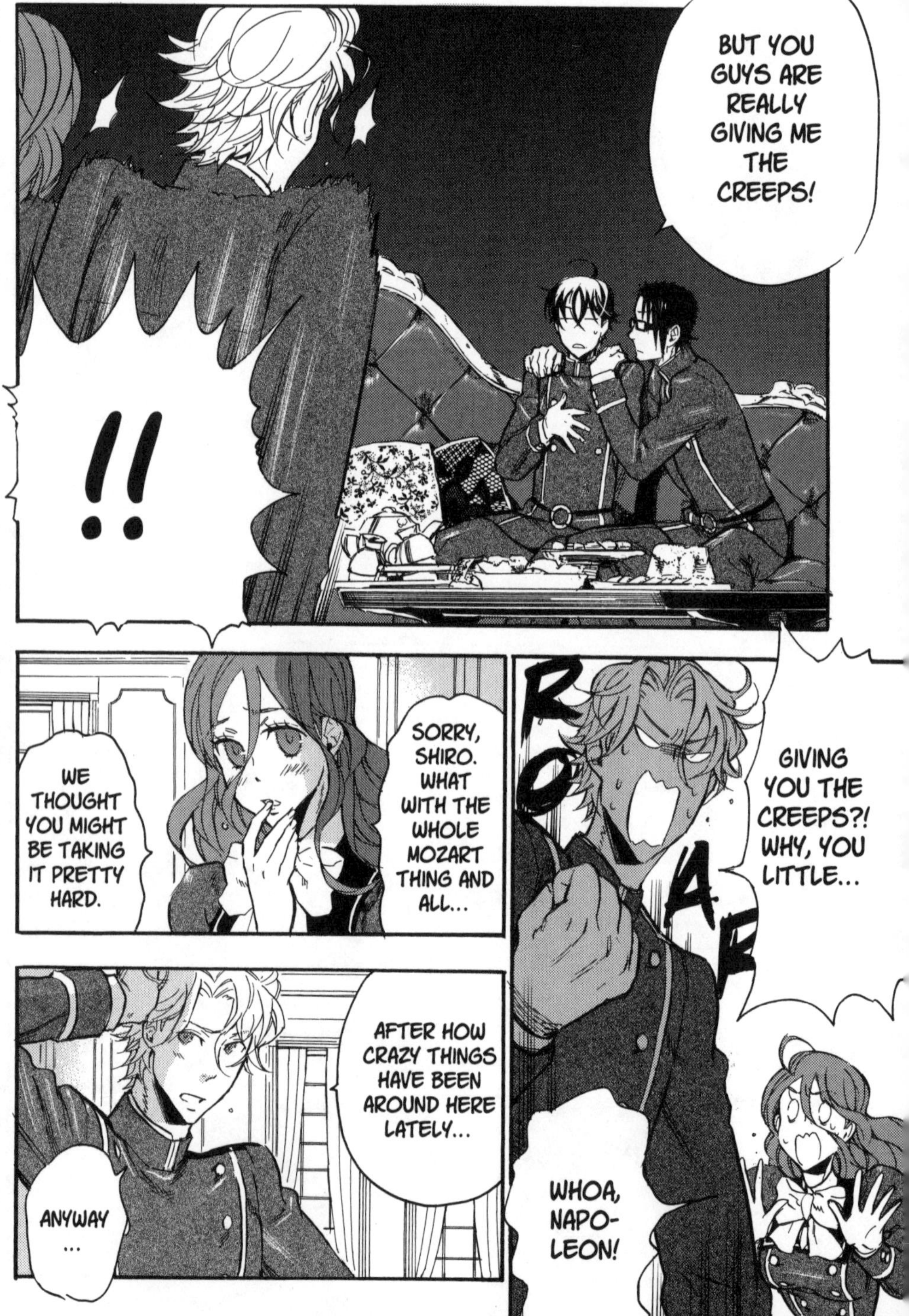
BUT YOU GUYS ARE REALLY GIVING ME THE CREEPS!
!!
GIVING YOU THE CREEPS?! WHY, YOU LITTLE...
ROAR
WHOA, NAPO-LEON!
SORRY, SHIRO. WHAT WITH THE WHOLE MOZART THING AND ALL...
WE THOUGHT YOU MIGHT BE TAKING IT PRETTY HARD.
AFTER HOW CRAZY THINGS HAVE BEEN AROUND HERE LATELY...
ANYWAY...

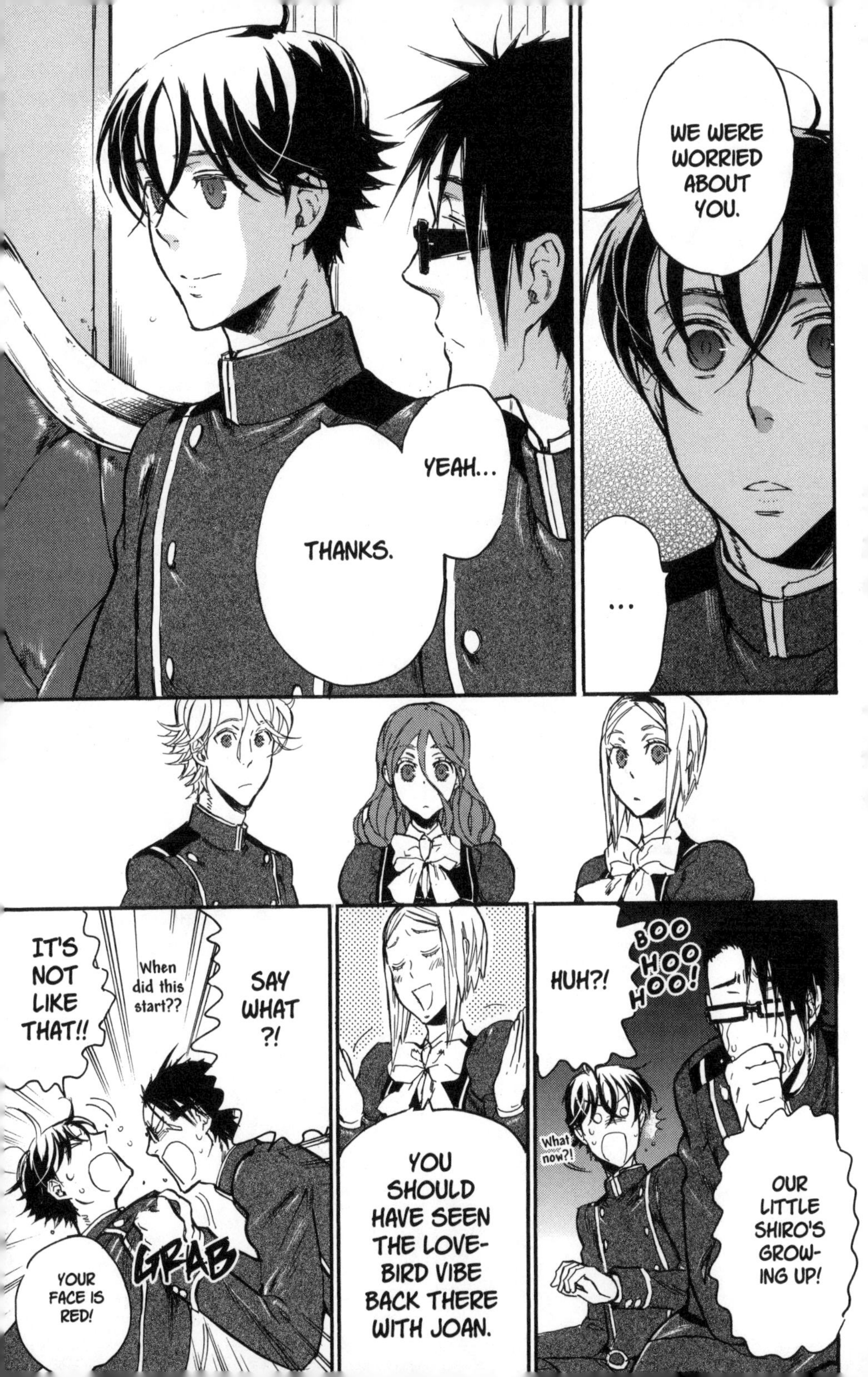
WE WERE WORRIED ABOUT YOU.
...
YEAH... THANKS.
BOO HOO HOO!
HUH?!
OUR LITTLE SHIRO'S GROW-ING UP!
What now?!
YOU SHOULD HAVE SEEN THE LOVE-BIRD VIBE BACK THERE WITH JOAN.
SAY WHAT?!
When did this start??
IT'S NOT LIKE THAT!!
GRAB
YOUR FACE IS RED!

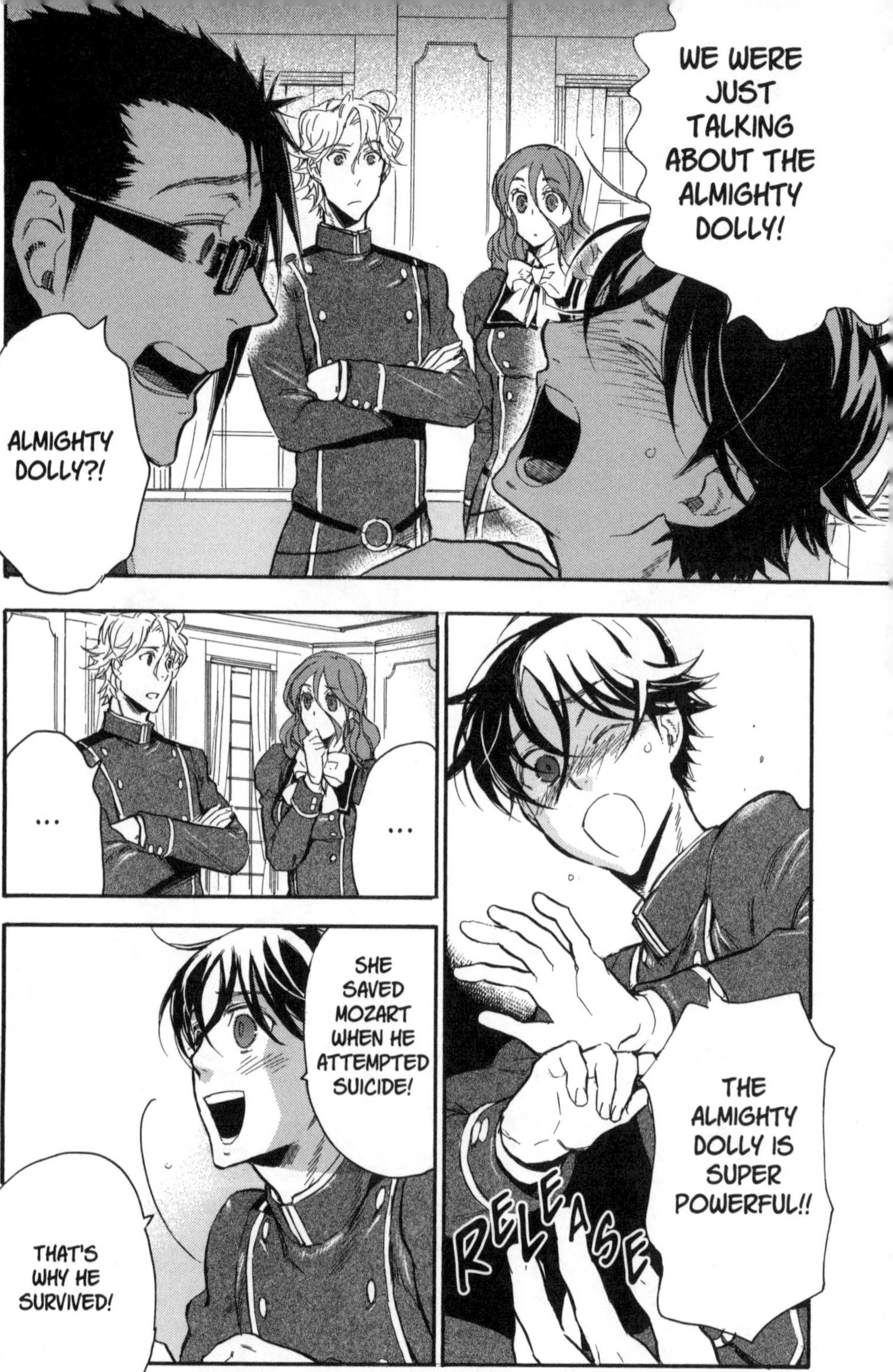
WE WERE JUST TALKING ABOUT THE ALMIGHTY DOLLY!
ALMIGHTY DOLLY?!
THE ALMIGHTY DOLLY IS SUPER POWERFUL!!
RELEASE
...
...
SHE SAVED MOZART WHEN HE ATTEMPTED SUICIDE!
THAT'S WHY HE SURVIVED!

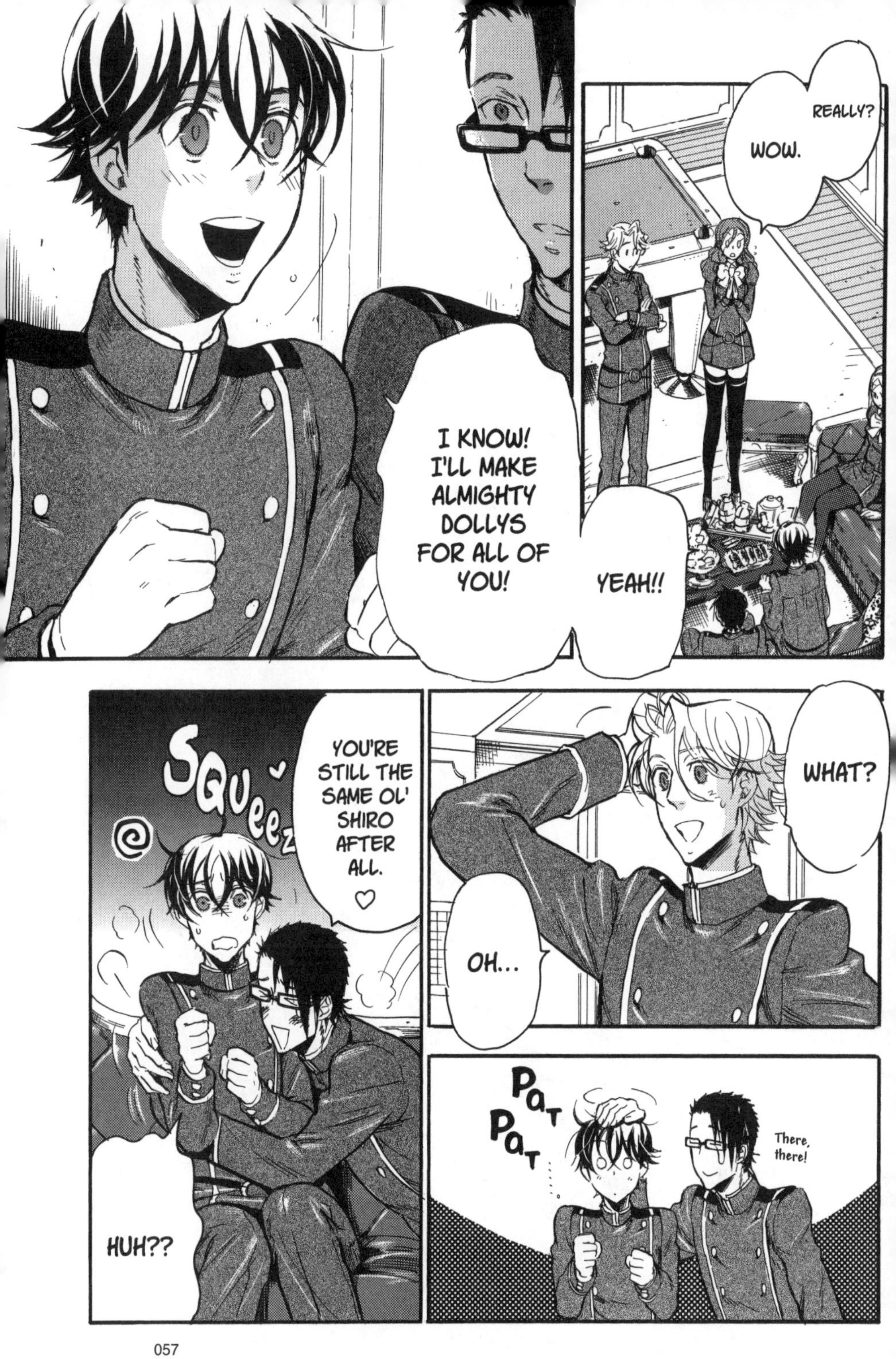
REALLY?
WOW.
I KNOW! I'LL MAKE ALMIGHTY DOLLYS FOR ALL OF YOU!
YEAH!!
WHAT?
OH...
Pat Pat
There, there!
SQueez
YOU'RE STILL THE SAME OL' SHIRO AFTER ALL. ♡
HUH??

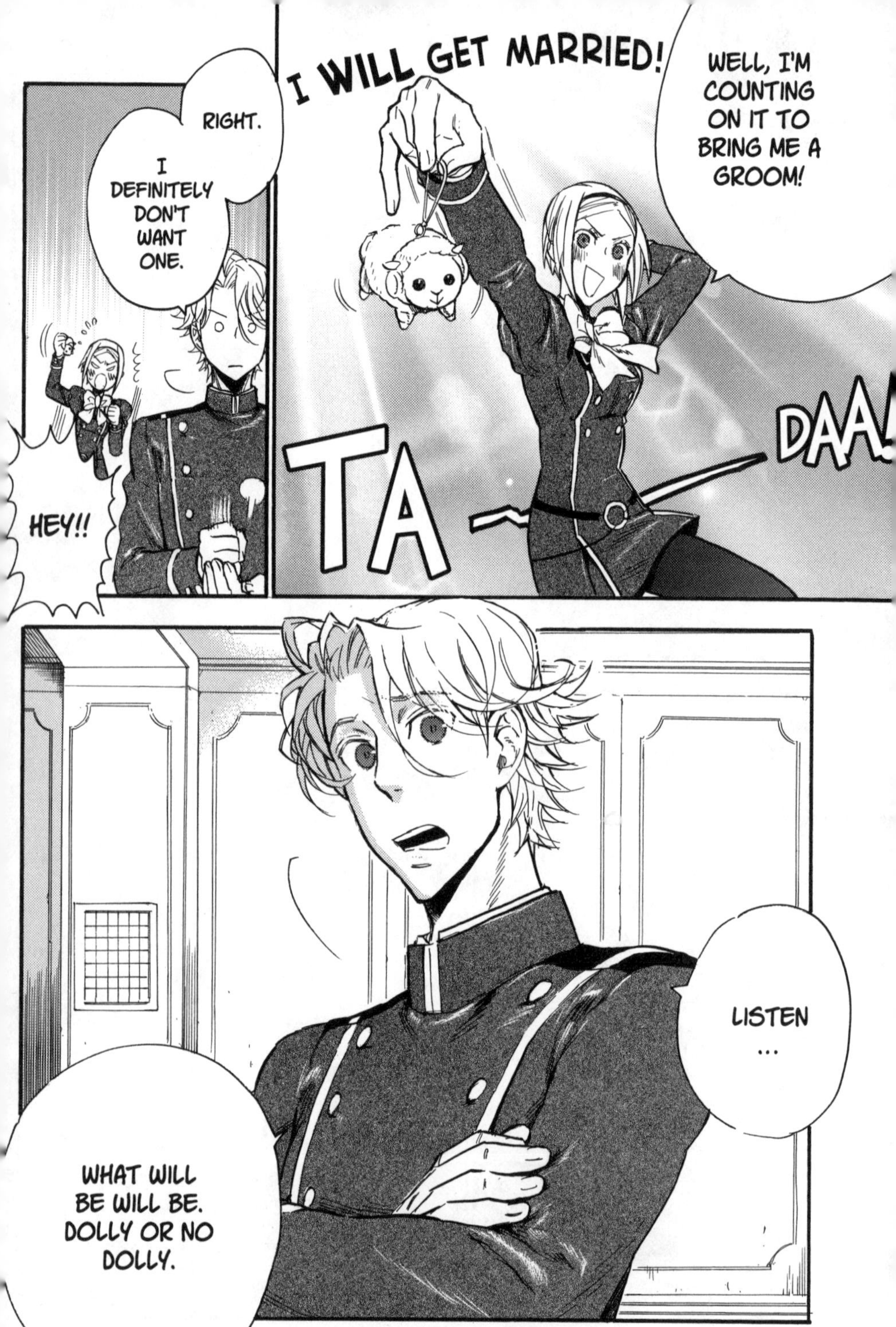
WELL, I'M COUNTING ON IT TO BRING ME A GROOM!
I WILL GET MARRIED!
TA~
DAA!
RIGHT.
I DEFINITELY DON'T WANT ONE.
HEY!!
LISTEN ...
WHAT WILL BE WILL BE. DOLLY OR NO DOLLY.

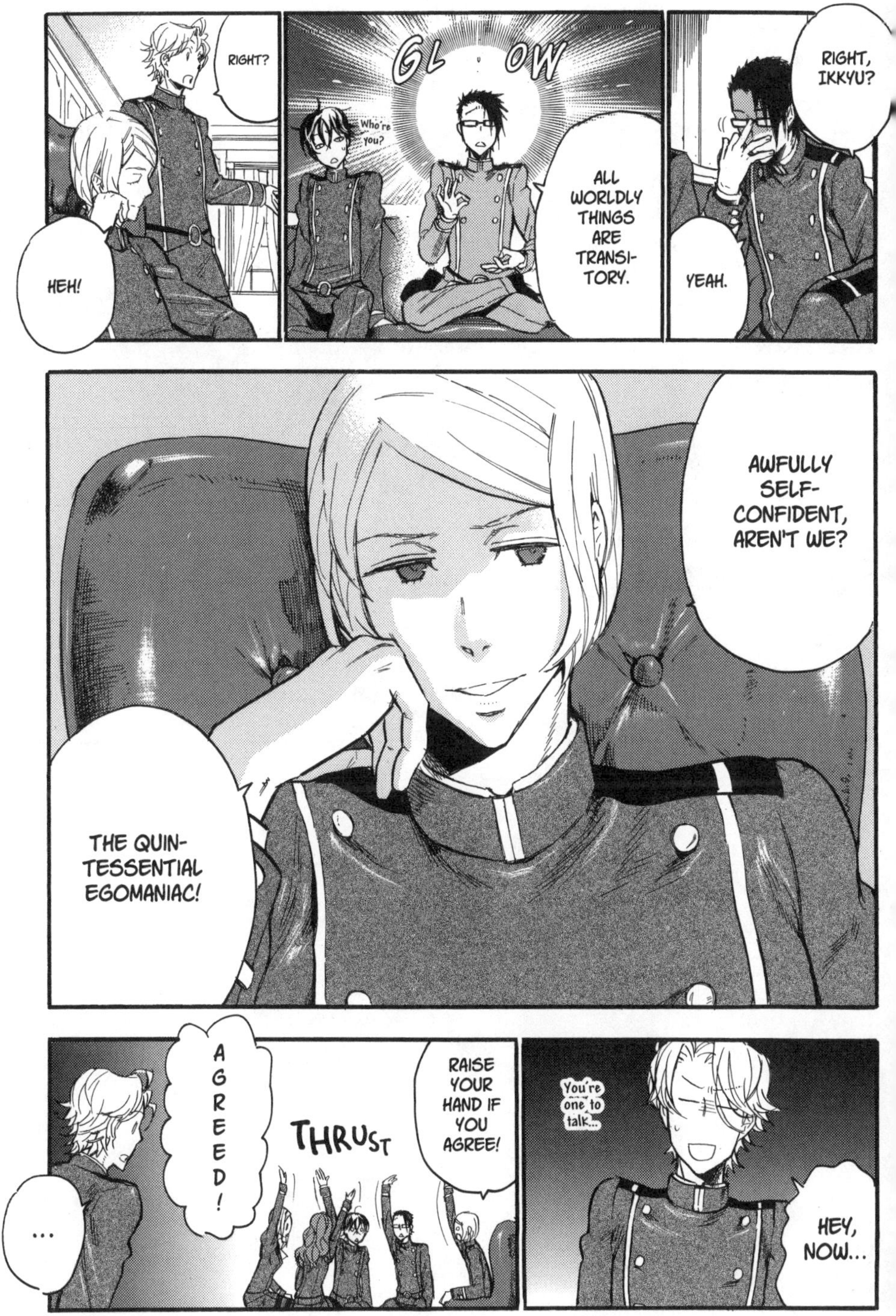
RIGHT, IKKYU?
YEAH.
GL OW
ALL WORLDLY THINGS ARE TRANSITORY.
Who're you?
RIGHT?
HEH!
AWFULLY SELF-CONFIDENT, AREN'T WE?
THE QUIN-TESSENTIAL EGOMANIAC!
You're one to talk...
HEY, NOW...
RAISE YOUR HAND IF YOU AGREE!
THRUST
AGREED!
...

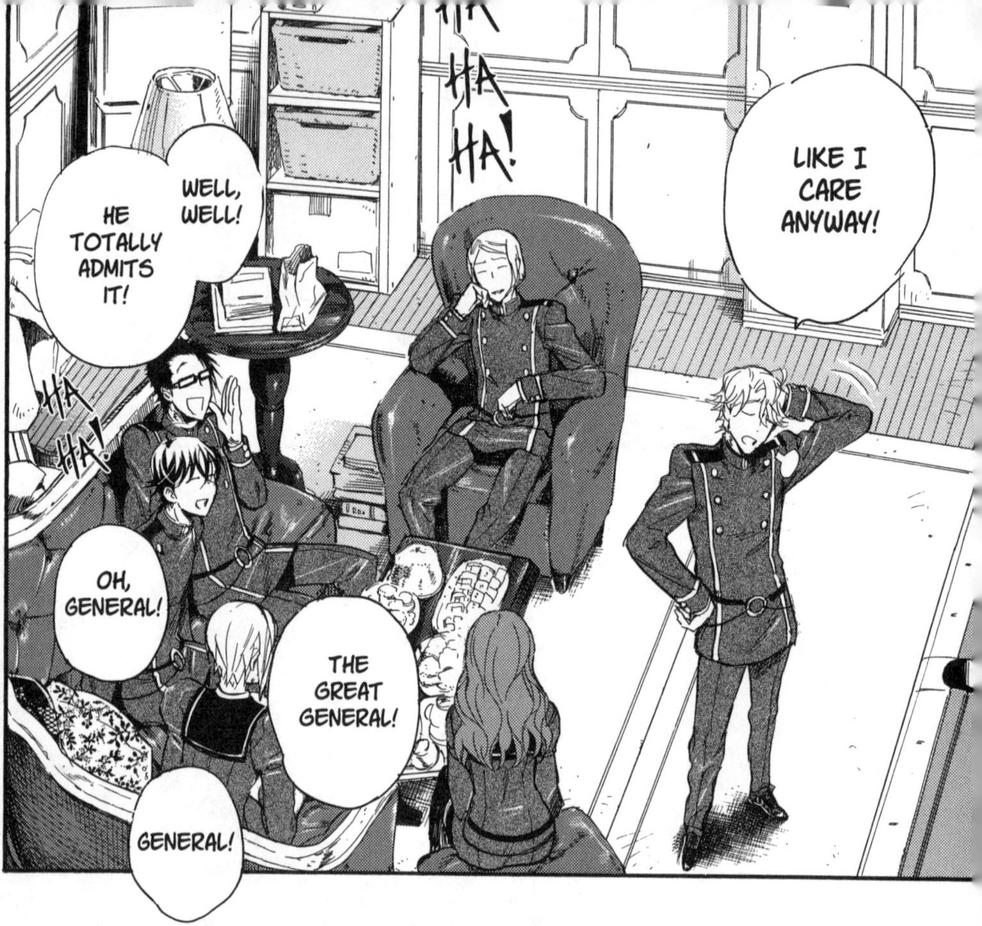
LIKE I CARE ANYWAY!
HA HA!
WELL, WELL!
HE TOTALLY ADMITS IT!
HA HA!
THE GREAT GENERAL!
OH, GENERAL!
GENERAL!

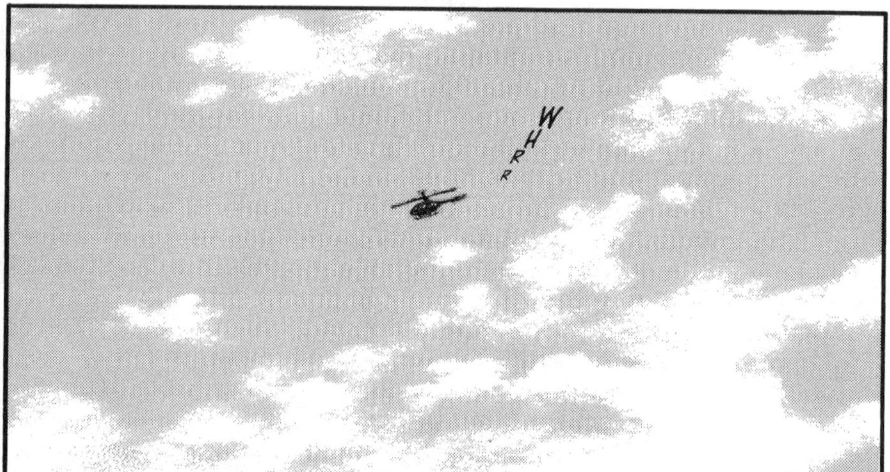
WHRR

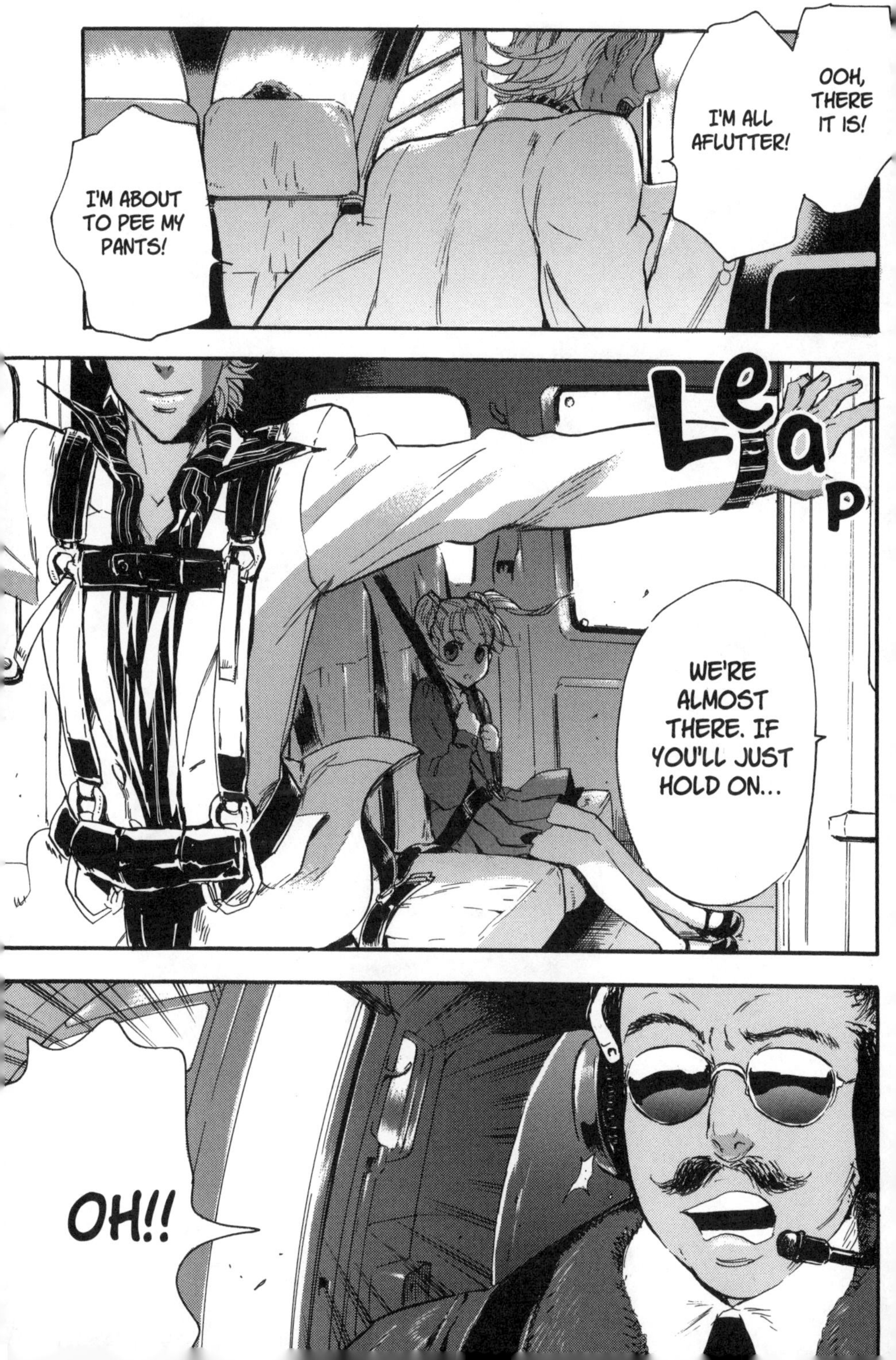
OOH, THERE IT IS!
I'M ALL AFLUTTER!
I'M ABOUT TO PEE MY PANTS!
LEAP
WE'RE ALMOST THERE. IF YOU'LL JUST HOLD ON...
OH!!

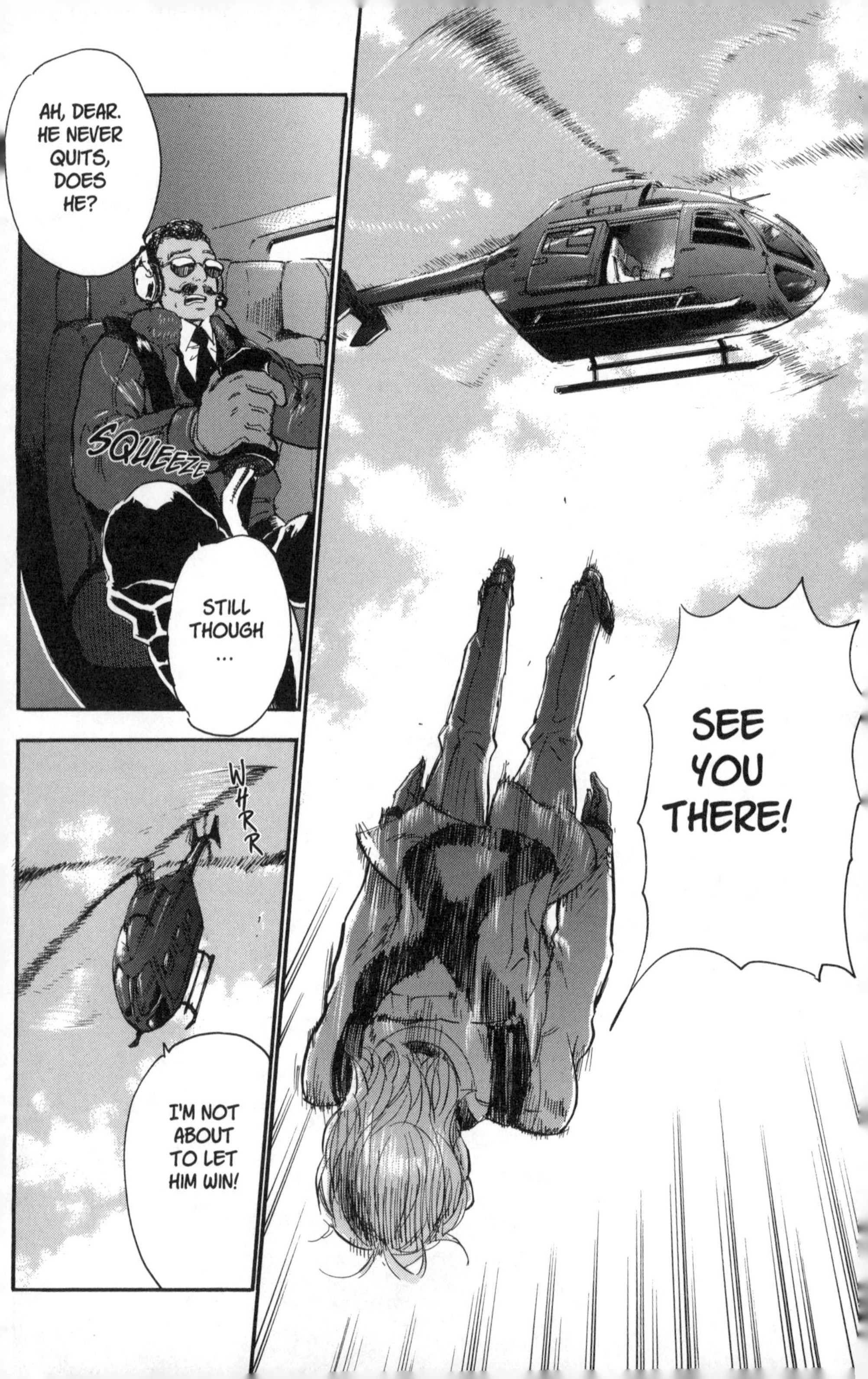
SEE YOU THERE!
AH, DEAR. HE NEVER QUITS, DOES HE?
SQUEEZE
STILL THOUGH ...
WHRR
I'M NOT ABOUT TO LET HIM WIN!

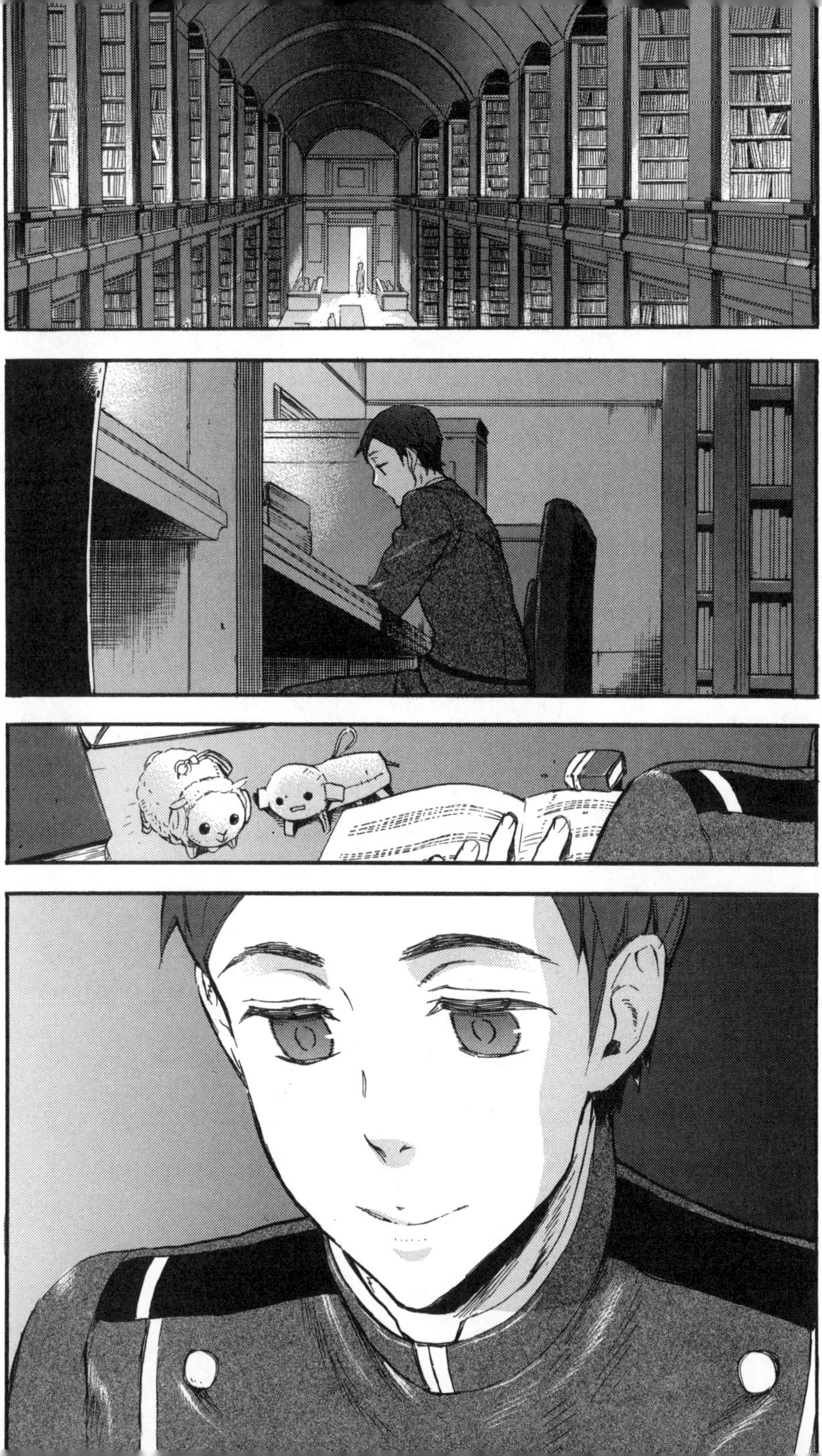

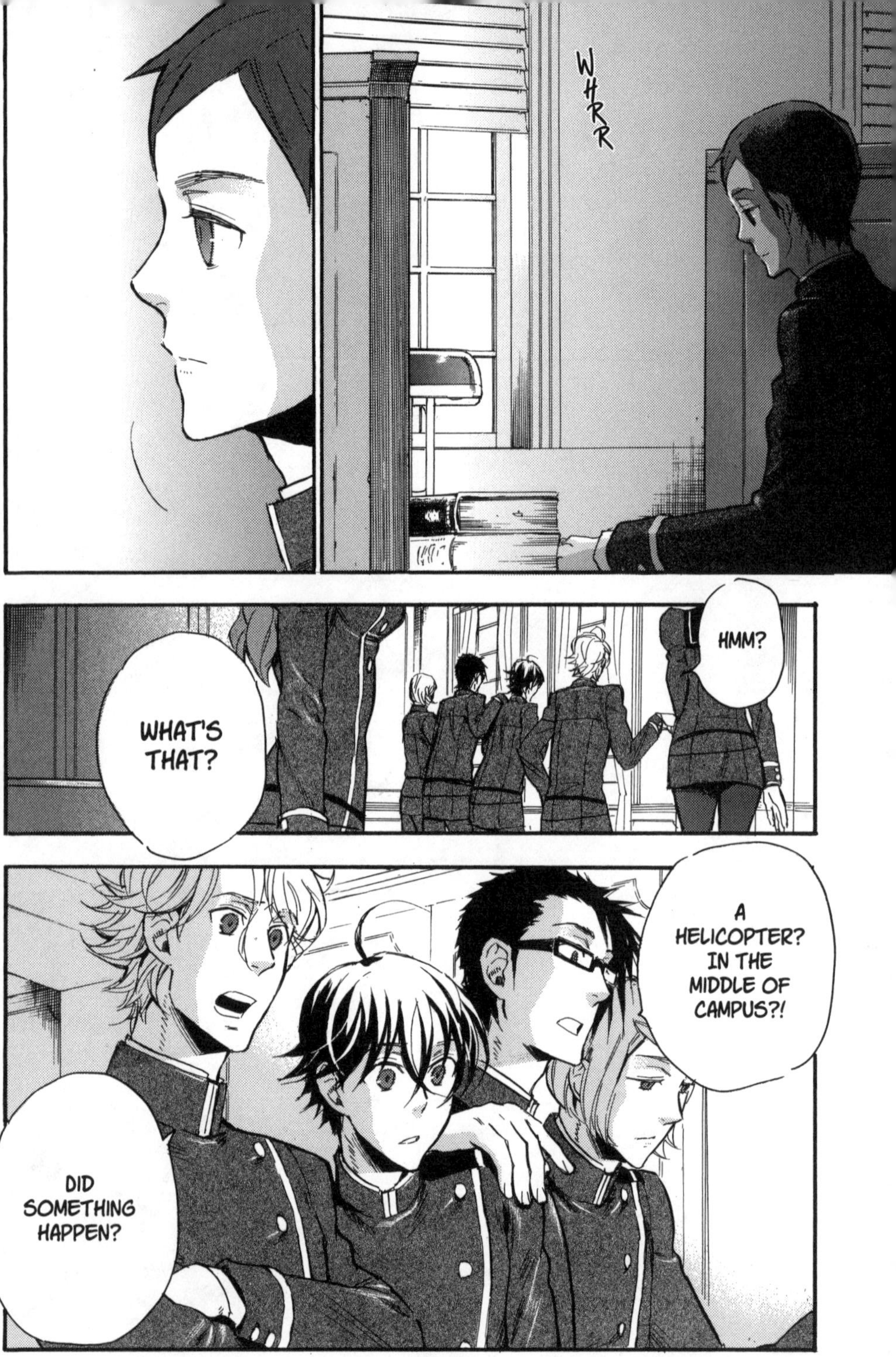
WHRR
HMM?
WHAT'S THAT?
A HELICOPTER? IN THE MIDDLE OF CAMPUS?!
DID SOMETHING HAPPEN?

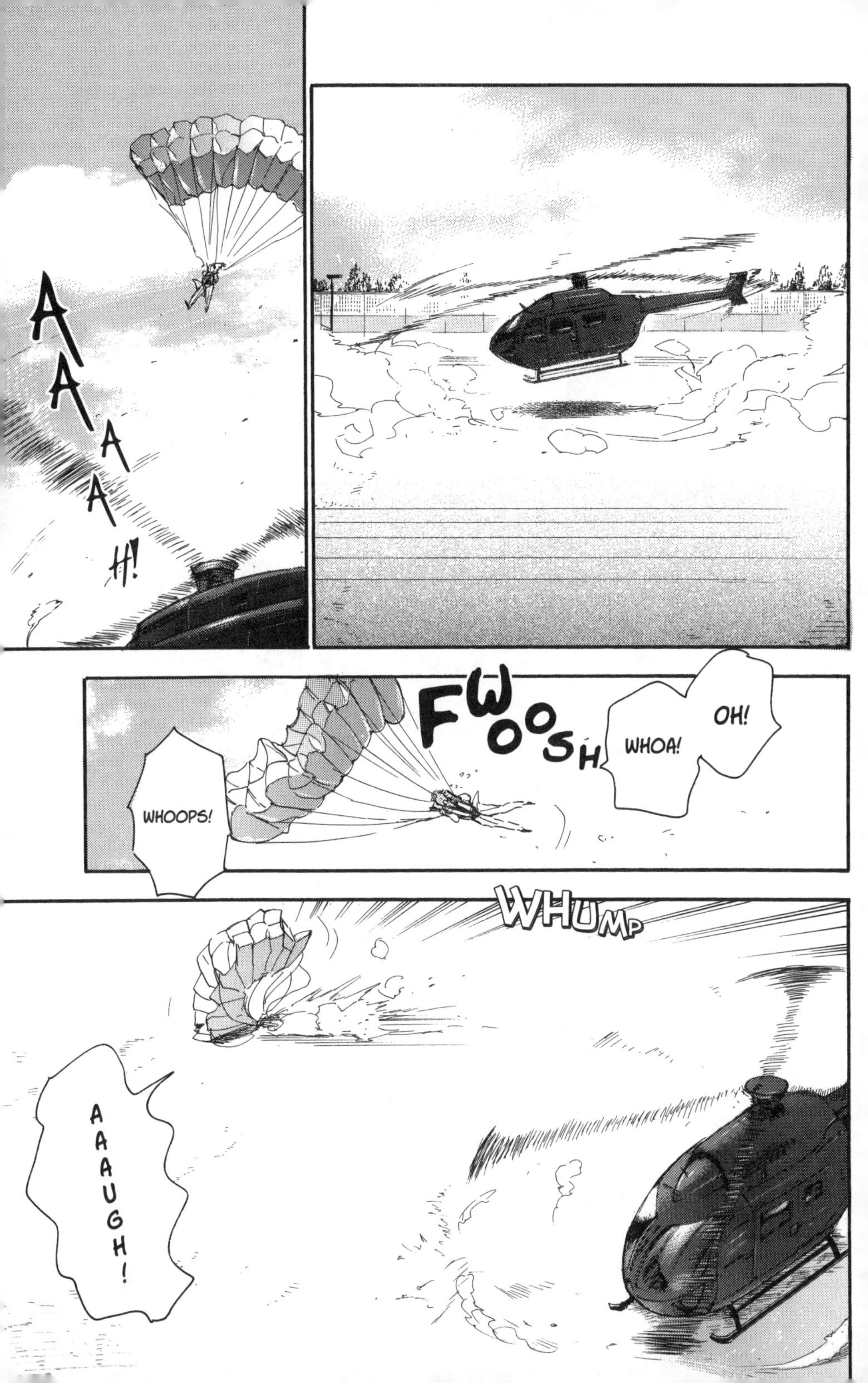
AAAAH!
OH!
WHOA!
FWOOSH
WHOOPS!
WHUMP
AAAUGH!

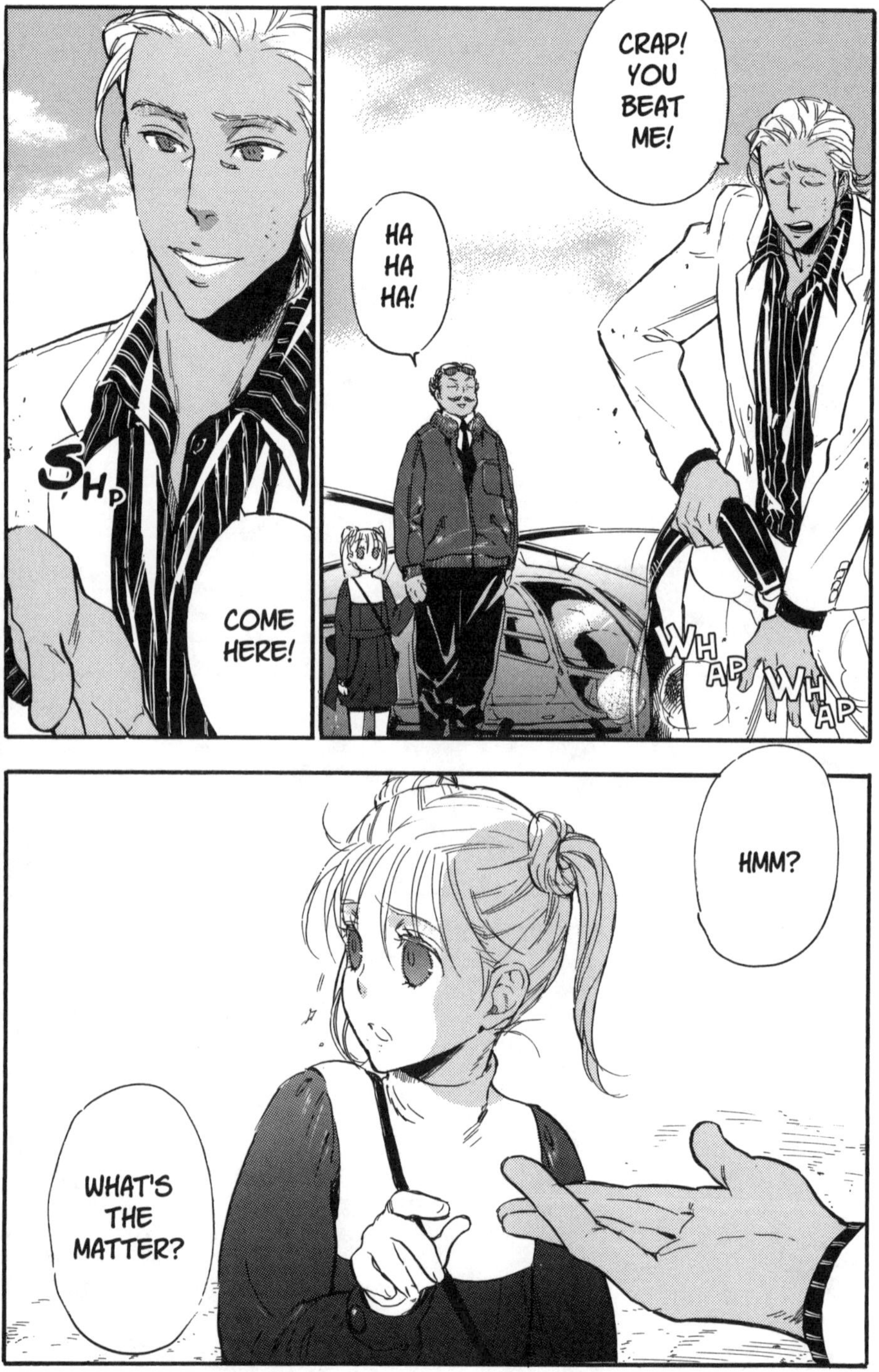
CRAP! YOU BEAT ME!
HA HA HA!
WHAP
WHAP
SHP
COME HERE!
HMM?
WHAT'S THE MATTER?

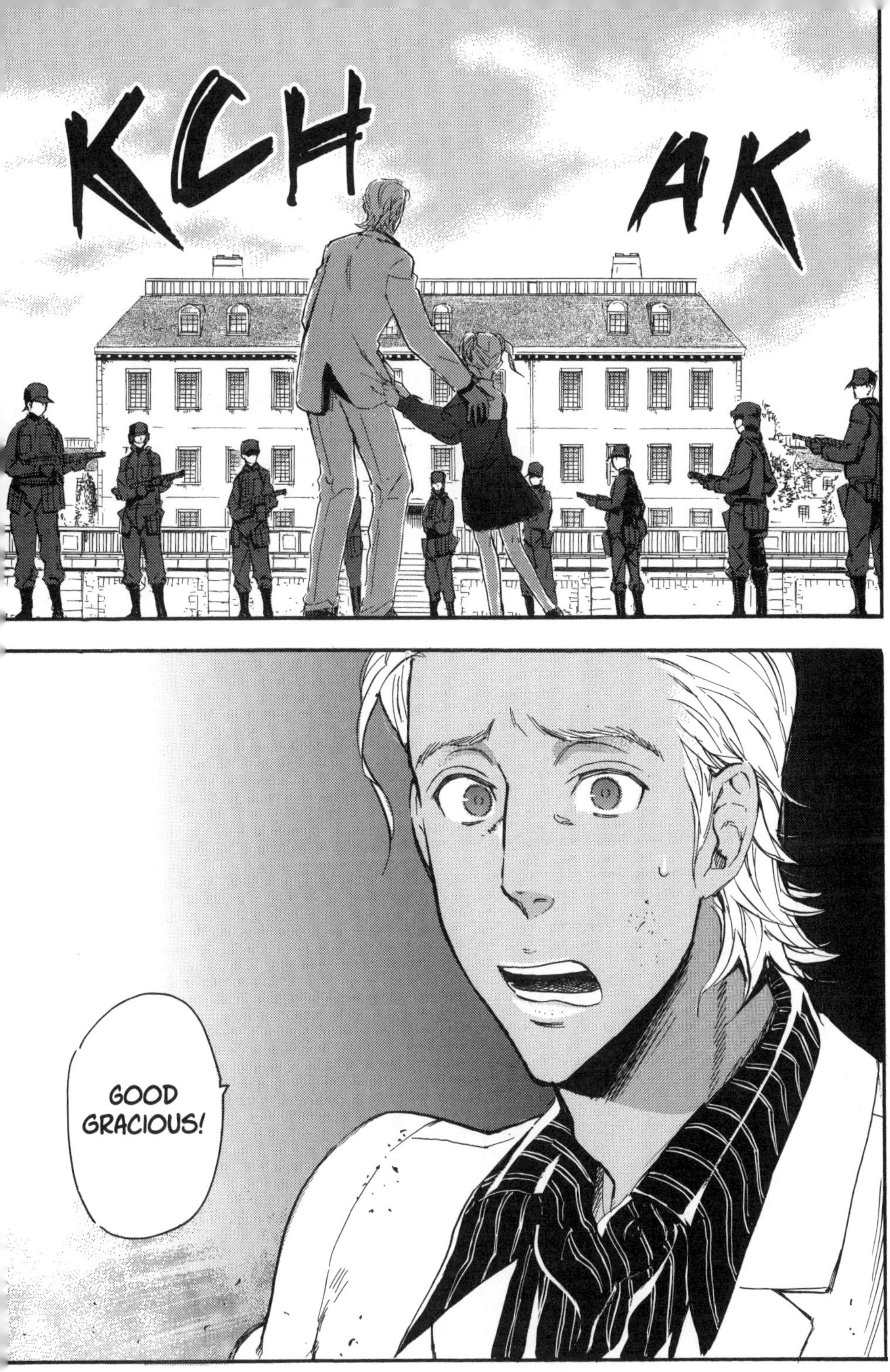
KCH
AK
GOOD GRACIOUS!

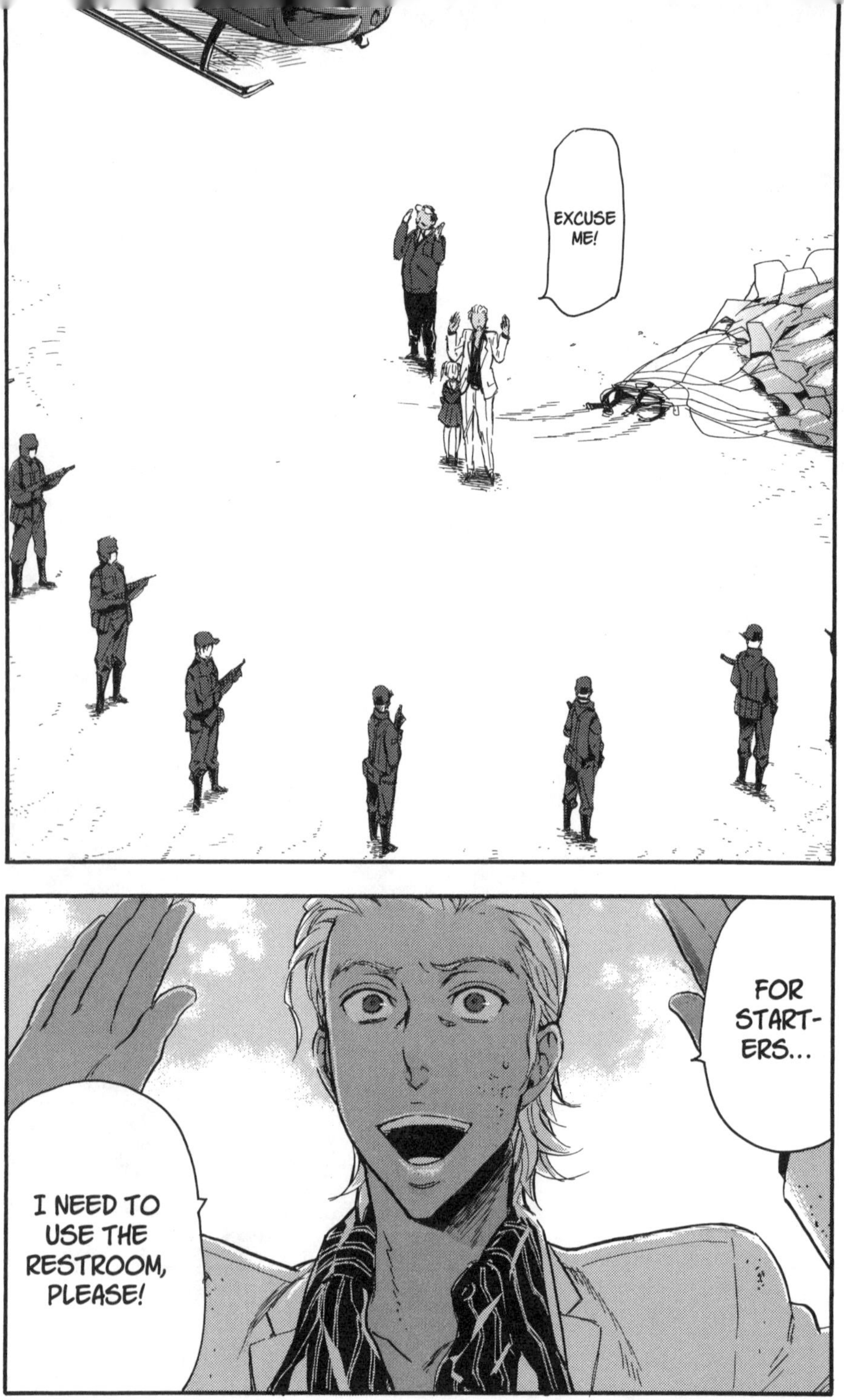
EXCUSE ME!
FOR START-ERS...
I NEED TO USE THE RESTROOM, PLEASE!

Chapter nine

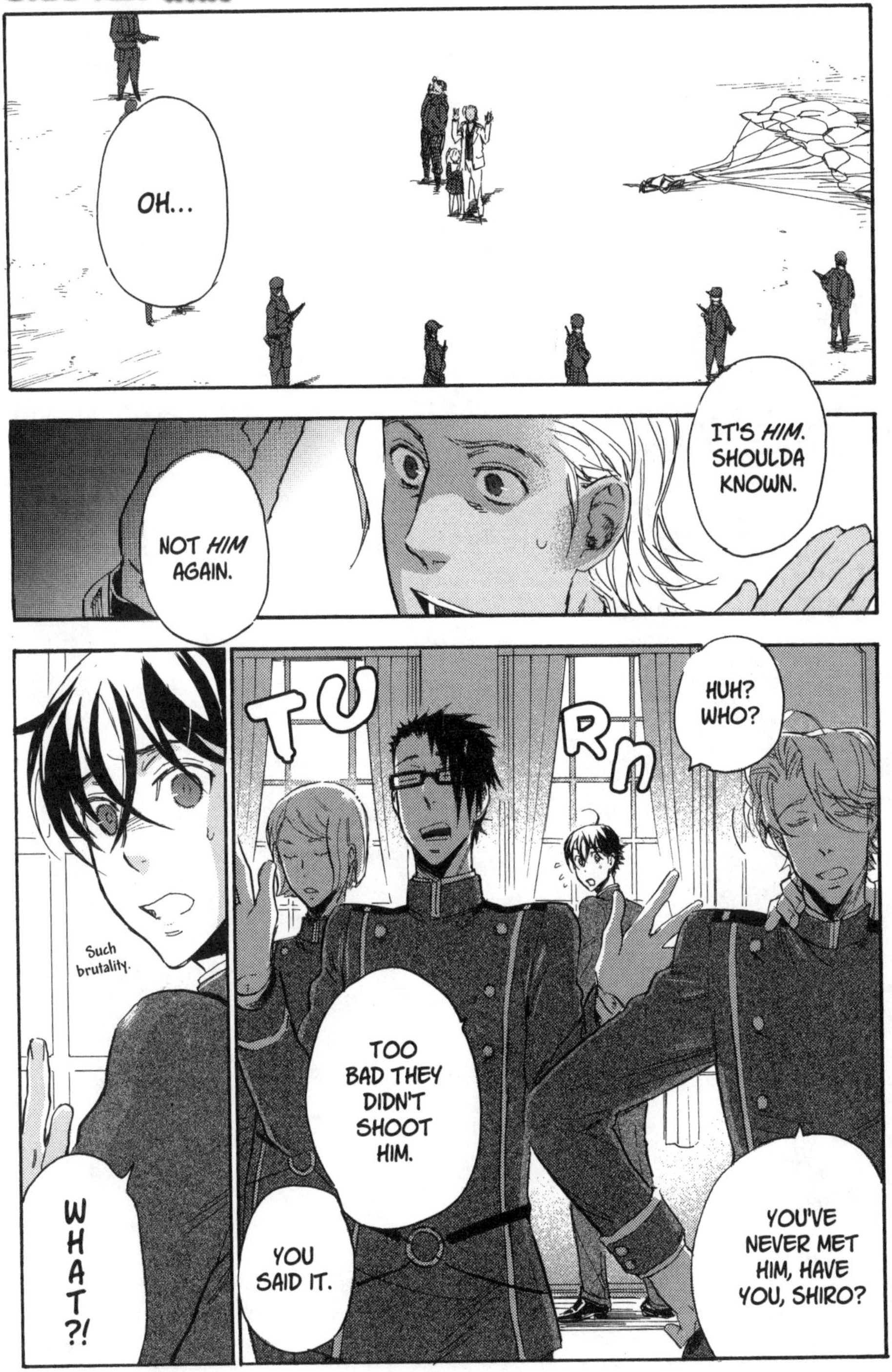
OH...
IT'S HIM. SHOULDA KNOWN.
NOT HIM AGAIN.
HUH? WHO?
TURN
TOO BAD THEY DIDN'T SHOOT HIM.
YOU SAID IT.
YOU'VE NEVER MET HIM, HAVE YOU, SHIRO?
Such brutality.
WHAT?!

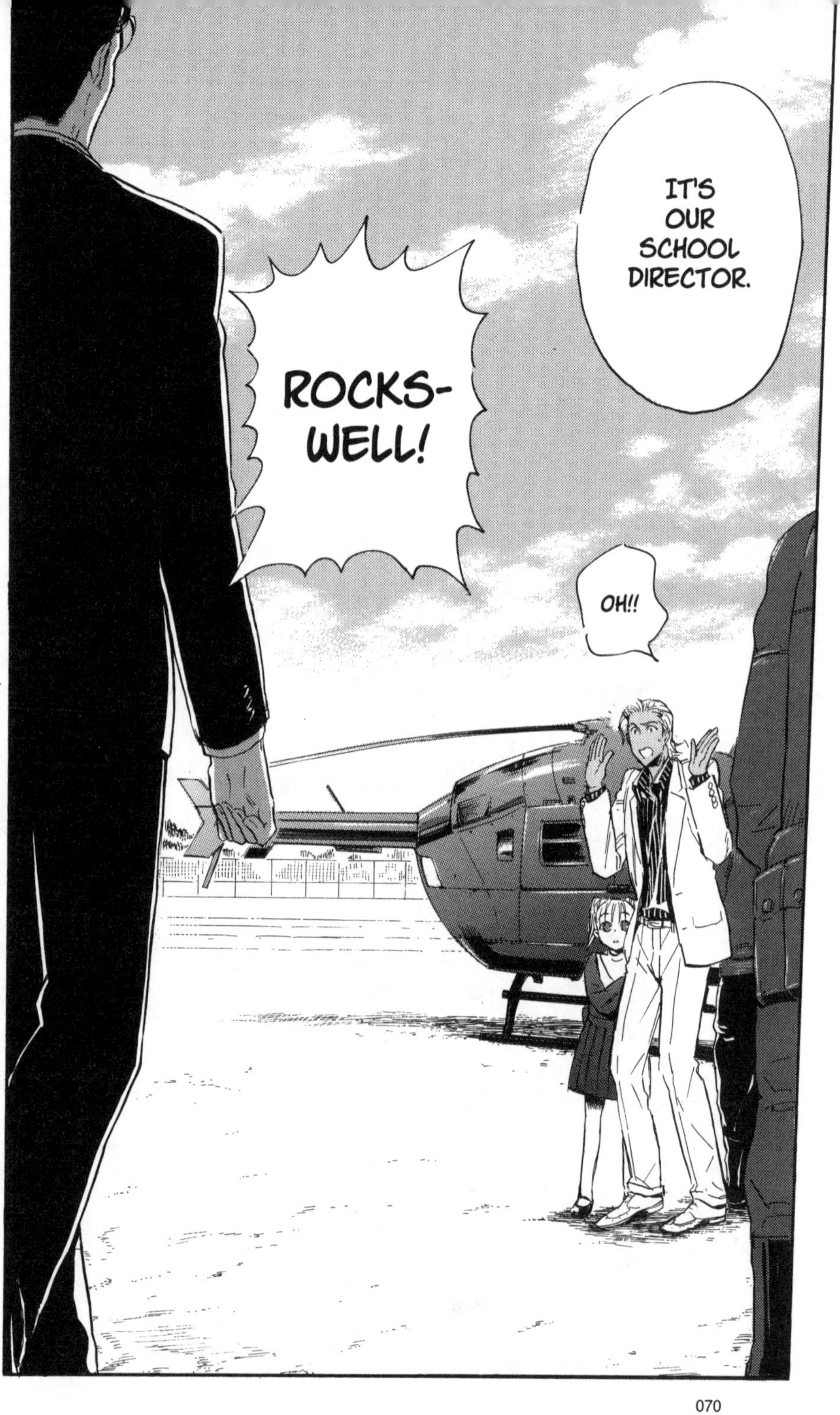
IT'S OUR SCHOOL DIRECTOR.
ROCKS-WELL!
OH!!

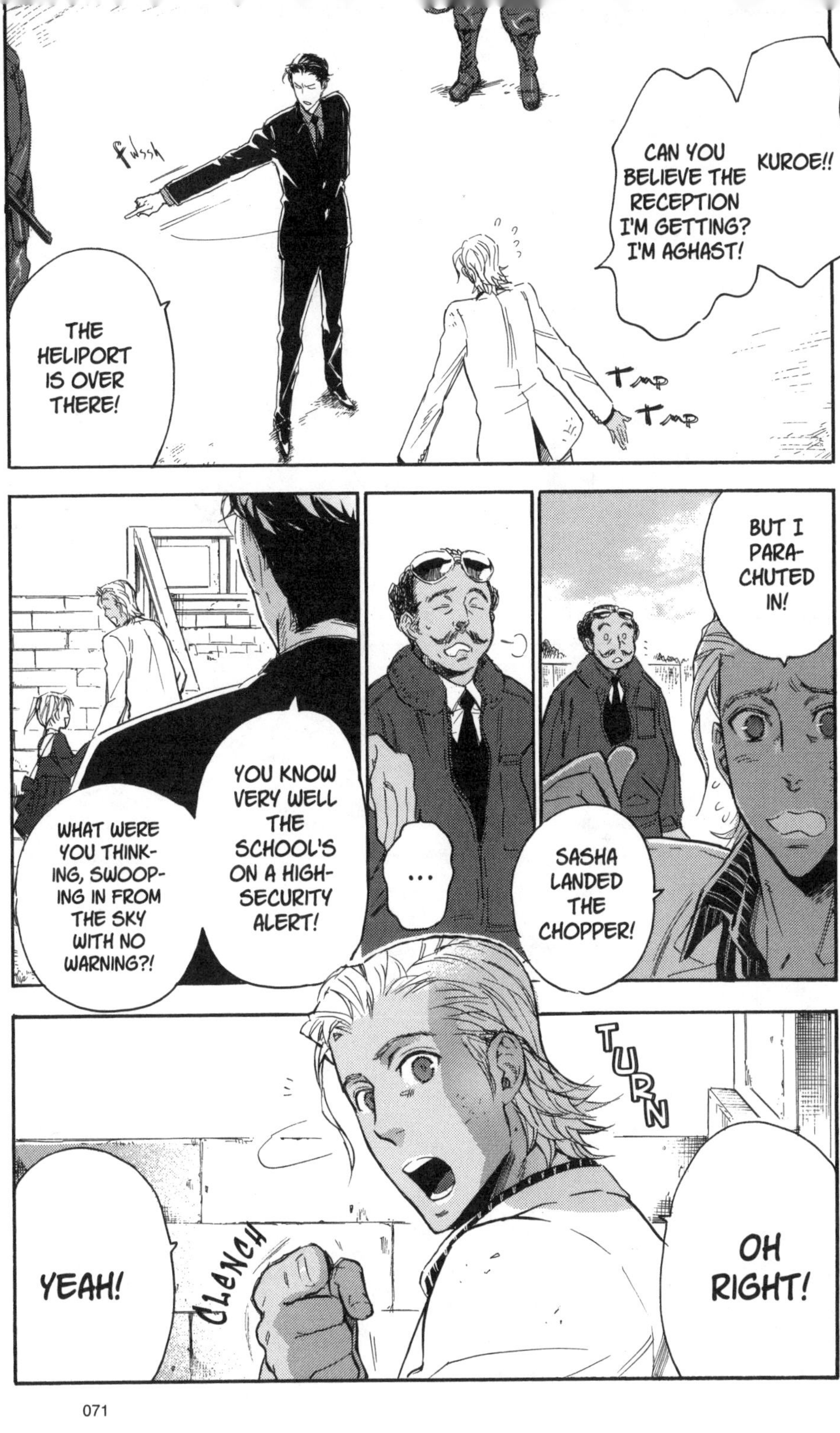
KUROE!!
CAN YOU BELIEVE THE RECEPTION I'M GETTING? I'M AGHAST!
Fwssh
Tmp Tmp
THE HELIPORT IS OVER THERE!
BUT I PARA-CHUTED IN!
SASHA LANDED THE CHOPPER!
...
YOU KNOW VERY WELL THE SCHOOL'S ON A HIGH-SECURITY ALERT!
WHAT WERE YOU THINK-ING, SWOOP-ING IN FROM THE SKY WITH NO WARNING?!
TURN
OH RIGHT!
CLENCH
YEAH!

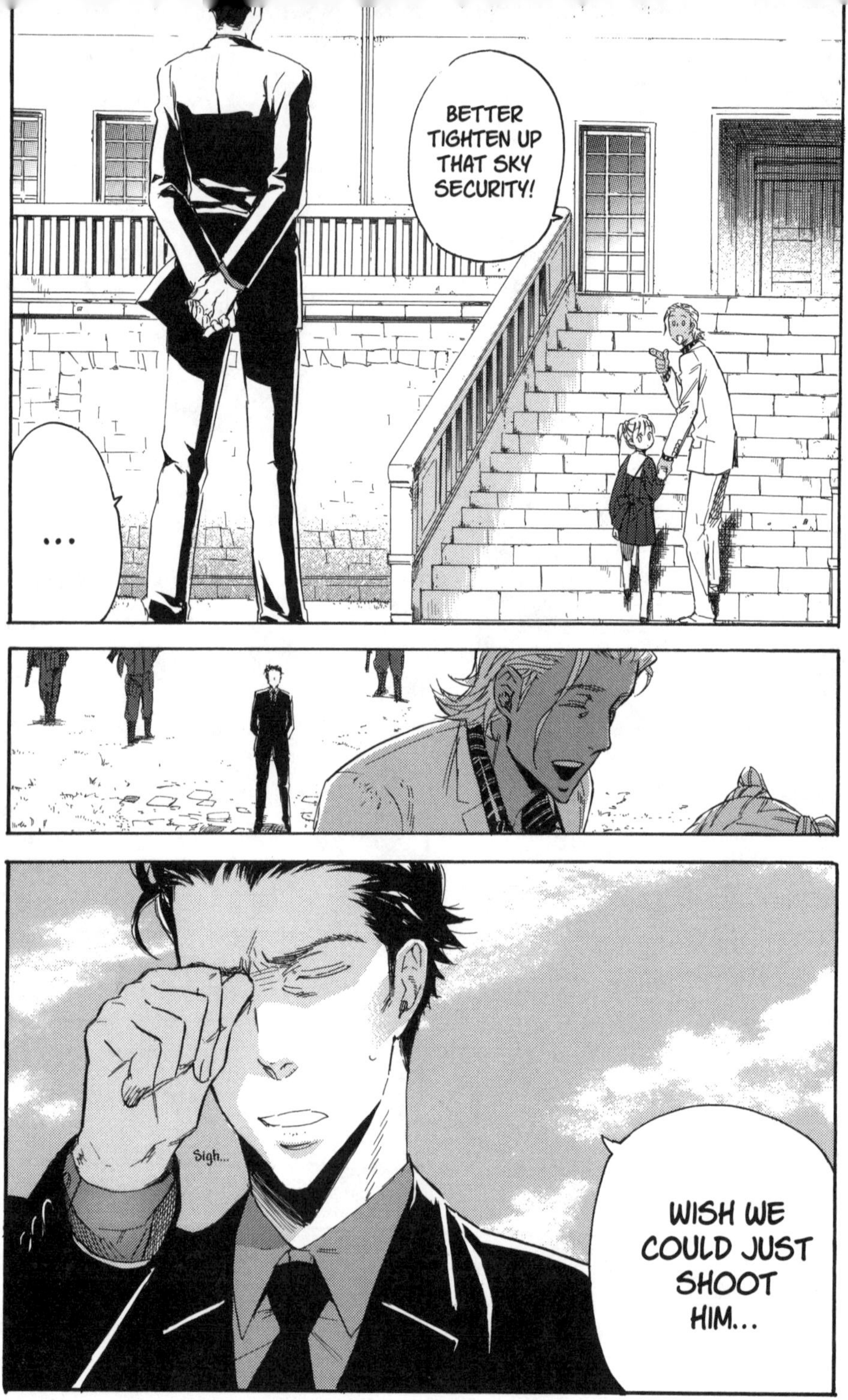
BETTER TIGHTEN UP THAT SKY SECURITY!
...
WISH WE COULD JUST SHOOT HIM...
Sigh...

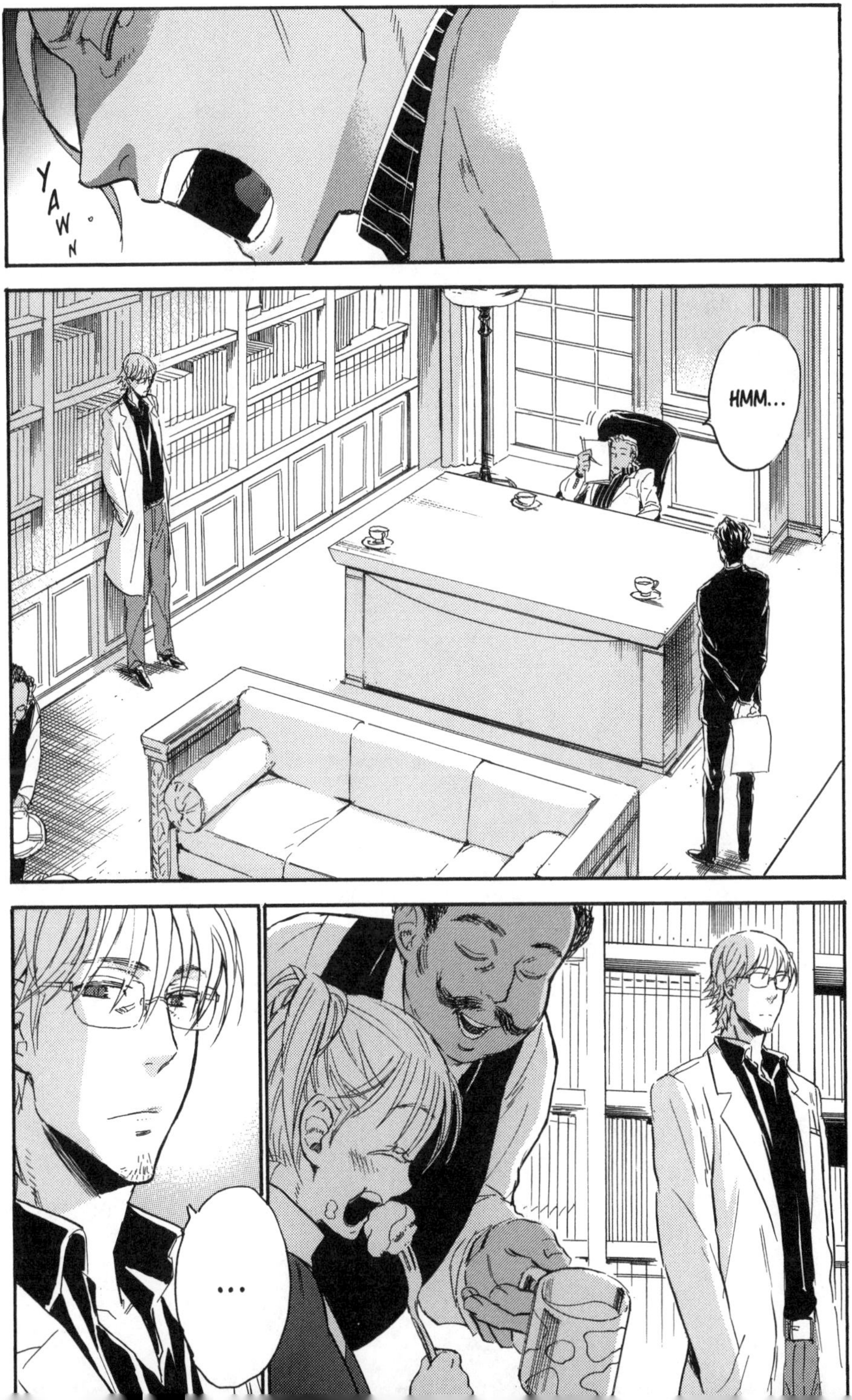
YAWN
HMM...
...

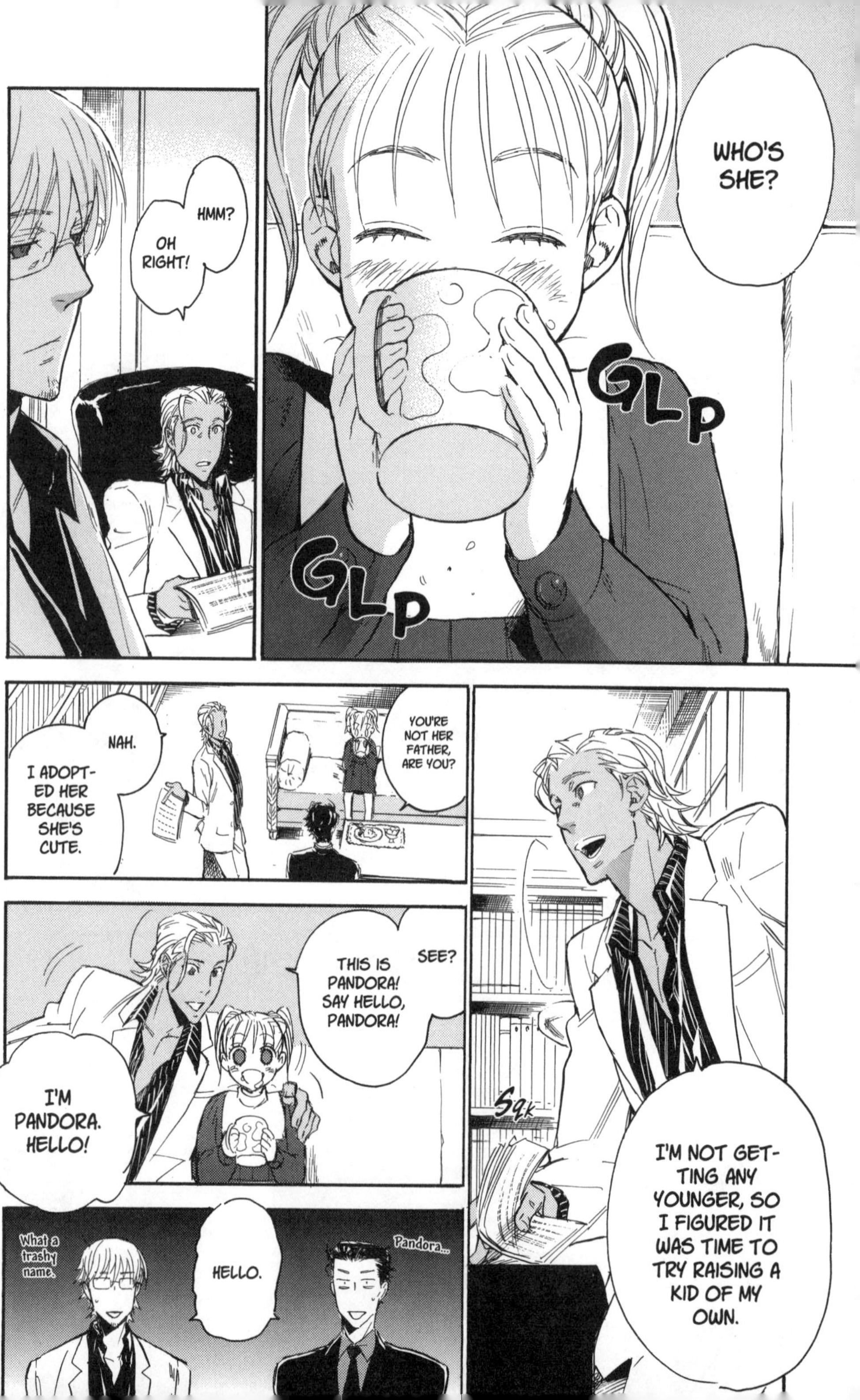
WHO'S SHE?
GLP
GLP
HMM?
OH RIGHT!
Sqk
I'M NOT GET-TING ANY YOUNGER, SO I FIGURED IT WAS TIME TO TRY RAISING A KID OF MY OWN.
YOU'RE NOT HER FATHER, ARE YOU?
NAH.
I ADOPT-ED HER BECAUSE SHE'S CUTE.
SEE?
THIS IS PANDORA! SAY HELLO, PANDORA!
I'M PANDORA. HELLO!
Pandora...
HELLO.
What a trashy name.

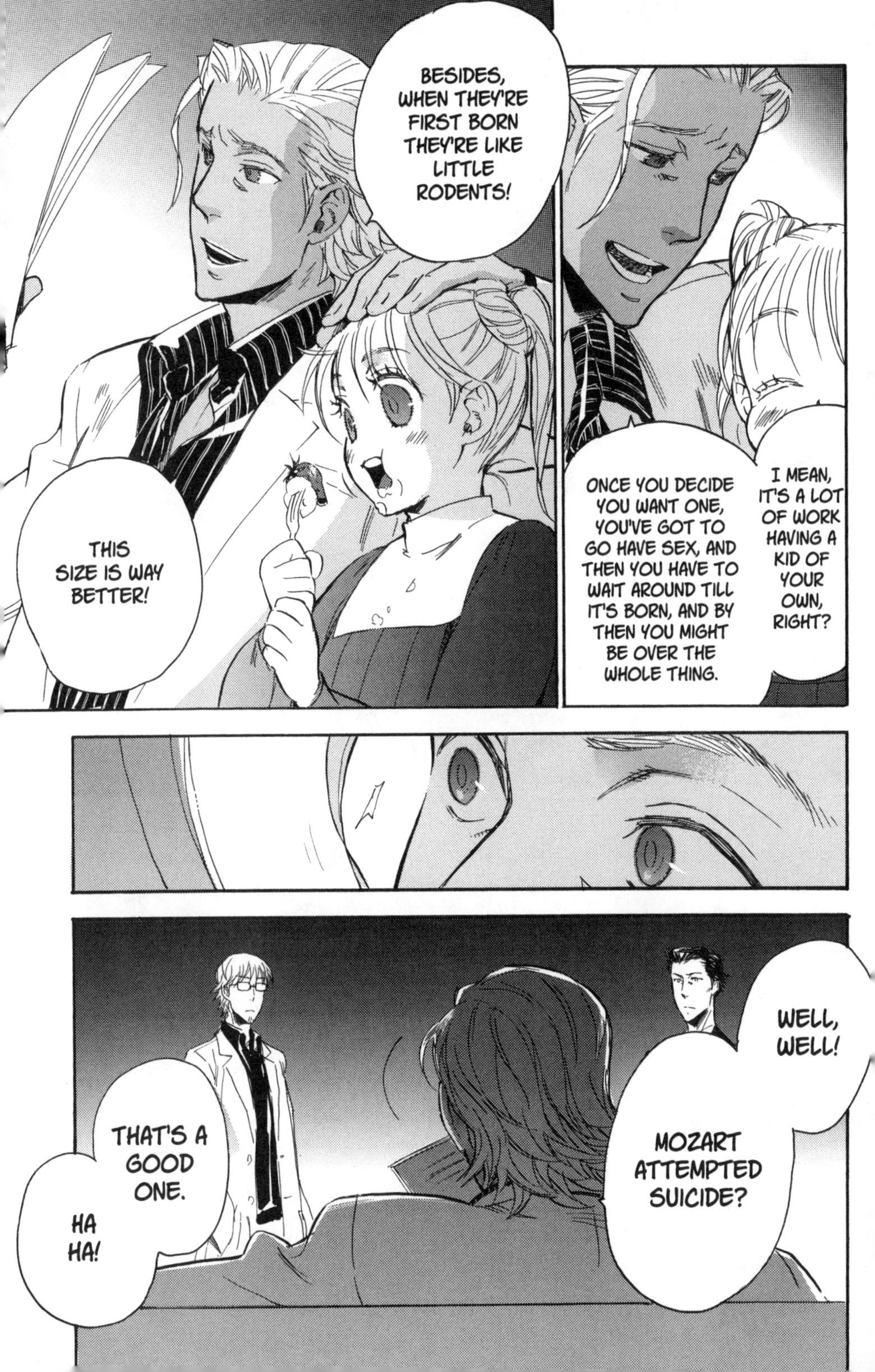
I MEAN, IT'S A LOT OF WORK HAVING A KID OF YOUR OWN, RIGHT?
ONCE YOU DECIDE YOU WANT ONE, YOU'VE GOT TO GO HAVE SEX, AND THEN YOU HAVE TO WAIT AROUND TILL IT'S BORN, AND BY THEN YOU MIGHT BE OVER THE WHOLE THING.
BESIDES, WHEN THEY'RE FIRST BORN THEY'RE LIKE LITTLE RODENTS!
THIS SIZE IS WAY BETTER!
WELL, WELL!
MOZART ATTEMPTED SUICIDE?
THAT'S A GOOD ONE.
HA HA!

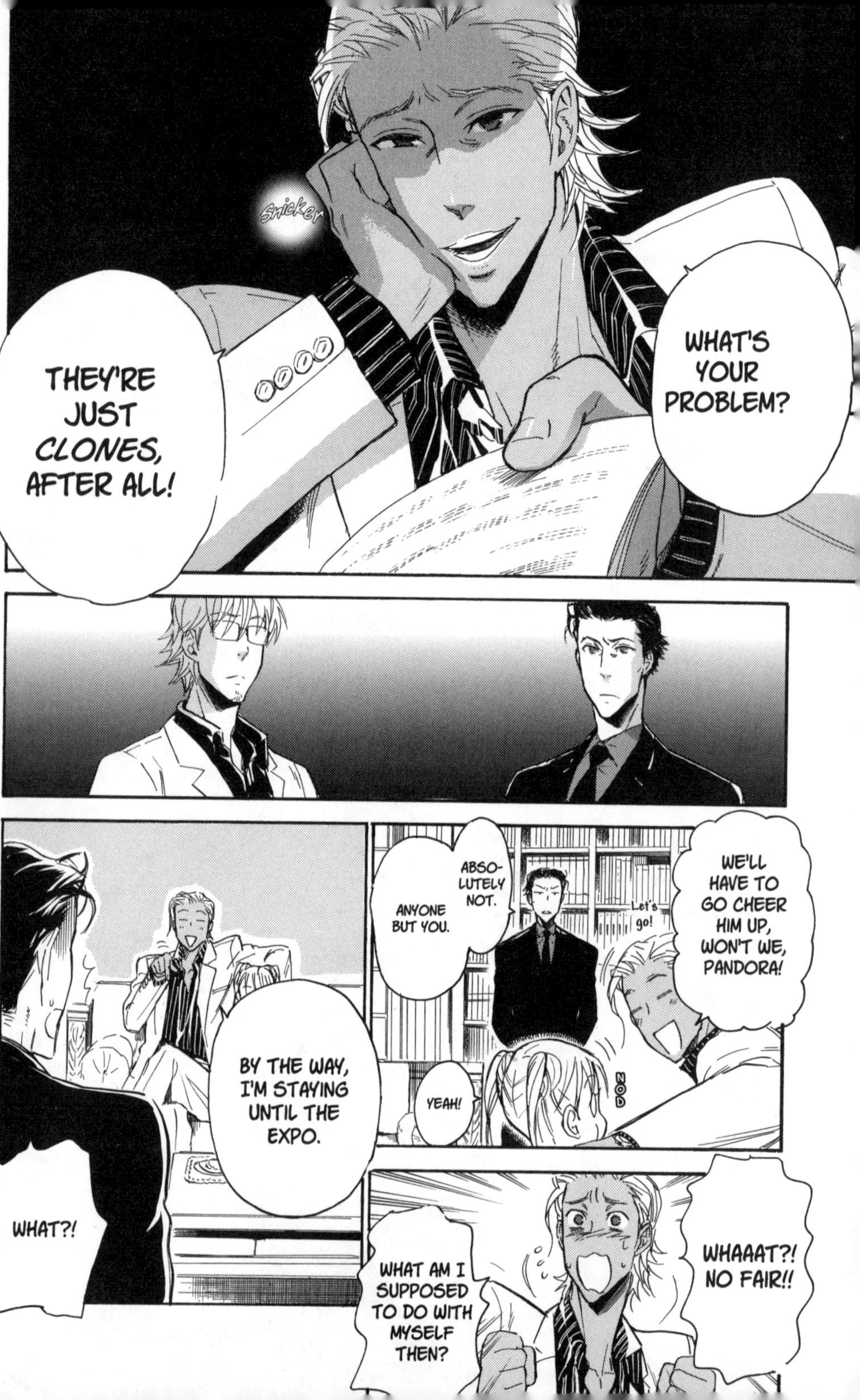
WHAT'S YOUR PROBLEM?
Snicker
THEY'RE JUST CLONES, AFTER ALL!
WE'LL HAVE TO GO CHEER HIM UP, WON'T WE, PANDORA!
Let's go!
ABSO-LUTELY NOT.
ANYONE BUT YOU.
NOD
YEAH!
WHAAAT?! NO FAIR!!
WHAT AM I SUPPOSED TO DO WITH MYSELF THEN?
BY THE WAY, I'M STAYING UNTIL THE EXPO.
WHAT?!

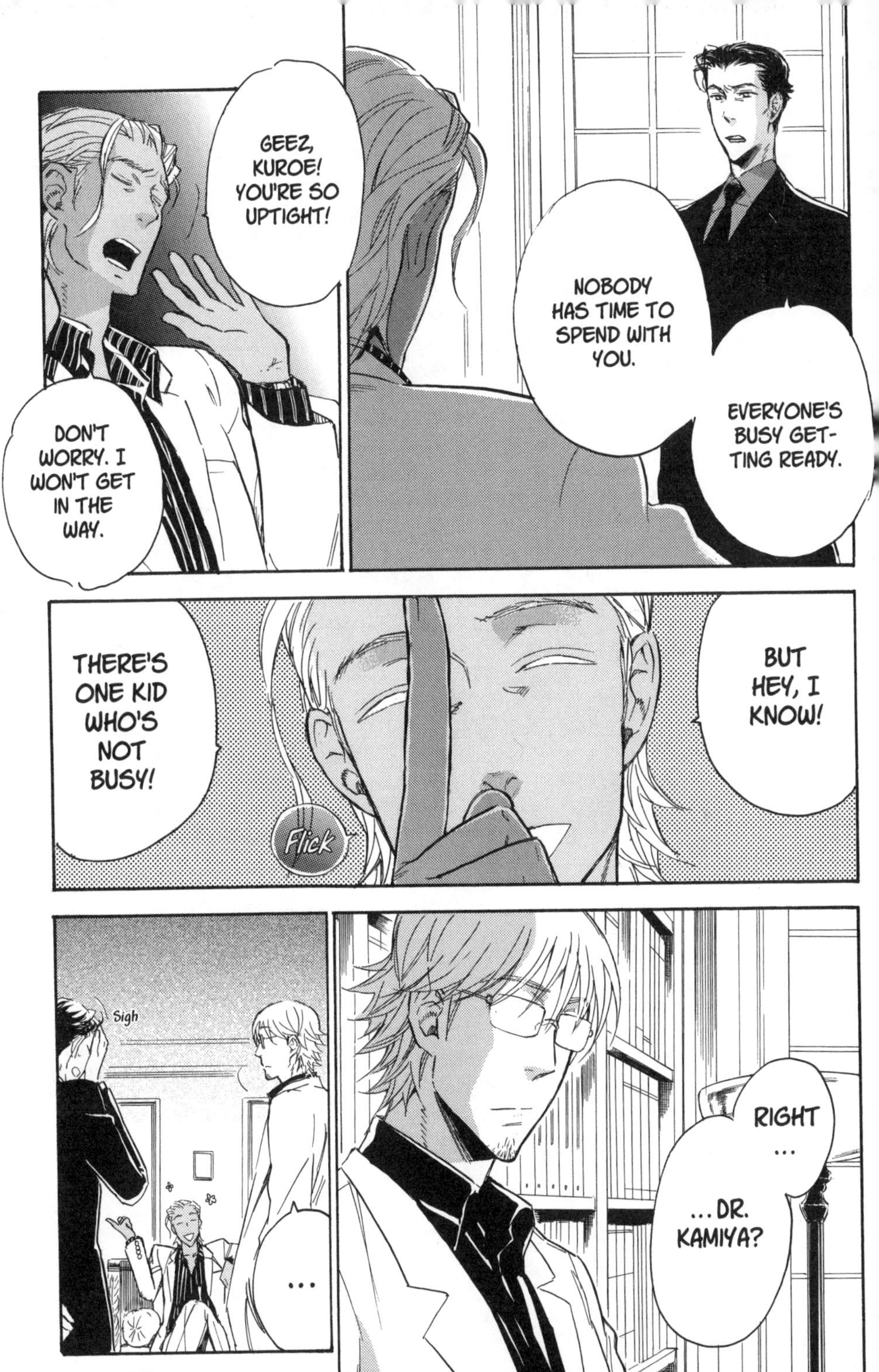
EVERYONE'S BUSY GET-TING READY.
NOBODY HAS TIME TO SPEND WITH YOU.
GEEZ, KUROE! YOU'RE SO UPTIGHT!
DON'T WORRY. I WON'T GET IN THE WAY.
BUT HEY, I KNOW!
Flick
THERE'S ONE KID WHO'S NOT BUSY!
RIGHT ...
... DR. KAMIYA?
Sigh
...

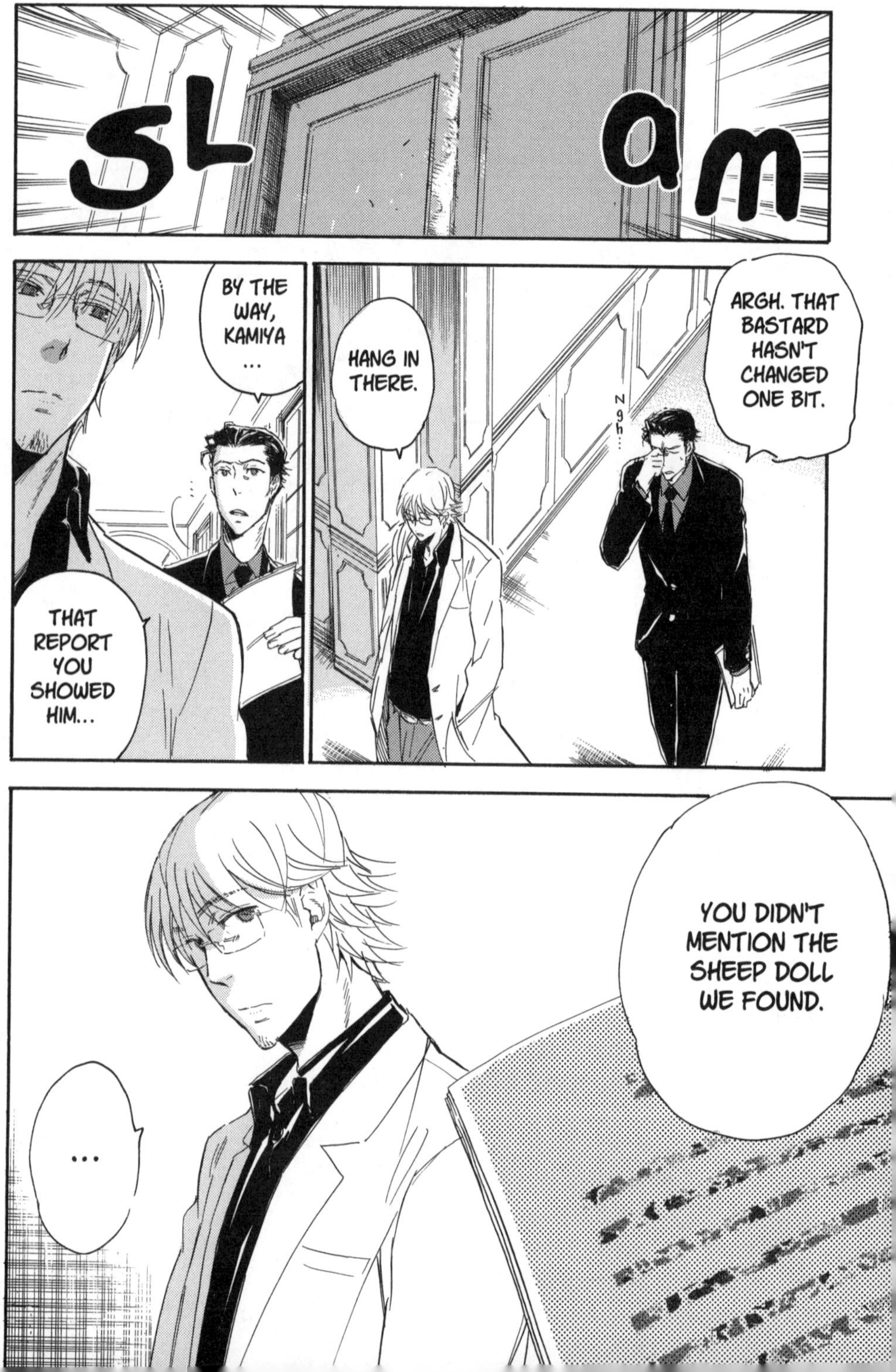
SLAM
ARGH. THAT BASTARD HASN'T CHANGED ONE BIT.
Ngh...
HANG IN THERE.
BY THE WAY, KAMIYA...
THAT REPORT YOU SHOWED HIM...
YOU DIDN'T MENTION THE SHEEP DOLL WE FOUND.
...

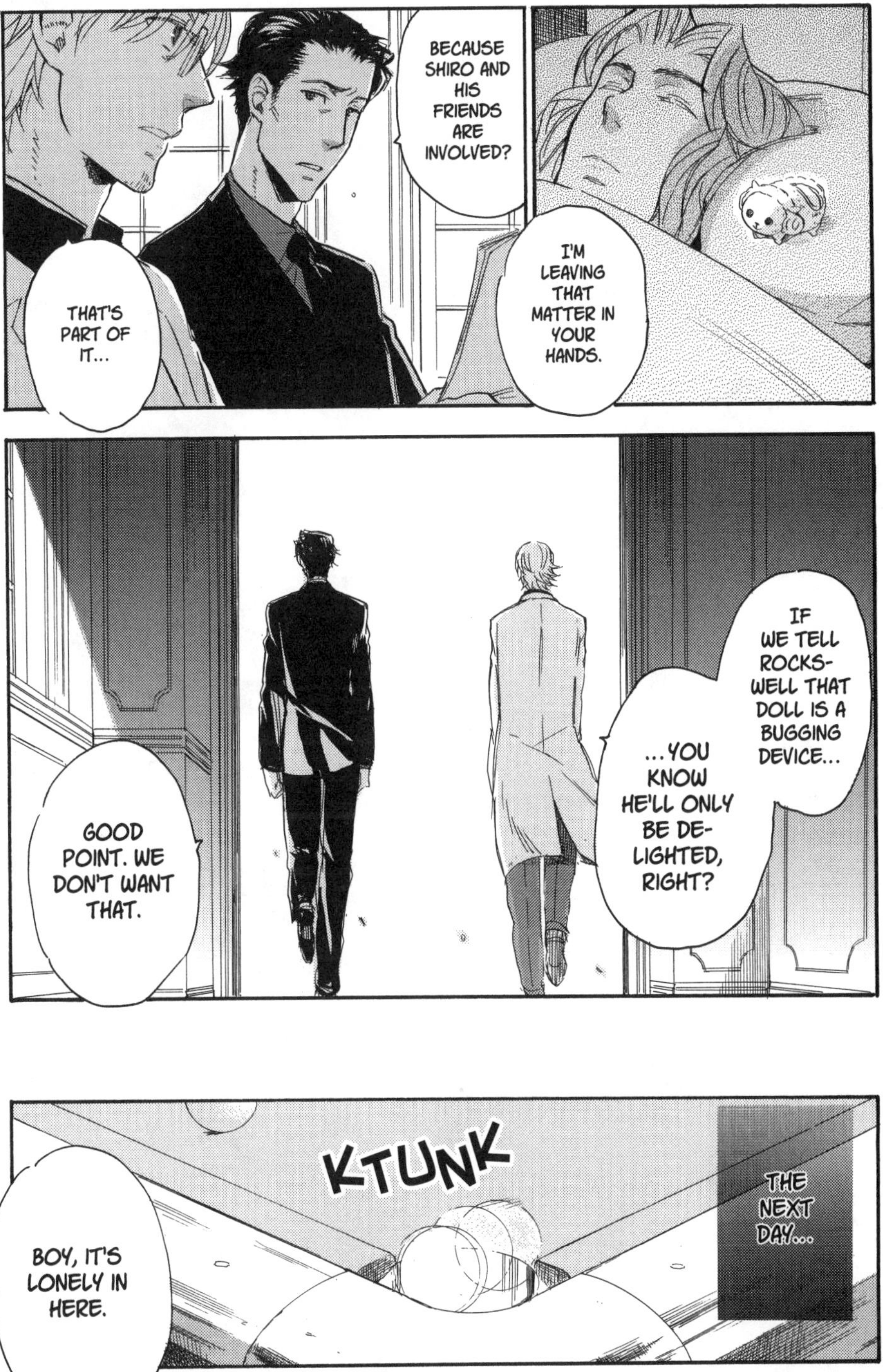
I'M LEAVING THAT MATTER IN YOUR HANDS.
BECAUSE SHIRO AND HIS FRIENDS ARE INVOLVED?
THAT'S PART OF IT...
IF WE TELL ROCKS-WELL THAT DOLL IS A BUGGING DEVICE...
...YOU KNOW HE'LL ONLY BE DE-LIGHTED, RIGHT?
GOOD POINT. WE DON'T WANT THAT.
THE NEXT DAY...
KTUNK
BOY, IT'S LONELY IN HERE.

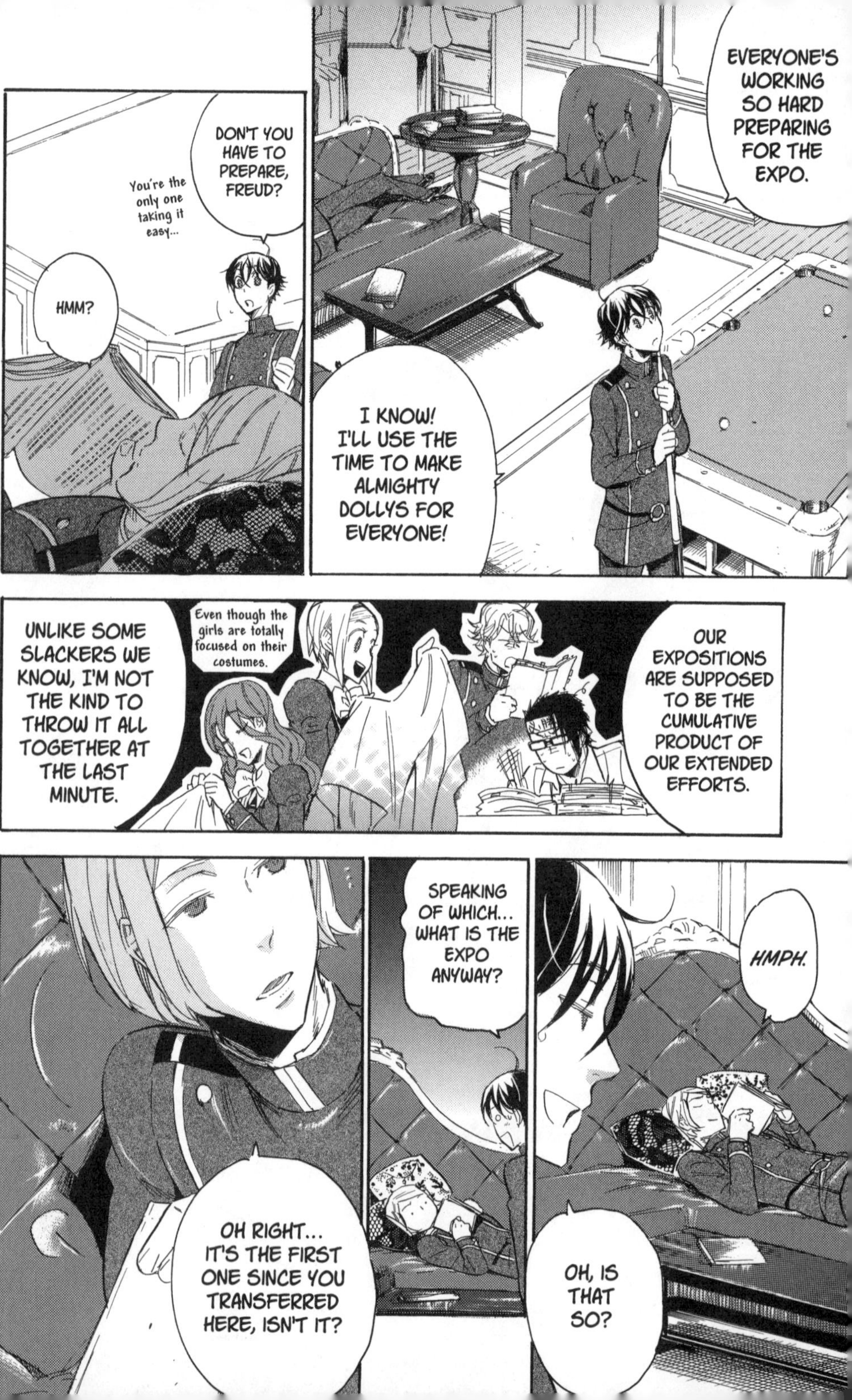
EVERYONE'S WORKING SO HARD PREPARING FOR THE EXPO.
I KNOW! I'LL USE THE TIME TO MAKE ALMIGHTY DOLLYS FOR EVERYONE!
DON'T YOU HAVE TO PREPARE, FREUD?
You're the only one taking it easy...
HMM?
OUR EXPOSITIONS ARE SUPPOSED TO BE THE CUMULATIVE PRODUCT OF OUR EXTENDED EFFORTS.
Even though the girls are totally focused on their costumes.
UNLIKE SOME SLACKERS WE KNOW, I'M NOT THE KIND TO THROW IT ALL TOGETHER AT THE LAST MINUTE.
HMPH.
OH, IS THAT SO?
SPEAKING OF WHICH... WHAT IS THE EXPO ANYWAY?
OH RIGHT... IT'S THE FIRST ONE SINCE YOU TRANSFERRED HERE, ISN'T IT?

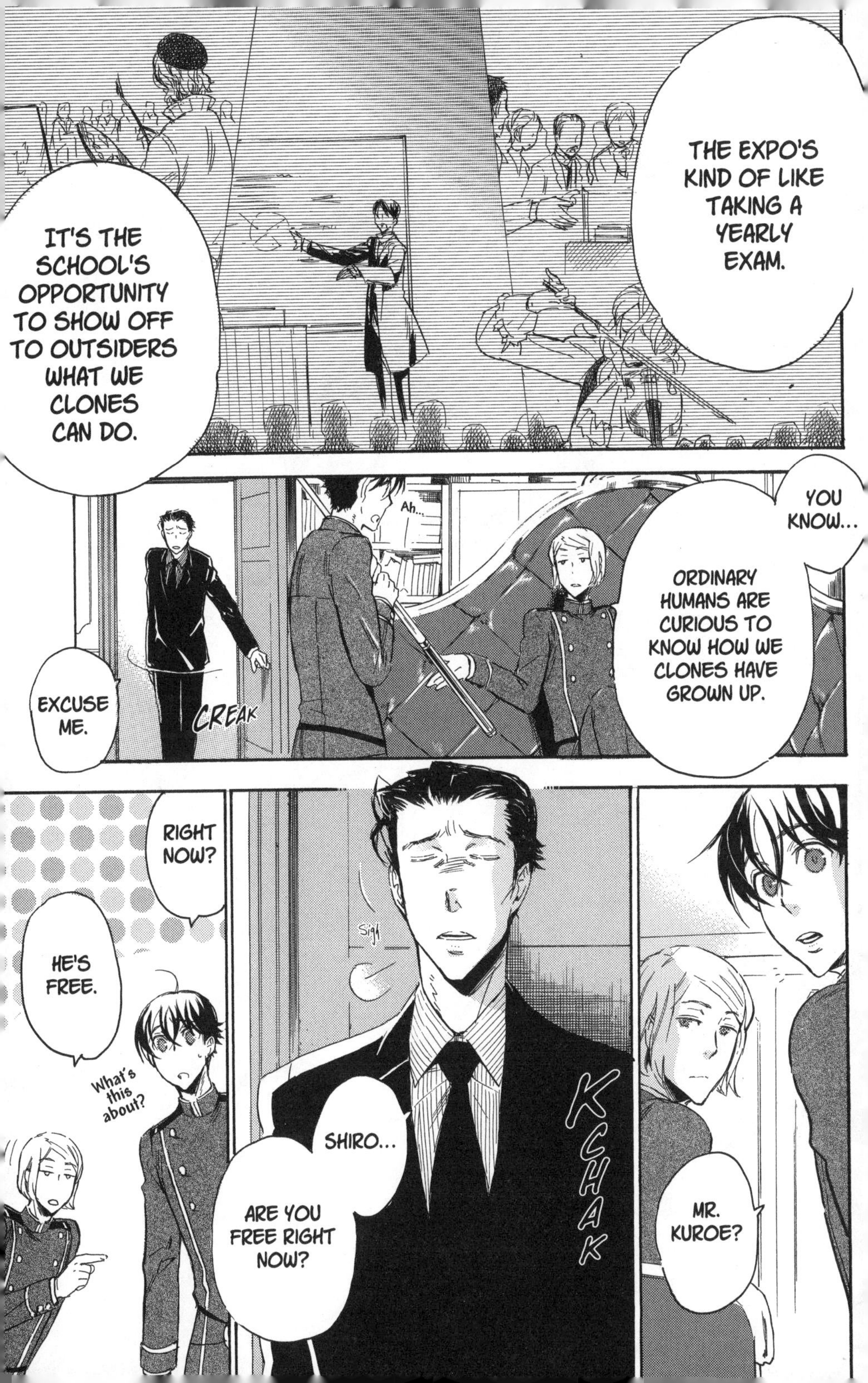
THE EXPO'S KIND OF LIKE TAKING A YEARLY EXAM.
IT'S THE SCHOOL'S OPPORTUNITY TO SHOW OFF TO OUTSIDERS WHAT WE CLONES CAN DO.
YOU KNOW...
ORDINARY HUMANS ARE CURIOUS TO KNOW HOW WE CLONES HAVE GROWN UP.
Ah...
CREAK
EXCUSE ME.
MR. KUROE?
Sigh
KCHAK
SHIRO...
ARE YOU FREE RIGHT NOW?
RIGHT NOW?
HE'S FREE.
What's this about?

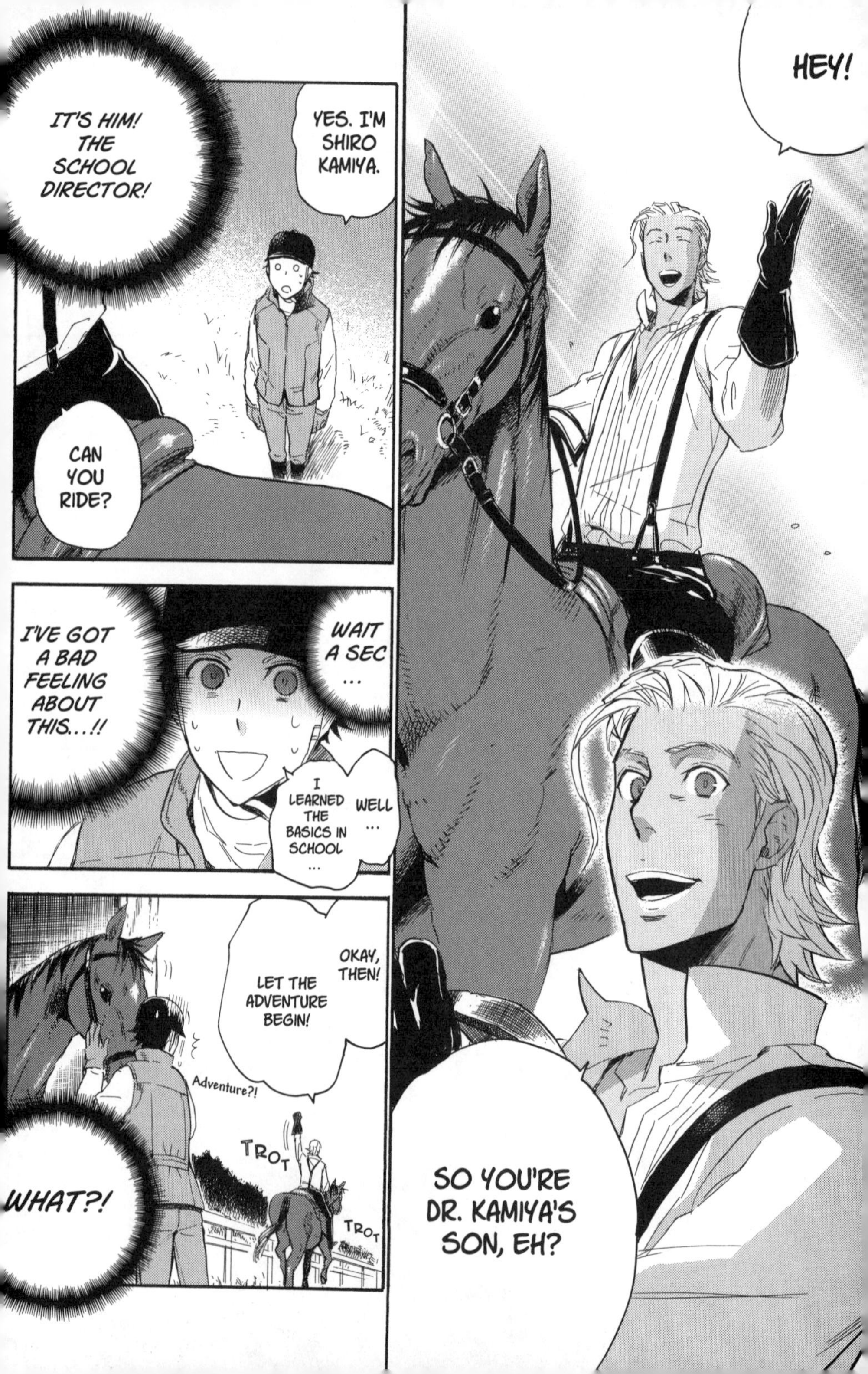
HEY!
SO YOU'RE DR. KAMIYA'S SON, EH?
YES. I'M SHIRO KAMIYA.
IT'S HIM! THE SCHOOL DIRECTOR!
CAN YOU RIDE?
WAIT A SEC...
I'VE GOT A BAD FEELING ABOUT THIS...!!
WELL...
I LEARNED THE BASICS IN SCHOOL...
OKAY, THEN!
LET THE ADVENTURE BEGIN!
Adventure?!
TROT
TROT
WHAT?!

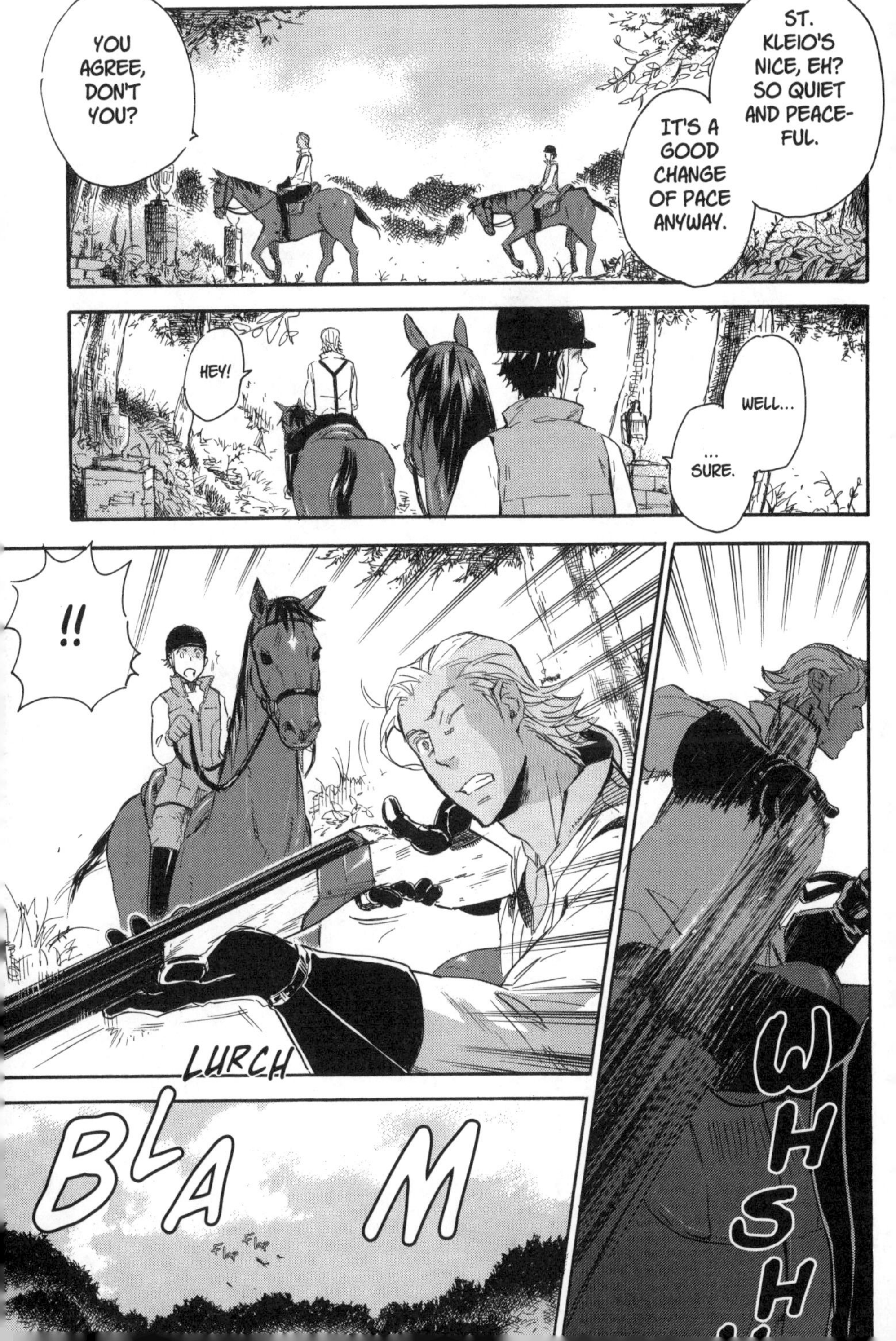
ST. KLEIO'S NICE, EH? SO QUIET AND PEACE-FUL.
IT'S A GOOD CHANGE OF PACE ANYWAY.
YOU AGREE, DON'T YOU?
WELL...
... SURE.
HEY!
WHSH
!!
LURCH
BLAM

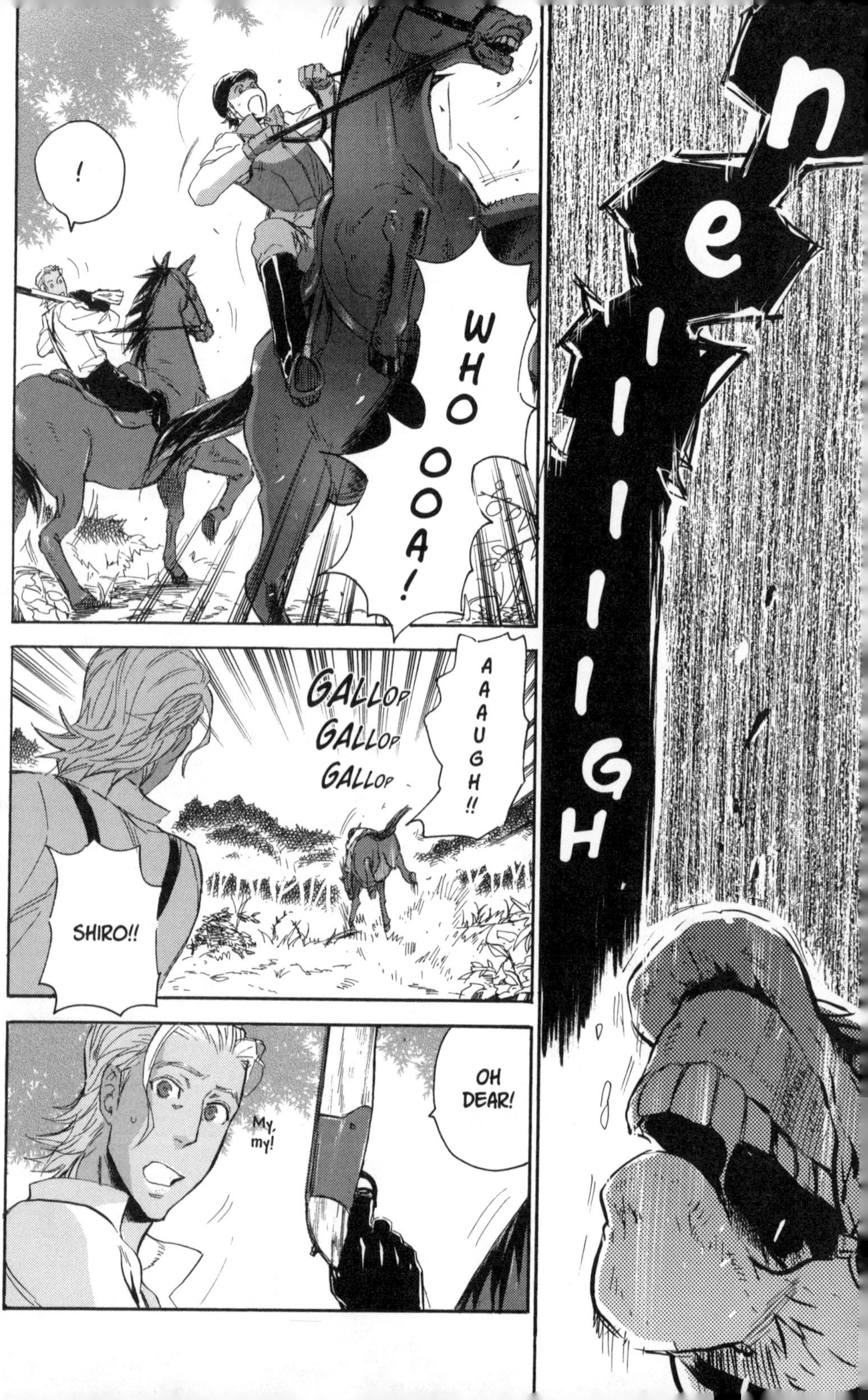
neIIIIIGH
!
WHOOOOA!
AAAAUGH!!
GALLop GALLop GALLop
SHIRO!!
OH DEAR!
My, my!

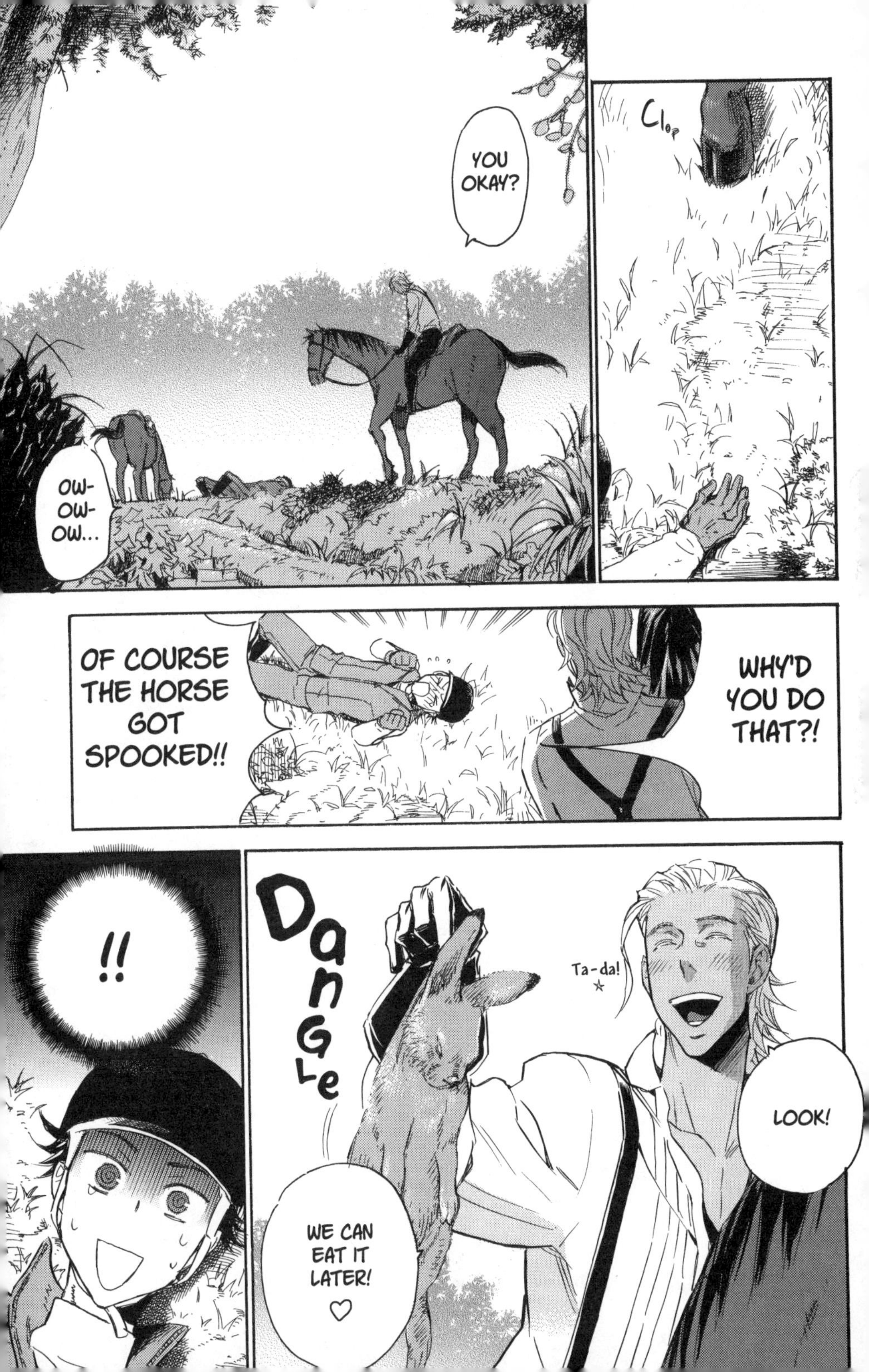
Clop
YOU OKAY?
OW-OW-OW...
WHY'D YOU DO THAT?!
OF COURSE THE HORSE GOT SPOOKED!!
Dangle
Ta-da!
LOOK!
WE CAN EAT IT LATER! ♡
!!

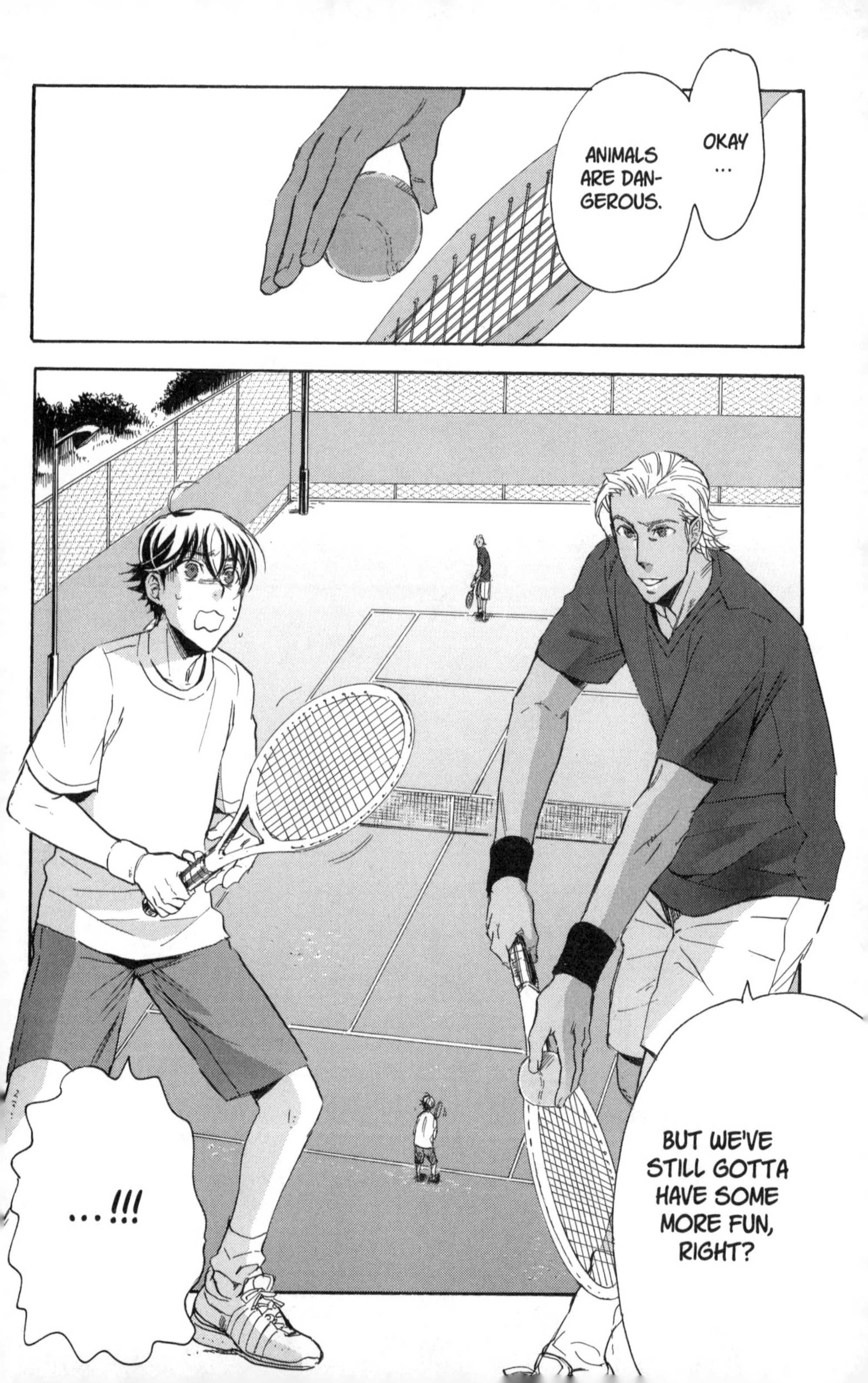
OKAY ...
ANIMALS ARE DAN-GEROUS.
BUT WE'VE STILL GOTTA HAVE SOME MORE FUN, RIGHT?
...!!!

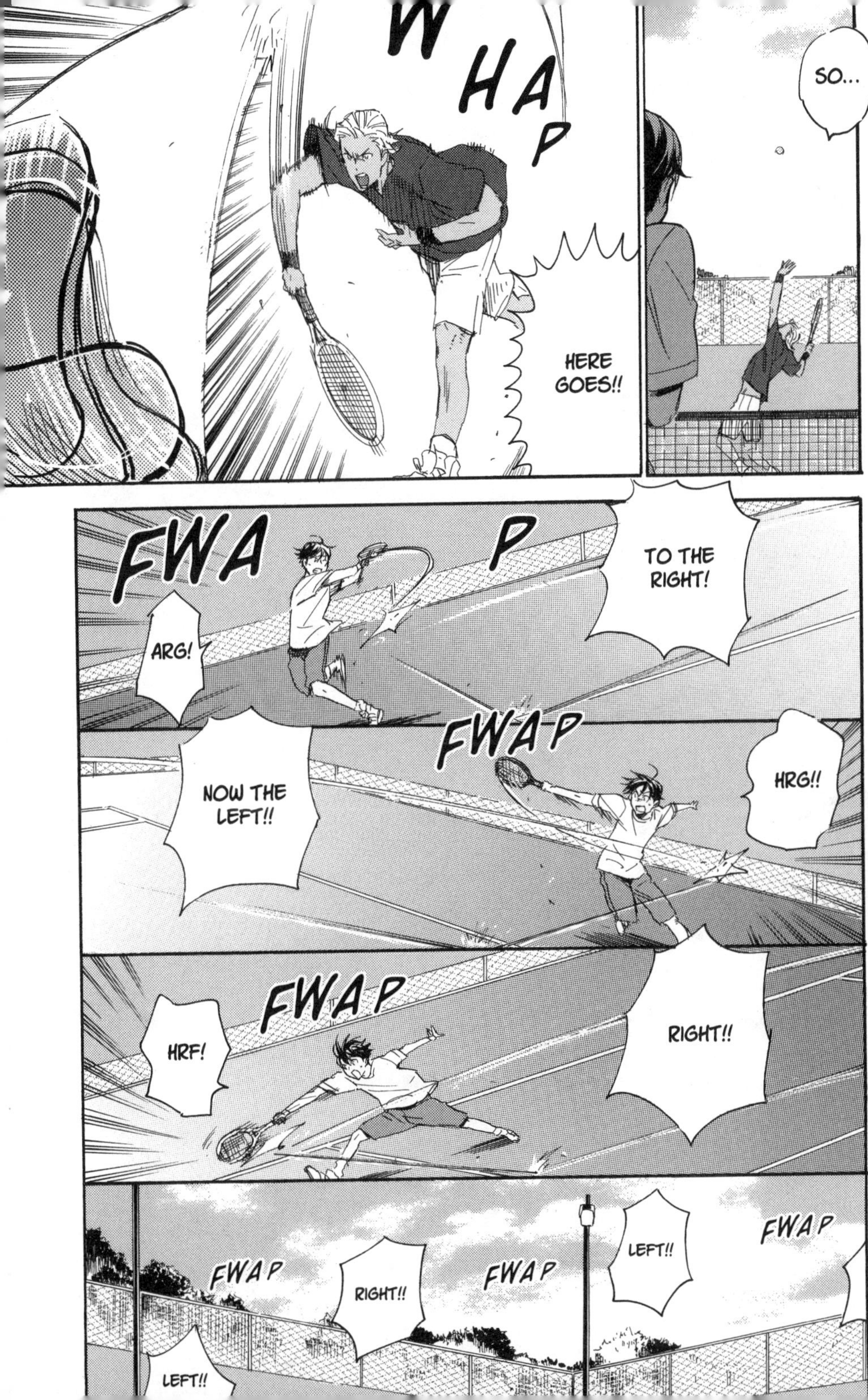
SO...
WHAP
HERE GOES!!
TO THE RIGHT!
FWAP
ARG!
HRG!!
FWAP
NOW THE LEFT!!
RIGHT!!
FWAP
HRF!
FWAP
LEFT!!
FWAP
RIGHT!!
FWAP
LEFT!!

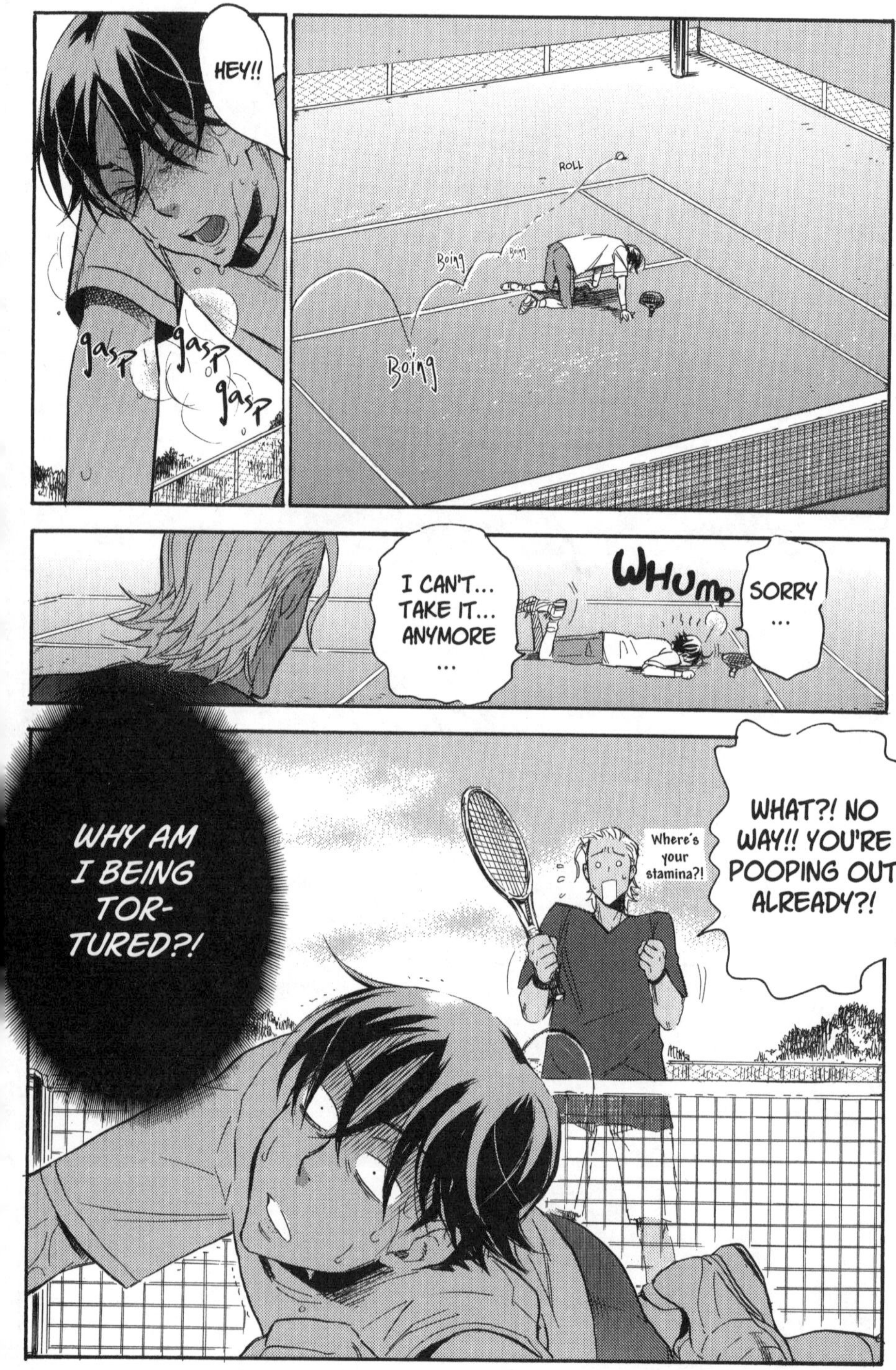
ROLL
Boing
Boing
Boing
HEY!!
gasp
gasp
gasp
SORRY ...
WHUmp
I CAN'T... TAKE IT... ANYMORE ...
WHAT?! NO WAY!! YOU'RE POOPING OUT ALREADY?!
Where's your stamina?!
WHY AM I BEING TOR- TURED?!

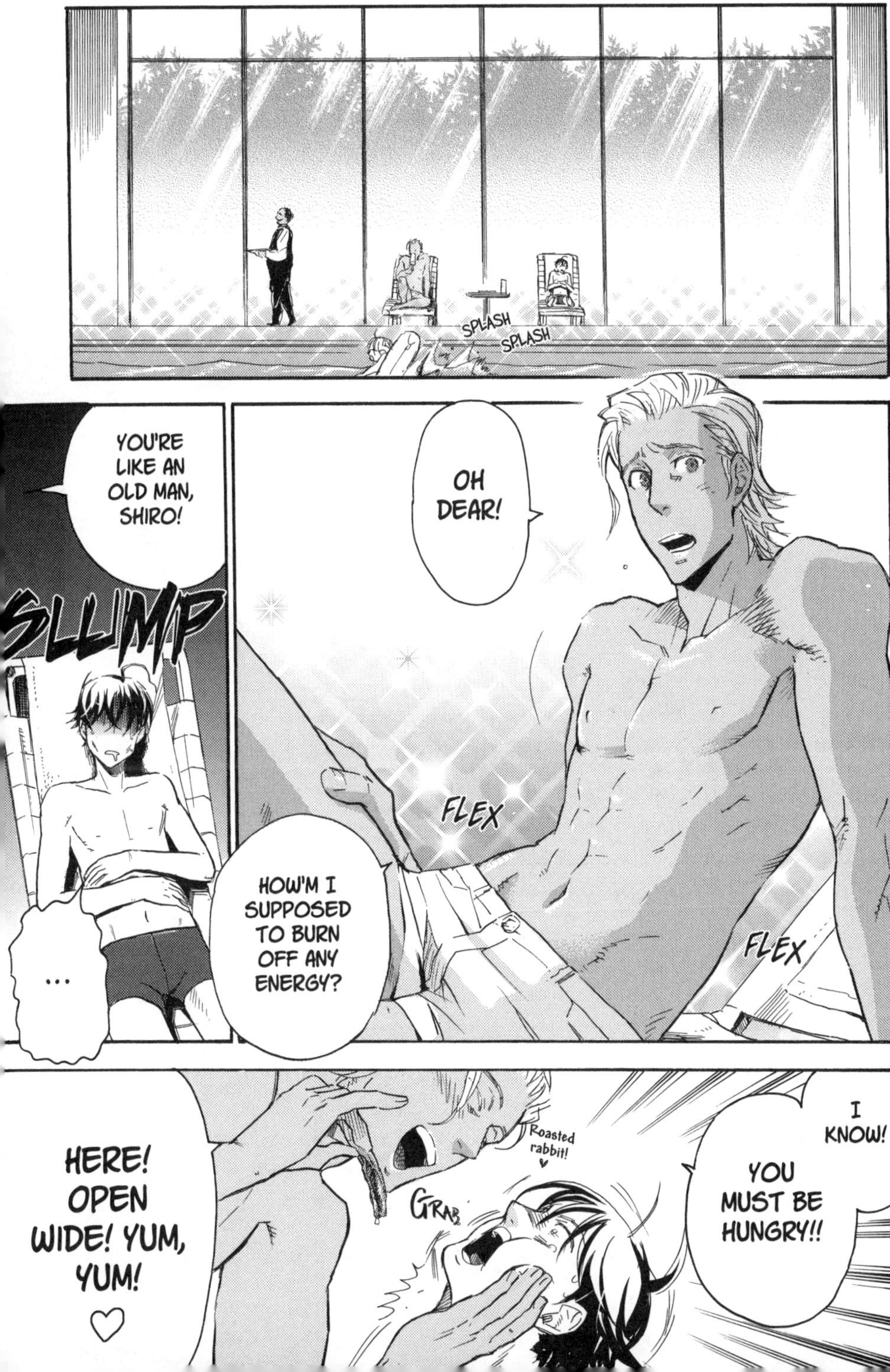
SPLASH
SPLASH
OH DEAR!
FLEX
FLEX
HOW'M I SUPPOSED TO BURN OFF ANY ENERGY?
YOU'RE LIKE AN OLD MAN, SHIRO!
SLUMP
...
I KNOW!
YOU MUST BE HUNGRY!!
Roasted rabbit! ♥
GRAB
HERE! OPEN WIDE! YUM, YUM! ♡

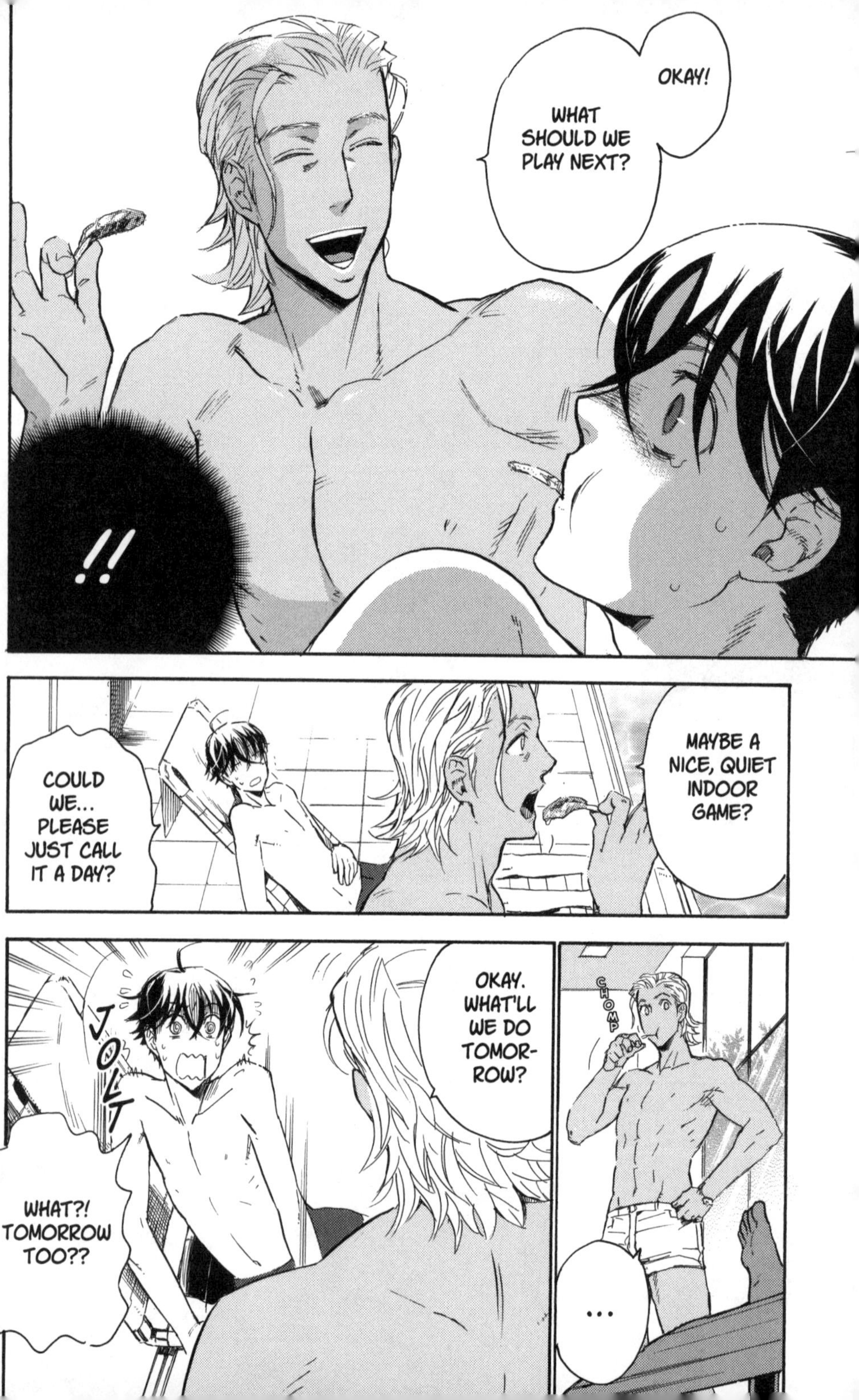
OKAY!
WHAT SHOULD WE PLAY NEXT?
!!
MAYBE A NICE, QUIET INDOOR GAME?
COULD WE... PLEASE JUST CALL IT A DAY?
CHOMP
...
OKAY. WHAT'LL WE DO TOMOR-ROW?
JOLT
WHAT?! TOMORROW TOO??

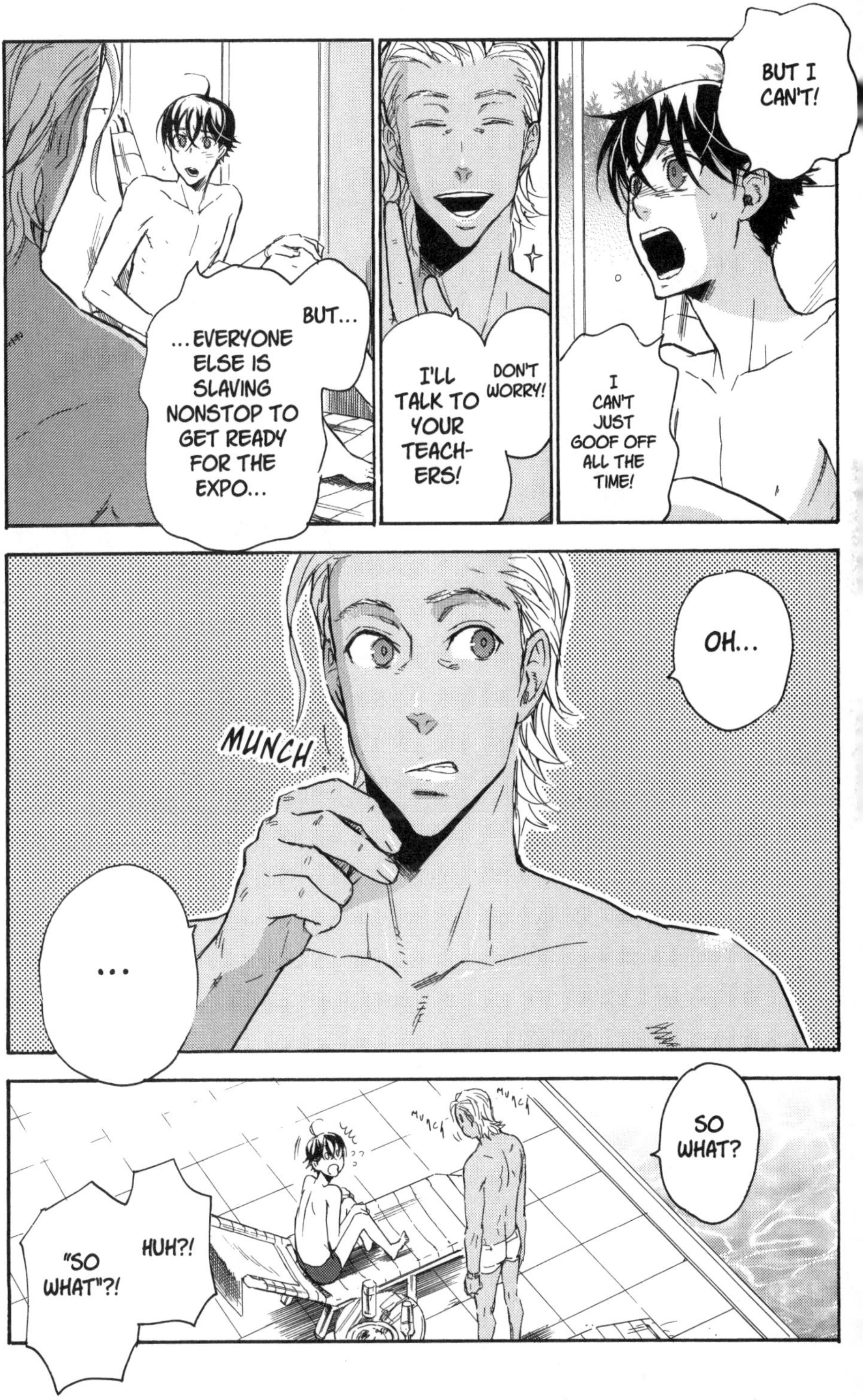
BUT I CAN'T!
I CAN'T JUST GOOF OFF ALL THE TIME!
DON'T WORRY!
I'LL TALK TO YOUR TEACHERS!
BUT...
...EVERYONE ELSE IS SLAVING NONSTOP TO GET READY FOR THE EXPO...
OH...
MUNCH
...
SO WHAT?
MUNCH
MUNCH
HUH?!
"SO WHAT"?!

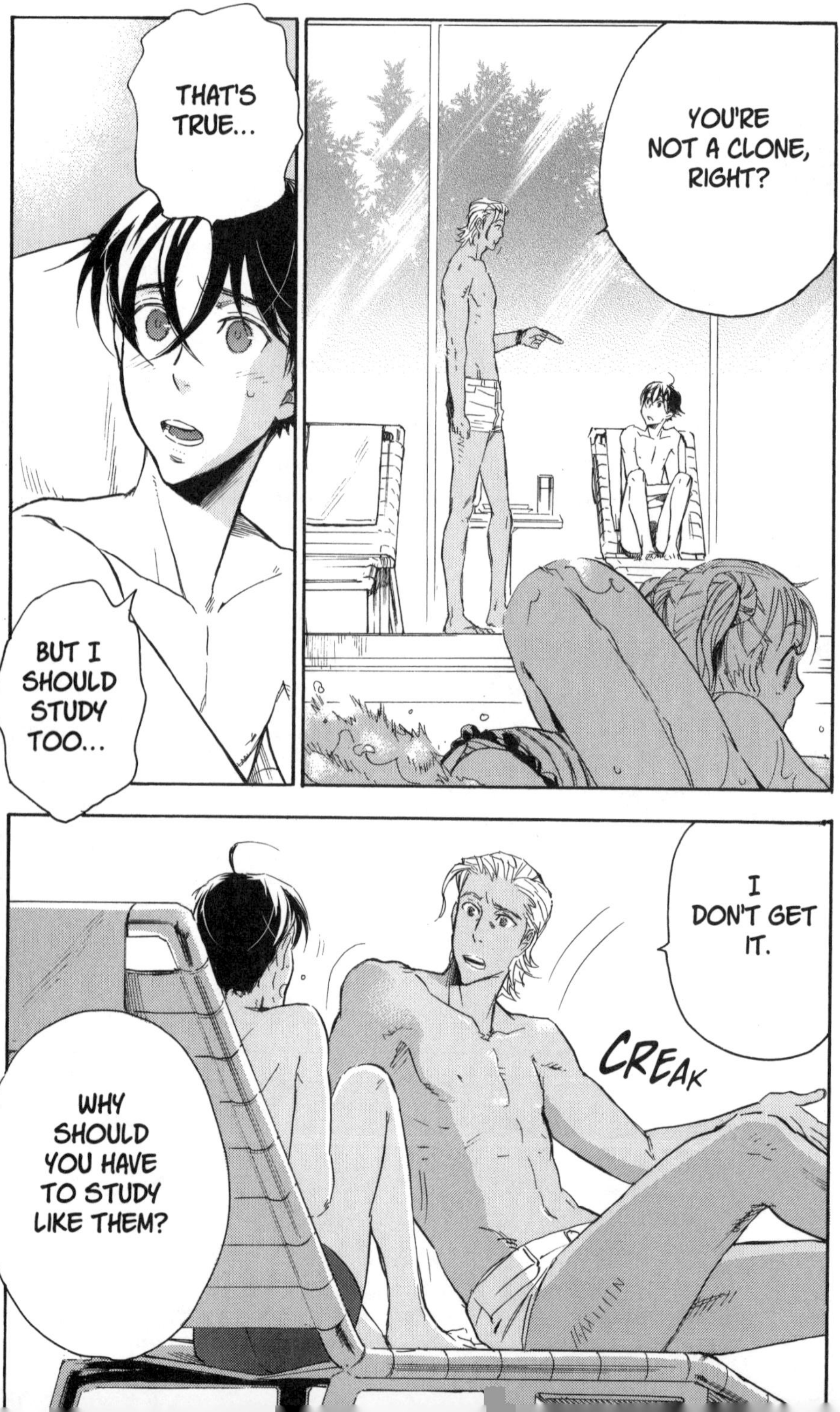
YOU'RE NOT A CLONE, RIGHT?
THAT'S TRUE...
BUT I SHOULD STUDY TOO...
I DON'T GET IT.
CREAK
WHY SHOULD YOU HAVE TO STUDY LIKE THEM?

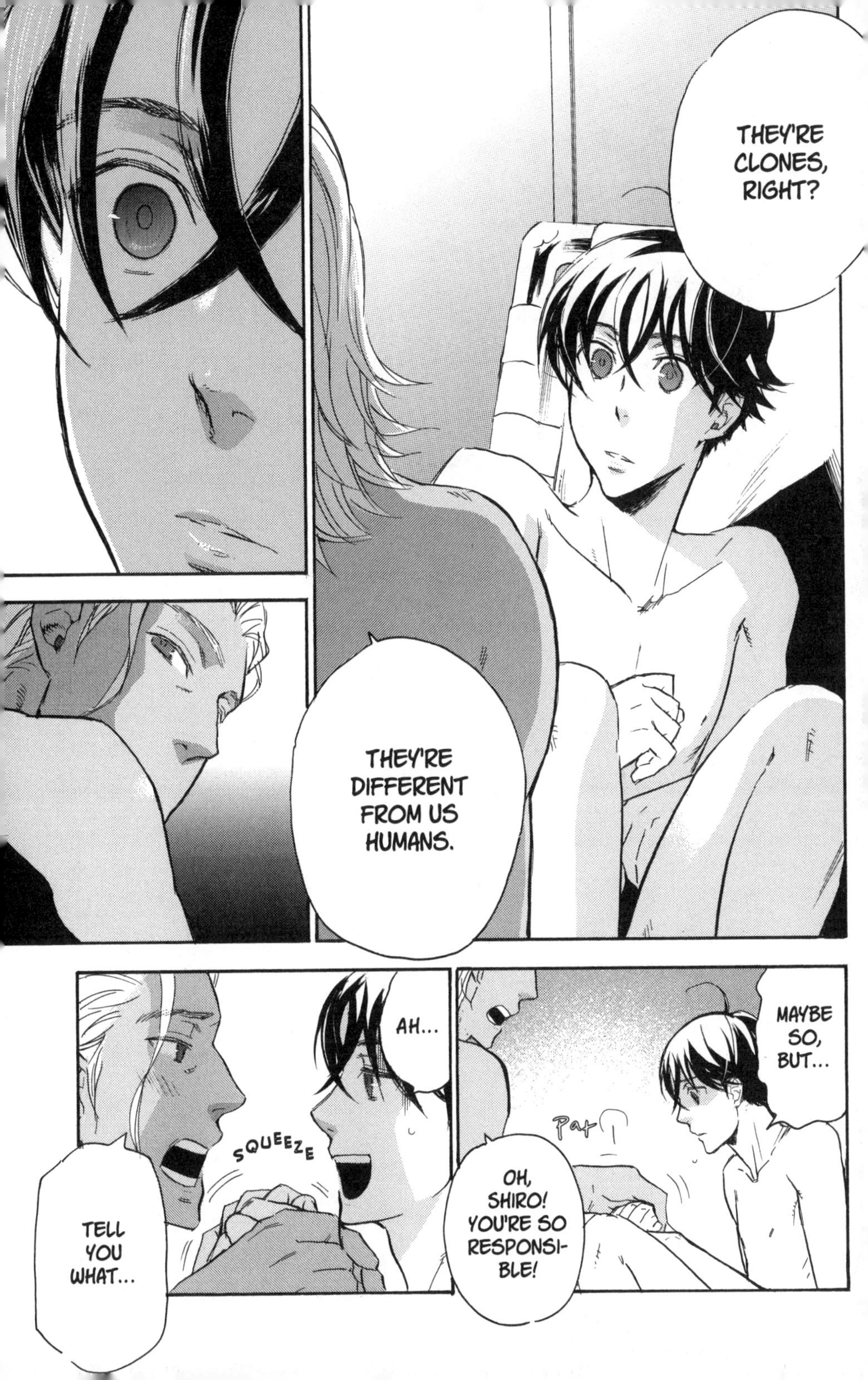
THEY'RE CLONES, RIGHT?
THEY'RE DIFFERENT FROM US HUMANS.
MAYBE SO, BUT...
Pat
OH, SHIRO! YOU'RE SO RESPONSI-BLE!
AH...
SQUEEZE
TELL YOU WHAT...

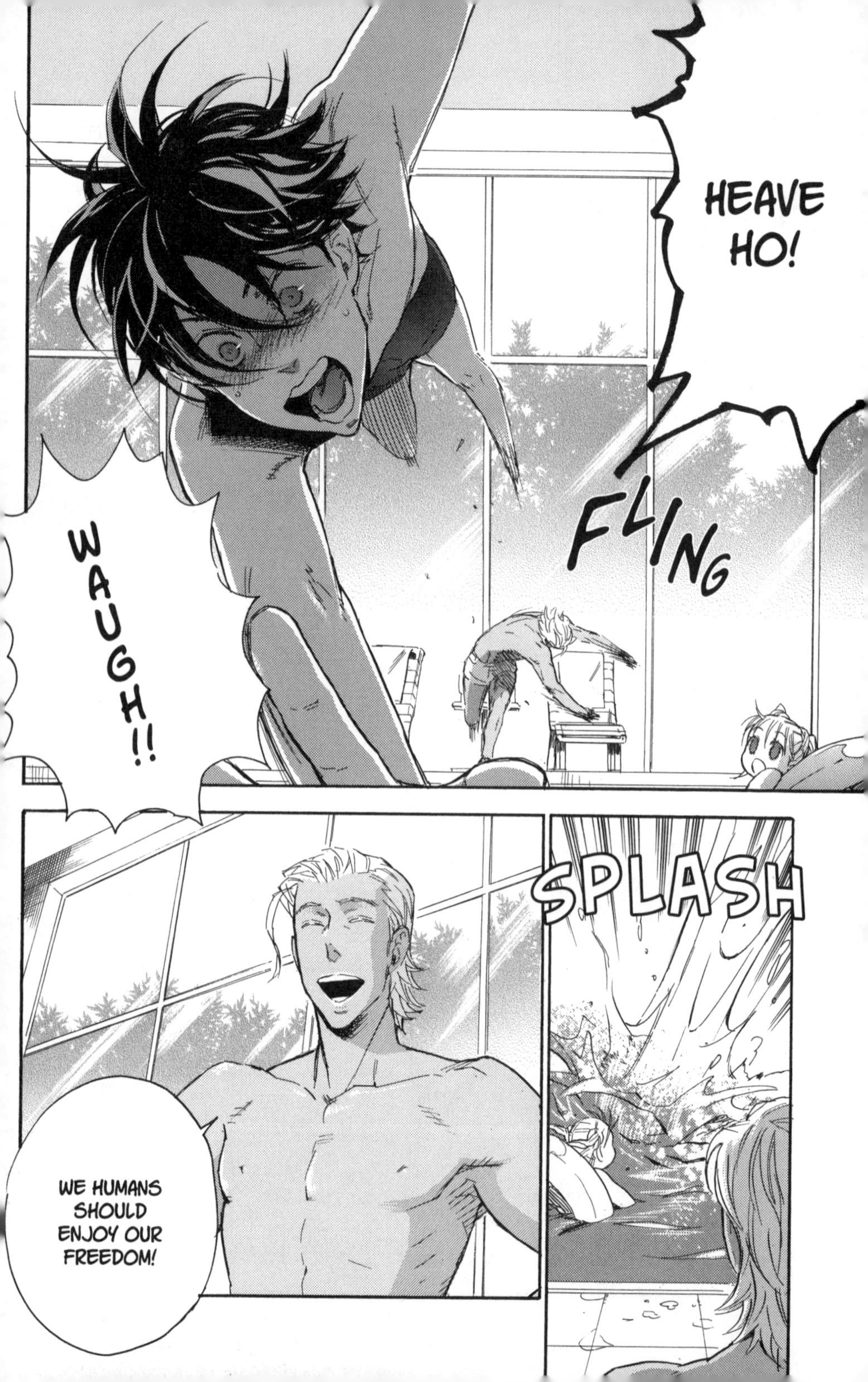
HEAVE HO!
FLING
WAUGH!!
SPLASH
WE HUMANS SHOULD ENJOY OUR FREEDOM!

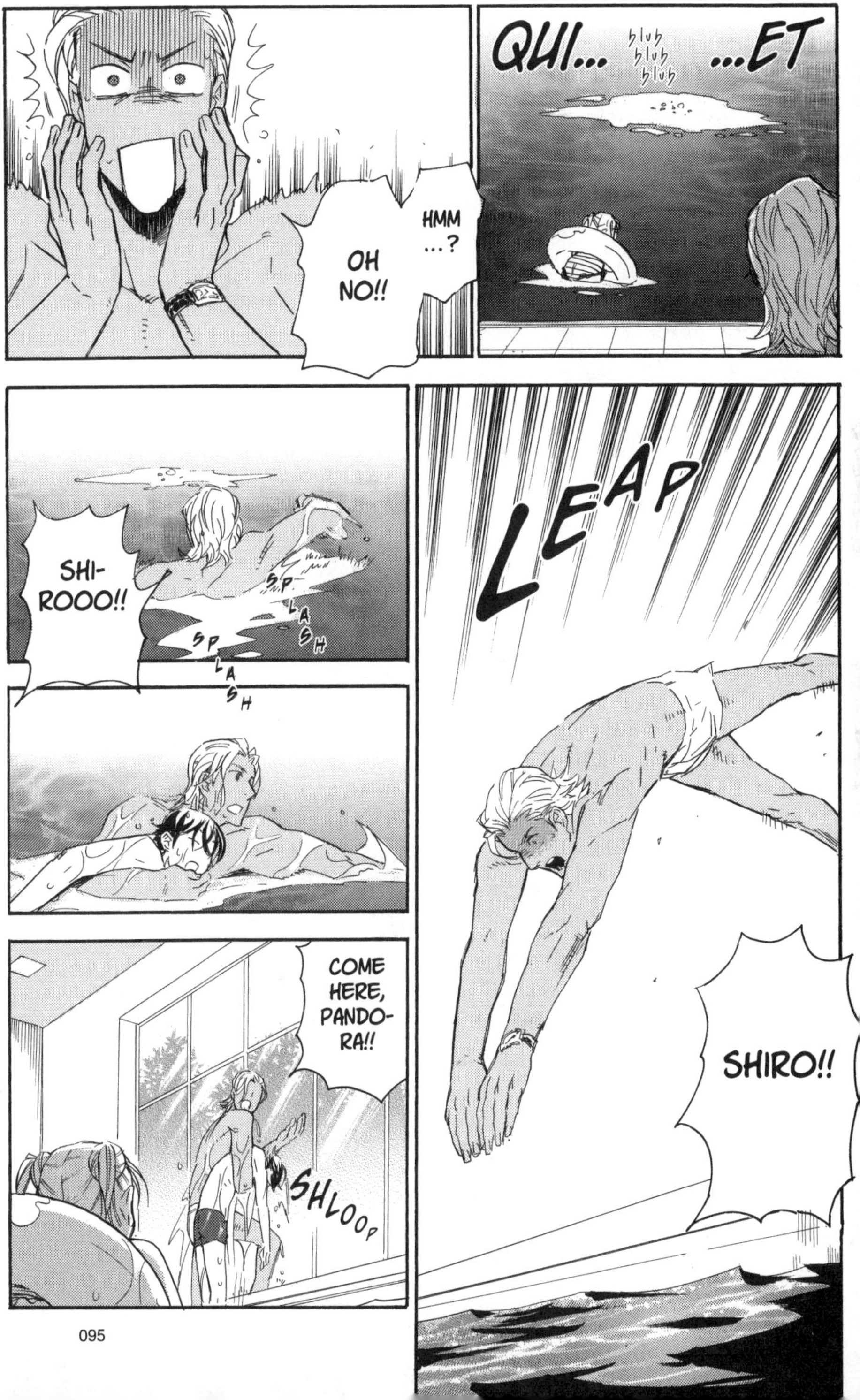
QUI... blub blub blub ...ET
HMM ...?
OH NO!!
LEAP
SHIRO!!
SHI-ROOO!!
SPLASH
SPLASH
COME HERE, PANDORA!!
SHLOOP

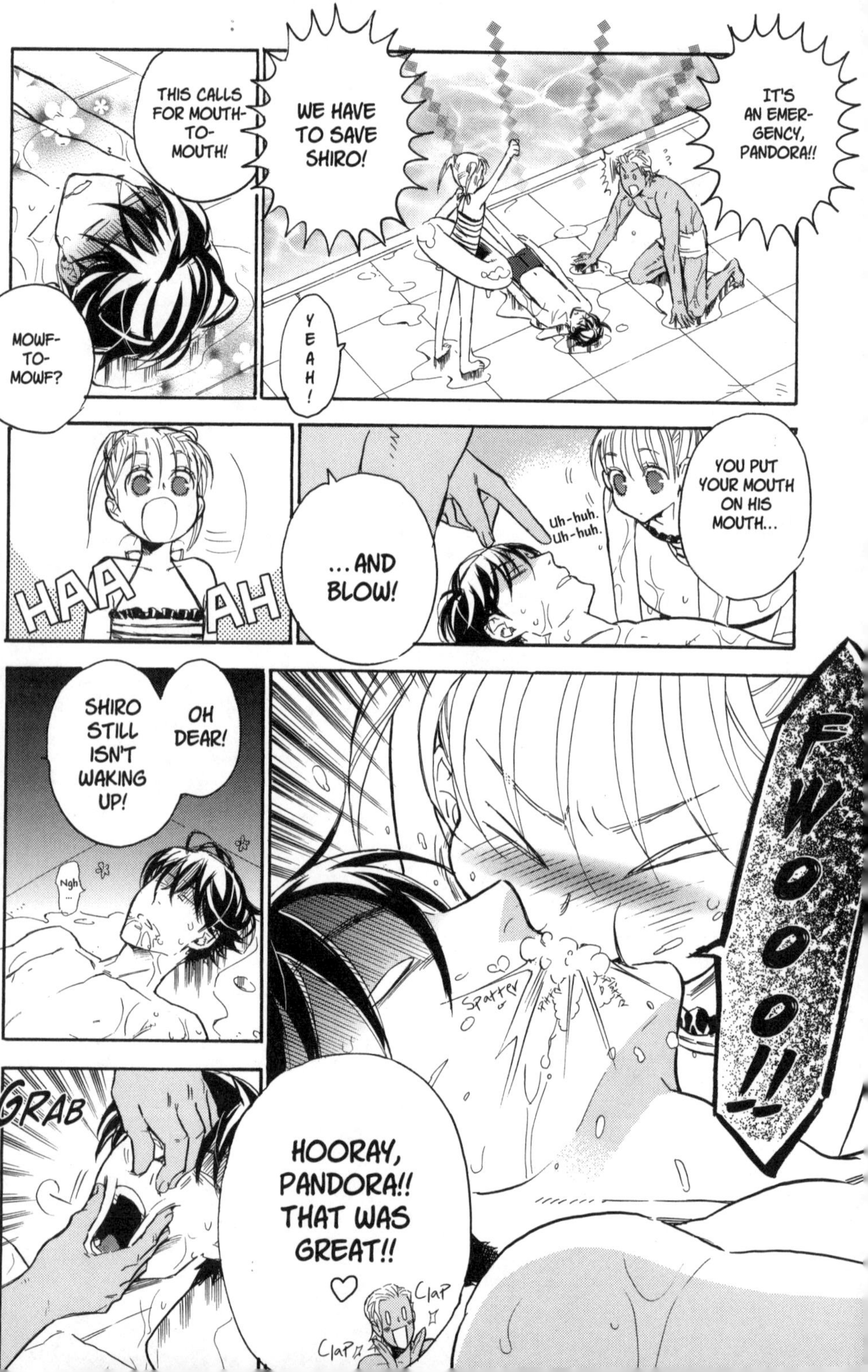
IT'S AN EMER-GENCY, PANDORA!!
WE HAVE TO SAVE SHIRO!
YEAH!
THIS CALLS FOR MOUTH-TO-MOUTH!
MOWF-TO-MOWF?
YOU PUT YOUR MOUTH ON HIS MOUTH...
Uh-huh. Uh-huh.
...AND BLOW!
HAAAH
FWOOOO!!
Spatter
OH DEAR!
SHIRO STILL ISN'T WAKING UP!
Ngh...
GRAB
HOORAY, PANDORA!! THAT WAS GREAT!!
Clap
Clap

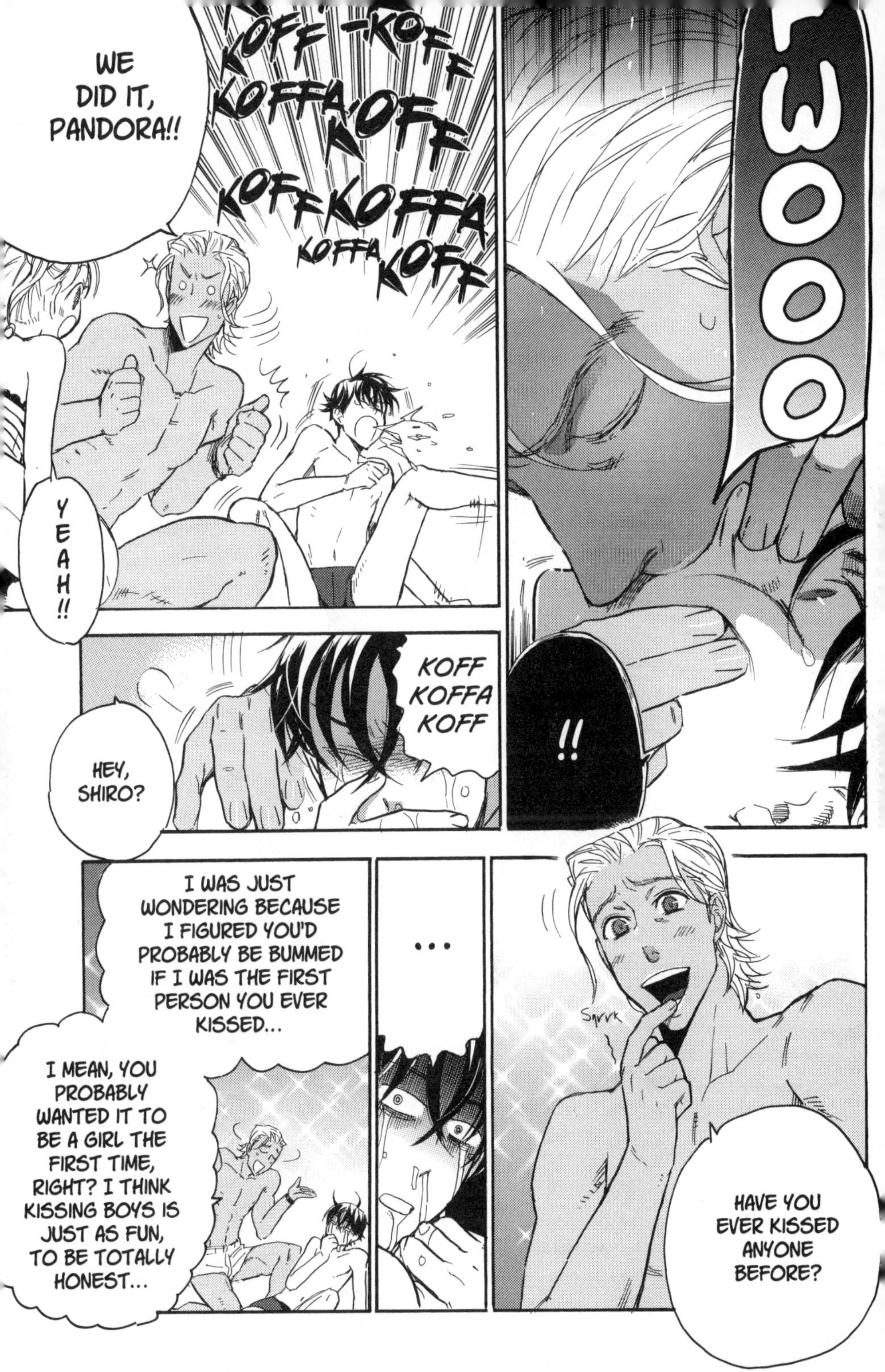
WOOO
!!
WE DID IT, PANDORA!!
KOFF-KOFF KOFFA KOFF KOFF
KOFF KOFFA
KOFFA KOFF
YEAH!!
KOFF KOFFA KOFF
HEY, SHIRO?
Snrk
HAVE YOU EVER KISSED ANYONE BEFORE?
...
I WAS JUST WONDERING BECAUSE I FIGURED YOU'D PROBABLY BE BUMMED IF I WAS THE FIRST PERSON YOU EVER KISSED...
I MEAN, YOU PROBABLY WANTED IT TO BE A GIRL THE FIRST TIME, RIGHT? I THINK KISSING BOYS IS JUST AS FUN, TO BE TOTALLY HONEST...

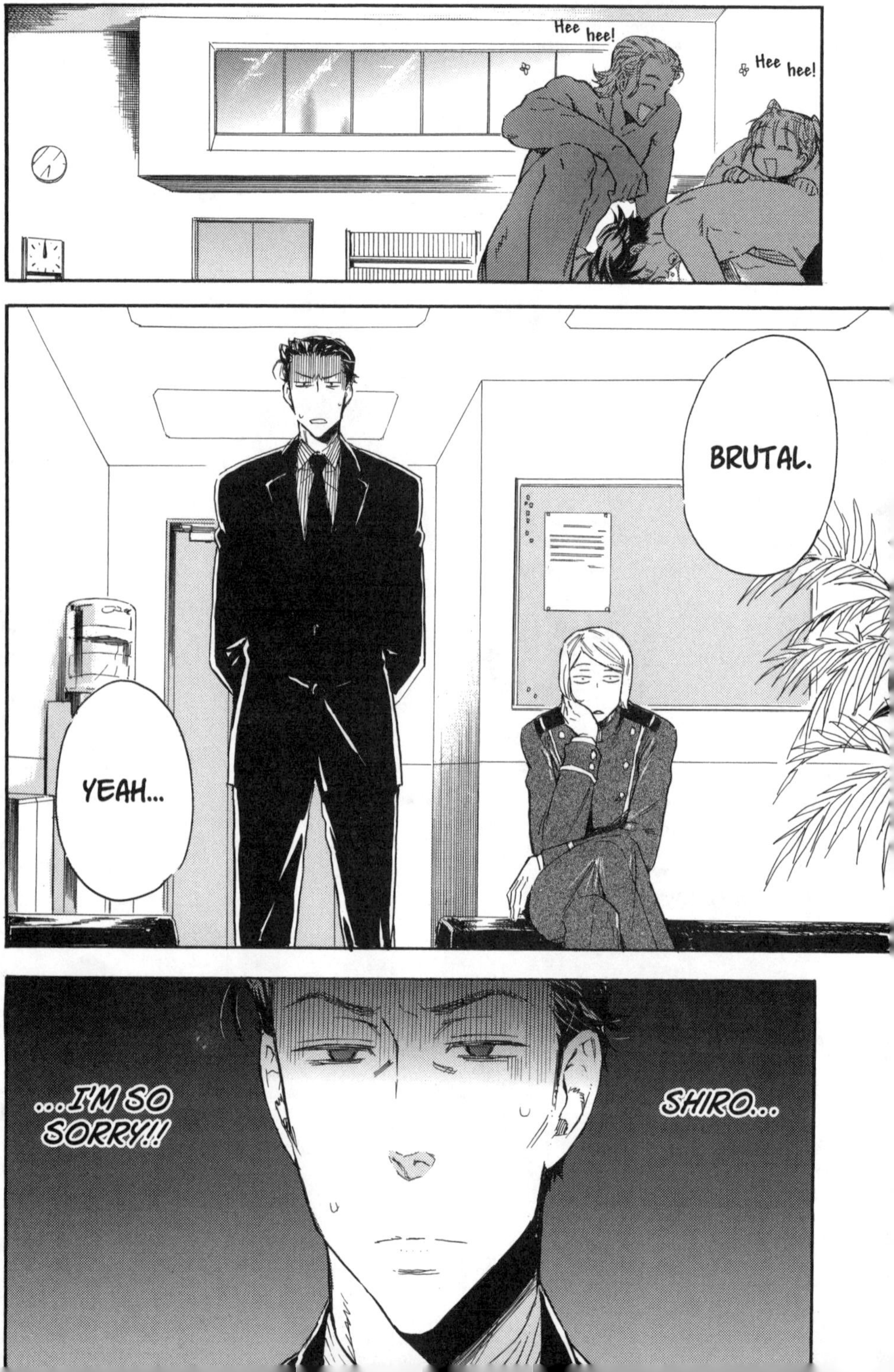
Hee hee!
Hee hee!
BRUTAL.
YEAH...
SHIRO...
...I'M SO SORRY!!

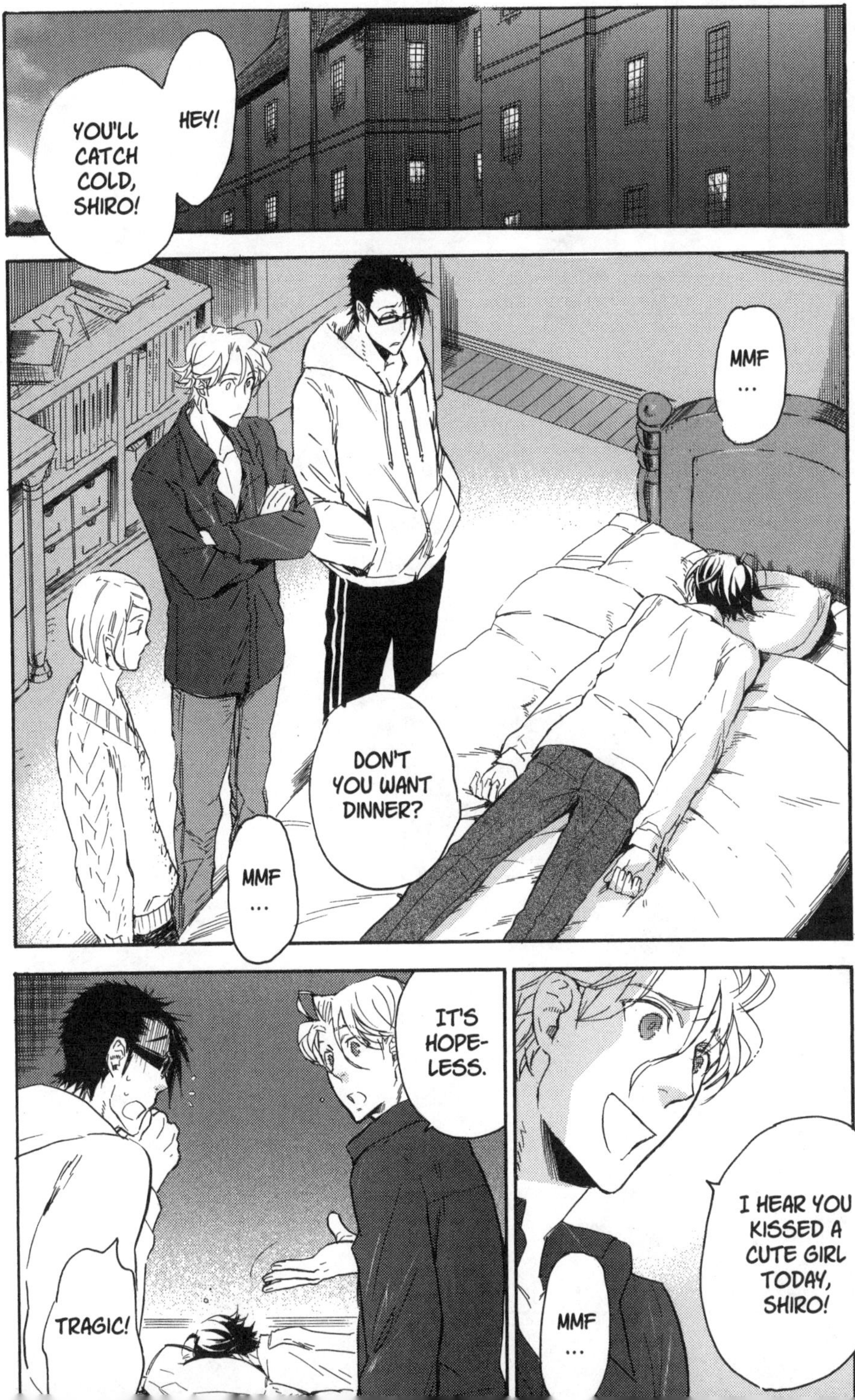
HEY!
YOU'LL CATCH COLD, SHIRO!
MMF ...
DON'T YOU WANT DINNER?
MMF ...
I HEAR YOU KISSED A CUTE GIRL TODAY, SHIRO!
MMF ...
IT'S HOPE-LESS.
TRAGIC!

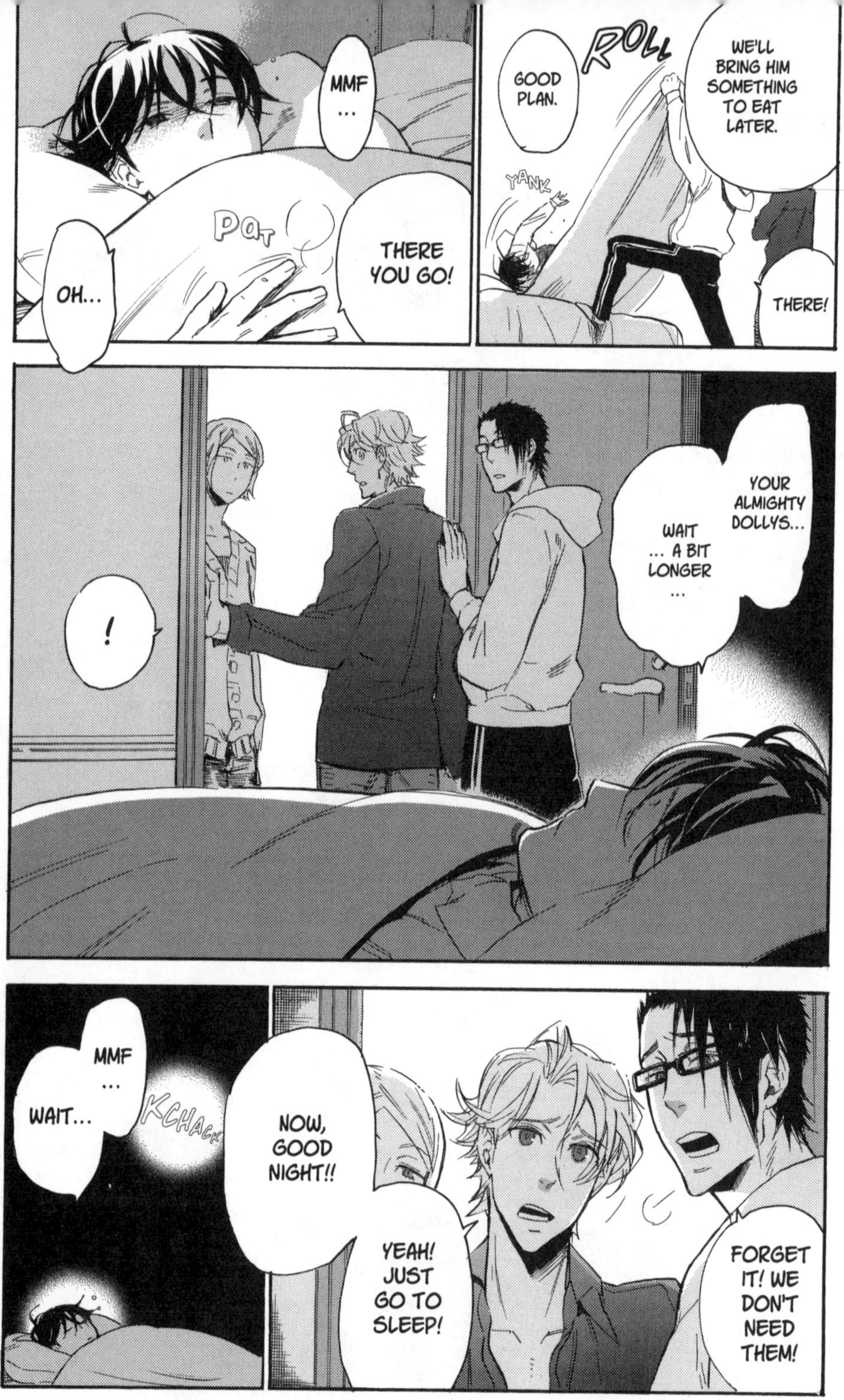
WE'LL BRING HIM SOMETHING TO EAT LATER.
ROLL
GOOD PLAN.
YANK
THERE!
MMF ...
PAT
THERE YOU GO!
OH...
YOUR ALMIGHTY DOLLYS...
WAIT ... A BIT LONGER ...
!
FORGET IT! WE DON'T NEED THEM!
NOW, GOOD NIGHT!!
YEAH! JUST GO TO SLEEP!
KCHACK
MMF ... WAIT...

CHAPTER ten

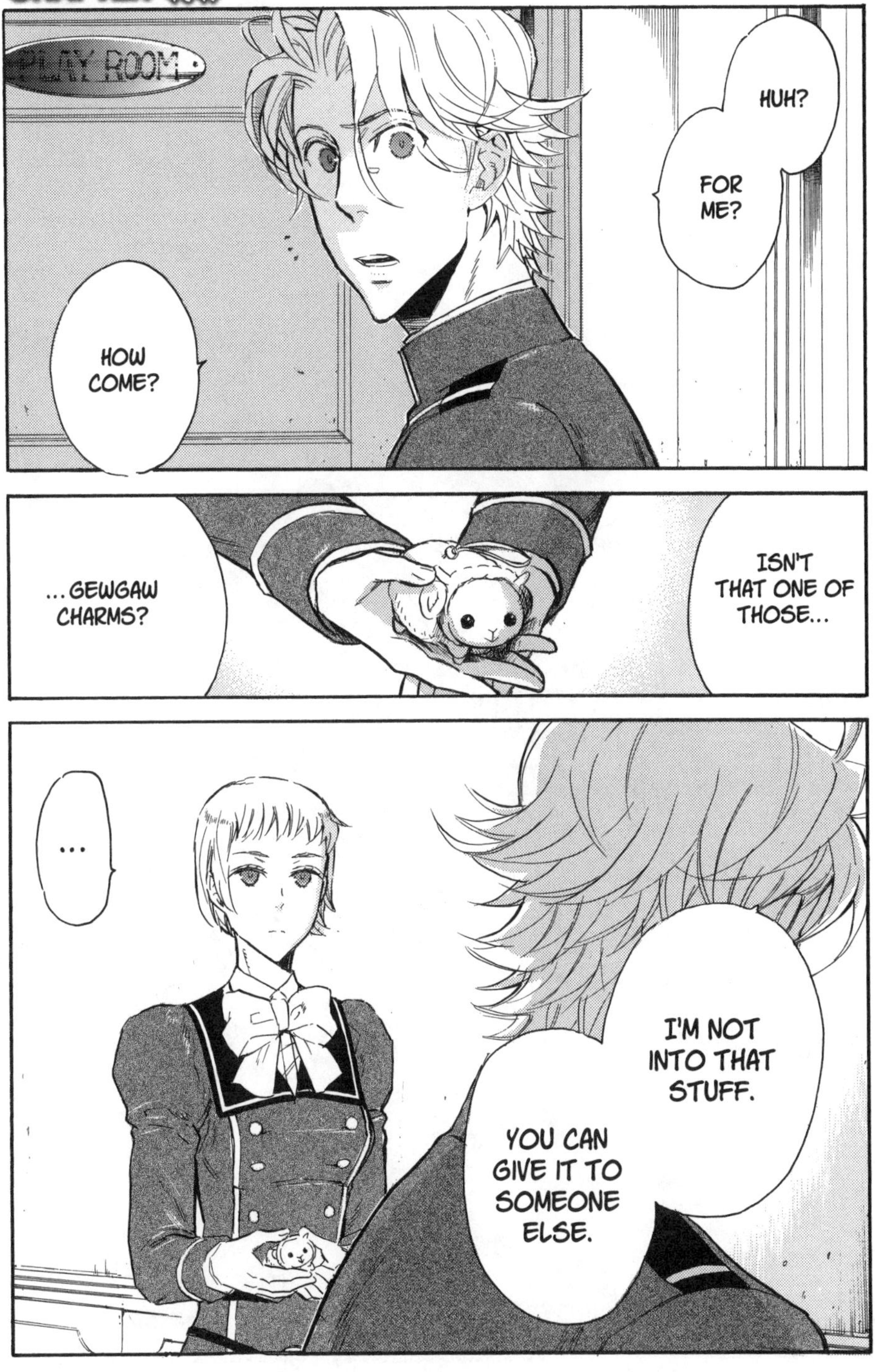
PLAY ROOM
HUH?
FOR ME?
HOW COME?
ISN'T THAT ONE OF THOSE...
...GEWGAW CHARMS?
I'M NOT INTO THAT STUFF.
YOU CAN GIVE IT TO SOMEONE ELSE.
...

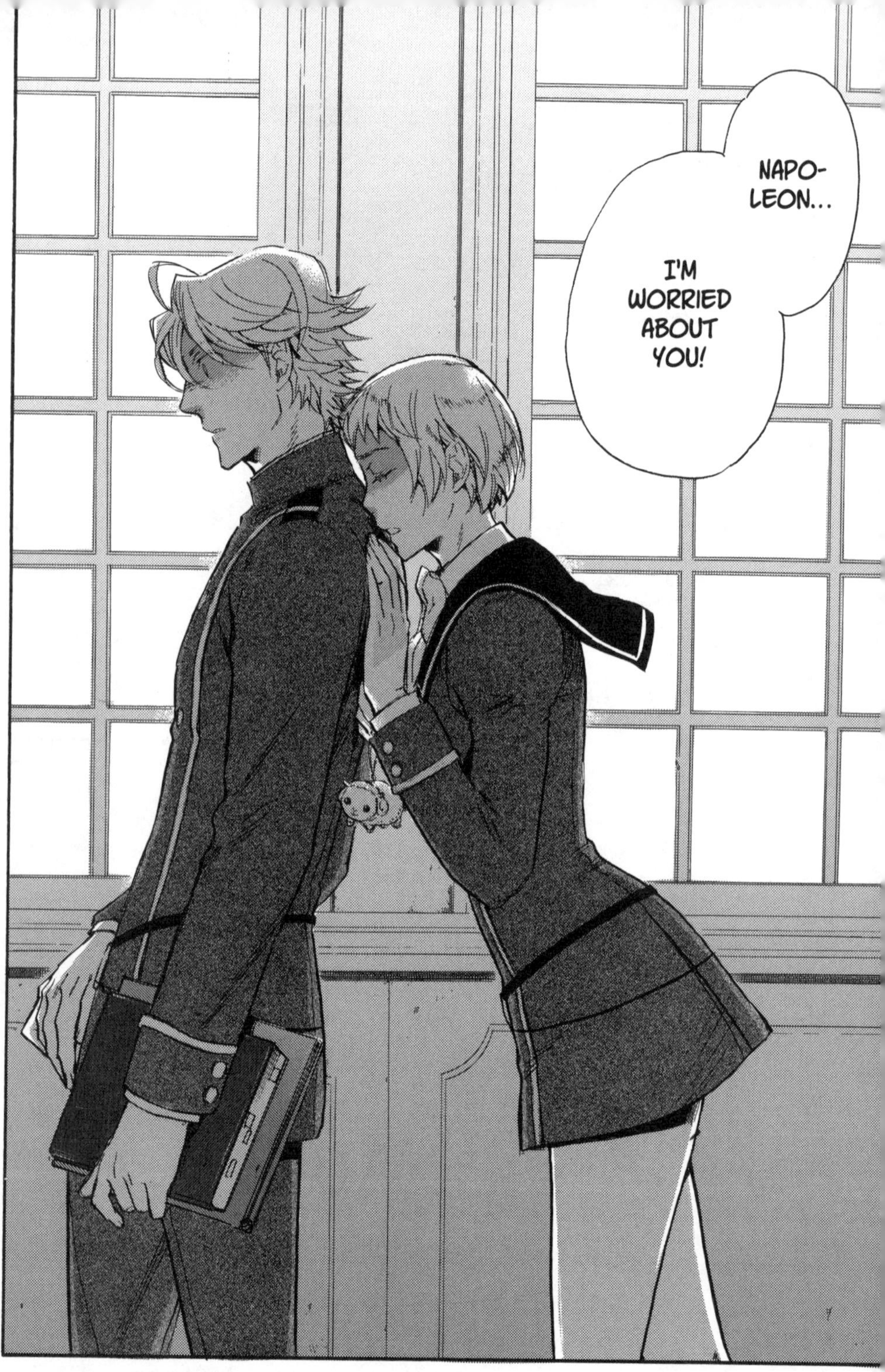
NAPO-LEON...
I'M WORRIED ABOUT YOU!

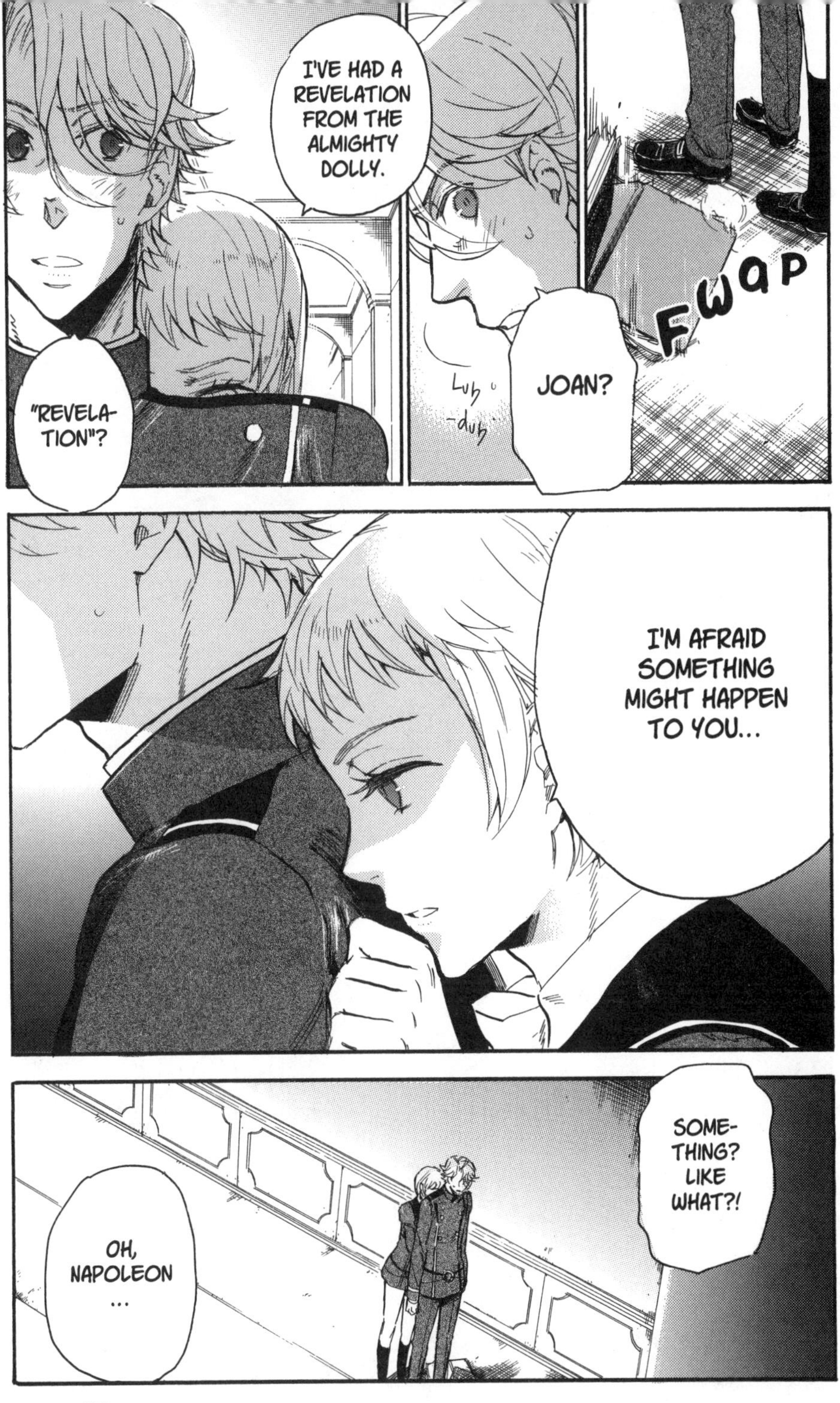
FWAP
Luh-dub
JOAN?
I'VE HAD A REVELATION FROM THE ALMIGHTY DOLLY.
"REVELATION"?
I'M AFRAID SOMETHING MIGHT HAPPEN TO YOU...
SOMETHING? LIKE WHAT?!
OH, NAPOLEON...

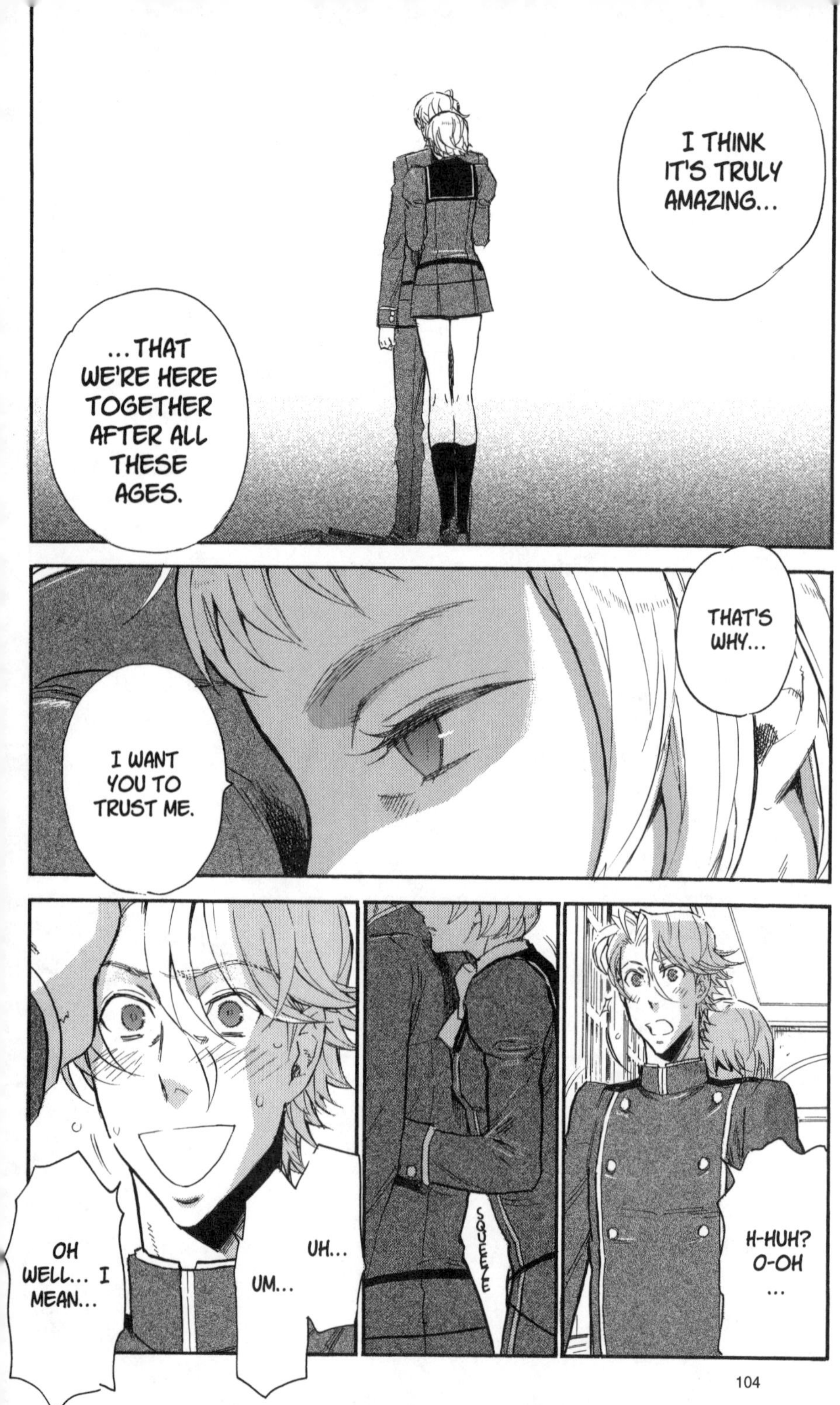
I THINK IT'S TRULY AMAZING...
...THAT WE'RE HERE TOGETHER AFTER ALL THESE AGES.
THAT'S WHY...
I WANT YOU TO TRUST ME.
H-HUH? O-OH ...
SQUEEZE
UH...
UM...
OH WELL... I MEAN...

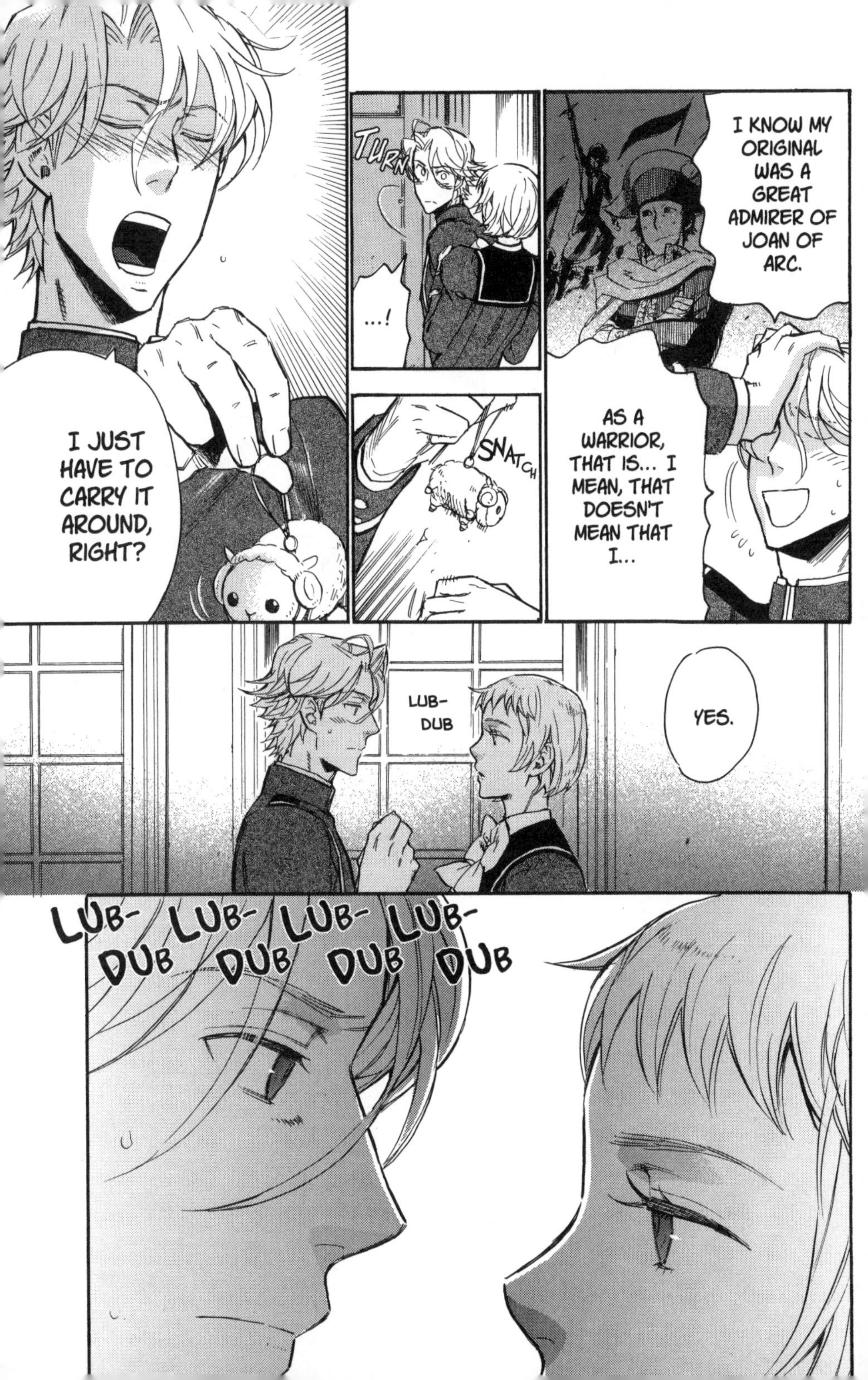
I KNOW MY ORIGINAL WAS A GREAT ADMIRER OF JOAN OF ARC.
AS A WARRIOR, THAT IS... I MEAN, THAT DOESN'T MEAN THAT I...
TURN
...!
SNATCH
I JUST HAVE TO CARRY IT AROUND, RIGHT?
YES.
LUB-DUB
LUB-DUB LUB-DUB LUB-DUB LUB-DUB

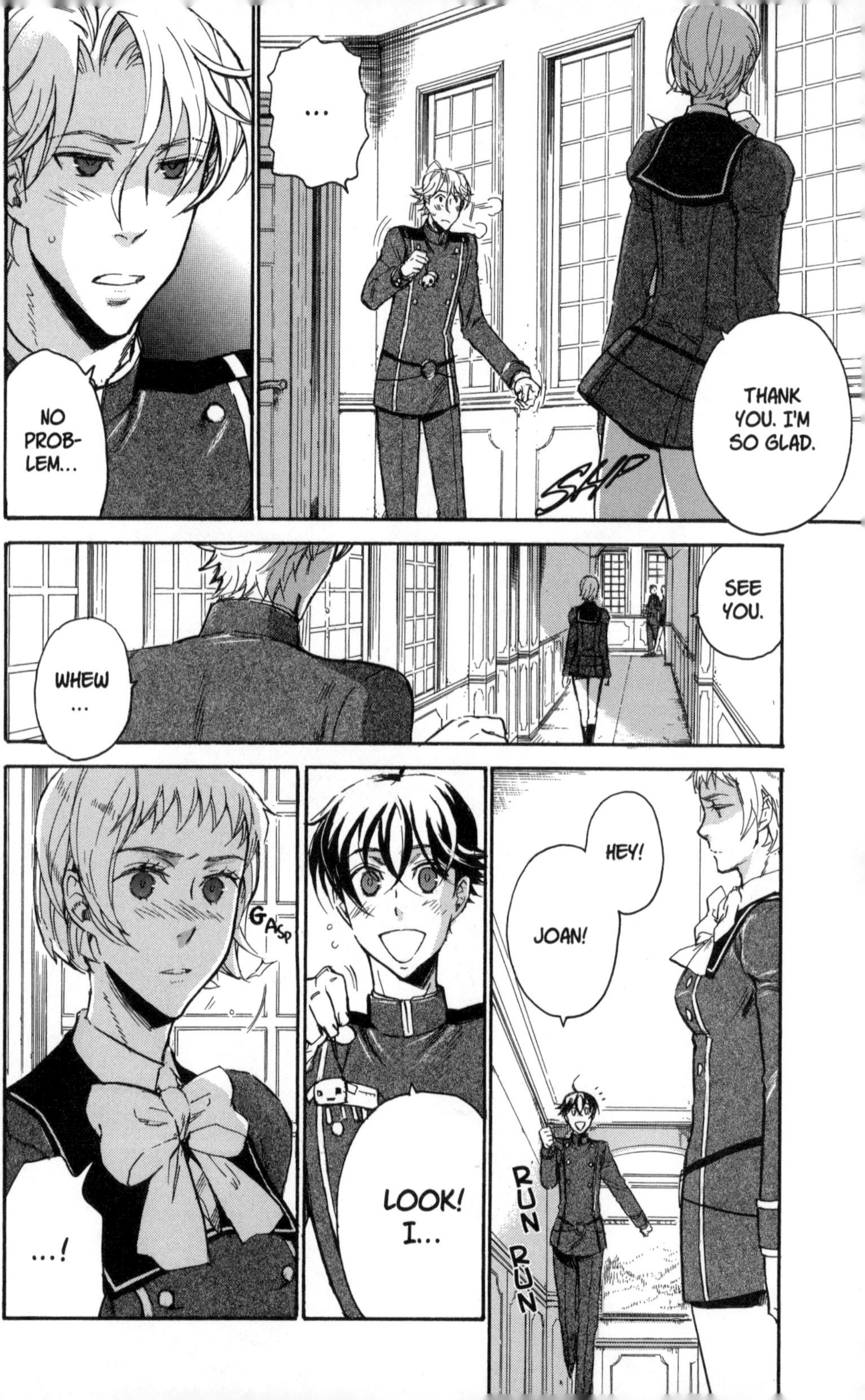
...
THANK YOU. I'M SO GLAD.
SHP
NO PROBLEM...
SEE YOU.
WHEW ...
HEY!
JOAN!
RUN RUN
LOOK! I...
GASP
...!

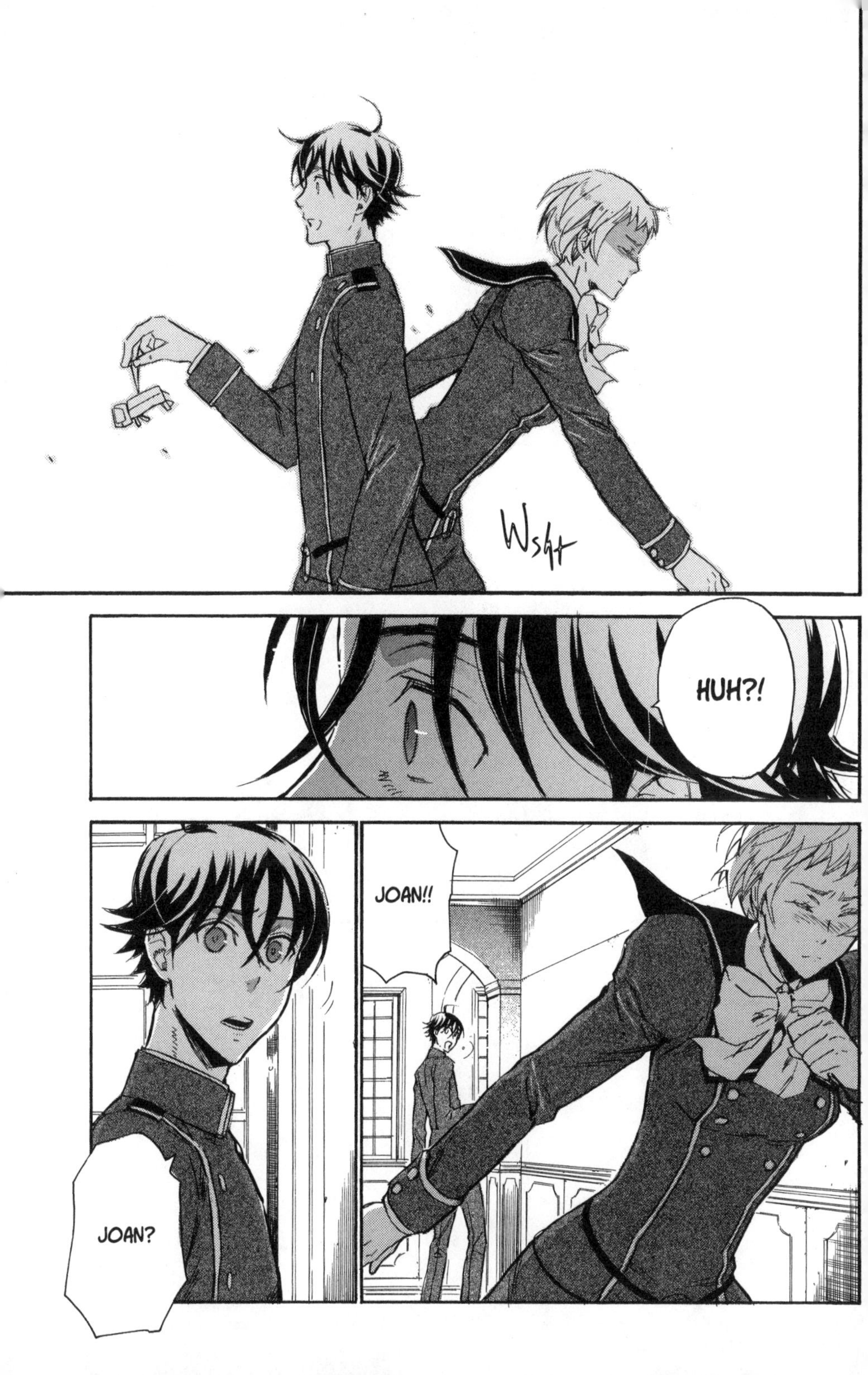
Wsht
HUH?!
JOAN!!
JOAN?

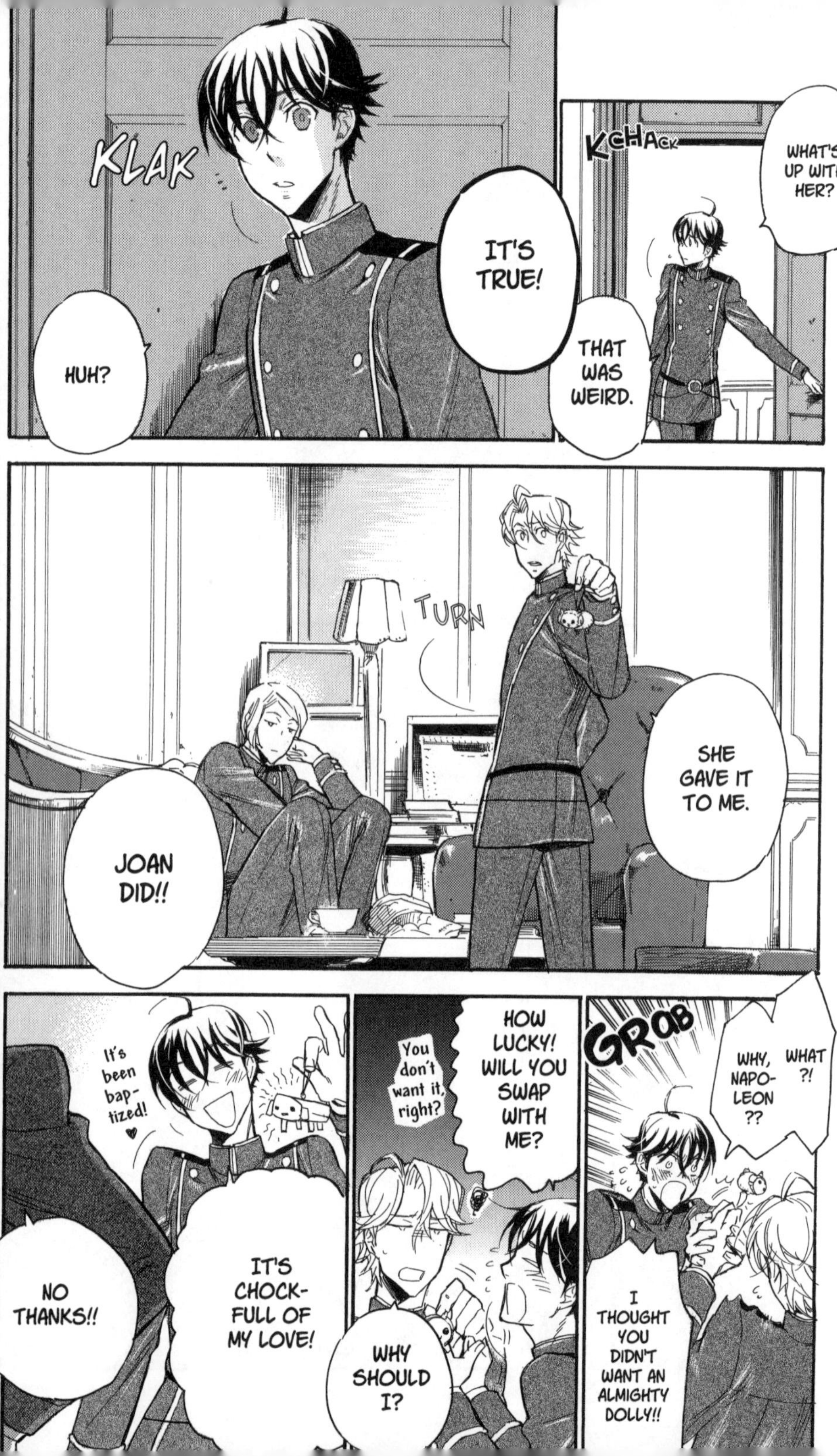
KCHACK
WHAT'S UP WITH HER?
THAT WAS WEIRD.
IT'S TRUE!
KLAK
HUH?
TURN
SHE GAVE IT TO ME.
JOAN DID!!
GRAB
WHAT?!
WHY, NAPOLEON??
I THOUGHT YOU DIDN'T WANT AN ALMIGHTY DOLLY!!
HOW LUCKY! WILL YOU SWAP WITH ME?
You don't want it, right?
WHY SHOULD I?
It's been baptized! ♥
IT'S CHOCK-FULL OF MY LOVE!
NO THANKS!!

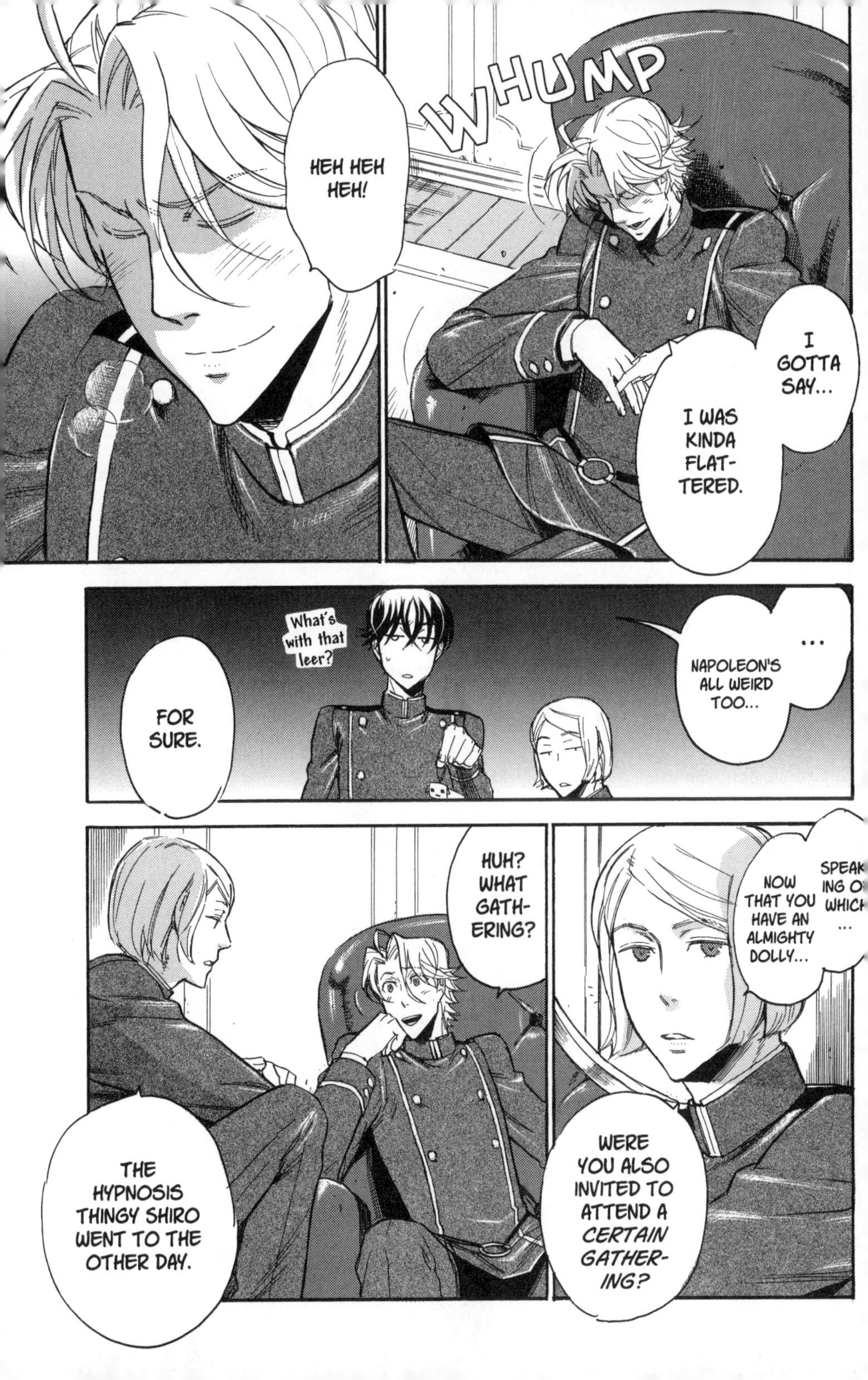
WHUMP
I GOTTA SAY...
I WAS KINDA FLATTERED.
HEH HEH HEH!
... NAPOLEON'S ALL WEIRD TOO...
What's with that leer?
FOR SURE.
SPEAK ING O WHICH ...
NOW THAT YOU HAVE AN ALMIGHTY DOLLY...
WERE YOU ALSO INVITED TO ATTEND A CERTAIN GATHERING?
HUH? WHAT GATHERING?
THE HYPNOSIS THINGY SHIRO WENT TO THE OTHER DAY.

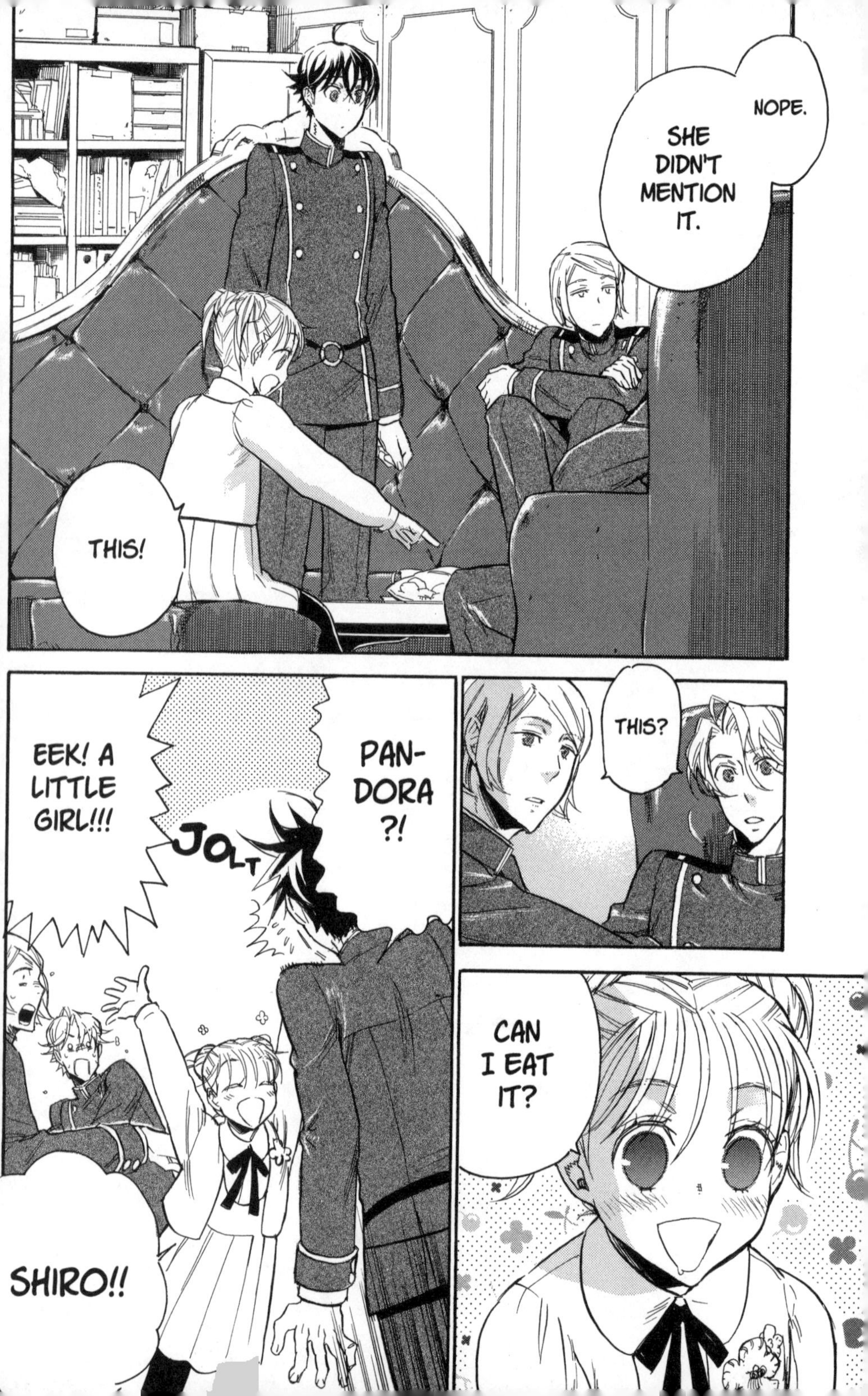
NOPE.
SHE DIDN'T MENTION IT.
THIS!
THIS?
CAN I EAT IT?
PAN-DORA?!
EEK! A LITTLE GIRL!!!
JOLT
SHIRO!!

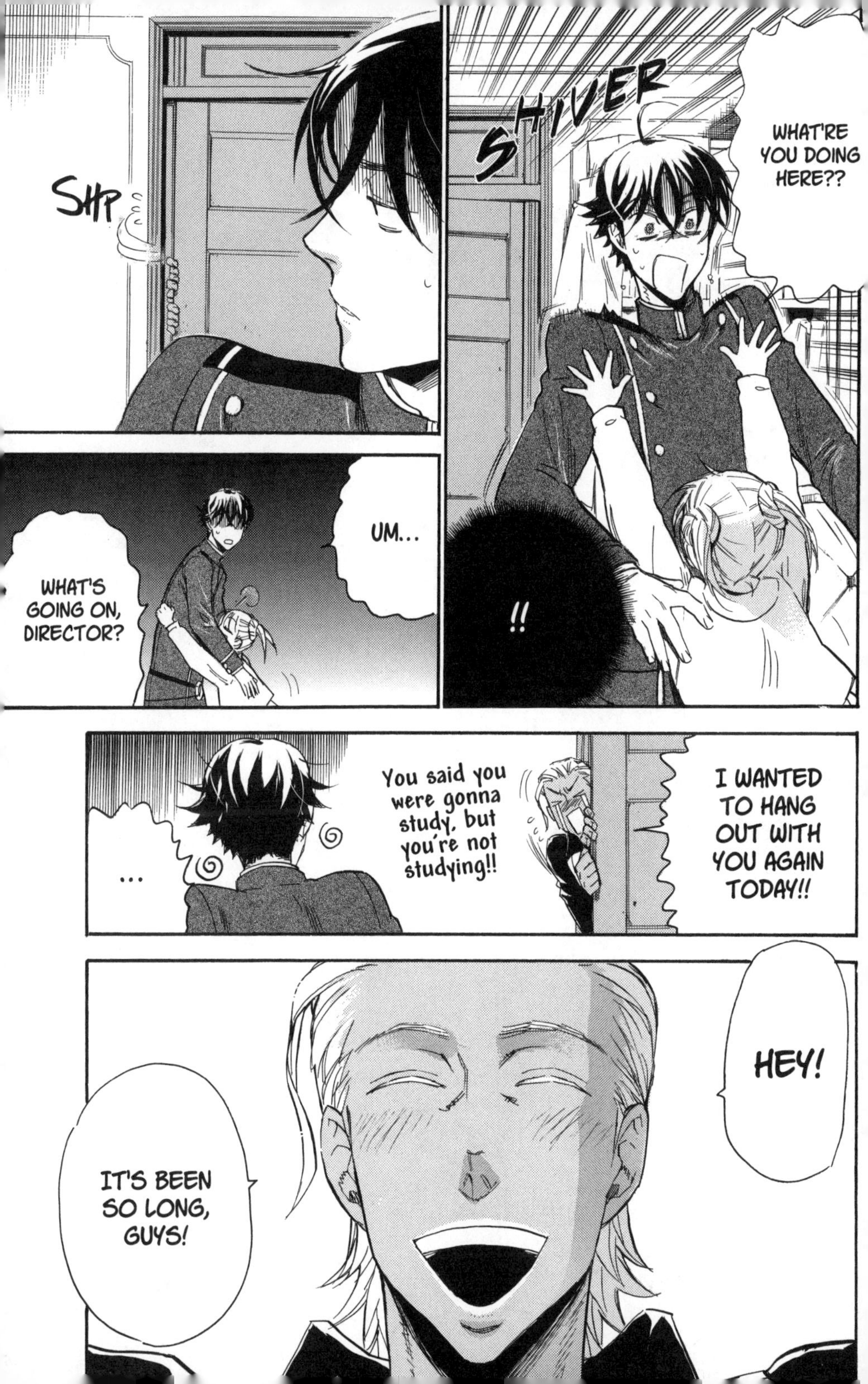
SHIVER
WHAT'RE YOU DOING HERE??
!!
SHP
UM...
WHAT'S GOING ON, DIRECTOR?
I WANTED TO HANG OUT WITH YOU AGAIN TODAY!!
You said you were gonna study, but you're not studying!!
...
HEY!
IT'S BEEN SO LONG, GUYS!

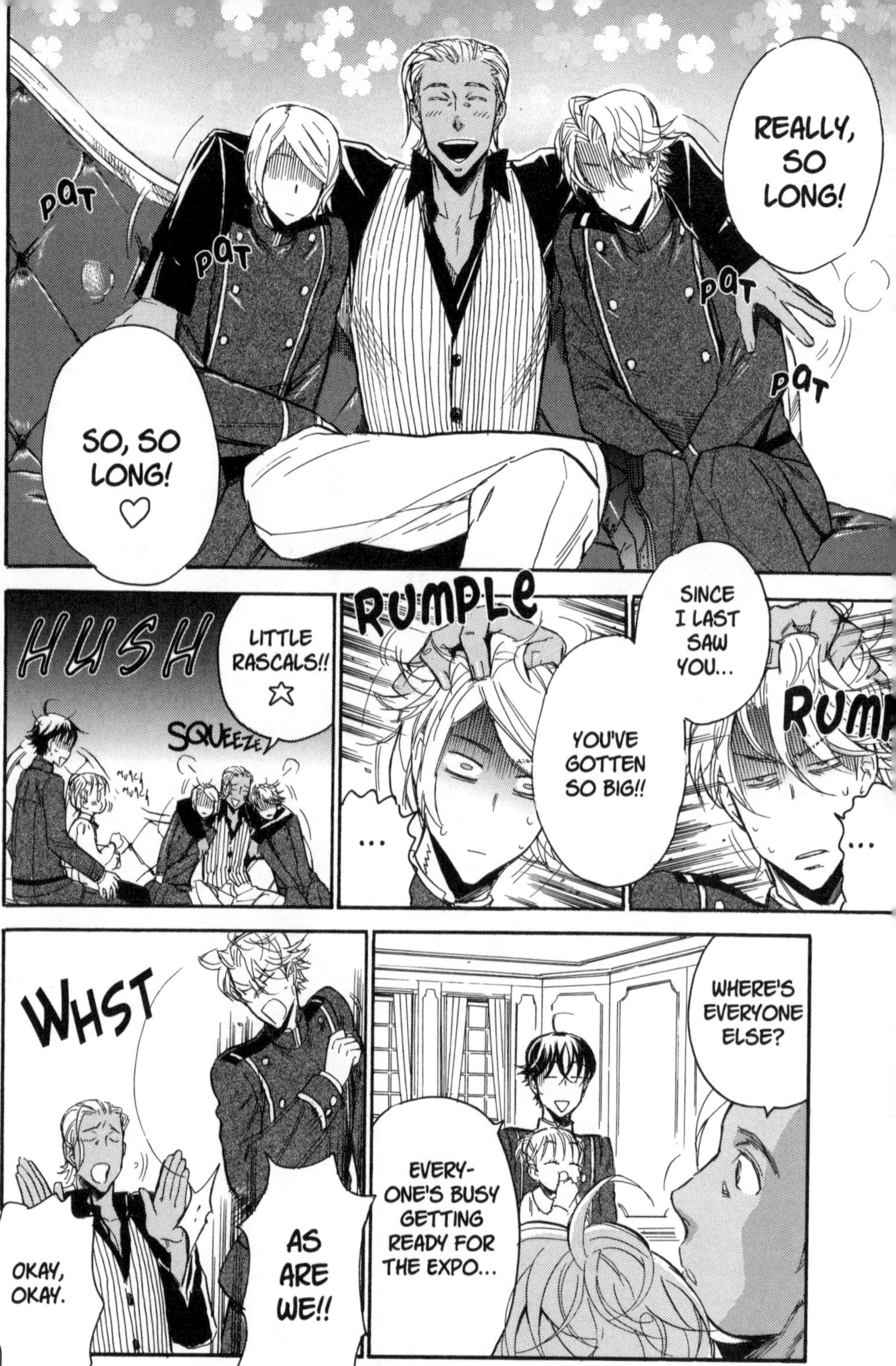
REALLY, SO LONG!
PAT
PAT
PAT
PAT
SO, SO LONG! ♡
SINCE I LAST SAW YOU...
YOU'VE GOTTEN SO BIG!!
RUMP
...
RUMPLE
...
LITTLE RASCALS!! ☆
HUSH
SQUEEZE
MUNCH MUNCH
WHERE'S EVERYONE ELSE?
EVERY-ONE'S BUSY GETTING READY FOR THE EXPO...
WHST
AS ARE WE!!
OKAY, OKAY.

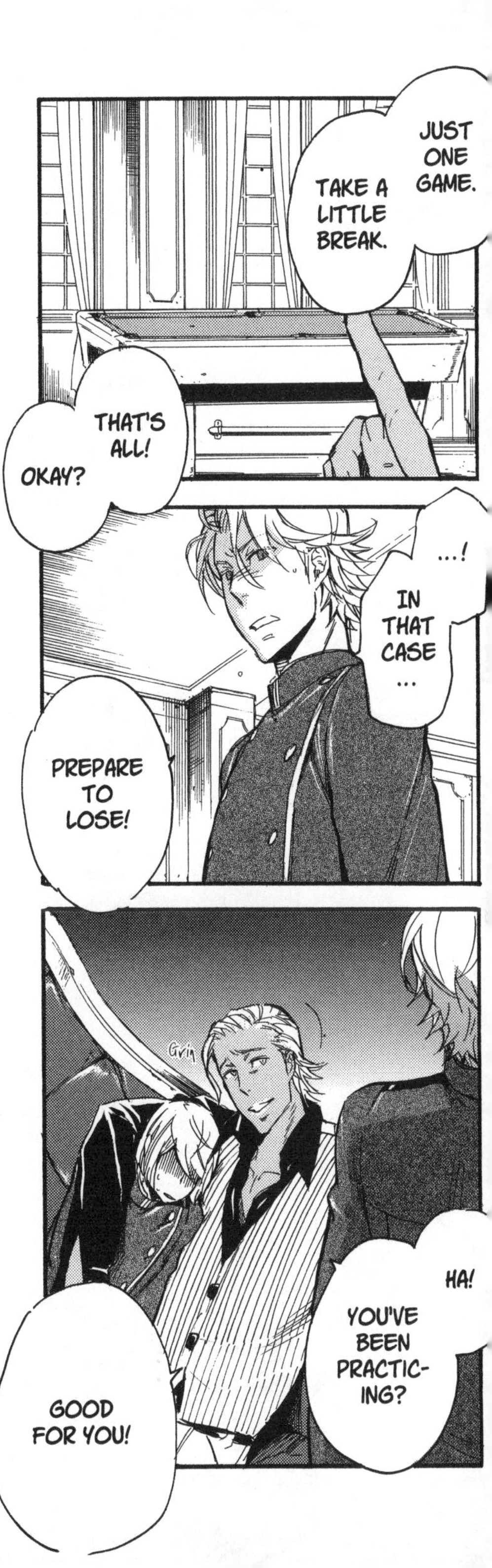
JUST ONE GAME.
TAKE A LITTLE BREAK.
THAT'S ALL!
OKAY?
...!
IN THAT CASE...
PREPARE TO LOSE!
Grin
HA!
YOU'VE BEEN PRACTIC- ING?
GOOD FOR YOU!

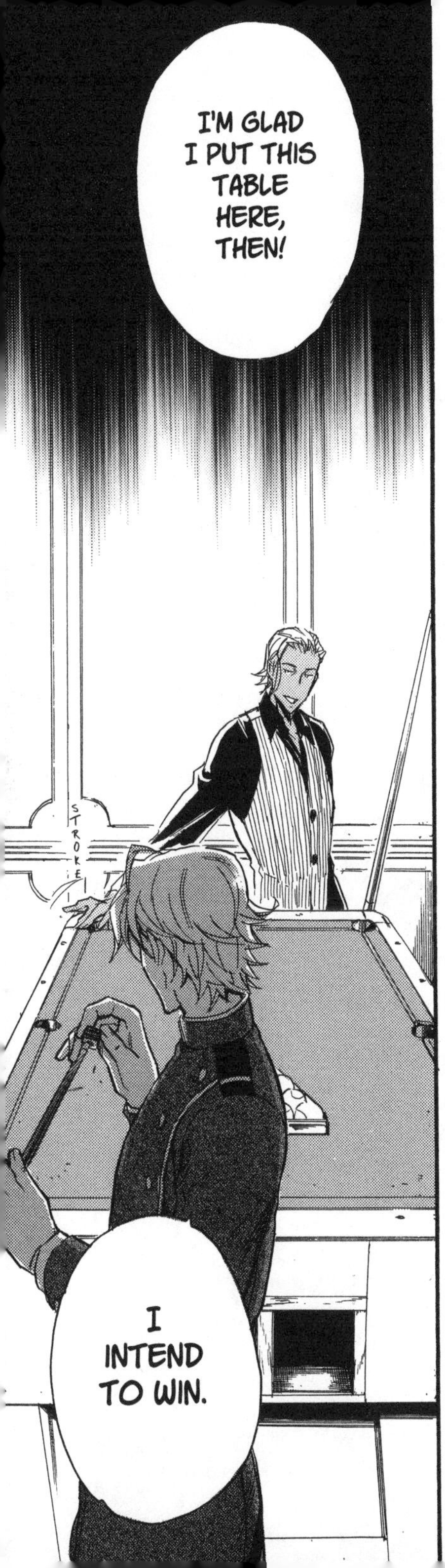
I'M GLAD I PUT THIS TABLE HERE, THEN!
STROKE
I INTEND TO WIN.

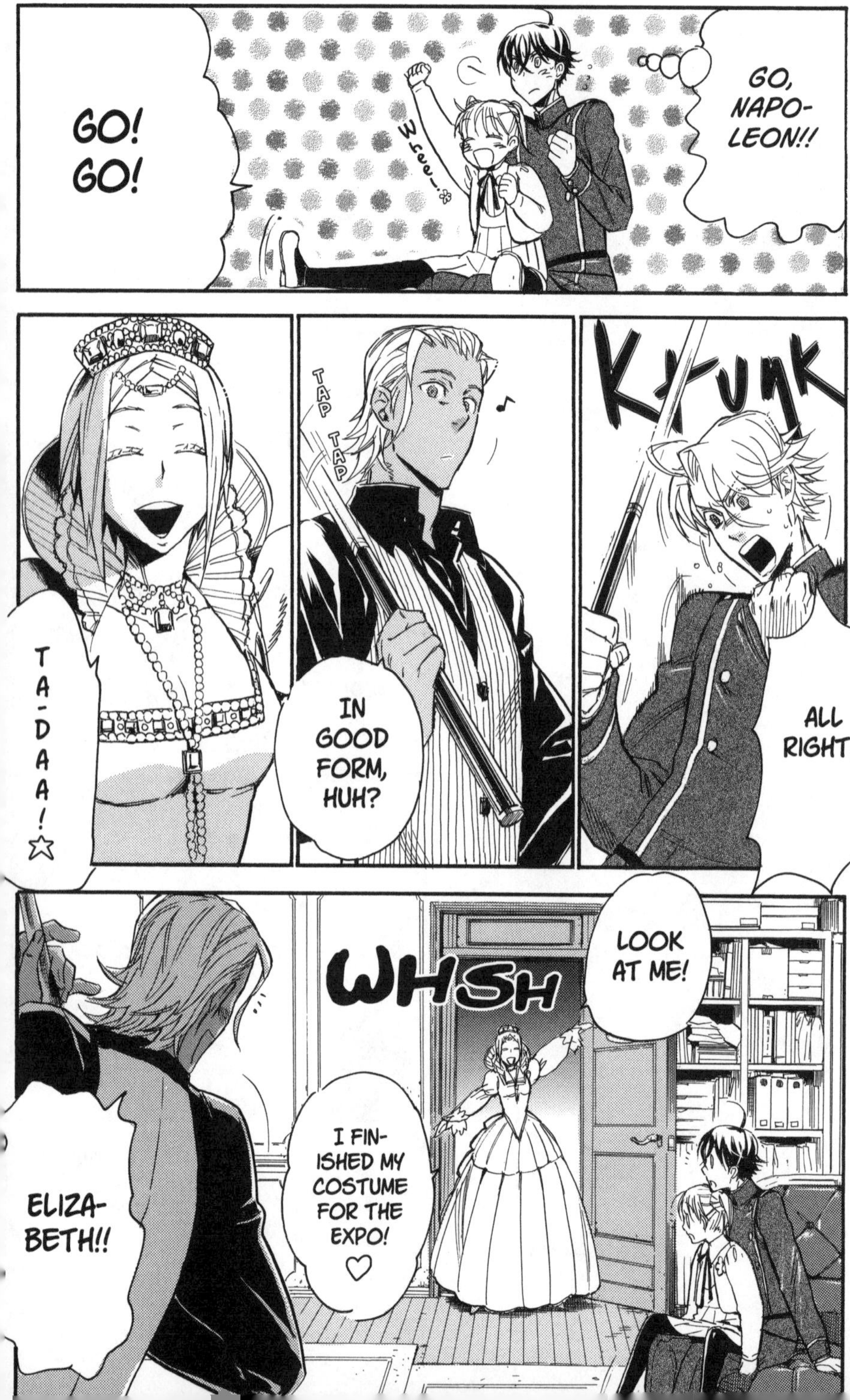
GO, NAPO-LEON!!
Wheee...
GO! GO!
KRUNK
ALL RIGHT!!
TAP TAP
IN GOOD FORM, HUH?
TA-DAAA! ☆
LOOK AT ME!
WHSH
I FIN-ISHED MY COSTUME FOR THE EXPO! ♡
ELIZA-BETH!!

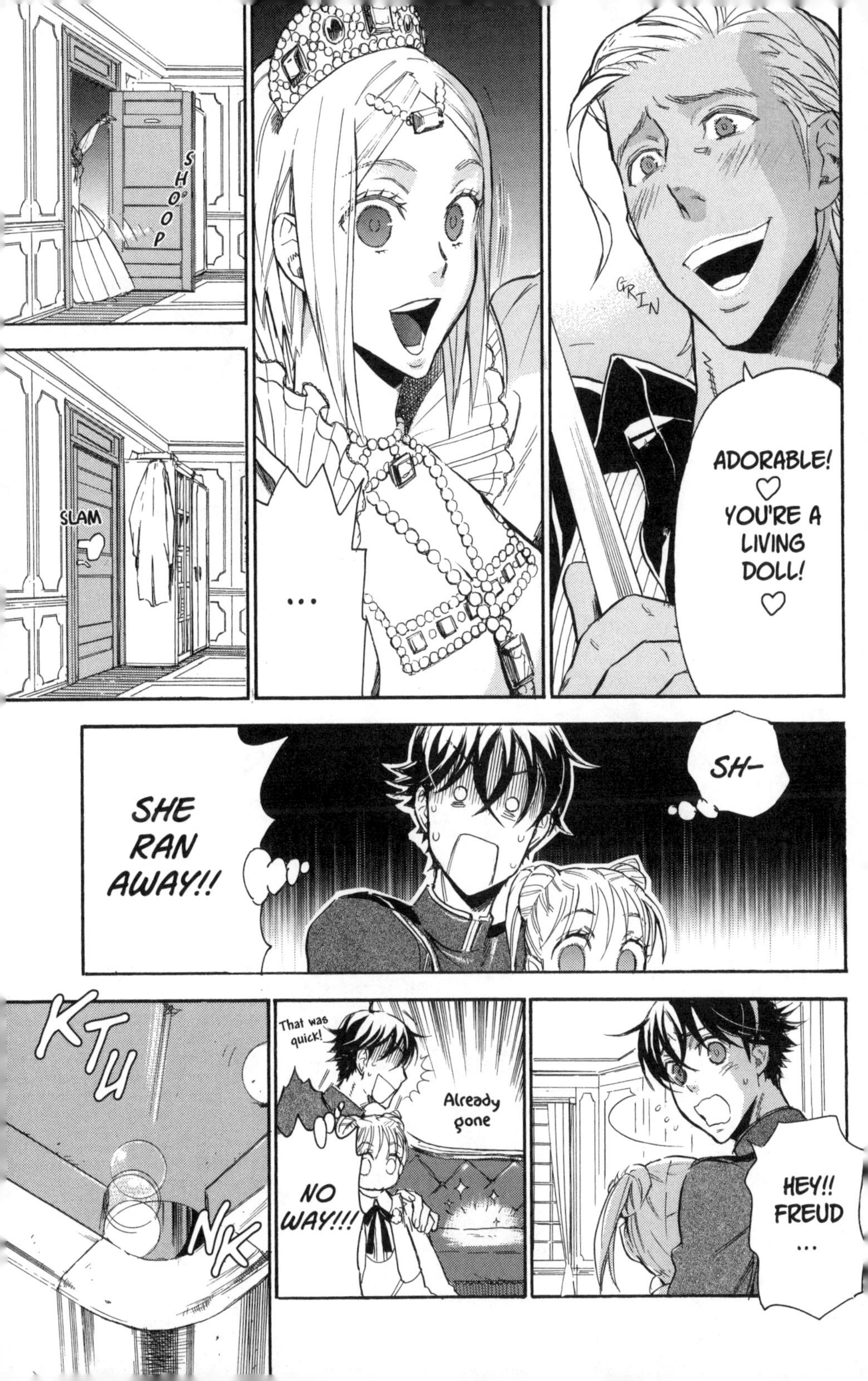
GRIN
ADORABLE! ♡ YOU'RE A LIVING DOLL! ♡
...
SHOOP
SLAM
SH-
SHE RAN AWAY!!
HEY!! FREUD ...
Already gone
That was quick!
NO WAY!!!
KTUNK

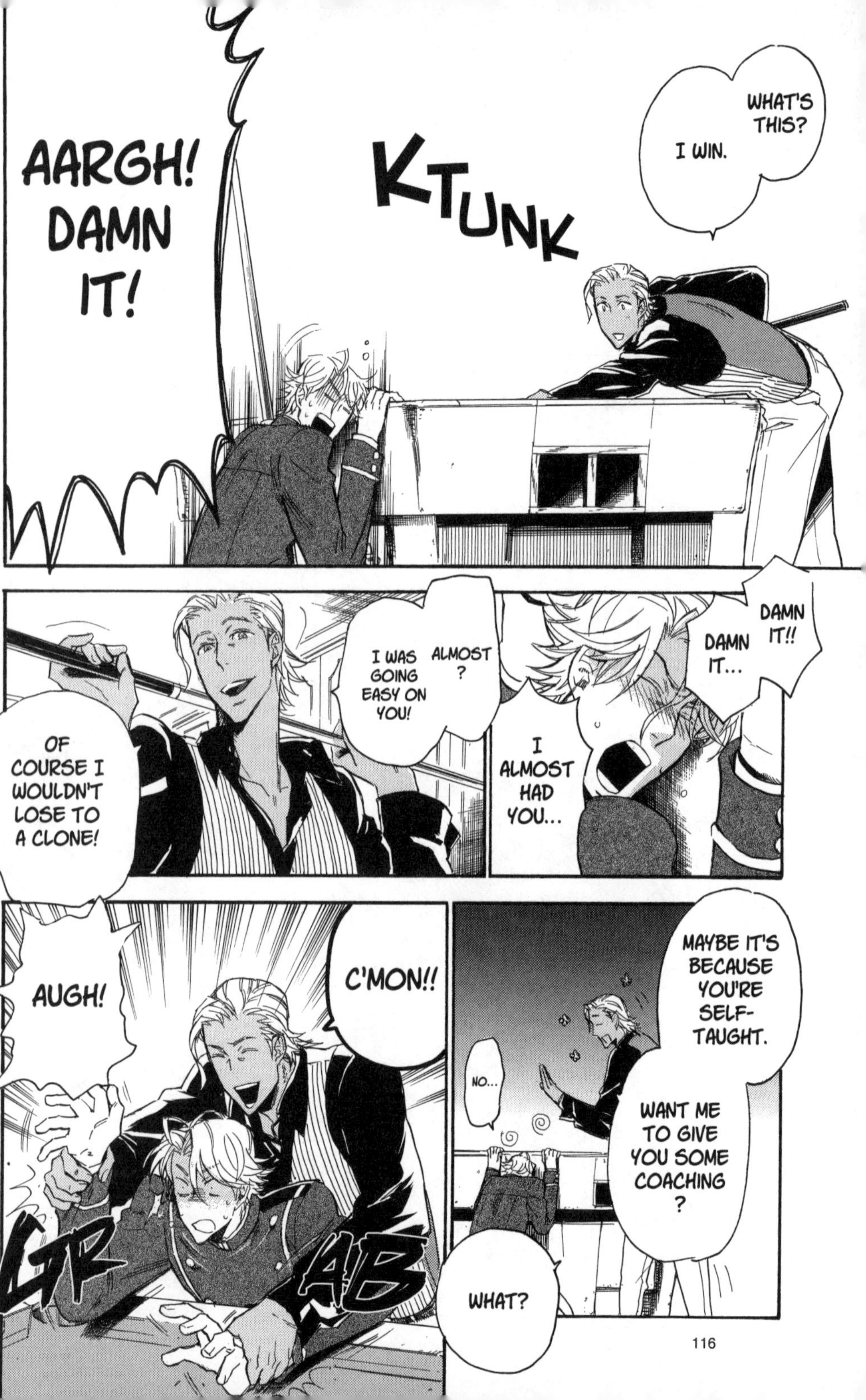
WHAT'S THIS?
I WIN.
KTUNK
AARGH! DAMN IT!
DAMN IT!!
DAMN IT...
I ALMOST HAD YOU...
ALMOST?
I WAS GOING EASY ON YOU!
OF COURSE I WOULDN'T LOSE TO A CLONE!
MAYBE IT'S BECAUSE YOU'RE SELF-TAUGHT.
NO...
WANT ME TO GIVE YOU SOME COACHING?
WHAT?
C'MON!!
AUGH!
GRAB

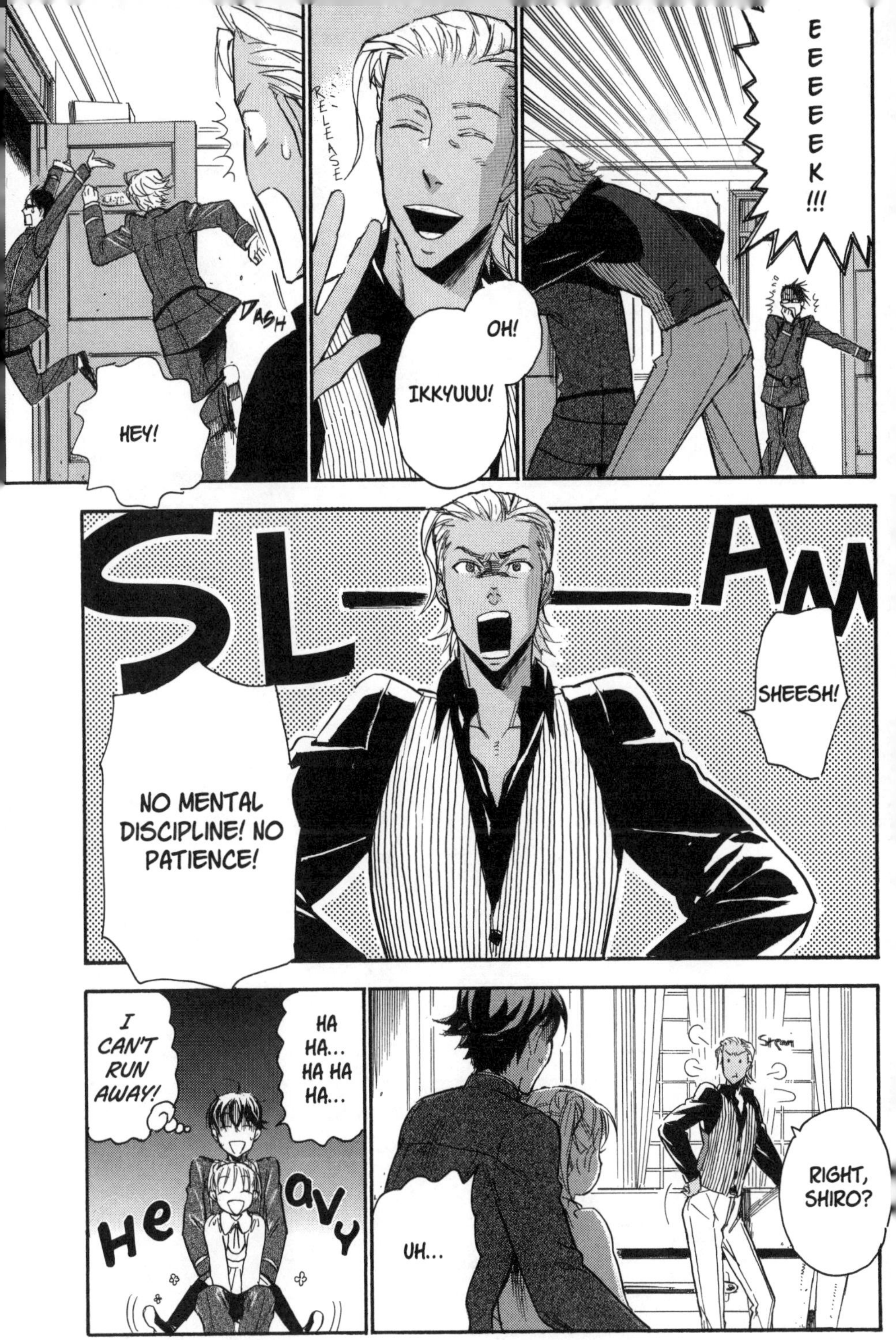
EEEEEEK!!!
RELEASE
OH!
IKKYUUU!
DASH
HEY!
SL—AM
SHEESH!
NO MENTAL DISCIPLINE! NO PATIENCE!
RIGHT, SHIRO?
UH...
HA HA... HA HA HA...
I CAN'T RUN AWAY!
HEAVY

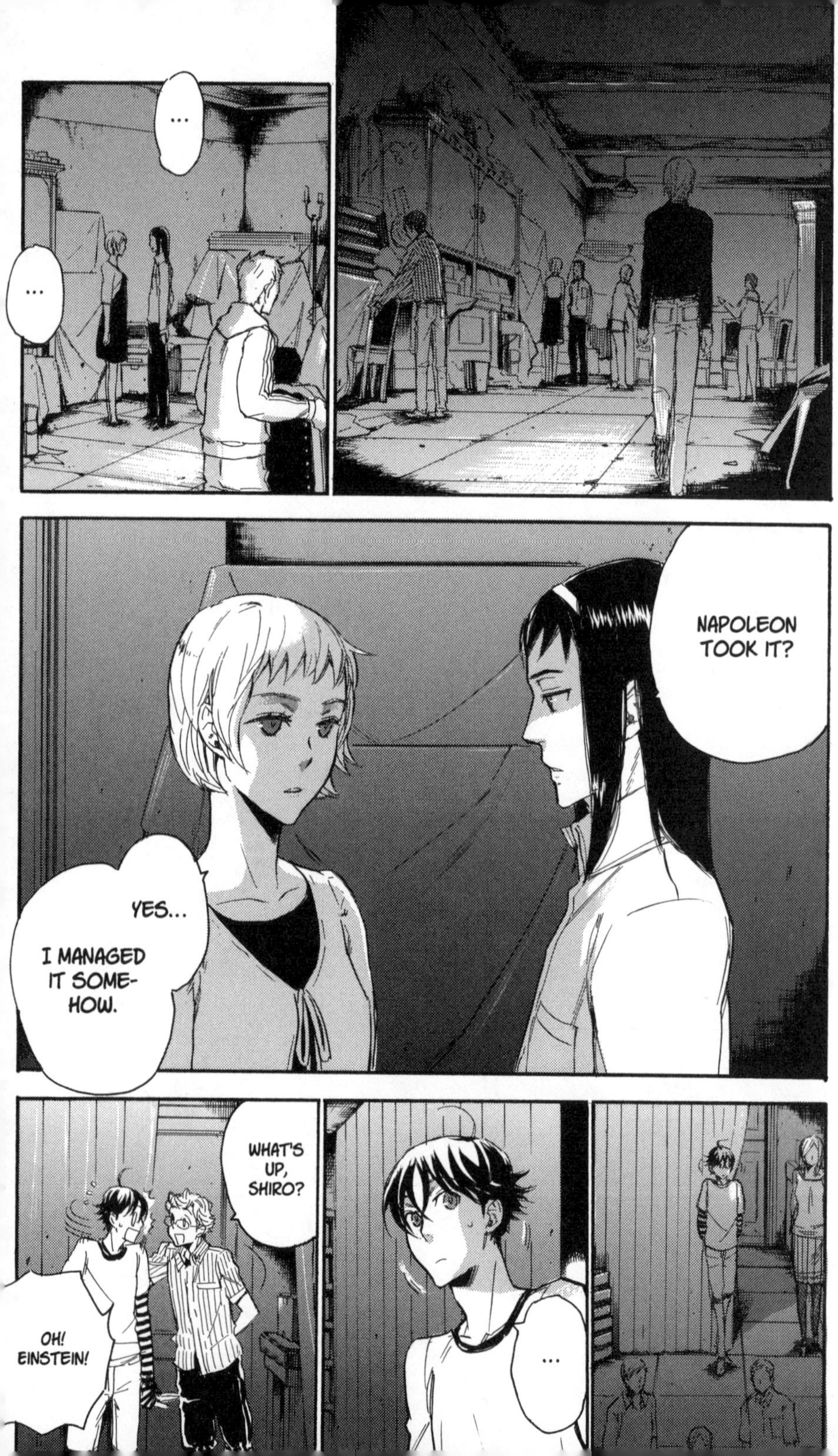
...
...
NAPOLEON TOOK IT?
YES...
I MANAGED IT SOME-HOW.
...
WHAT'S UP, SHIRO?
OH! EINSTEIN!

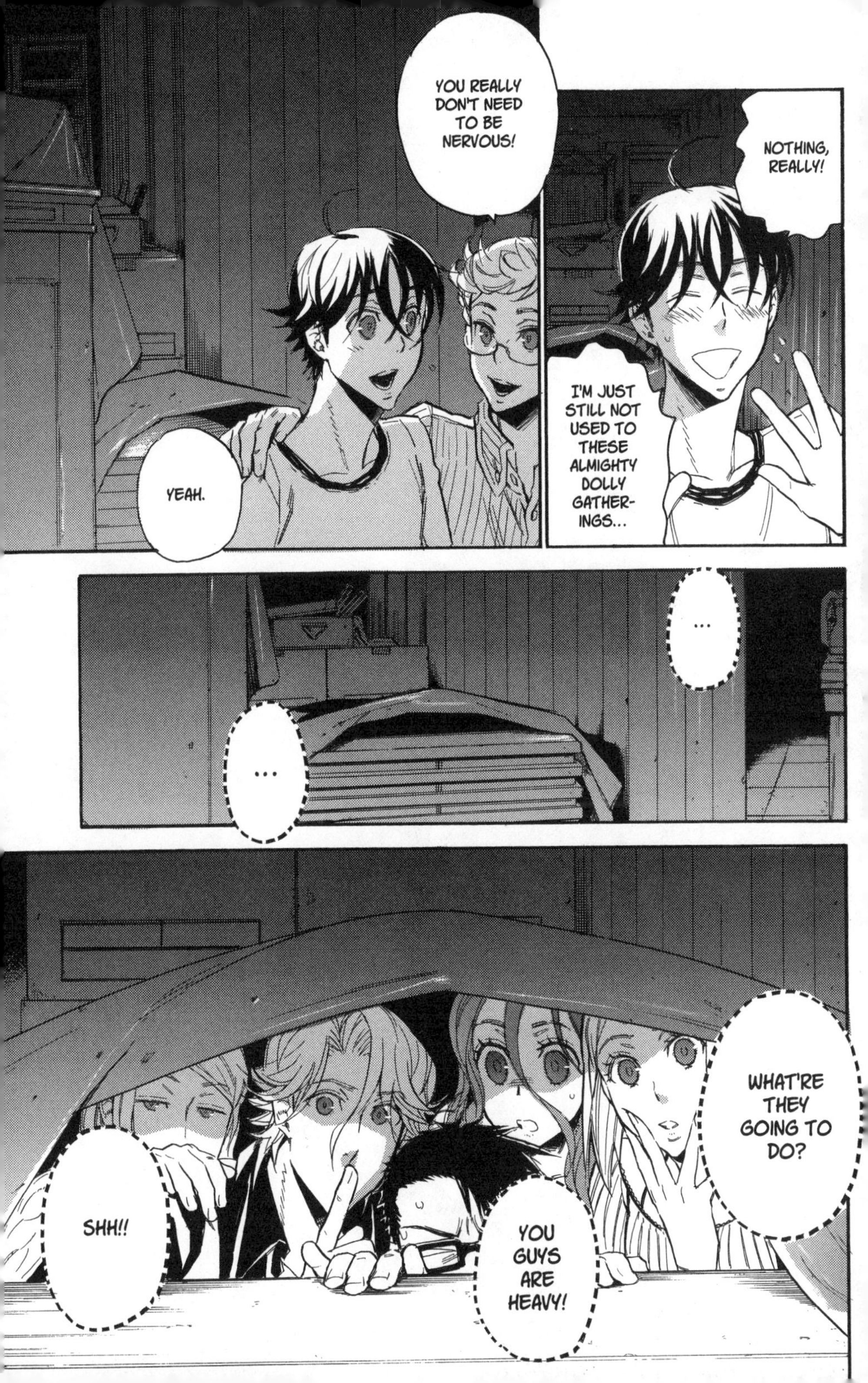
NOTHING, REALLY!
I'M JUST STILL NOT USED TO THESE ALMIGHTY DOLLY GATHER-INGS...
YOU REALLY DON'T NEED TO BE NERVOUS!
YEAH.
...
...
WHAT'RE THEY GOING TO DO?
YOU GUYS ARE HEAVY!
SHH!!

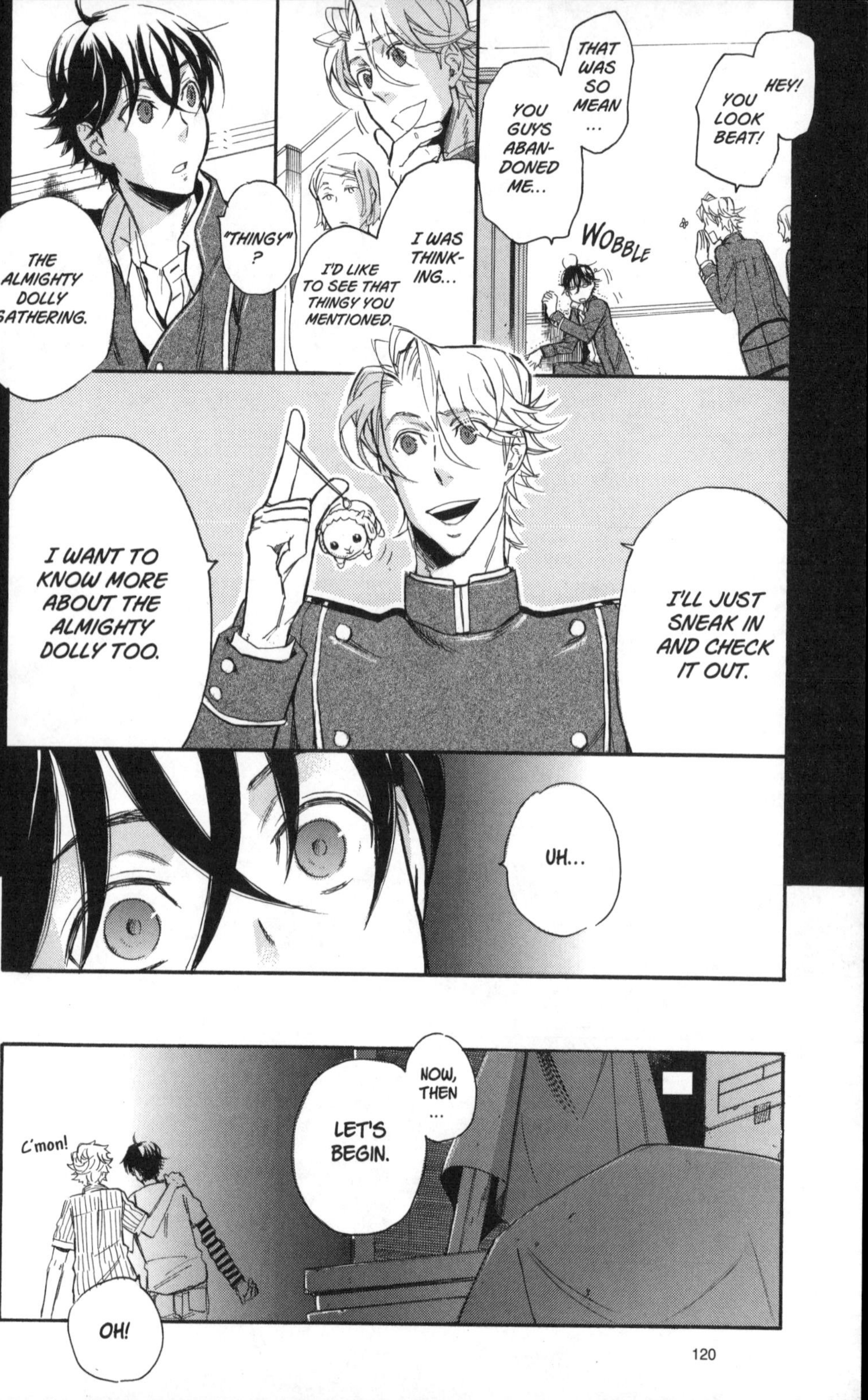
HEY! YOU LOOK BEAT!
THAT WAS SO MEAN...
YOU GUYS ABANDONED ME...
WOBBLE
I WAS THINKING...
I'D LIKE TO SEE THAT THINGY YOU MENTIONED.
"THINGY"?
THE ALMIGHTY DOLLY GATHERING.
I'LL JUST SNEAK IN AND CHECK IT OUT.
I WANT TO KNOW MORE ABOUT THE ALMIGHTY DOLLY TOO.
UH...
NOW, THEN...
LET'S BEGIN.
C'mon!
OH!

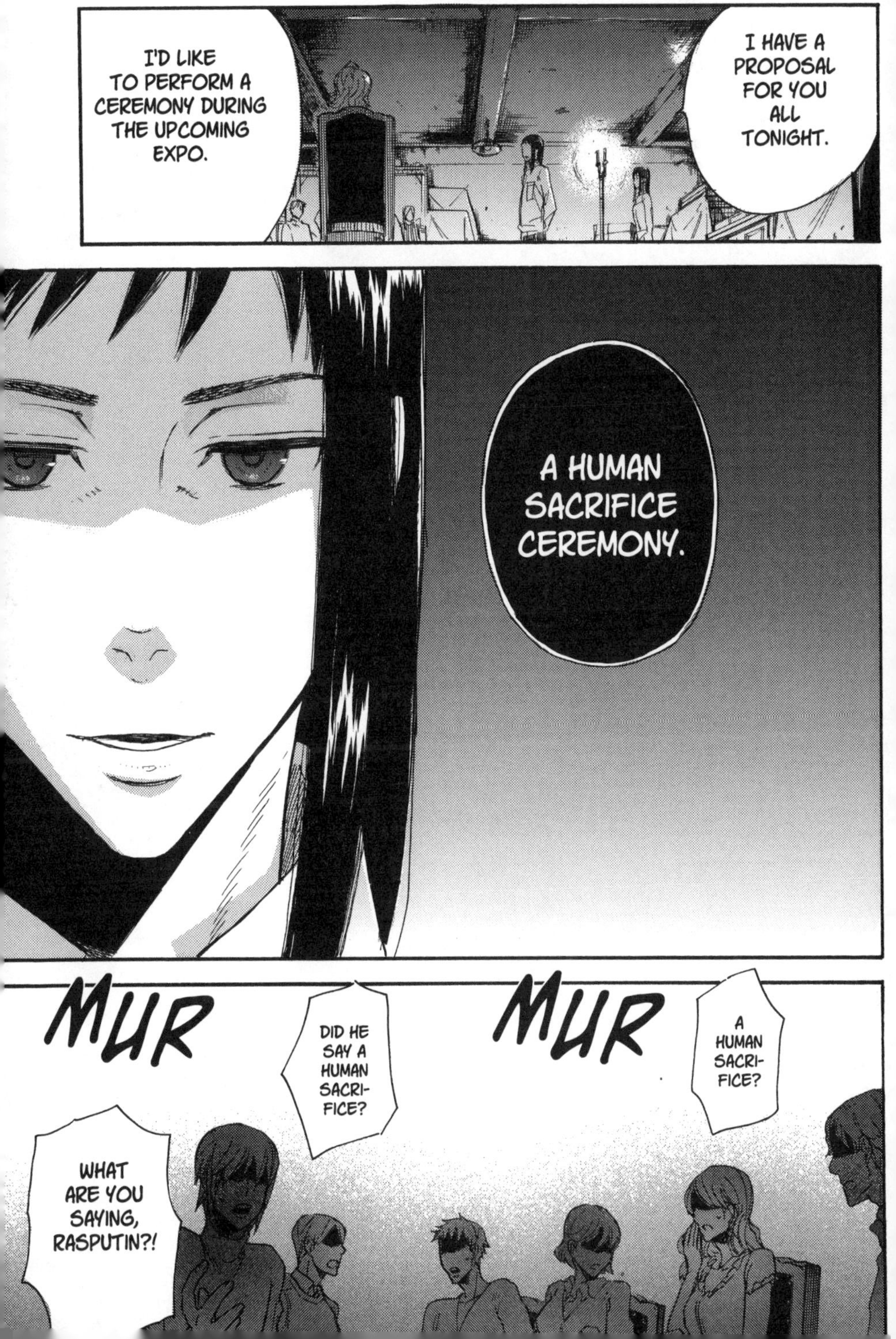
I HAVE A PROPOSAL FOR YOU ALL TONIGHT.
I'D LIKE TO PERFORM A CEREMONY DURING THE UPCOMING EXPO.
A HUMAN SACRIFICE CEREMONY.
A HUMAN SACRI-FICE?
MUR
DID HE SAY A HUMAN SACRI-FICE?
MUR
WHAT ARE YOU SAYING, RASPUTIN?!

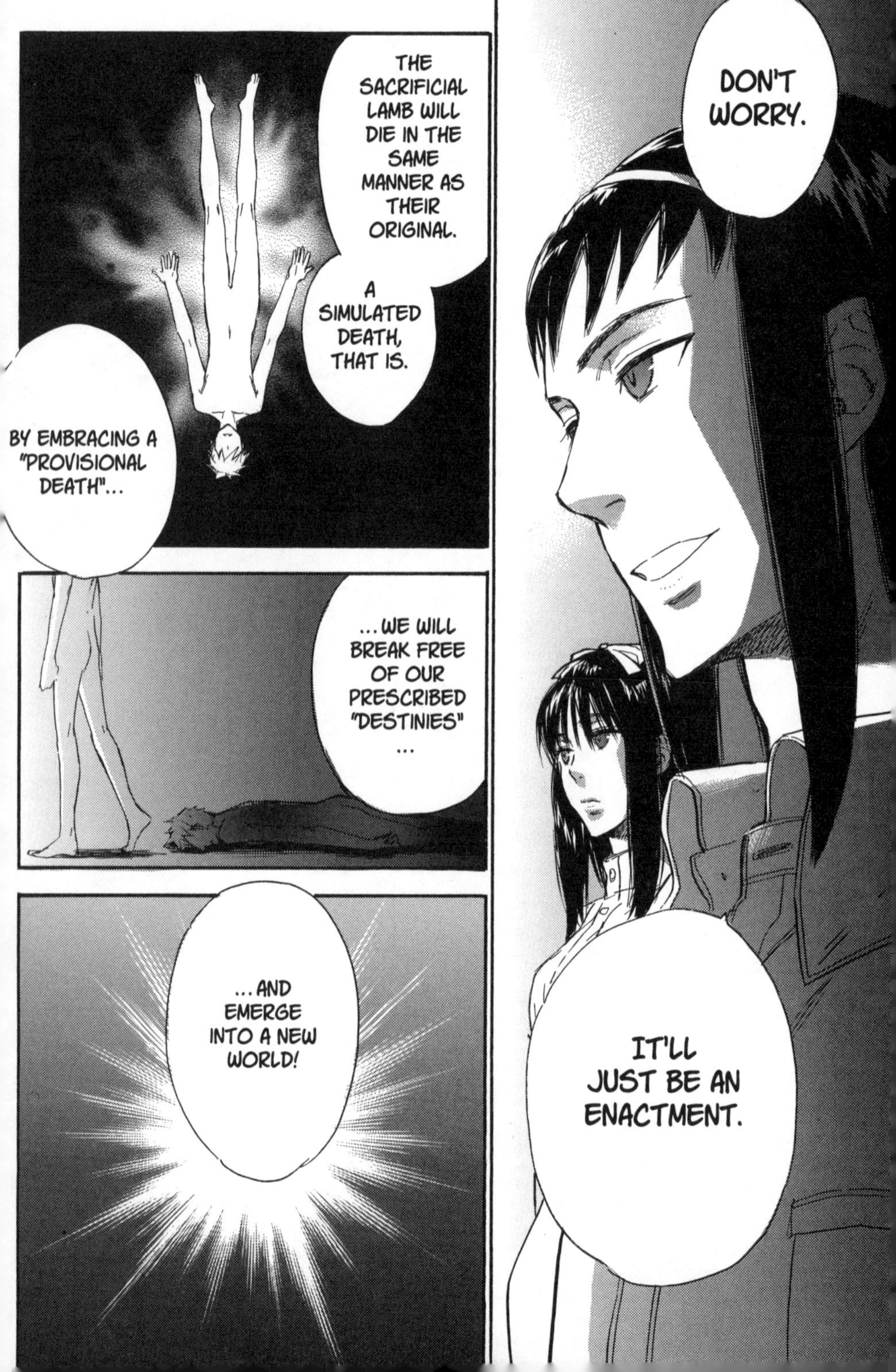
DON'T WORRY.
IT'LL JUST BE AN ENACTMENT.
THE SACRIFICIAL LAMB WILL DIE IN THE SAME MANNER AS THEIR ORIGINAL.
A SIMULATED DEATH, THAT IS.
BY EMBRACING A "PROVISIONAL DEATH"...
...WE WILL BREAK FREE OF OUR PRESCRIBED "DESTINIES"...
...AND EMERGE INTO A NEW WORLD!

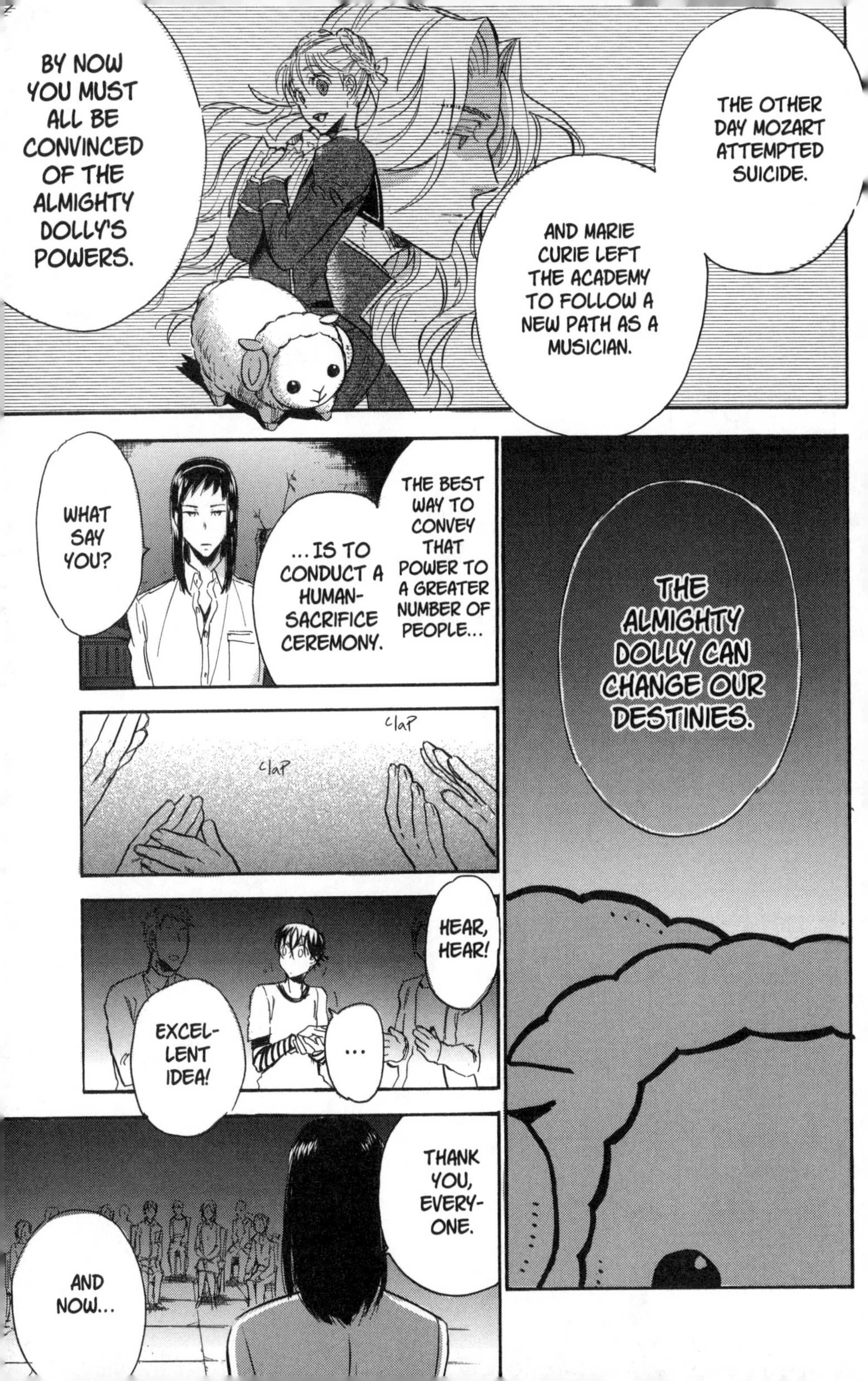
THE OTHER DAY MOZART ATTEMPTED SUICIDE.
AND MARIE CURIE LEFT THE ACADEMY TO FOLLOW A NEW PATH AS A MUSICIAN.
BY NOW YOU MUST ALL BE CONVINCED OF THE ALMIGHTY DOLLY'S POWERS.
THE ALMIGHTY DOLLY CAN CHANGE OUR DESTINIES.
THE BEST WAY TO CONVEY THAT POWER TO A GREATER NUMBER OF PEOPLE...
...IS TO CONDUCT A HUMAN-SACRIFICE CEREMONY.
WHAT SAY YOU?
CLAP
CLAP
HEAR, HEAR!
...
EXCEL-LENT IDEA!
THANK YOU, EVERY-ONE.
AND NOW...

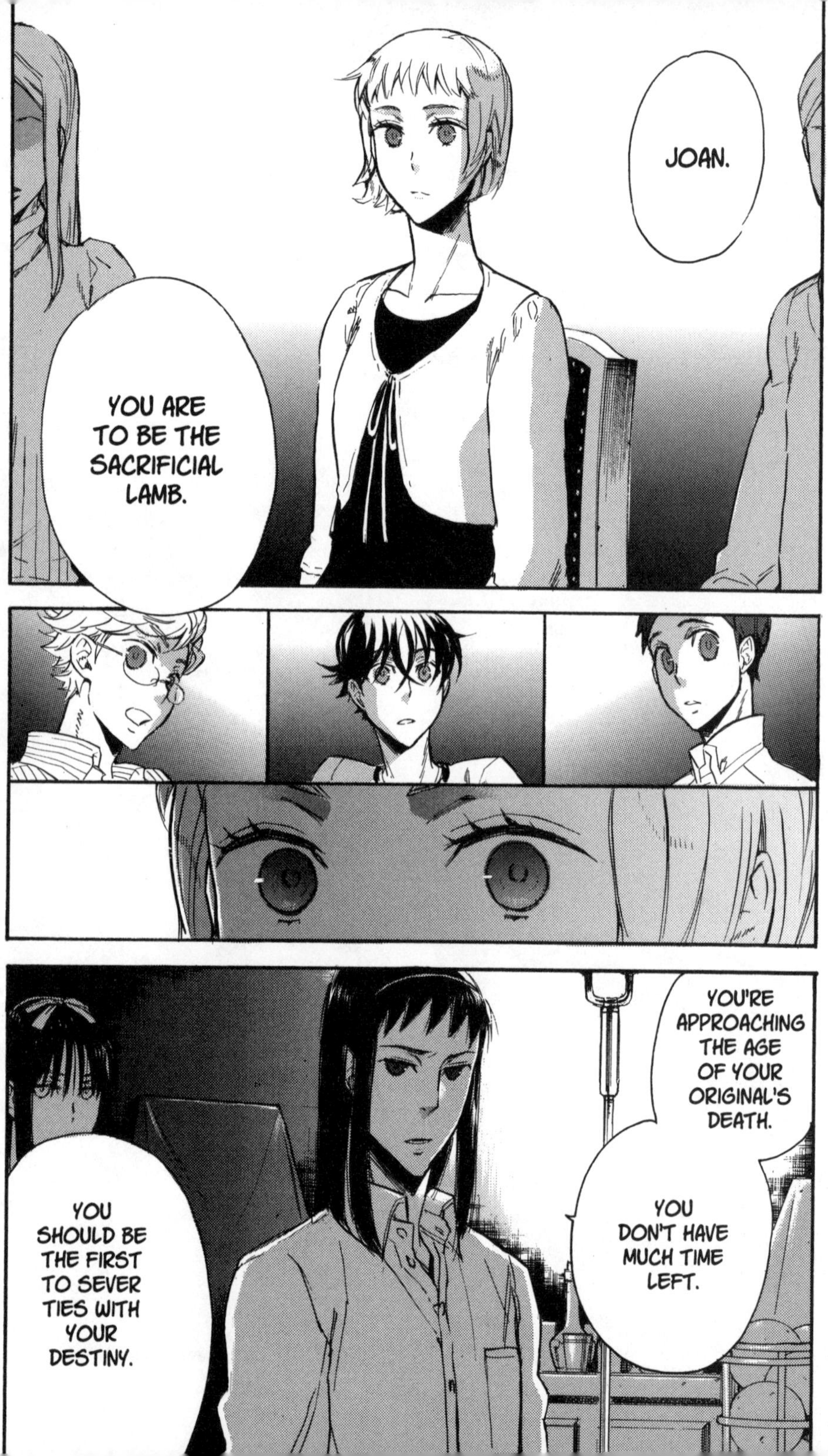
JOAN.
YOU ARE TO BE THE SACRIFICIAL LAMB.
YOU'RE APPROACHING THE AGE OF YOUR ORIGINAL'S DEATH.
YOU DON'T HAVE MUCH TIME LEFT.
YOU SHOULD BE THE FIRST TO SEVER TIES WITH YOUR DESTINY.

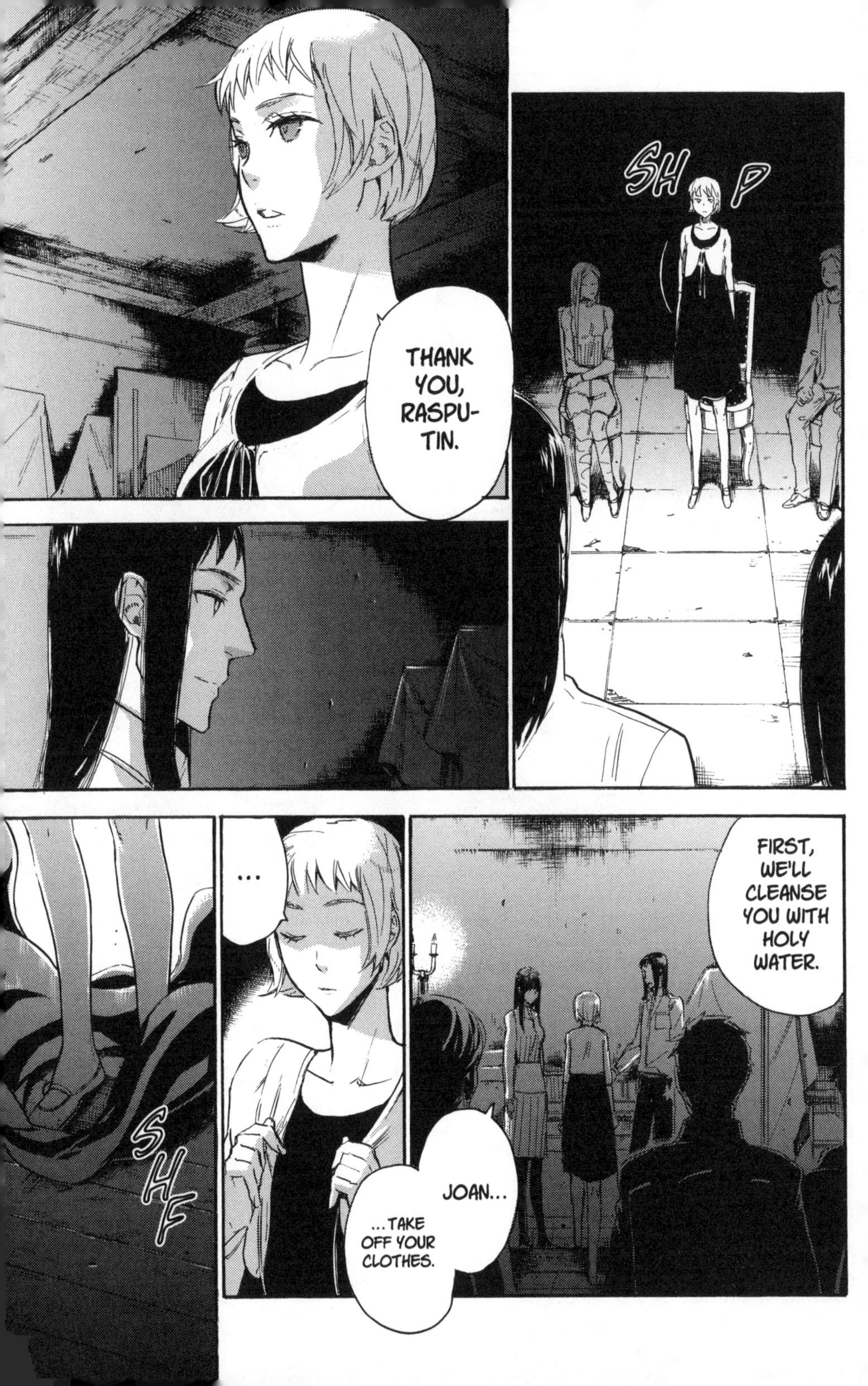
SHP
THANK YOU, RASPUTIN.
FIRST, WE'LL CLEANSE YOU WITH HOLY WATER.
...
JOAN... ...TAKE OFF YOUR CLOTHES.
SHF

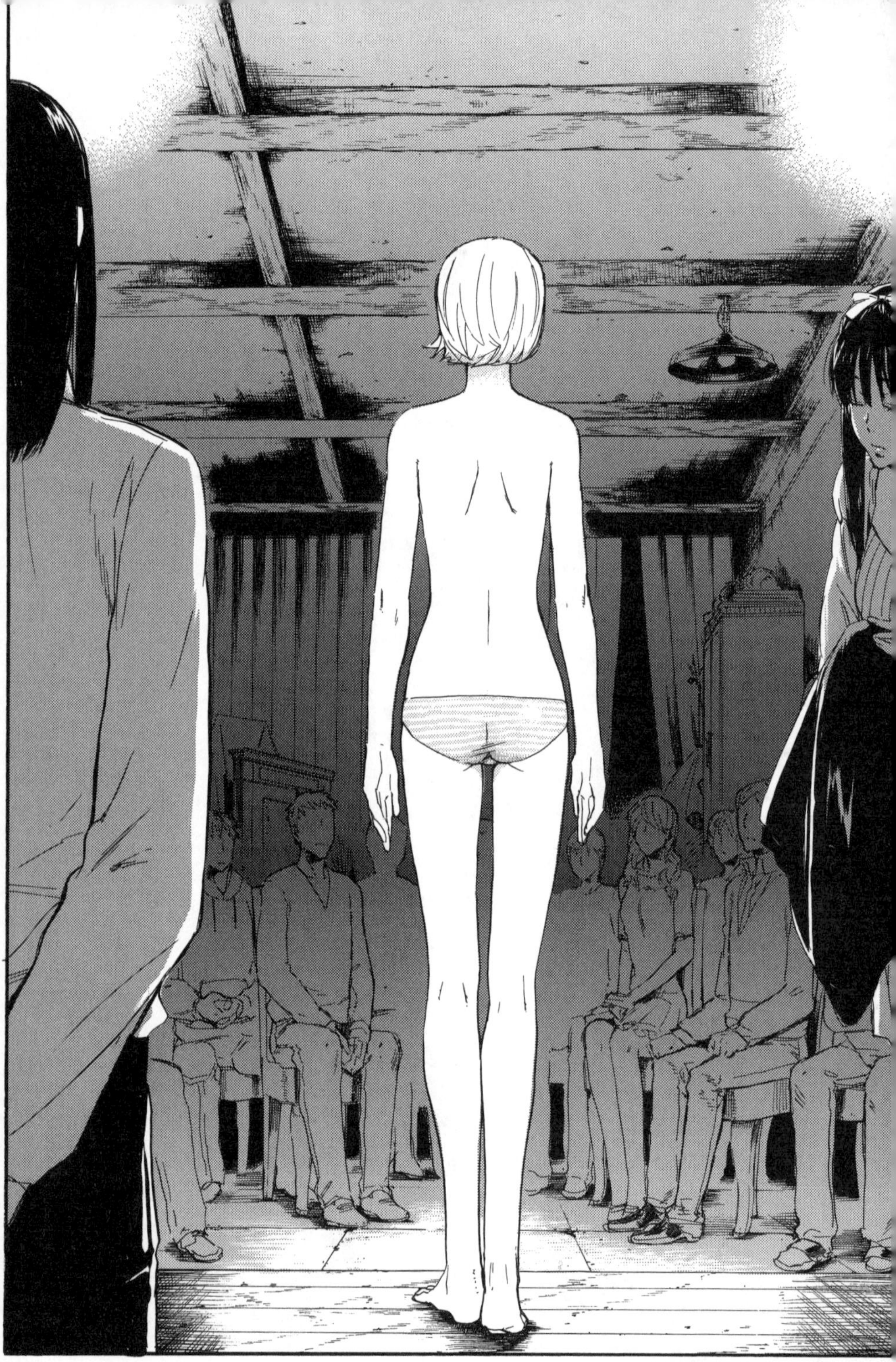

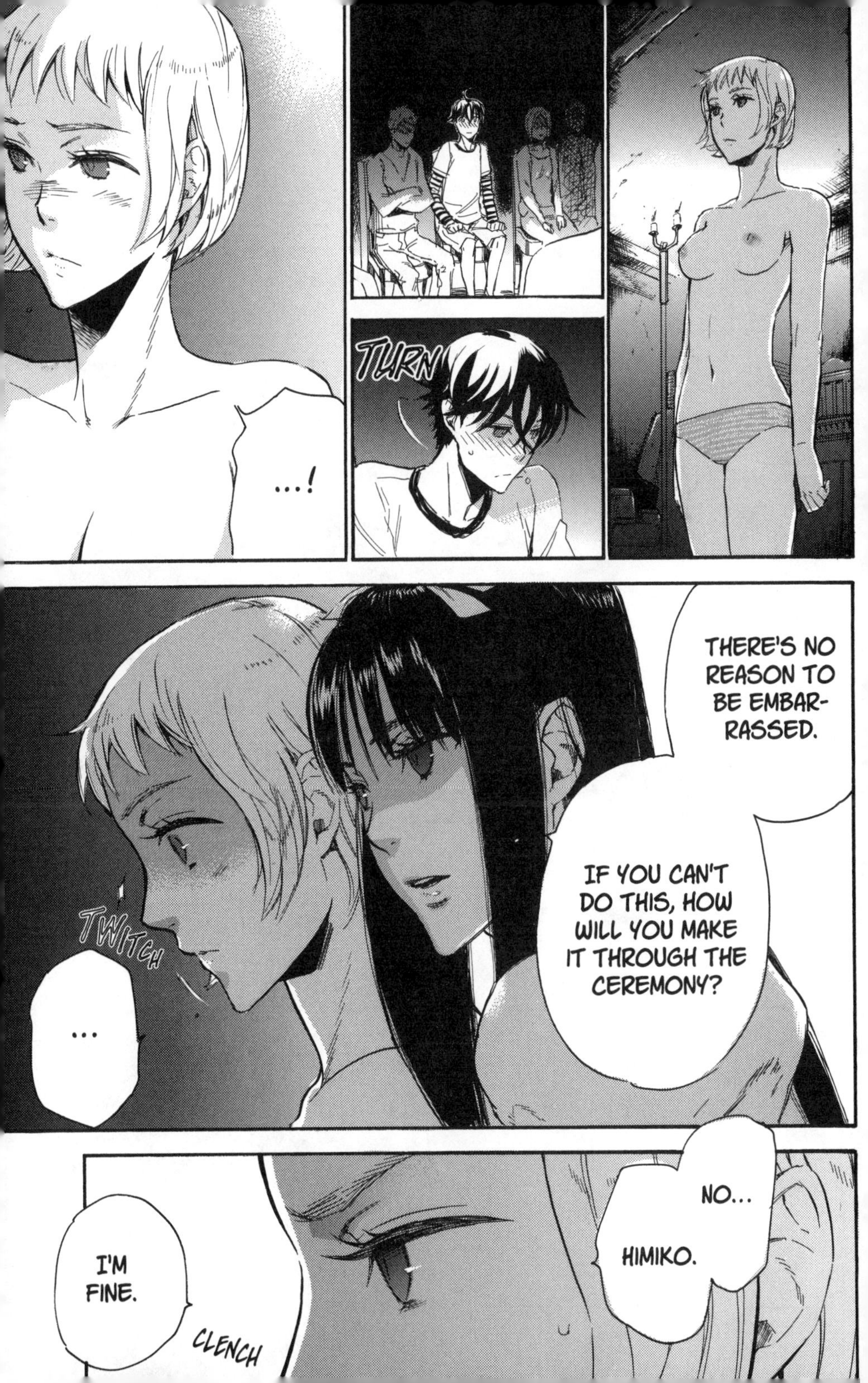
TURN
...!
THERE'S NO REASON TO BE EMBARRASSED.
IF YOU CAN'T DO THIS, HOW WILL YOU MAKE IT THROUGH THE CEREMONY?
TWITCH
...
NO...
HIMIKO.
I'M FINE.
CLENCH

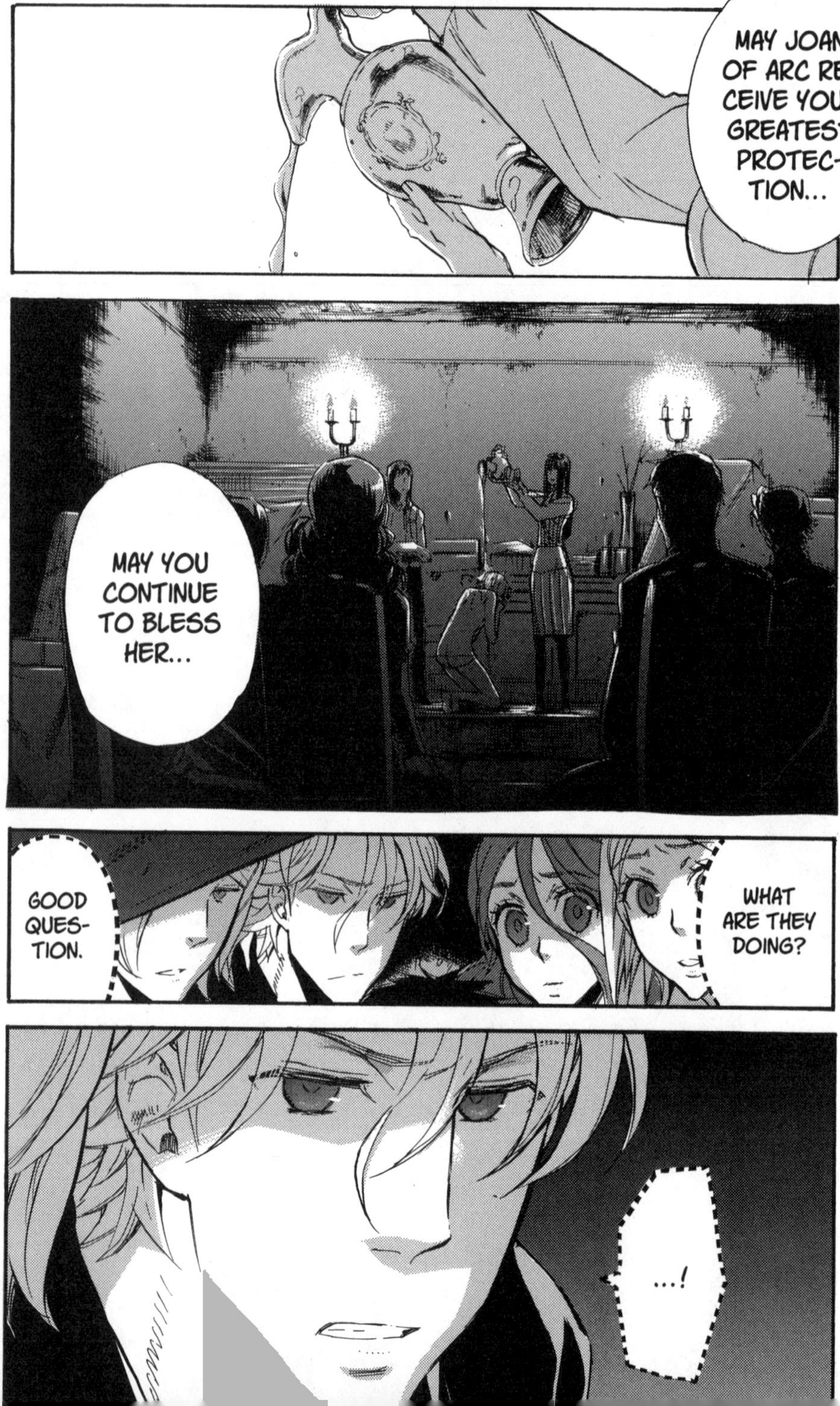
MAY JOAN OF ARC RE-CEIVE YOUR GREATEST PROTEC-TION...
MAY YOU CONTINUE TO BLESS HER...
WHAT ARE THEY DOING?
GOOD QUES-TION.
...!

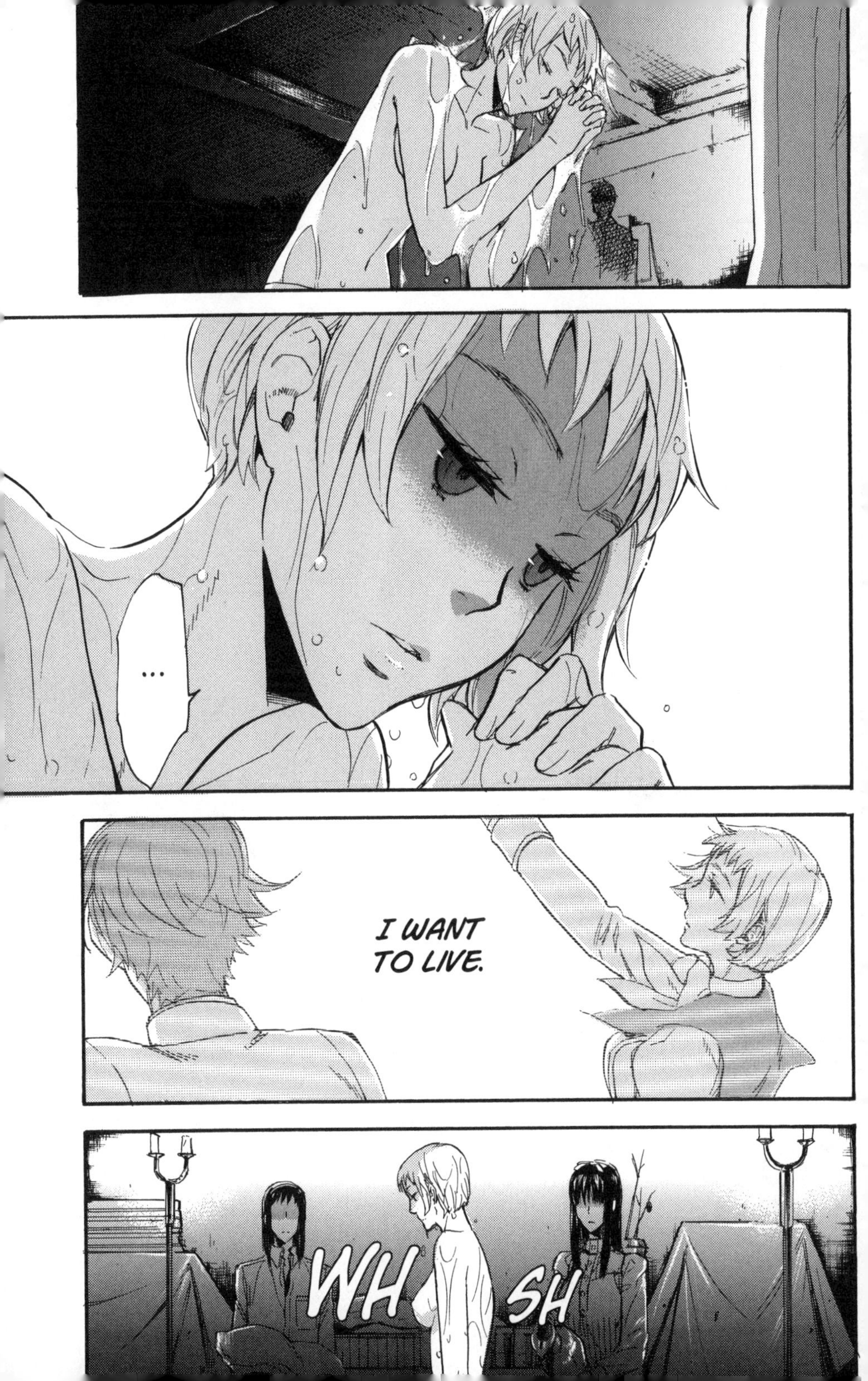
...
I WANT TO LIVE.
WH SH

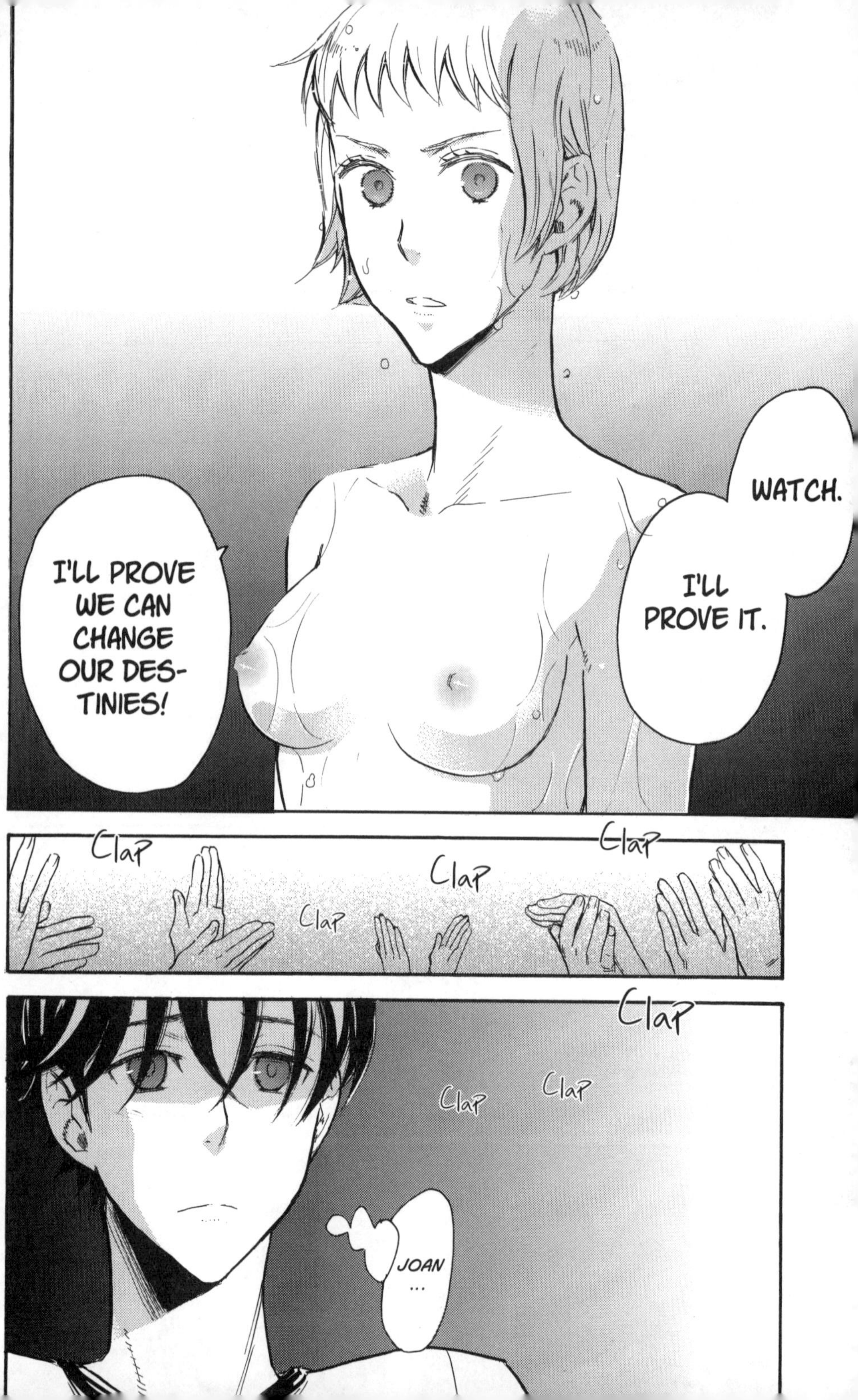
WATCH.
I'LL PROVE IT.
I'LL PROVE WE CAN CHANGE OUR DES-TINIES!
Clap
Clap
Clap
Clap
Clap
Clap
Clap
JOAN ...

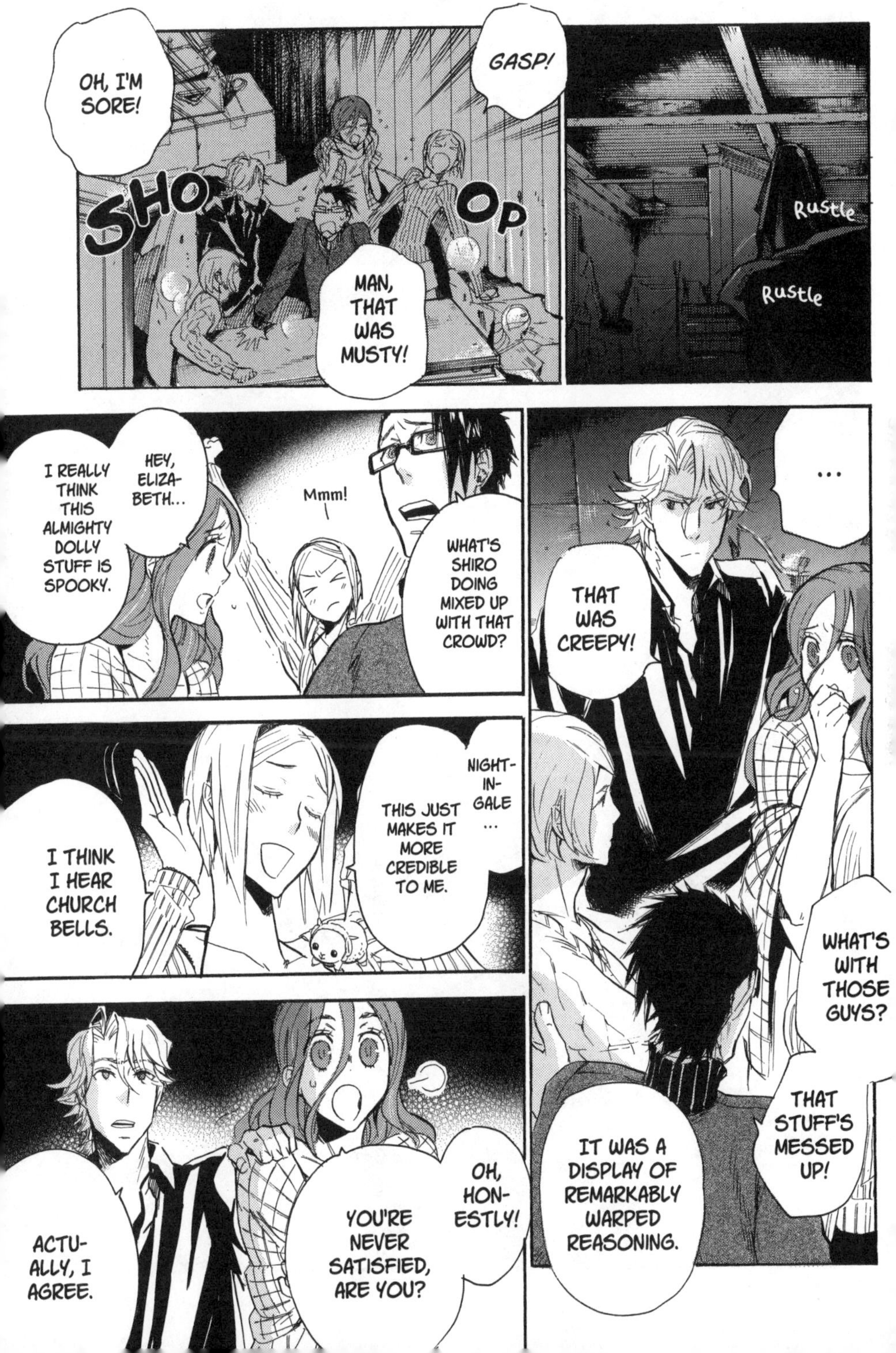
Rustle
Rustle
GASP!
OH, I'M SORE!
SHO OP
MAN, THAT WAS MUSTY!
...
THAT WAS CREEPY!
WHAT'S WITH THOSE GUYS?
THAT STUFF'S MESSED UP!
IT WAS A DISPLAY OF REMARKABLY WARPED REASONING.
WHAT'S SHIRO DOING MIXED UP WITH THAT CROWD?
Mmm!
HEY, ELIZA-BETH...
I REALLY THINK THIS ALMIGHTY DOLLY STUFF IS SPOOKY.
NIGHT-IN-GALE...
THIS JUST MAKES IT MORE CREDIBLE TO ME.
I THINK I HEAR CHURCH BELLS.
OH, HON-ESTLY!
YOU'RE NEVER SATISFIED, ARE YOU?
ACTU-ALLY, I AGREE.

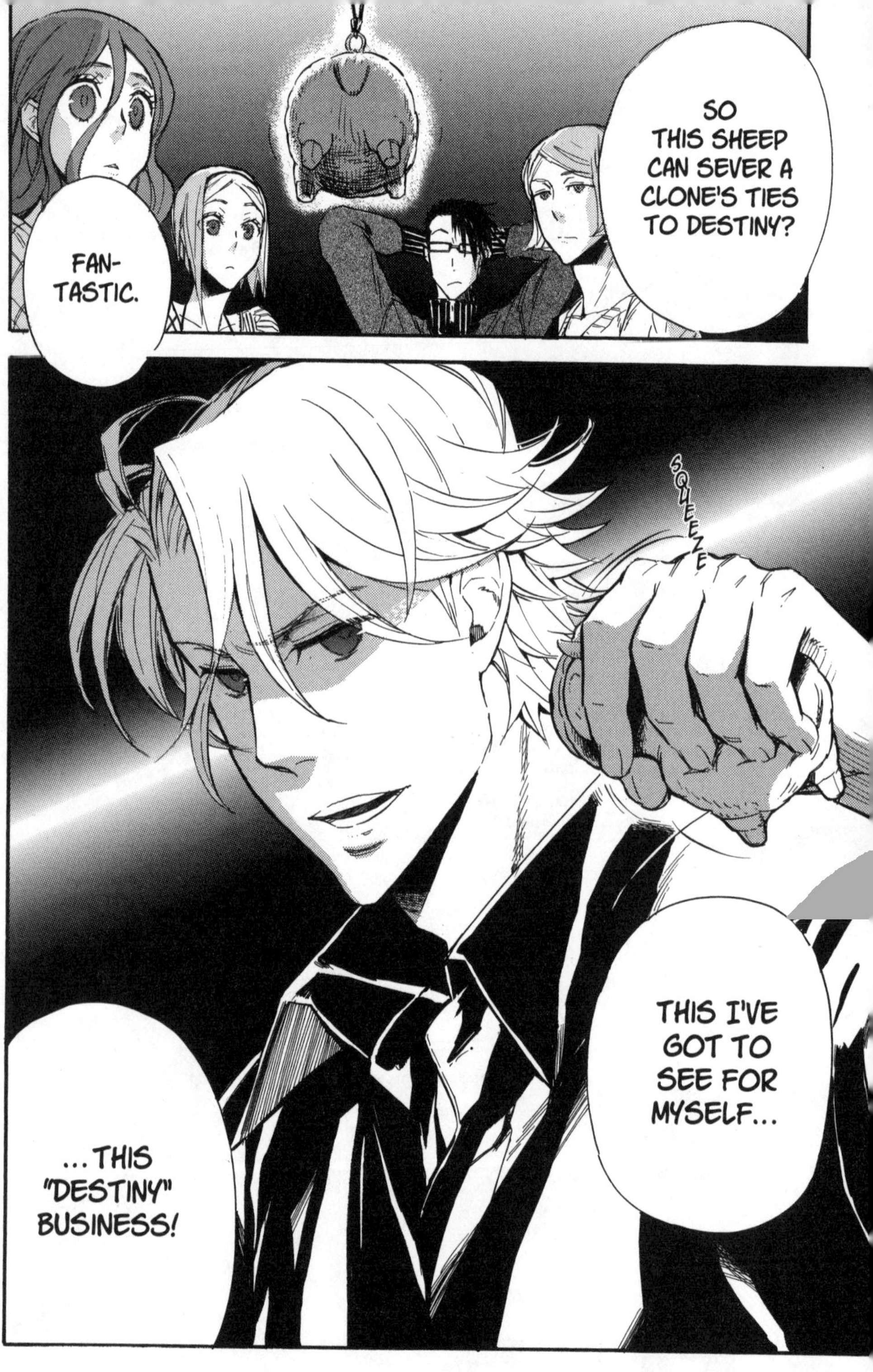
SO THIS SHEEP CAN SEVER A CLONE'S TIES TO DESTINY?
FAN-TASTIC.
SQUEEZE
THIS I'VE GOT TO SEE FOR MYSELF...
...THIS "DESTINY" BUSINESS!

Chapter eleven

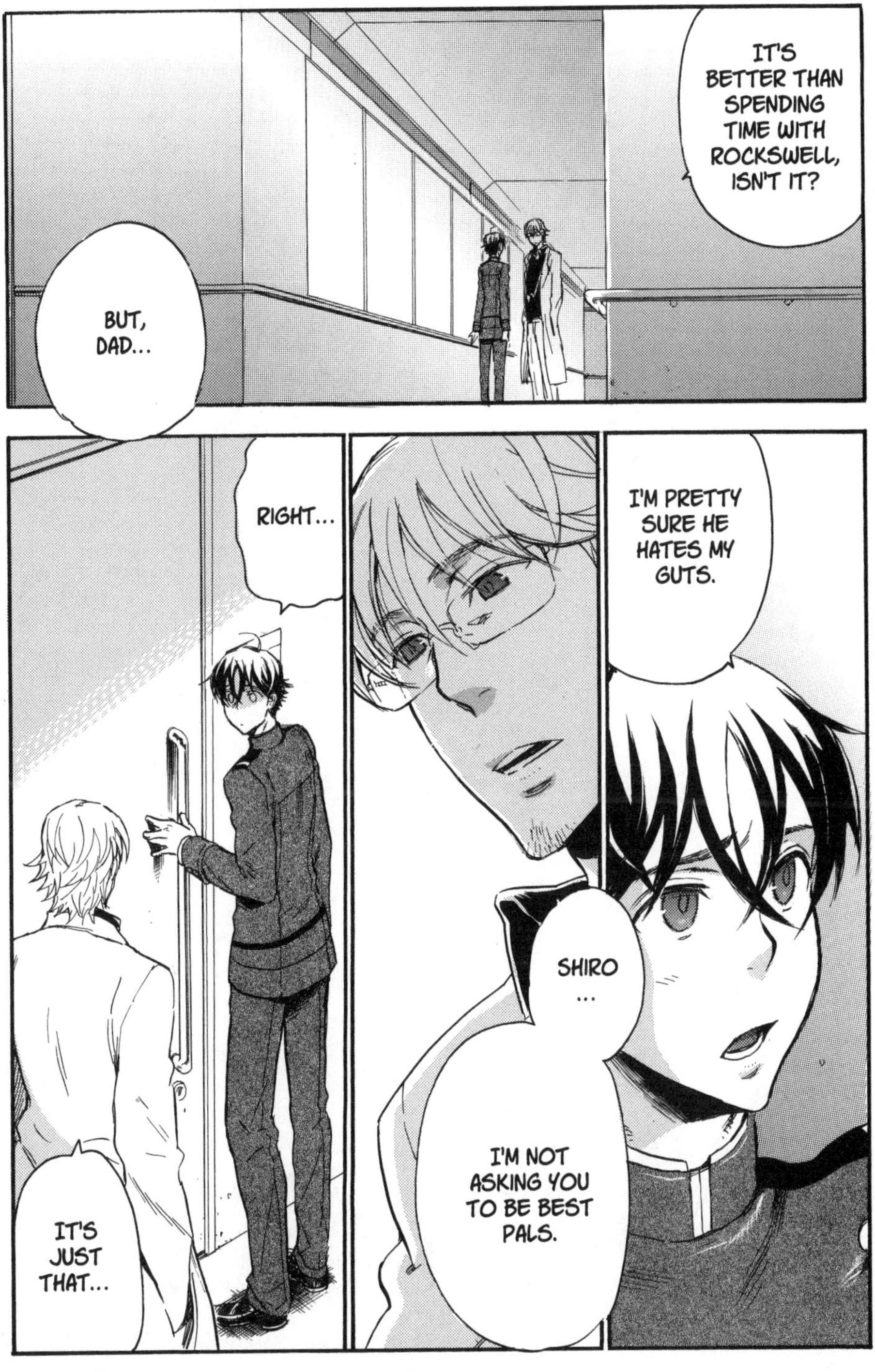

IT'S BETTER THAN SPENDING TIME WITH ROCKSWELL, ISN'T IT?
BUT, DAD...
I'M PRETTY SURE HE HATES MY GUTS.
SHIRO...
I'M NOT ASKING YOU TO BE BEST PALS.
RIGHT...
IT'S JUST THAT...

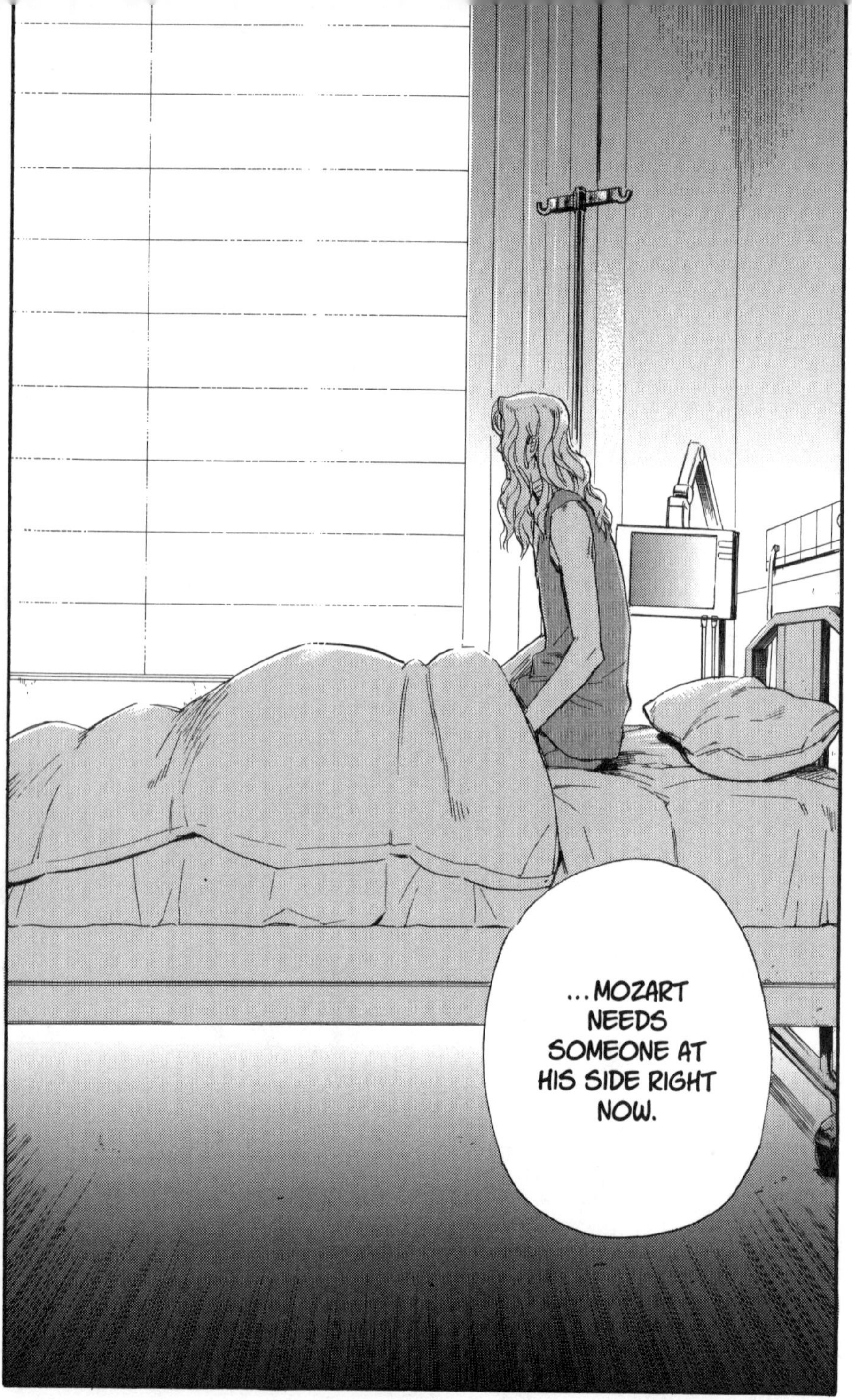
...MOZART NEEDS SOMEONE AT HIS SIDE RIGHT NOW.

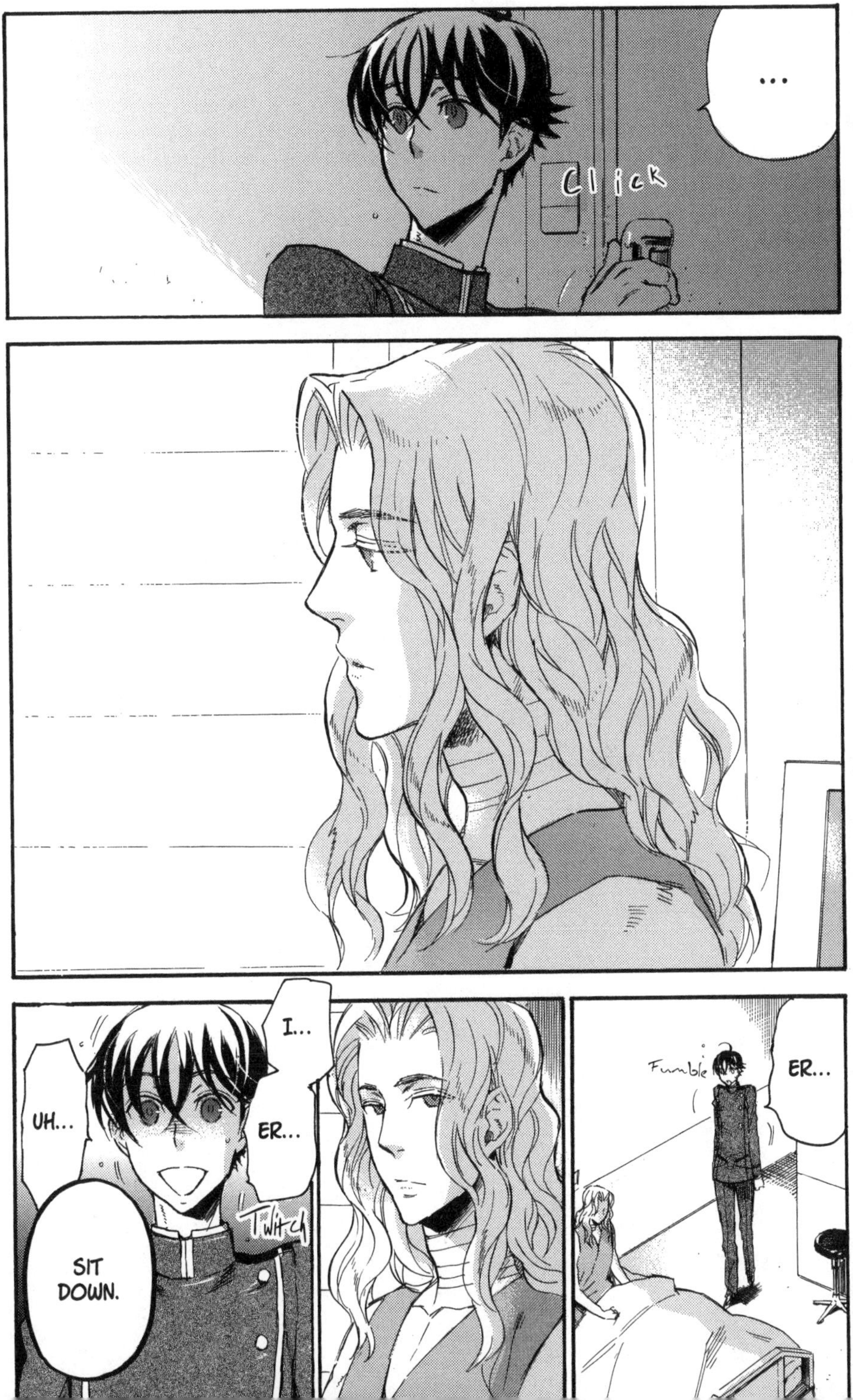
...
CLICK
Fumble
ER...
I...
ER...
UH...
TWITCH
SIT DOWN.

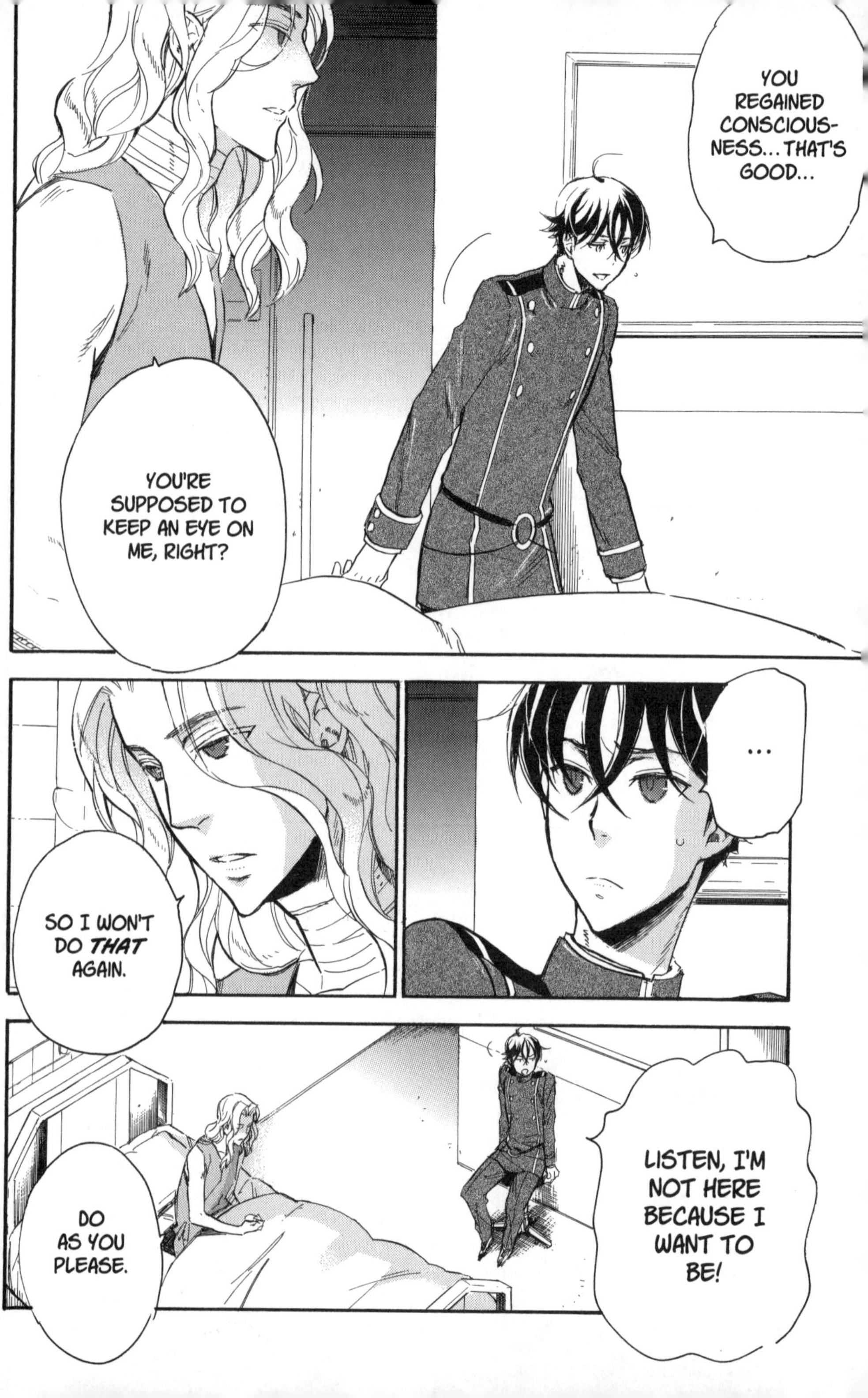
YOU REGAINED CONSCIOUS-NESS... THAT'S GOOD...
YOU'RE SUPPOSED TO KEEP AN EYE ON ME, RIGHT?
...
SO I WON'T DO *THAT* AGAIN.
LISTEN, I'M NOT HERE BECAUSE I WANT TO BE!
DO AS YOU PLEASE.

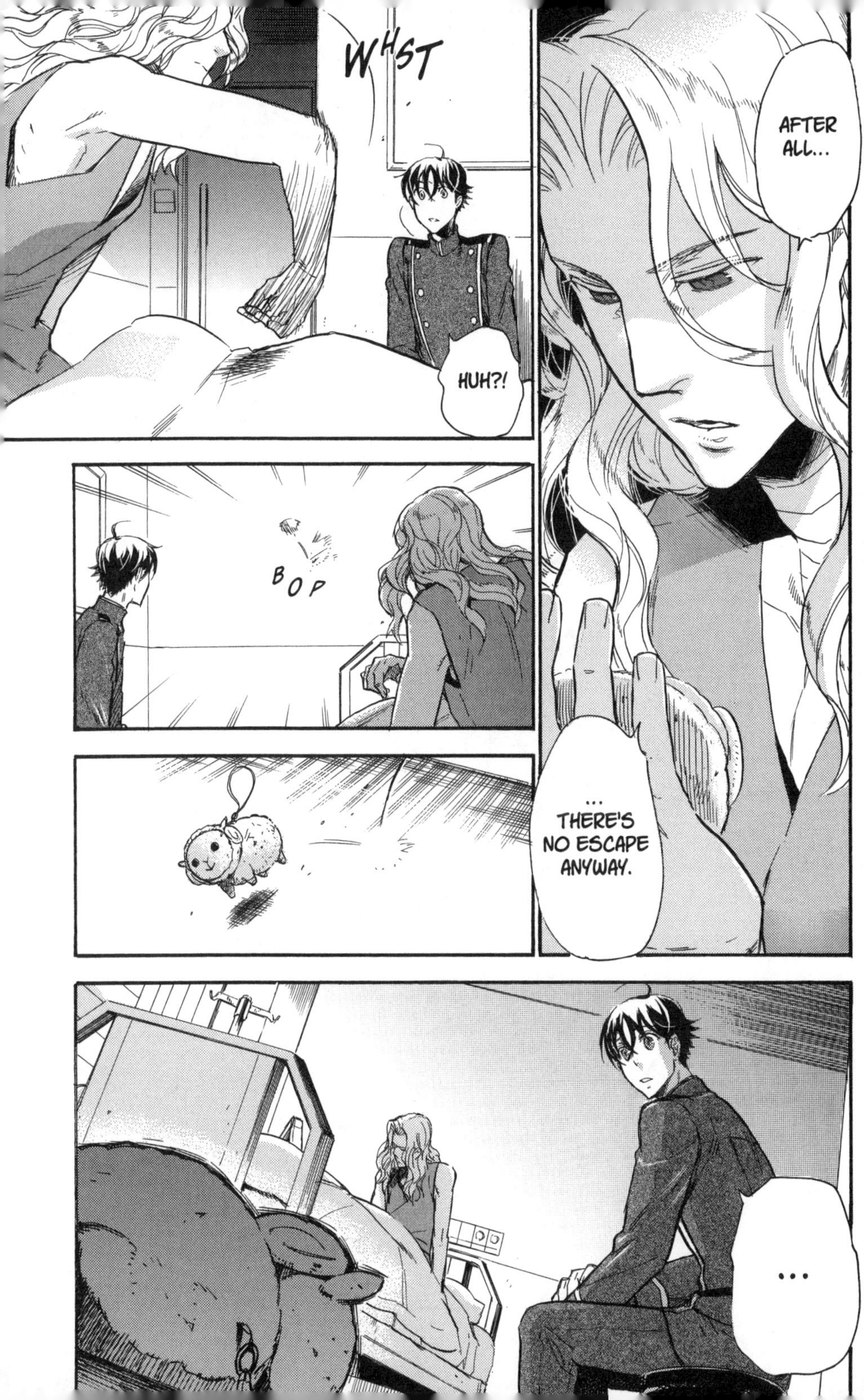
AFTER ALL...
... THERE'S NO ESCAPE ANYWAY.
WHST
HUH?!
BOP
...

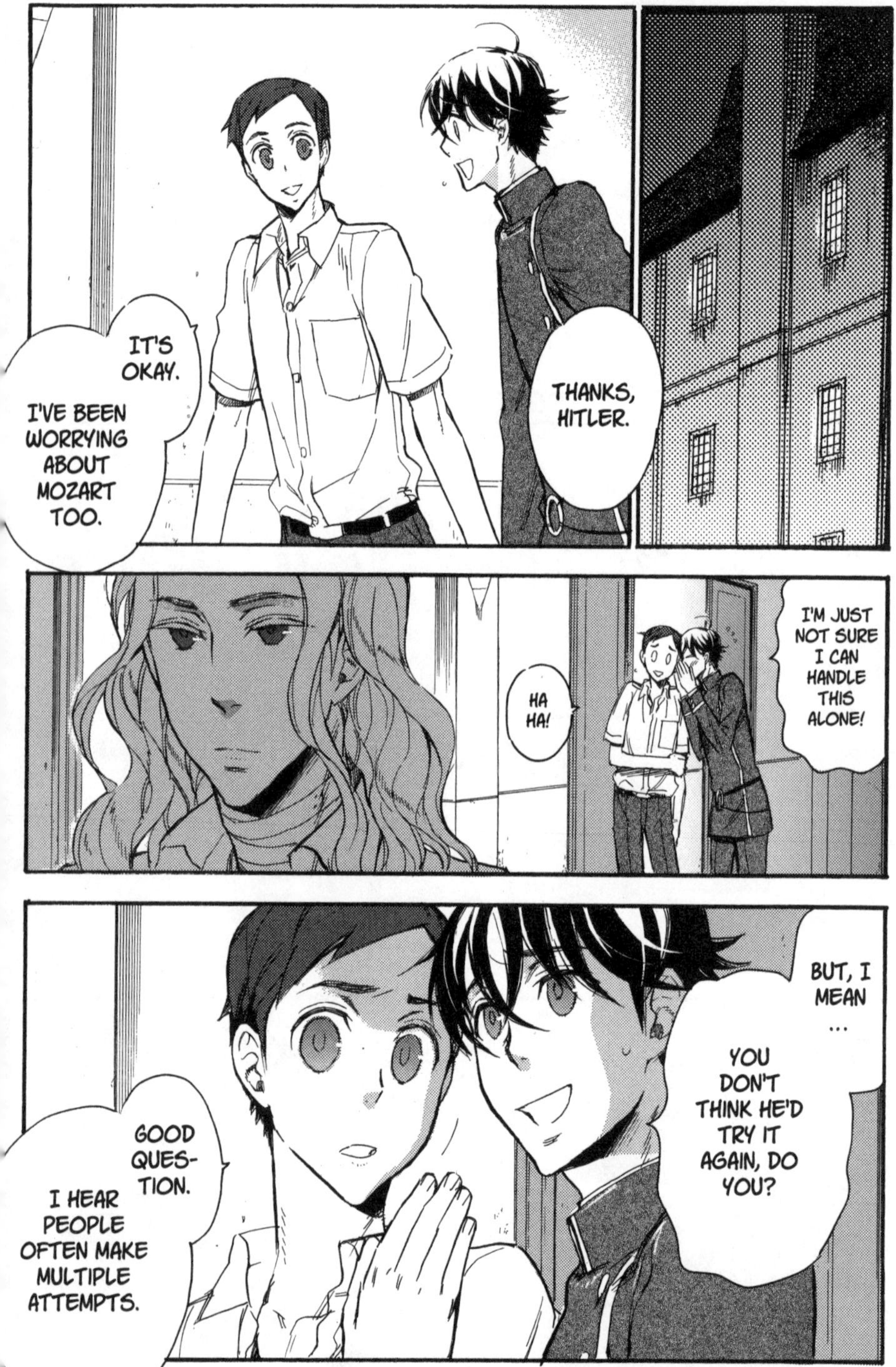
THANKS, HITLER.
IT'S OKAY.
I'VE BEEN WORRYING ABOUT MOZART TOO.
I'M JUST NOT SURE I CAN HANDLE THIS ALONE!
HA HA!
BUT, I MEAN ...
YOU DON'T THINK HE'D TRY IT AGAIN, DO YOU?
GOOD QUES-TION.
I HEAR PEOPLE OFTEN MAKE MULTIPLE ATTEMPTS.

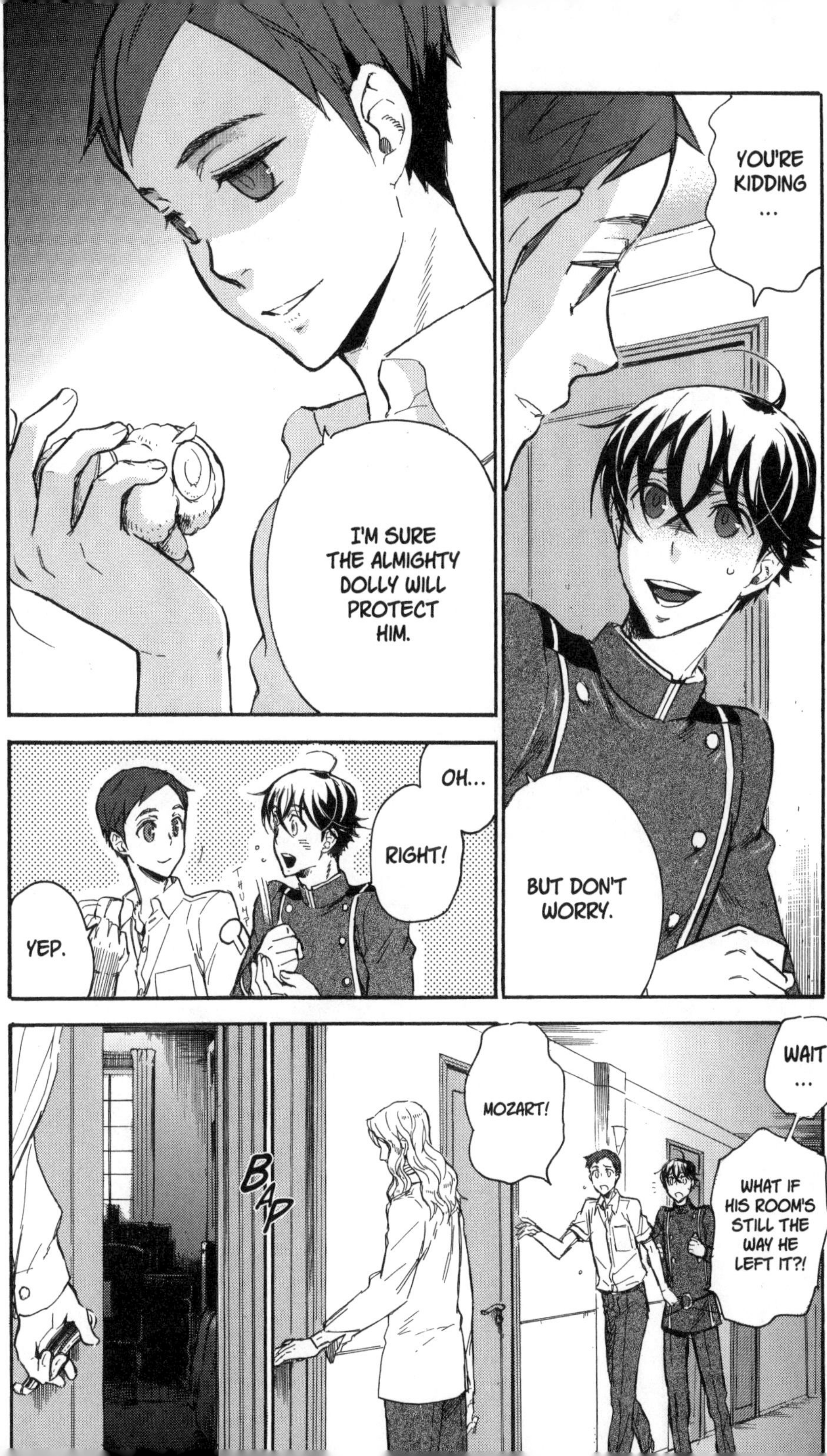
YOU'RE KIDDING ...
BUT DON'T WORRY.
I'M SURE THE ALMIGHTY DOLLY WILL PROTECT HIM.
OH...
RIGHT!
THUMP
YEP.
WAIT ...
WHAT IF HIS ROOM'S STILL THE WAY HE LEFT IT?!
MOZART!
BAP

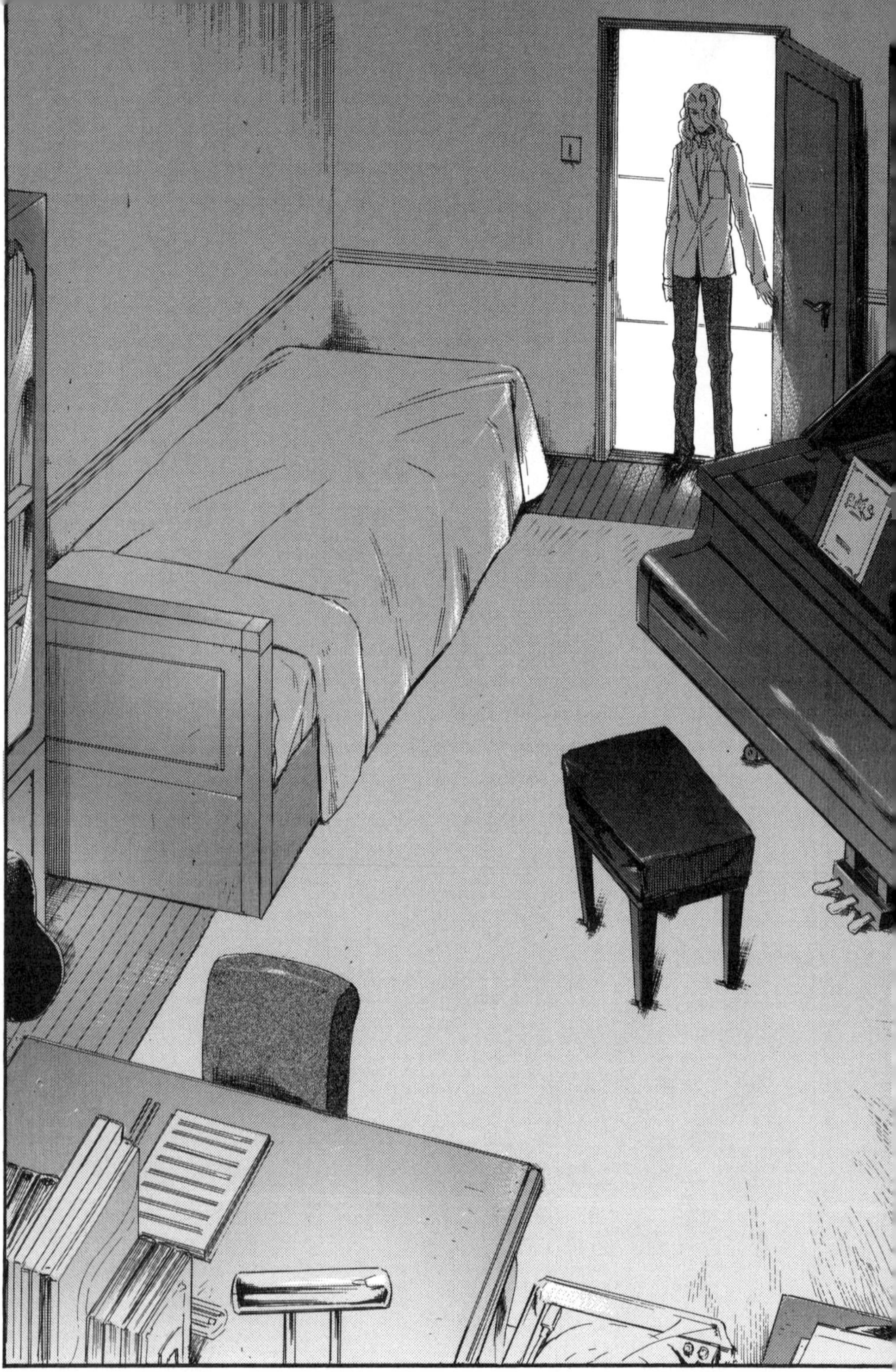

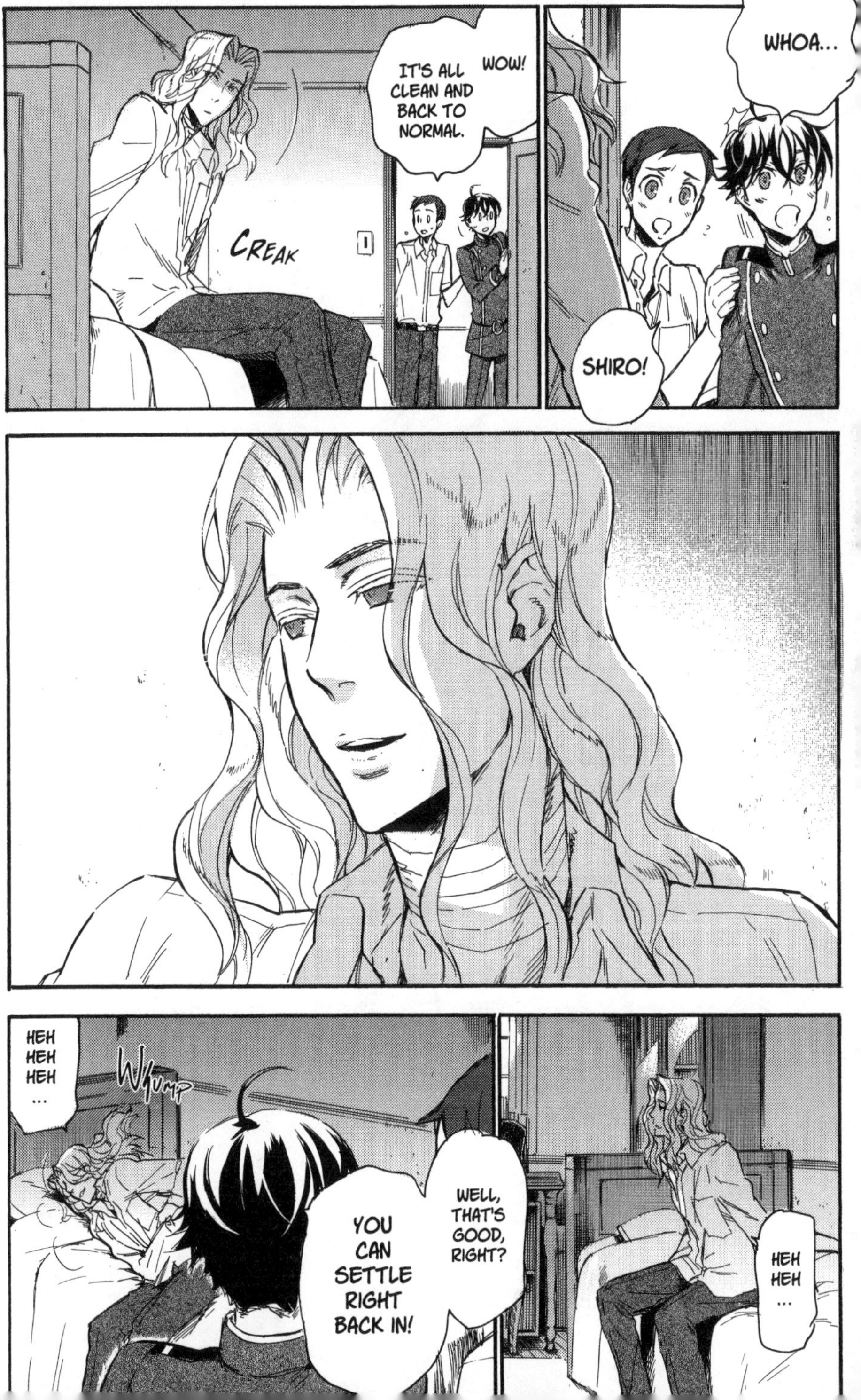
WHOA...
SHIRO!
WOW!
IT'S ALL CLEAN AND BACK TO NORMAL.
CREAK
HEH HEH ...
WELL, THAT'S GOOD, RIGHT?
YOU CAN SETTLE RIGHT BACK IN!
WHUMP
HEH HEH HEH ...

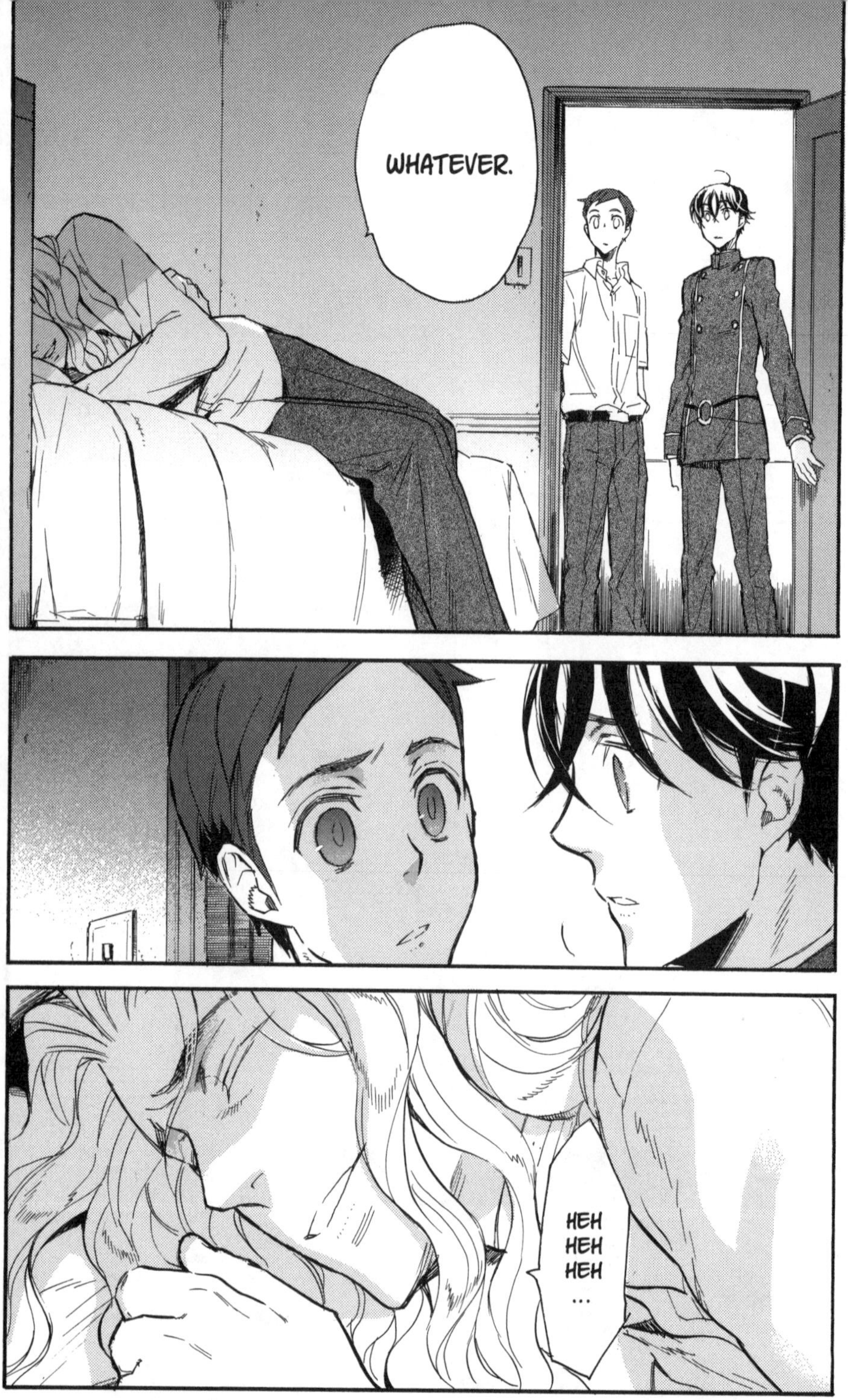
WHATEVER.
HEH HEH HEH ...

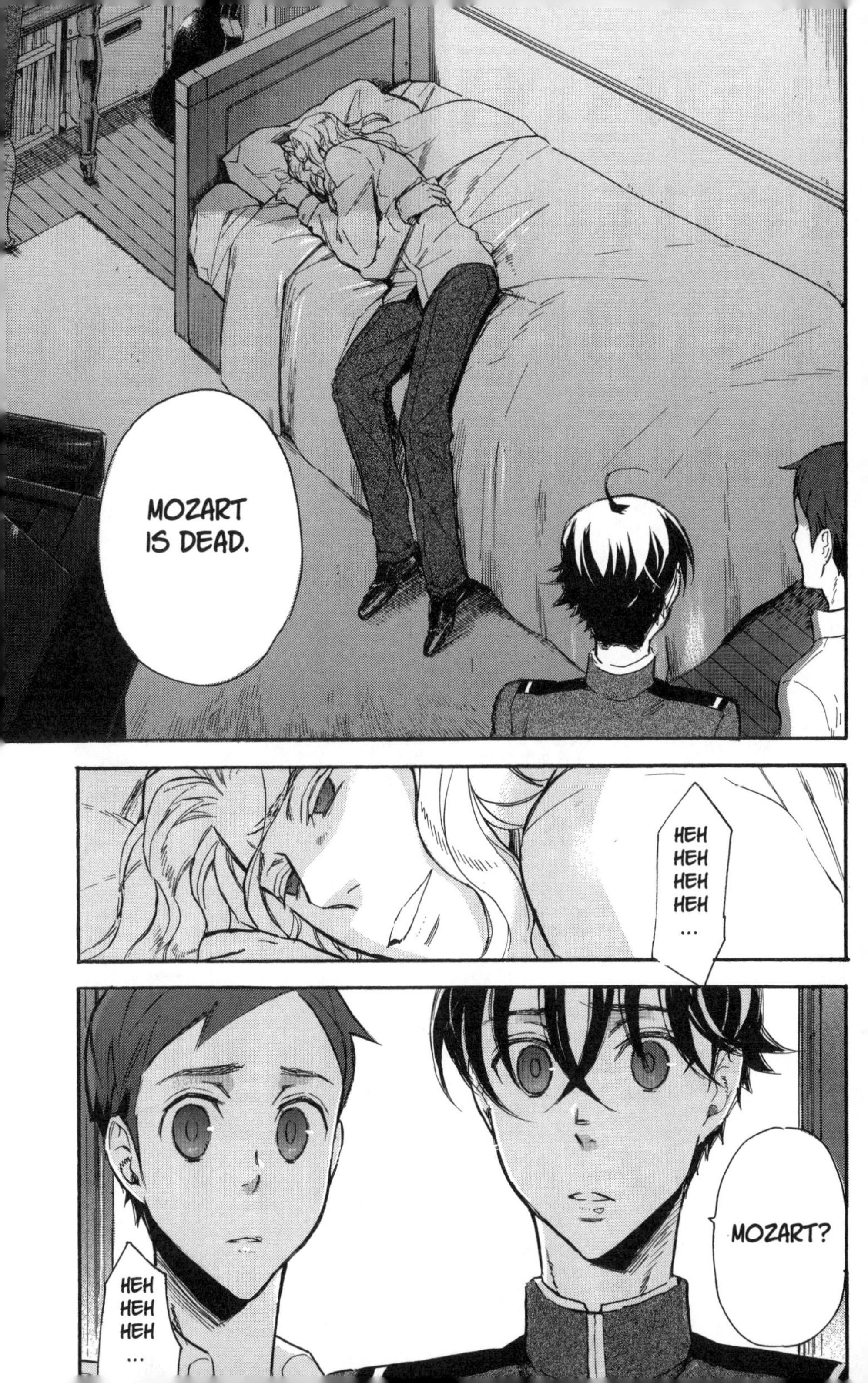
MOZART IS DEAD.
HEH HEH HEH HEH ...
MOZART?
HEH HEH HEH ...

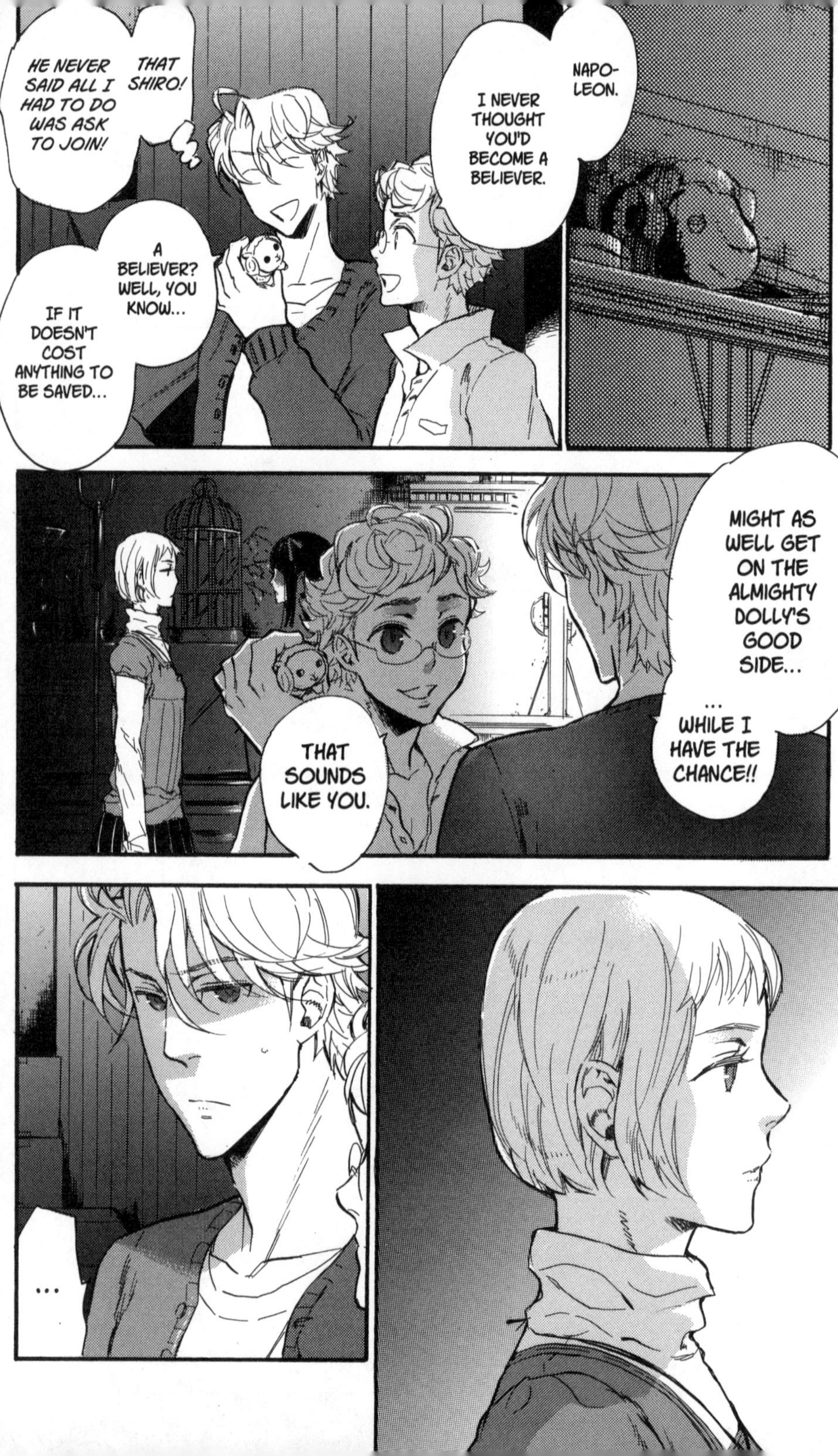

NAPO-LEON.
I NEVER THOUGHT YOU'D BECOME A BELIEVER.
THAT SHIRO!
HE NEVER SAID ALL I HAD TO DO WAS ASK TO JOIN!
A BELIEVER? WELL, YOU KNOW...
IF IT DOESN'T COST ANYTHING TO BE SAVED...
MIGHT AS WELL GET ON THE ALMIGHTY DOLLY'S GOOD SIDE...
... WHILE I HAVE THE CHANCE!!
THAT SOUNDS LIKE YOU.
...

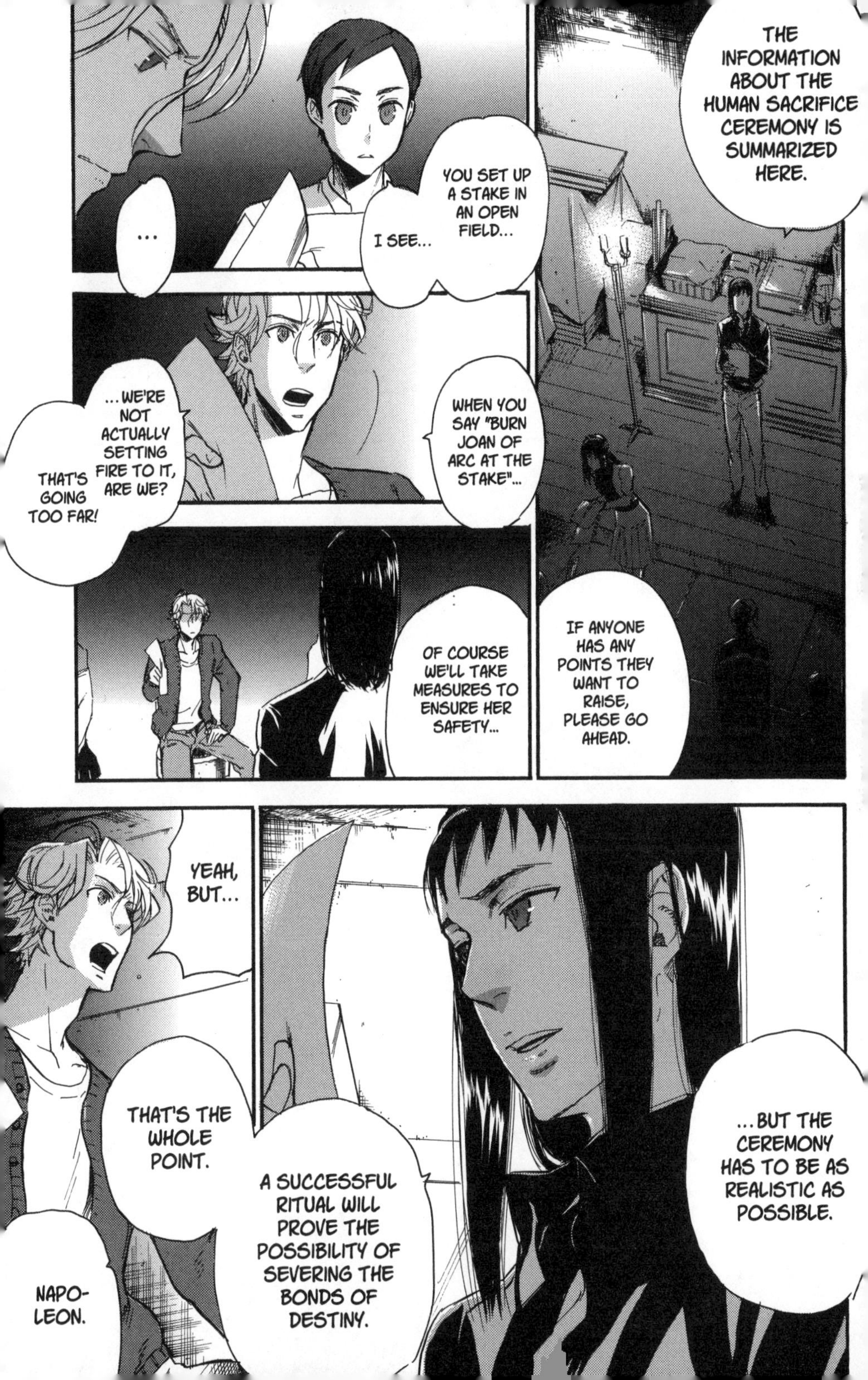
THE INFORMATION ABOUT THE HUMAN SACRIFICE CEREMONY IS SUMMARIZED HERE.
IF ANYONE HAS ANY POINTS THEY WANT TO RAISE, PLEASE GO AHEAD.
YOU SET UP A STAKE IN AN OPEN FIELD...
I SEE...
...
WHEN YOU SAY "BURN JOAN OF ARC AT THE STAKE"...
...WE'RE NOT ACTUALLY SETTING FIRE TO IT, ARE WE?
THAT'S GOING TOO FAR!
OF COURSE WE'LL TAKE MEASURES TO ENSURE HER SAFETY...
...BUT THE CEREMONY HAS TO BE AS REALISTIC AS POSSIBLE.
A SUCCESSFUL RITUAL WILL PROVE THE POSSIBILITY OF SEVERING THE BONDS OF DESTINY.
THAT'S THE WHOLE POINT.
YEAH, BUT...
NAPO-LEON.

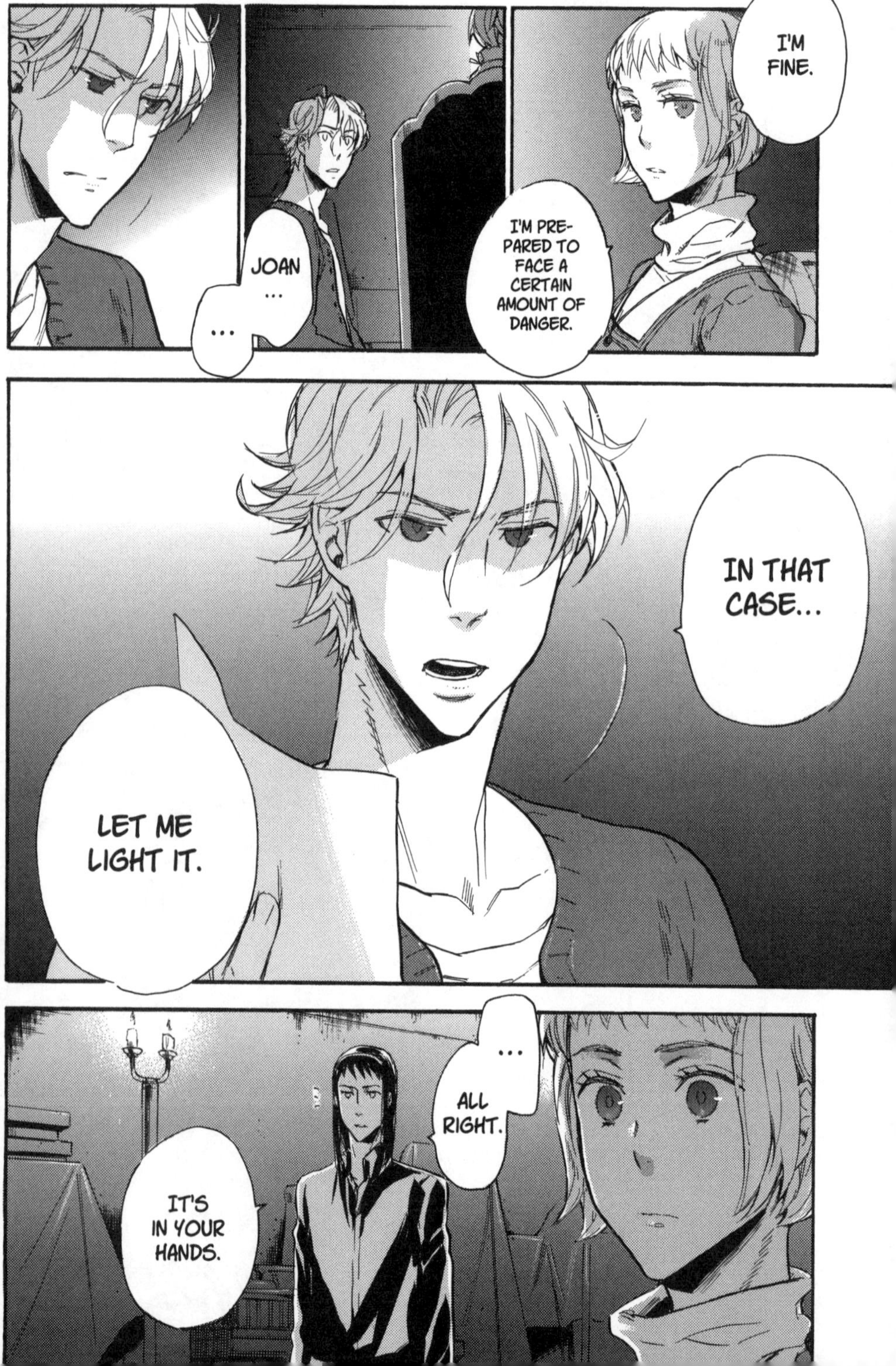
I'M FINE.
I'M PRE-PARED TO FACE A CERTAIN AMOUNT OF DANGER.
JOAN ...
...
IN THAT CASE...
LET ME LIGHT IT.
...
ALL RIGHT.
IT'S IN YOUR HANDS.

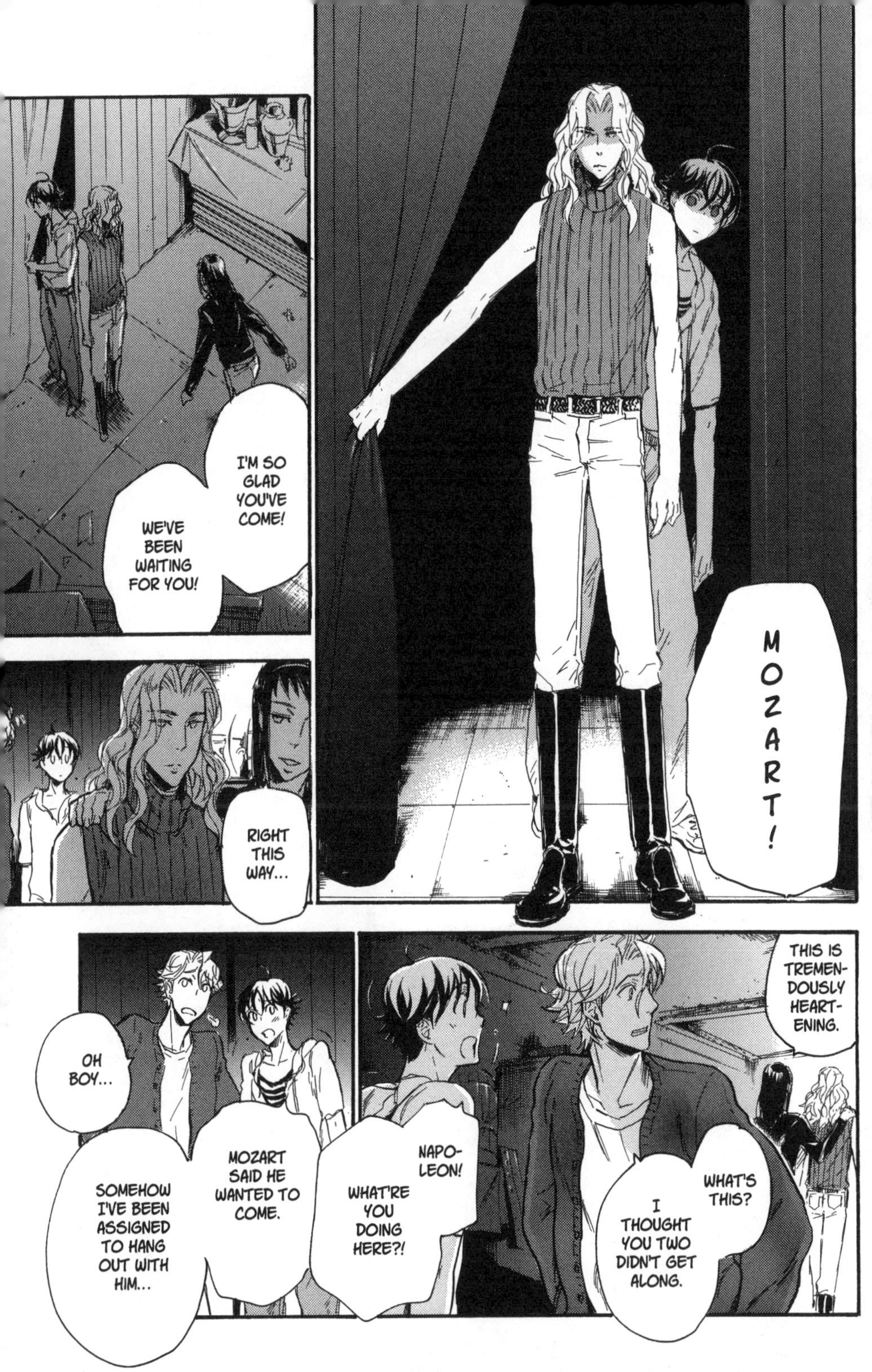
MOZART!
I'M SO GLAD YOU'VE COME!
WE'VE BEEN WAITING FOR YOU!
RIGHT THIS WAY...
THIS IS TREMENDOUSLY HEARTENING.
WHAT'S THIS?
I THOUGHT YOU TWO DIDN'T GET ALONG.
NAPOLEON!
WHAT'RE YOU DOING HERE?!
MOZART SAID HE WANTED TO COME.
OH BOY...
SOMEHOW I'VE BEEN ASSIGNED TO HANG OUT WITH HIM...

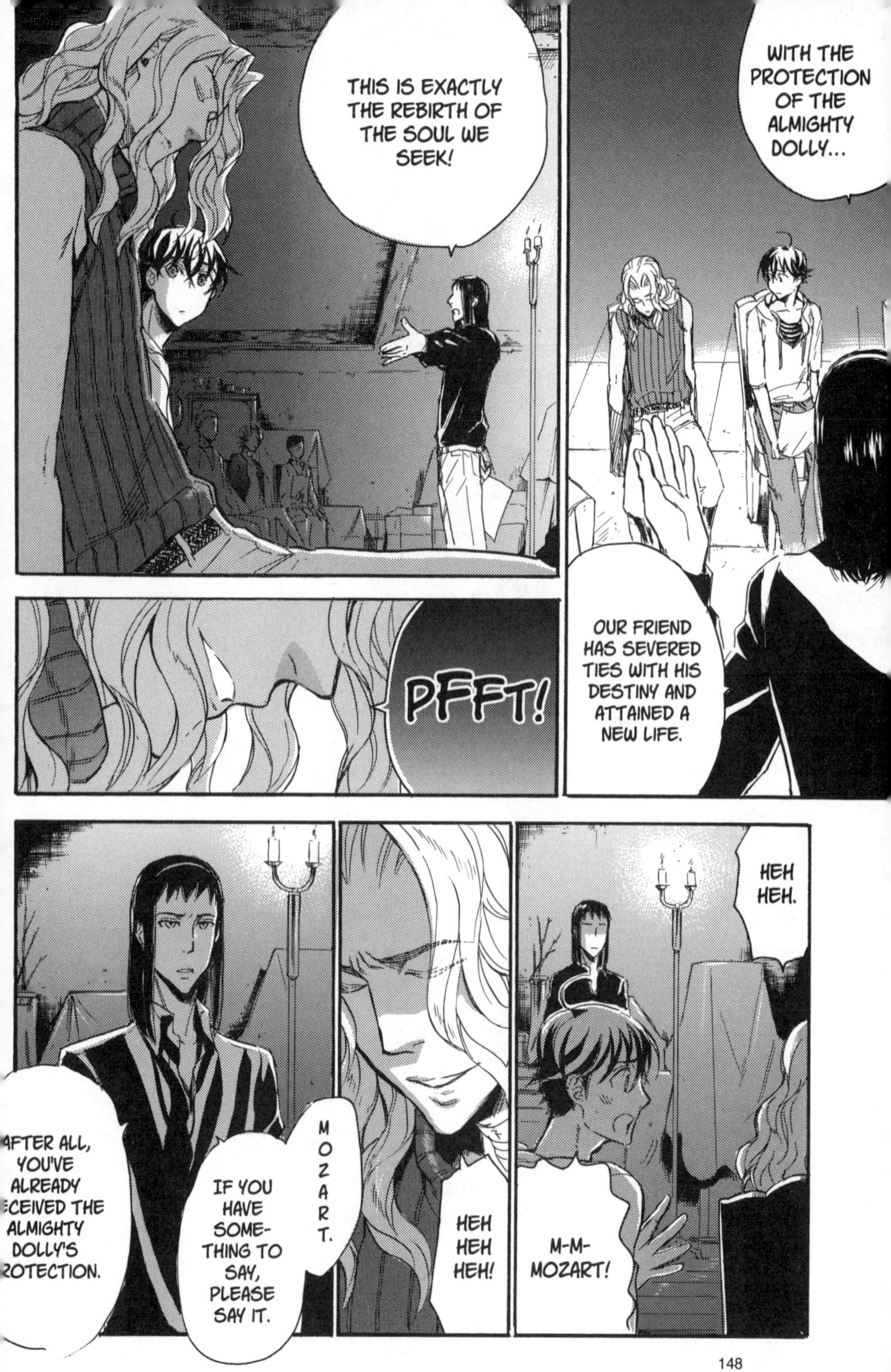
WITH THE PROTECTION OF THE ALMIGHTY DOLLY...
OUR FRIEND HAS SEVERED TIES WITH HIS DESTINY AND ATTAINED A NEW LIFE.
THIS IS EXACTLY THE REBIRTH OF THE SOUL WE SEEK!
PFFT!
HEH HEH.
M-M-MOZART!
HEH HEH HEH!
MOZART.
IF YOU HAVE SOME-THING TO SAY, PLEASE SAY IT.
AFTER ALL, YOU'VE ALREADY ECEIVED THE ALMIGHTY DOLLY'S ROTECTION.

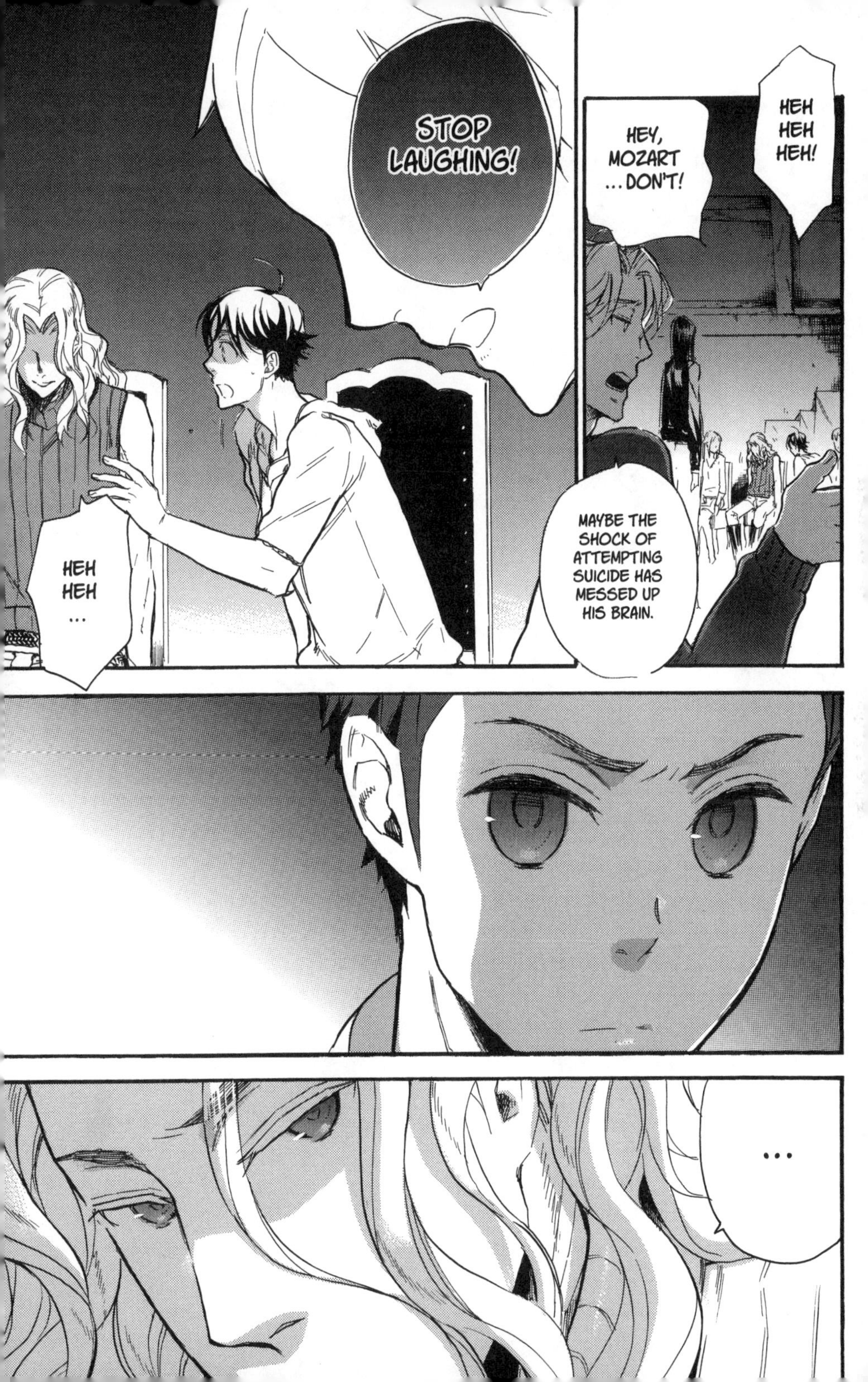
HEH HEH HEH!
HEY, MOZART ...DON'T!
MAYBE THE SHOCK OF ATTEMPTING SUICIDE HAS MESSED UP HIS BRAIN.
STOP LAUGHING!
HEH HEH ...
...

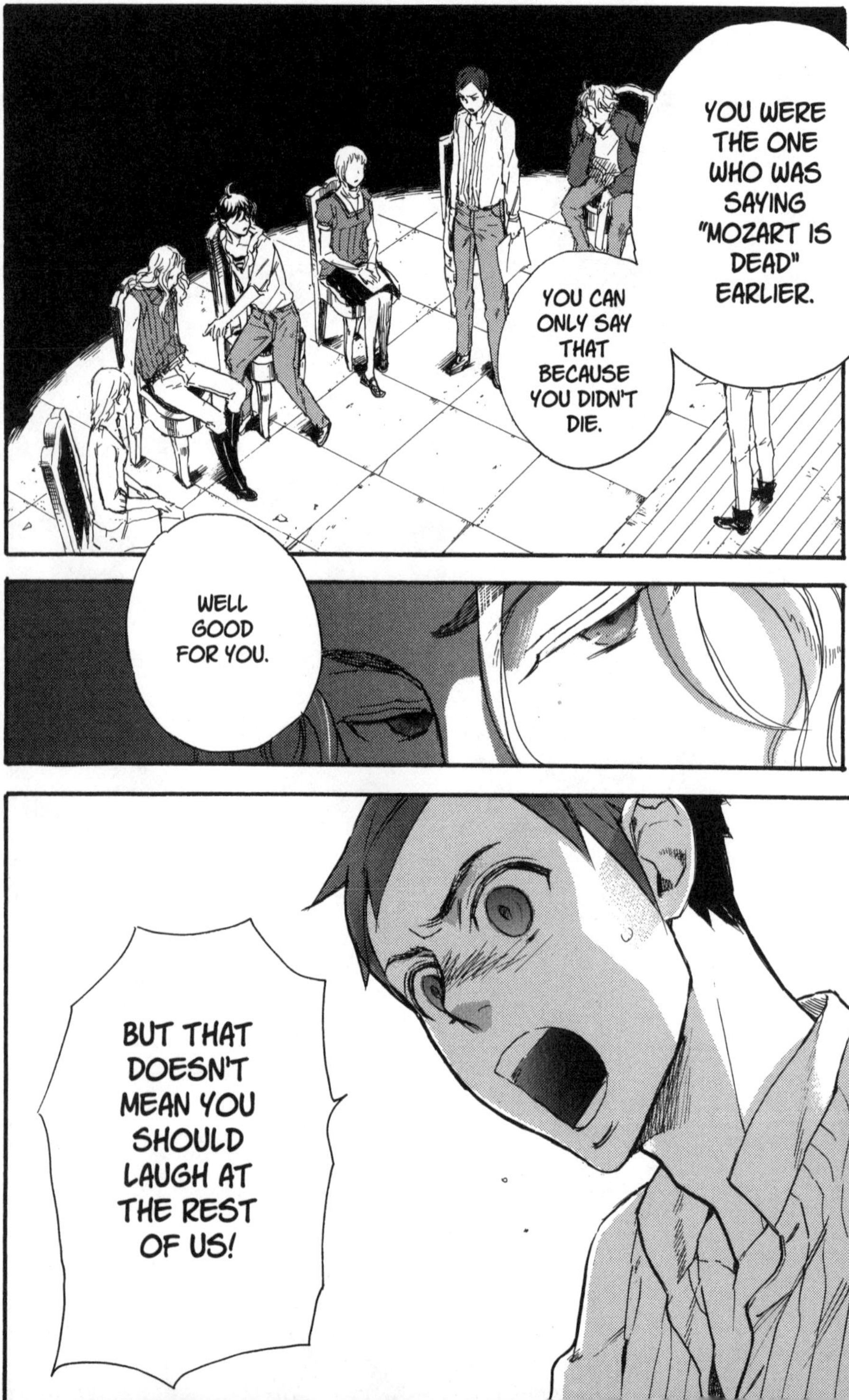
YOU WERE THE ONE WHO WAS SAYING "MOZART IS DEAD" EARLIER.
YOU CAN ONLY SAY THAT BECAUSE YOU DIDN'T DIE.
WELL GOOD FOR YOU.
BUT THAT DOESN'T MEAN YOU SHOULD LAUGH AT THE REST OF US!

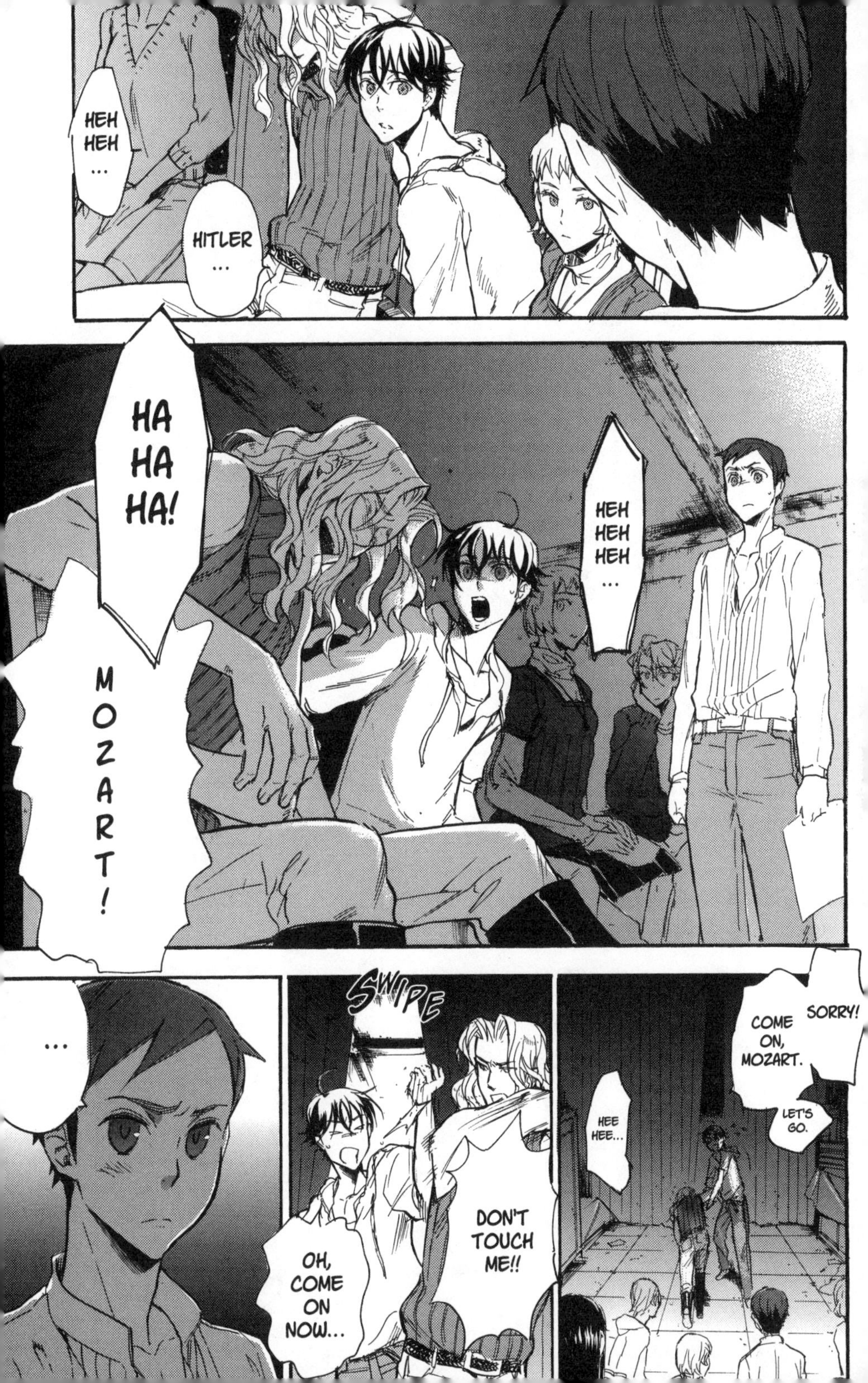
HEH HEH ...
HITLER ...
HEH HEH HEH ...
HA HA HA!
MOZART!
SORRY!
COME ON, MOZART.
LET'S GO.
HEE HEE...
SWIPE
DON'T TOUCH ME!!
OH, COME ON NOW...
...

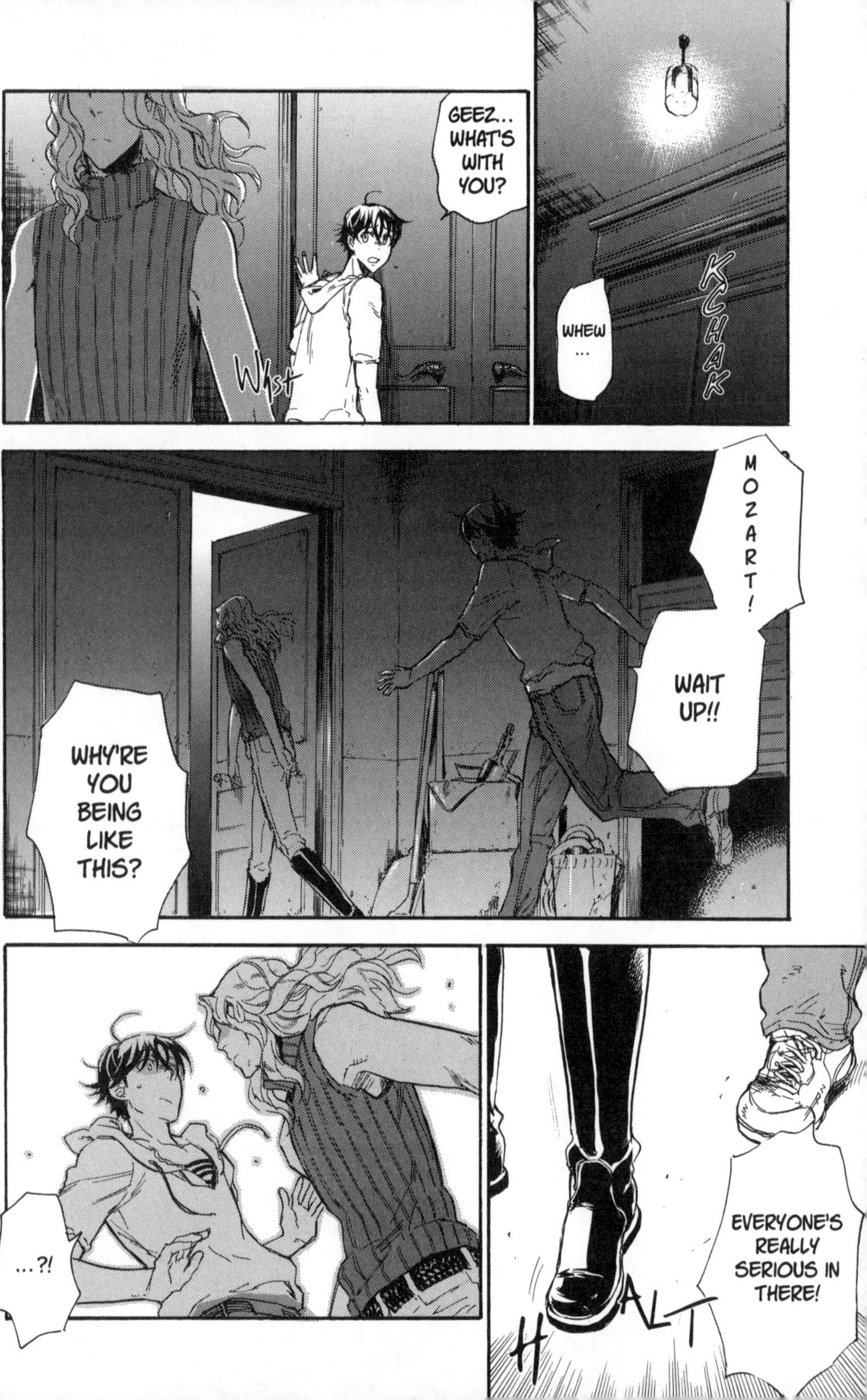
KCHAK
WHEW...
GEEZ... WHAT'S WITH YOU?
Whst
MOZART!
WAIT UP!!
WHY'RE YOU BEING LIKE THIS?
EVERYONE'S REALLY SERIOUS IN THERE!
HALT
...?!

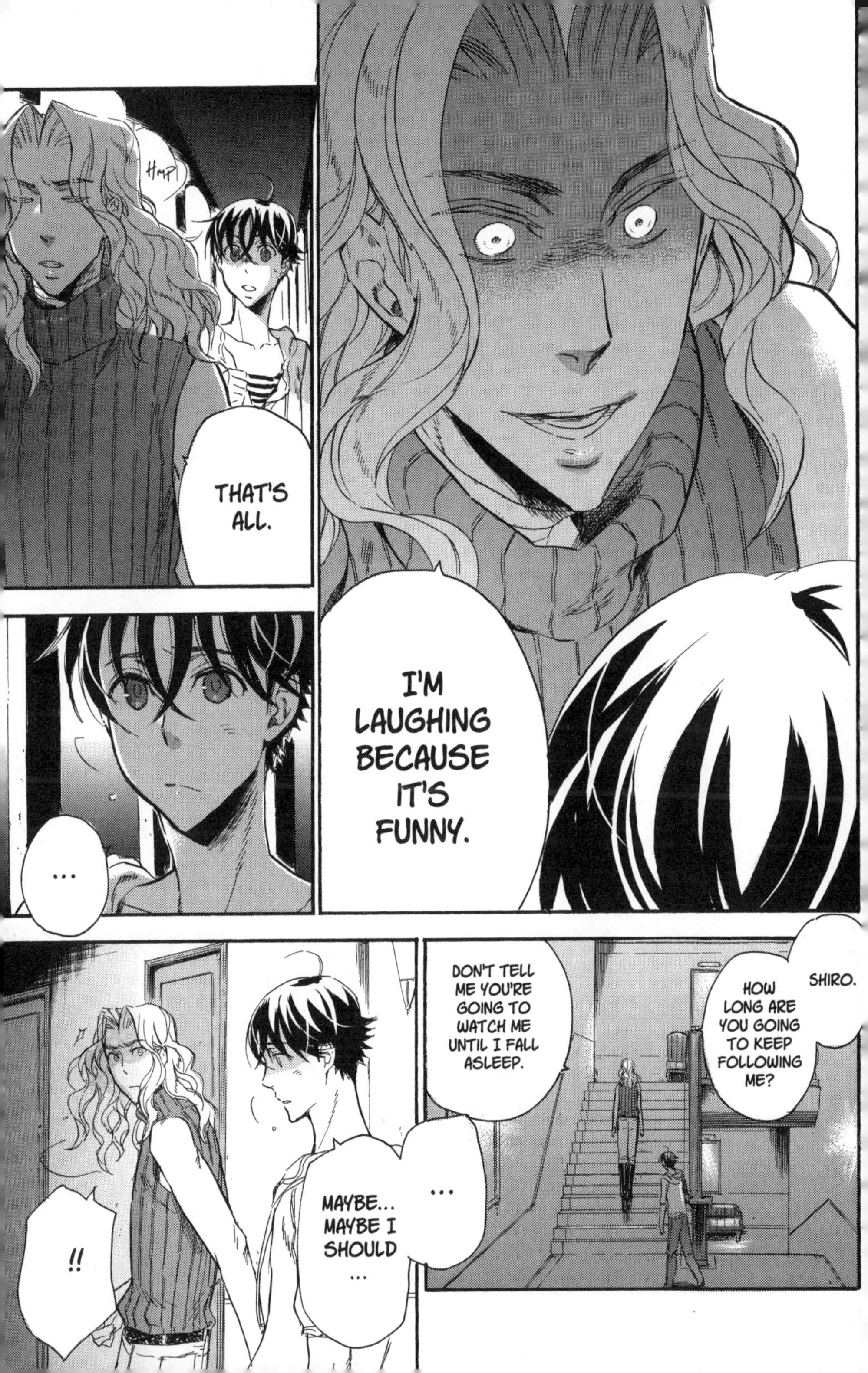
I'M LAUGHING BECAUSE IT'S FUNNY.
HMP
THAT'S ALL.
...
SHIRO.
HOW LONG ARE YOU GOING TO KEEP FOLLOWING ME?
DON'T TELL ME YOU'RE GOING TO WATCH ME UNTIL I FALL ASLEEP.
...
MAYBE... MAYBE I SHOULD ...
!!

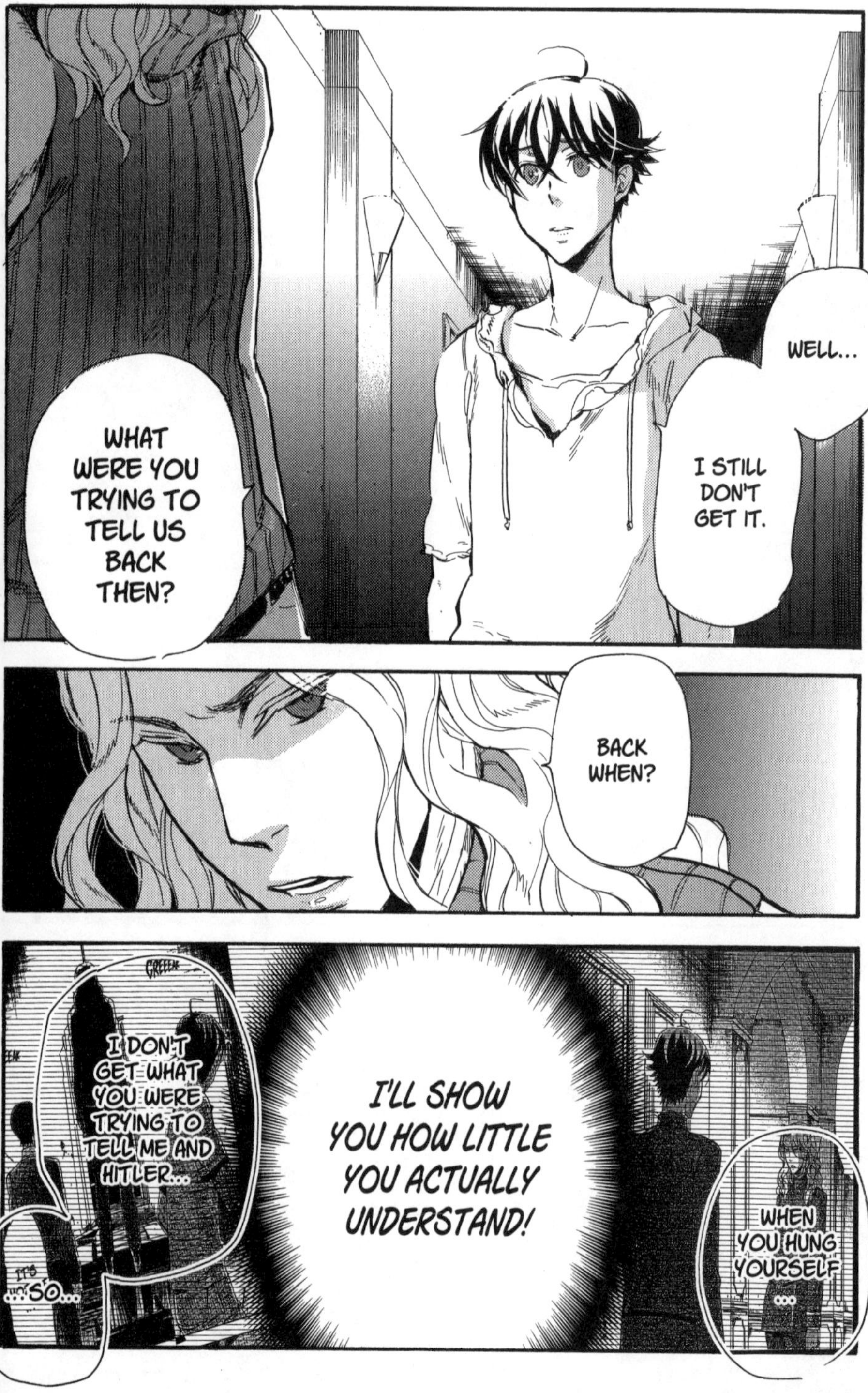

WELL...
I STILL DON'T GET IT.
WHAT WERE YOU TRYING TO TELL US BACK THEN?
BACK WHEN?
WHEN YOU HUNG YOURSELF...
I'LL SHOW YOU HOW LITTLE YOU ACTUALLY UNDERSTAND!
I DON'T GET WHAT YOU WERE TRYING TO TELL ME AND HITLER...
IT'S ...SO...

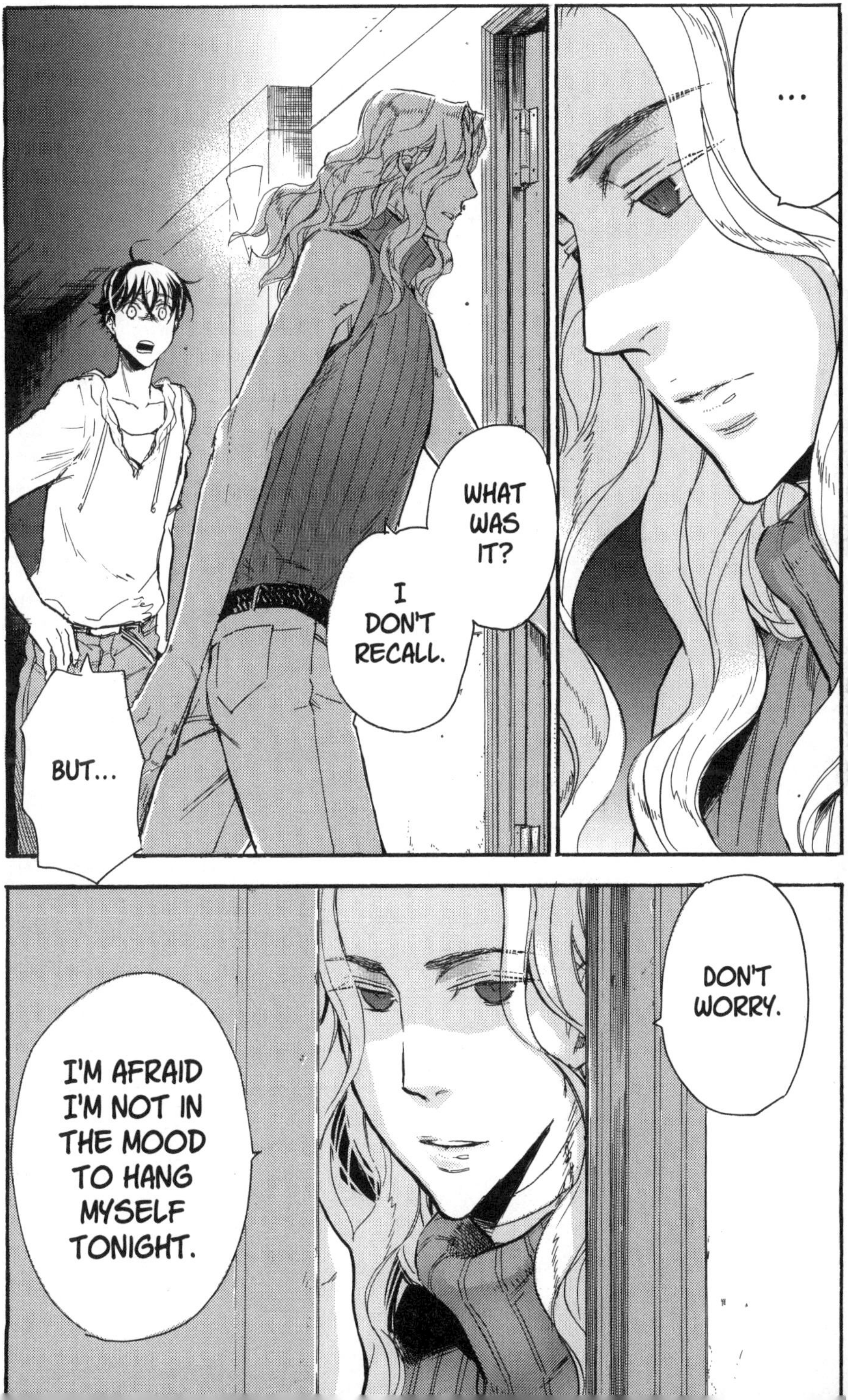
...
WHAT WAS IT?
I DON'T RECALL.
BUT...
DON'T WORRY.
I'M AFRAID I'M NOT IN THE MOOD TO HANG MYSELF TONIGHT.

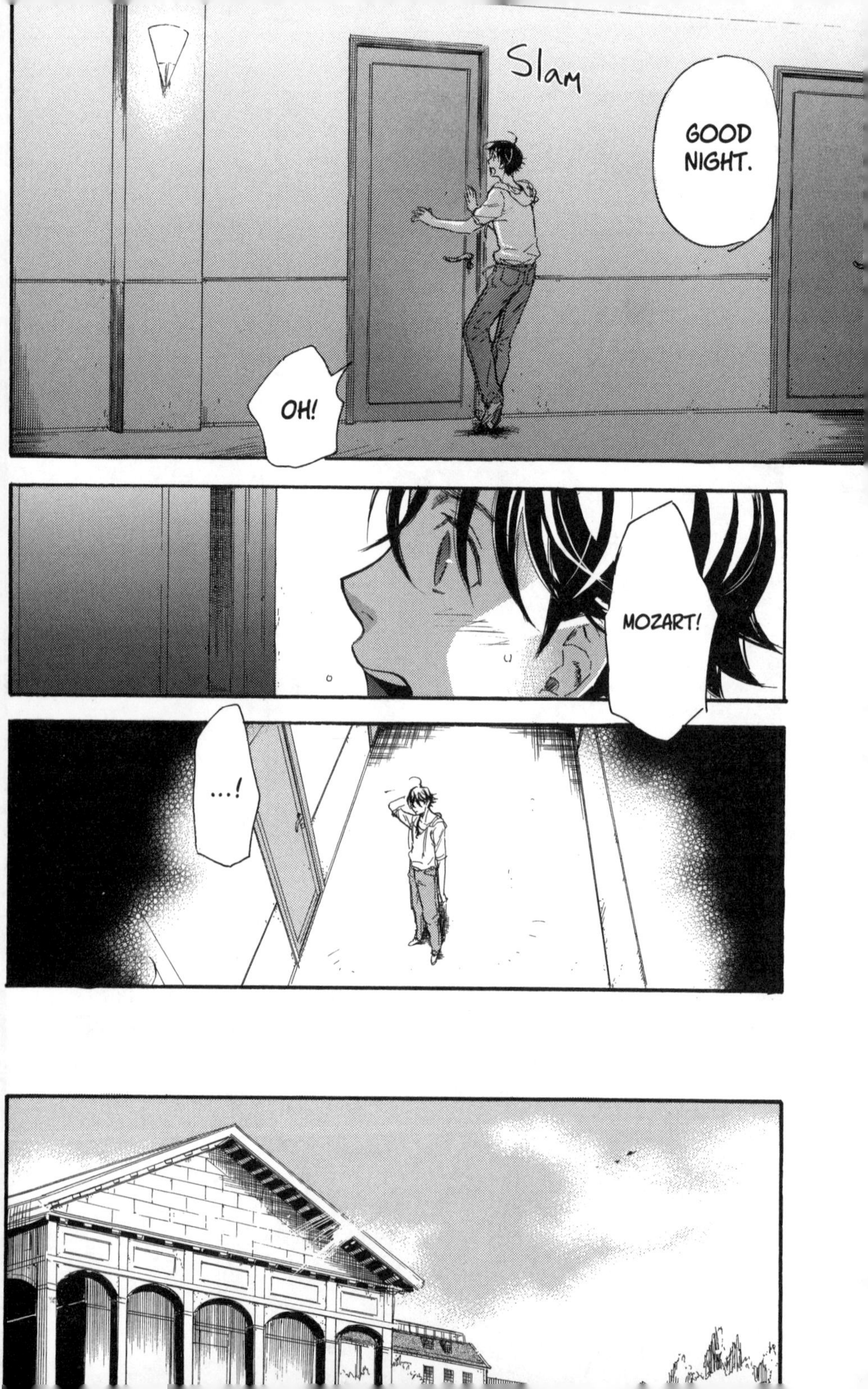
GOOD NIGHT.
Slam
OH!
MOZART!
...!

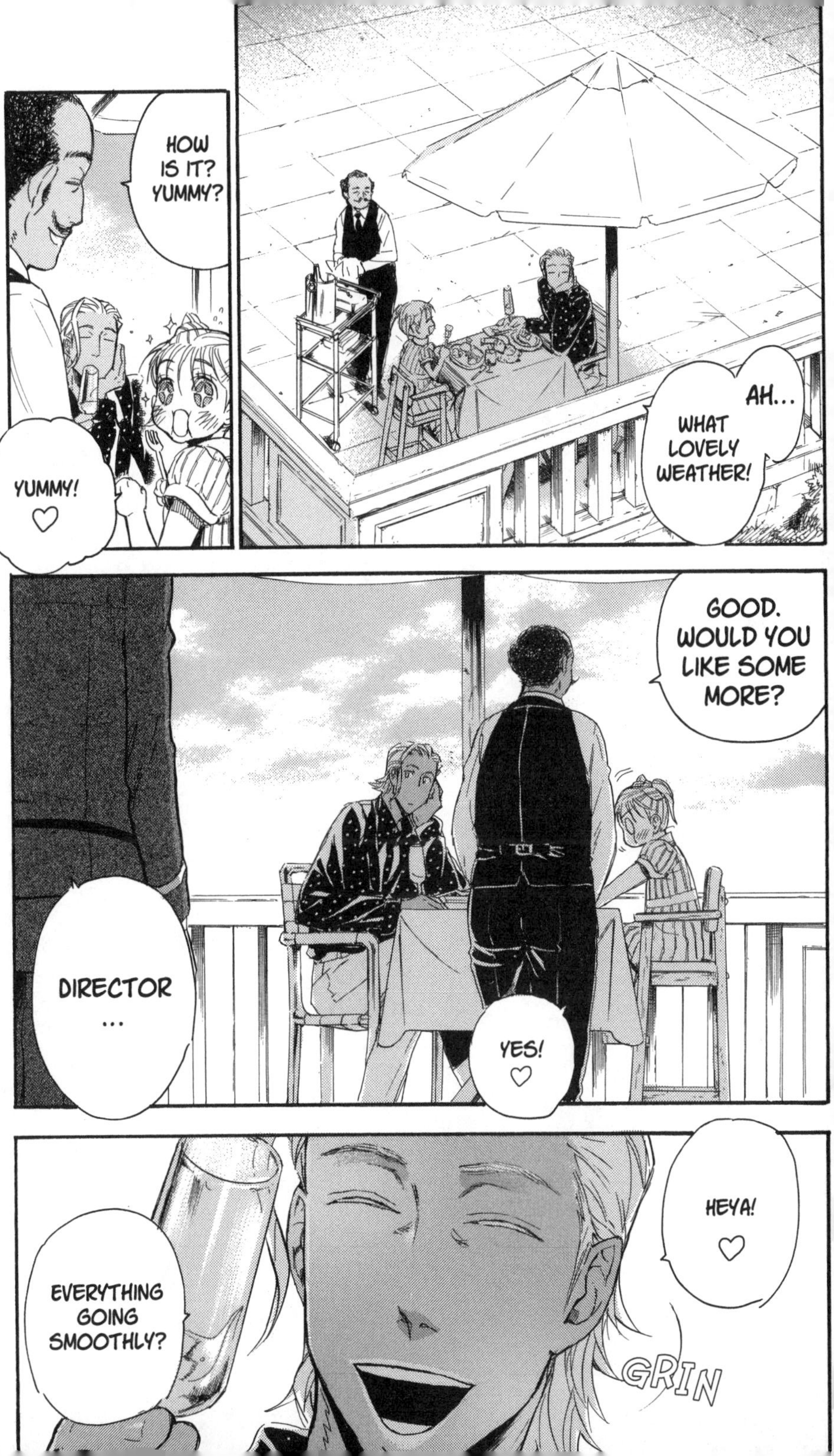
AH... WHAT LOVELY WEATHER!
HOW IS IT? YUMMY?
YUMMY! ♡
GOOD. WOULD YOU LIKE SOME MORE?
YES! ♡
DIRECTOR ...
HEYA! ♡
EVERYTHING GOING SMOOTHLY?
GRIN

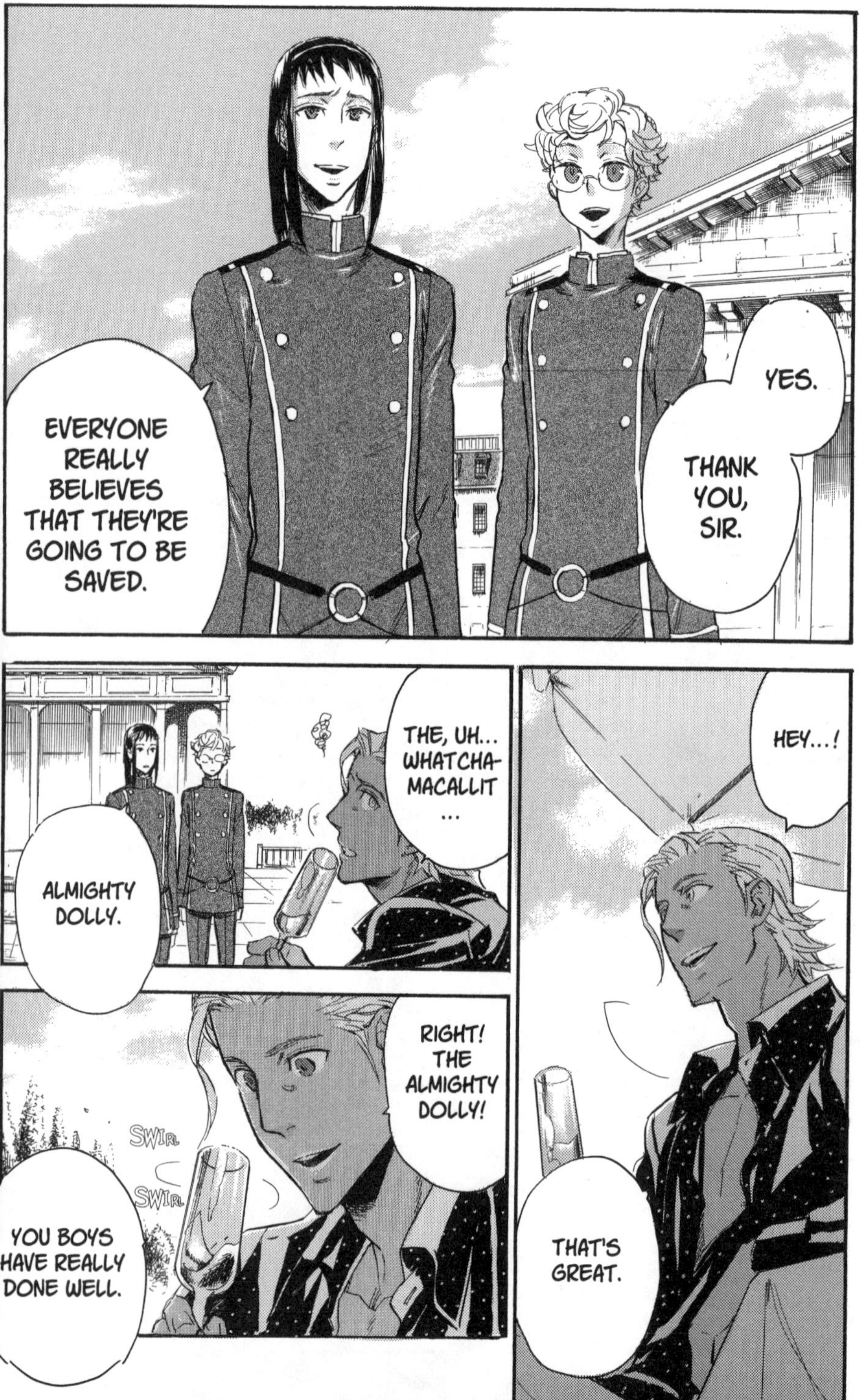
YES.
THANK YOU, SIR.
EVERYONE REALLY BELIEVES THAT THEY'RE GOING TO BE SAVED.
HEY...!
THAT'S GREAT.
THE, UH... WHATCHA-MACALLIT ...
ALMIGHTY DOLLY.
RIGHT! THE ALMIGHTY DOLLY!
SWIRL
SWIRL
YOU BOYS HAVE REALLY DONE WELL.

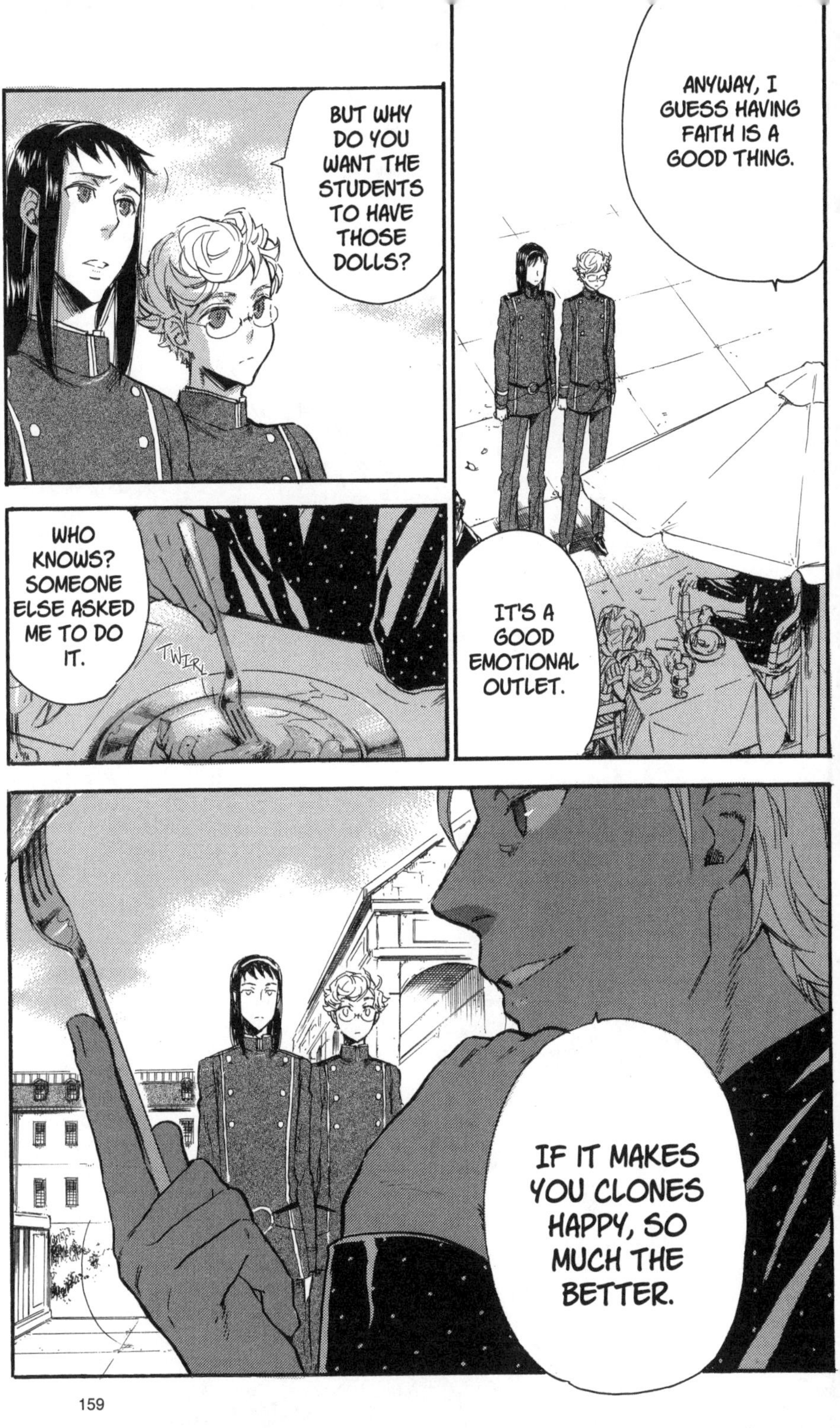
ANYWAY, I GUESS HAVING FAITH IS A GOOD THING.
IT'S A GOOD EMOTIONAL OUTLET.
BUT WHY DO YOU WANT THE STUDENTS TO HAVE THOSE DOLLS?
WHO KNOWS? SOMEONE ELSE ASKED ME TO DO IT.
TWIRL
IF IT MAKES YOU CLONES HAPPY, SO MUCH THE BETTER.

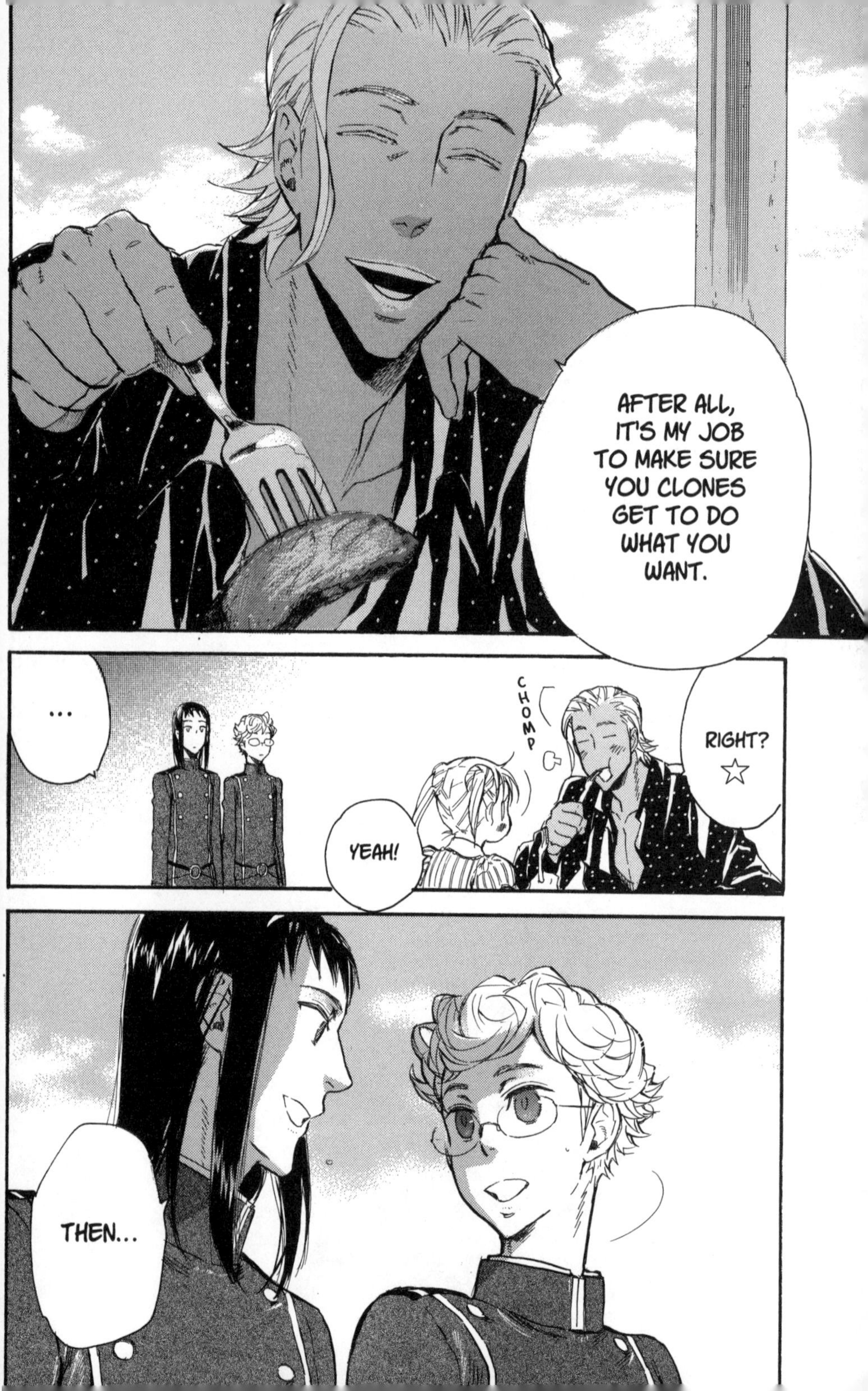
AFTER ALL, IT'S MY JOB TO MAKE SURE YOU CLONES GET TO DO WHAT YOU WANT.
RIGHT? ☆
CHOMP
YEAH!
...
THEN...

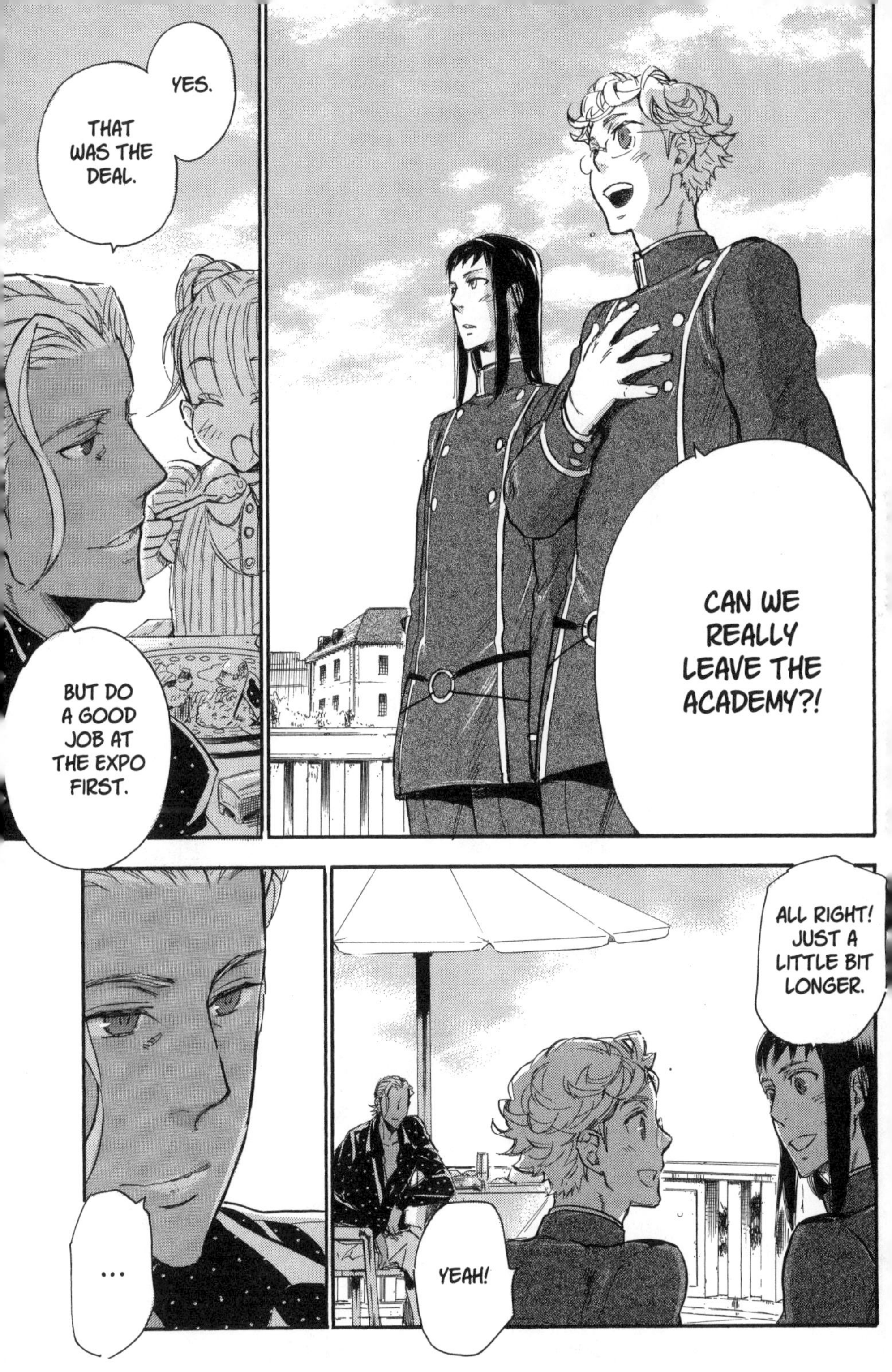
CAN WE REALLY LEAVE THE ACADEMY?!
YES.
THAT WAS THE DEAL.
BUT DO A GOOD JOB AT THE EXPO FIRST.
ALL RIGHT! JUST A LITTLE BIT LONGER.
YEAH!
...

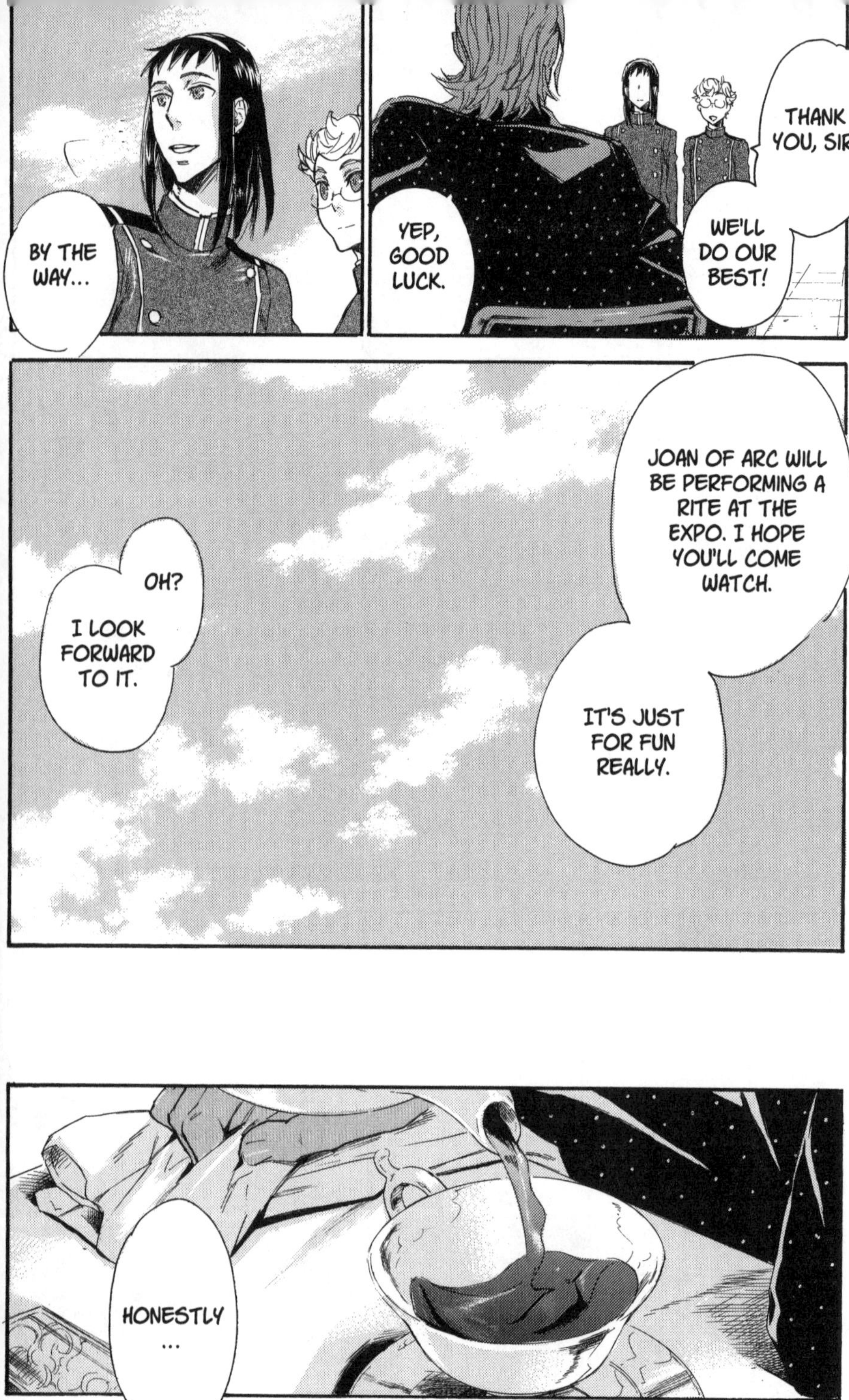
THANK YOU, SIR.
WE'LL DO OUR BEST!
YEP, GOOD LUCK.
BY THE WAY...
JOAN OF ARC WILL BE PERFORMING A RITE AT THE EXPO. I HOPE YOU'LL COME WATCH.
IT'S JUST FOR FUN REALLY.
OH?
I LOOK FORWARD TO IT.
HONESTLY ...

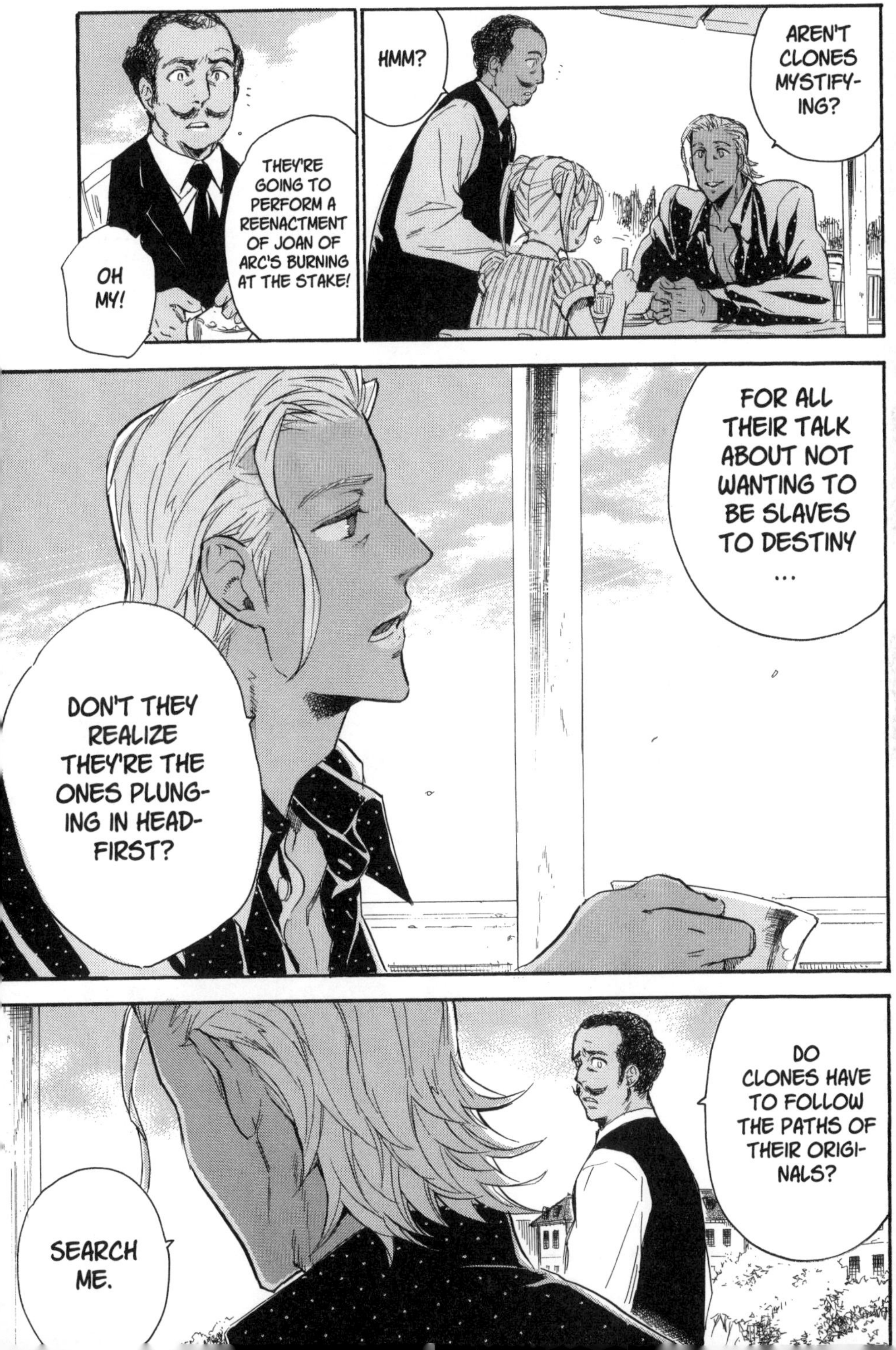
AREN'T CLONES MYSTIFYING?
HMM?
THEY'RE GOING TO PERFORM A REENACTMENT OF JOAN OF ARC'S BURNING AT THE STAKE!
OH MY!
FOR ALL THEIR TALK ABOUT NOT WANTING TO BE SLAVES TO DESTINY ...
DON'T THEY REALIZE THEY'RE THE ONES PLUNGING IN HEADFIRST?
DO CLONES HAVE TO FOLLOW THE PATHS OF THEIR ORIGINALS?
SEARCH ME.

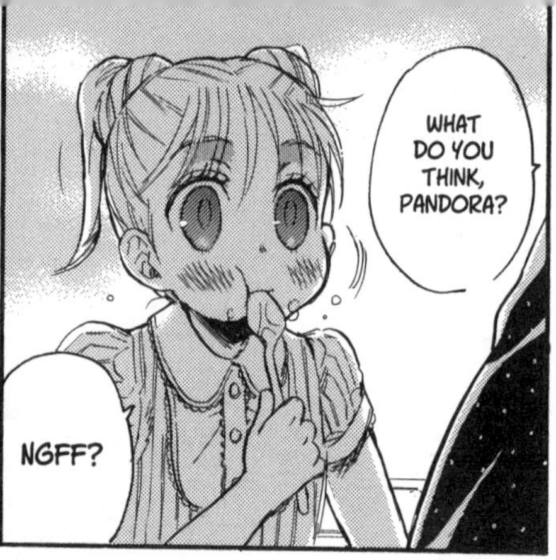
WHAT DO YOU THINK, PANDORA?
NGFF?

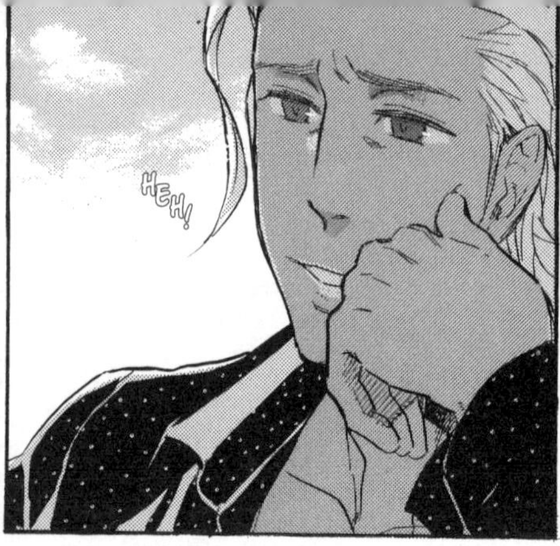
HEH!

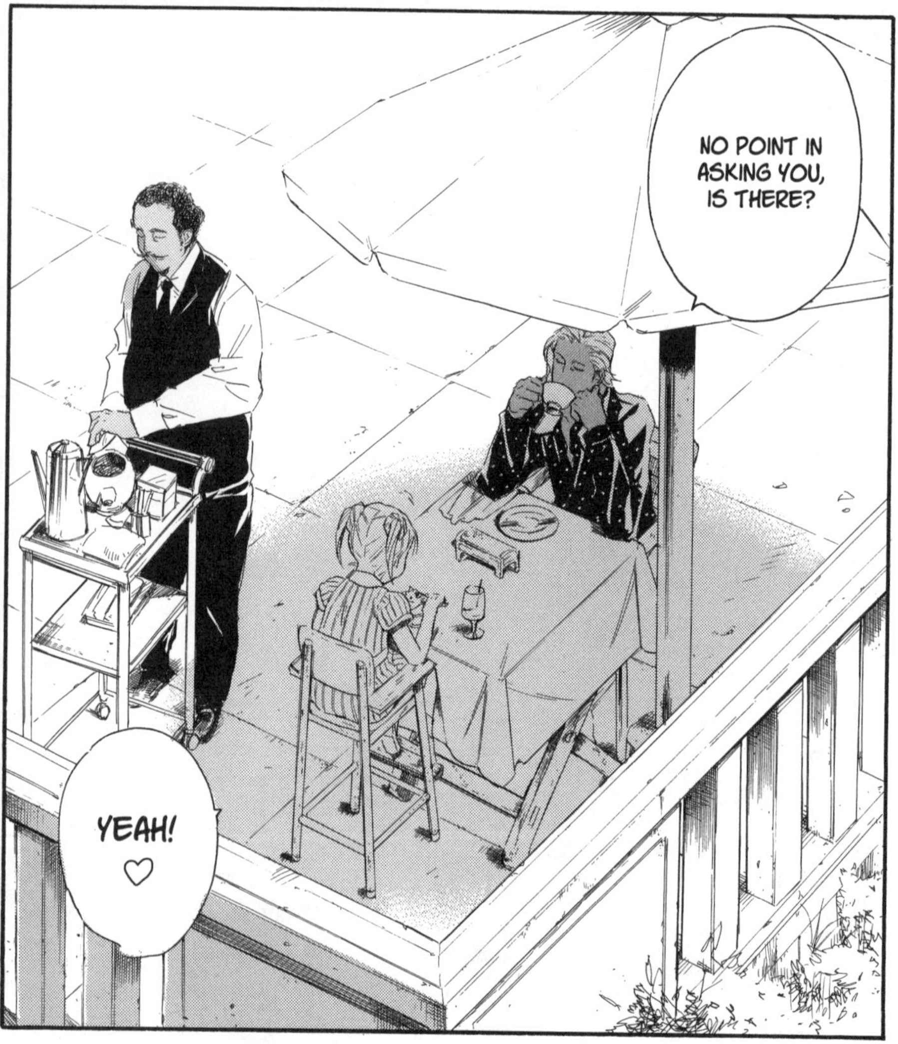
NO POINT IN ASKING YOU, IS THERE?
YEAH! ♡

CHAPTER twelve

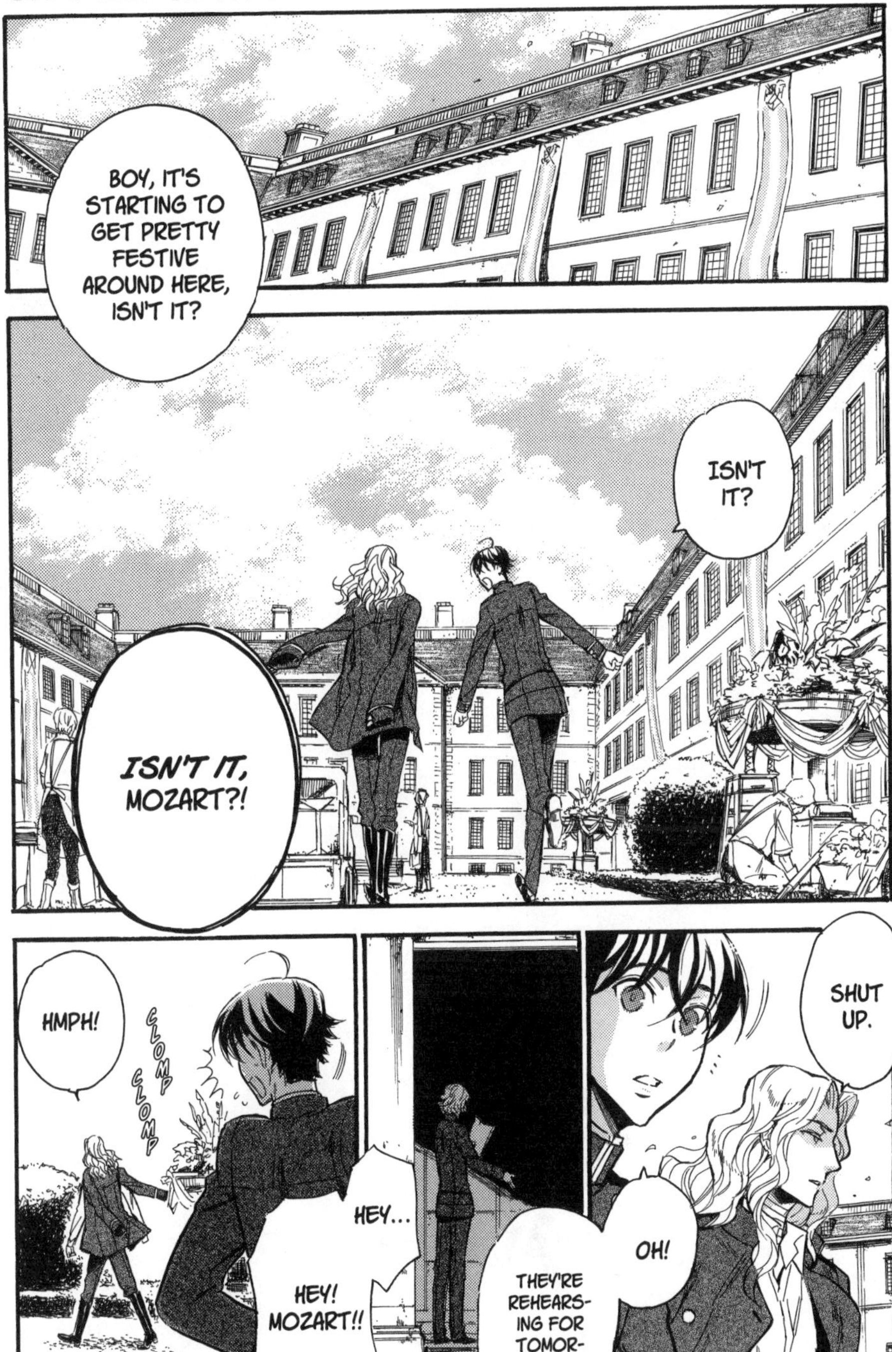
BOY, IT'S STARTING TO GET PRETTY FESTIVE AROUND HERE, ISN'T IT?
ISN'T IT?
ISN'T IT, MOZART?!
SHUT UP.
OH!
THEY'RE REHEARSING FOR TOMORROW!
HEY...
HEY! MOZART!!
HMPH!
CLOMP CLOMP

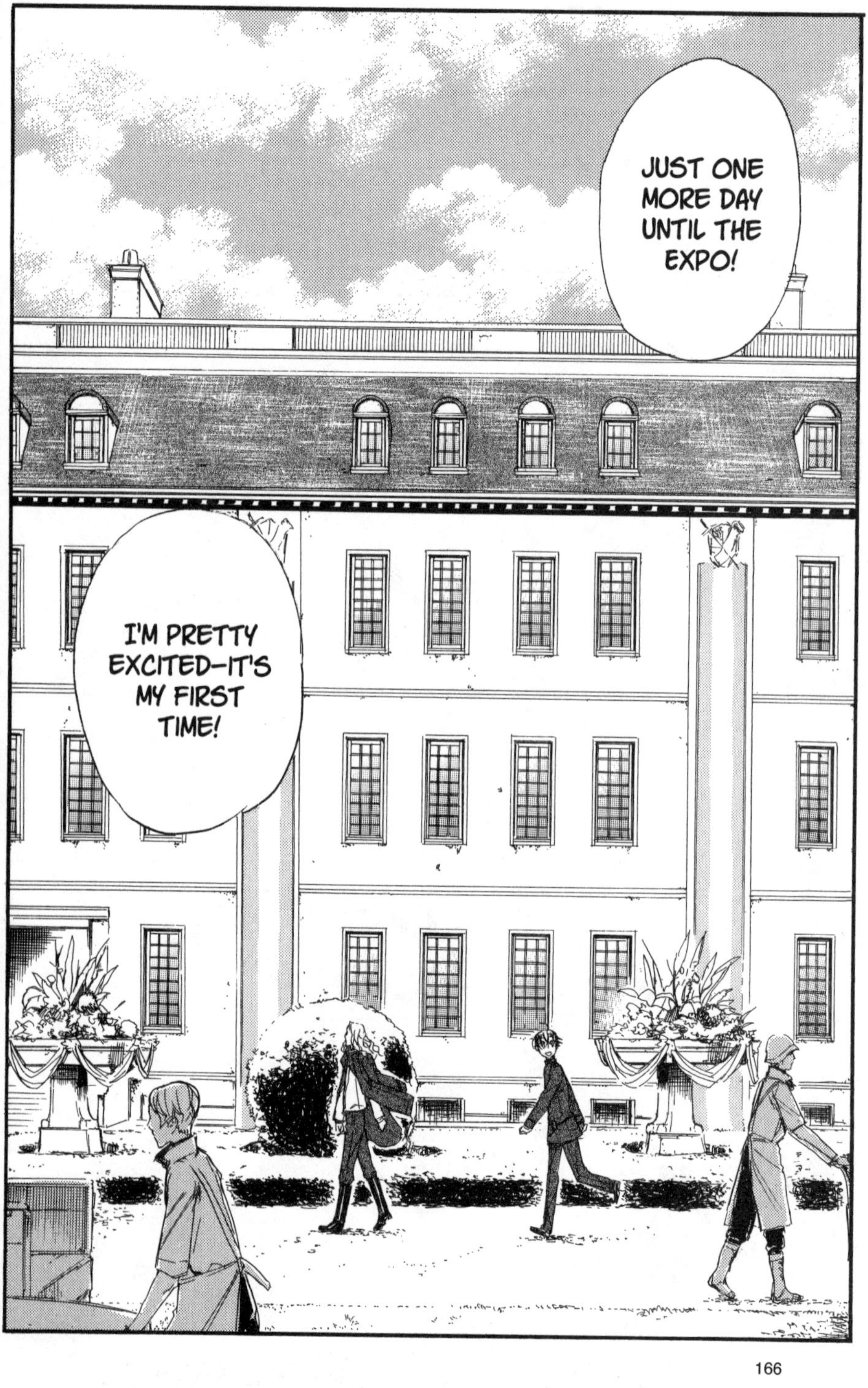
JUST ONE MORE DAY UNTIL THE EXPO!
I'M PRETTY EXCITED—IT'S MY FIRST TIME!

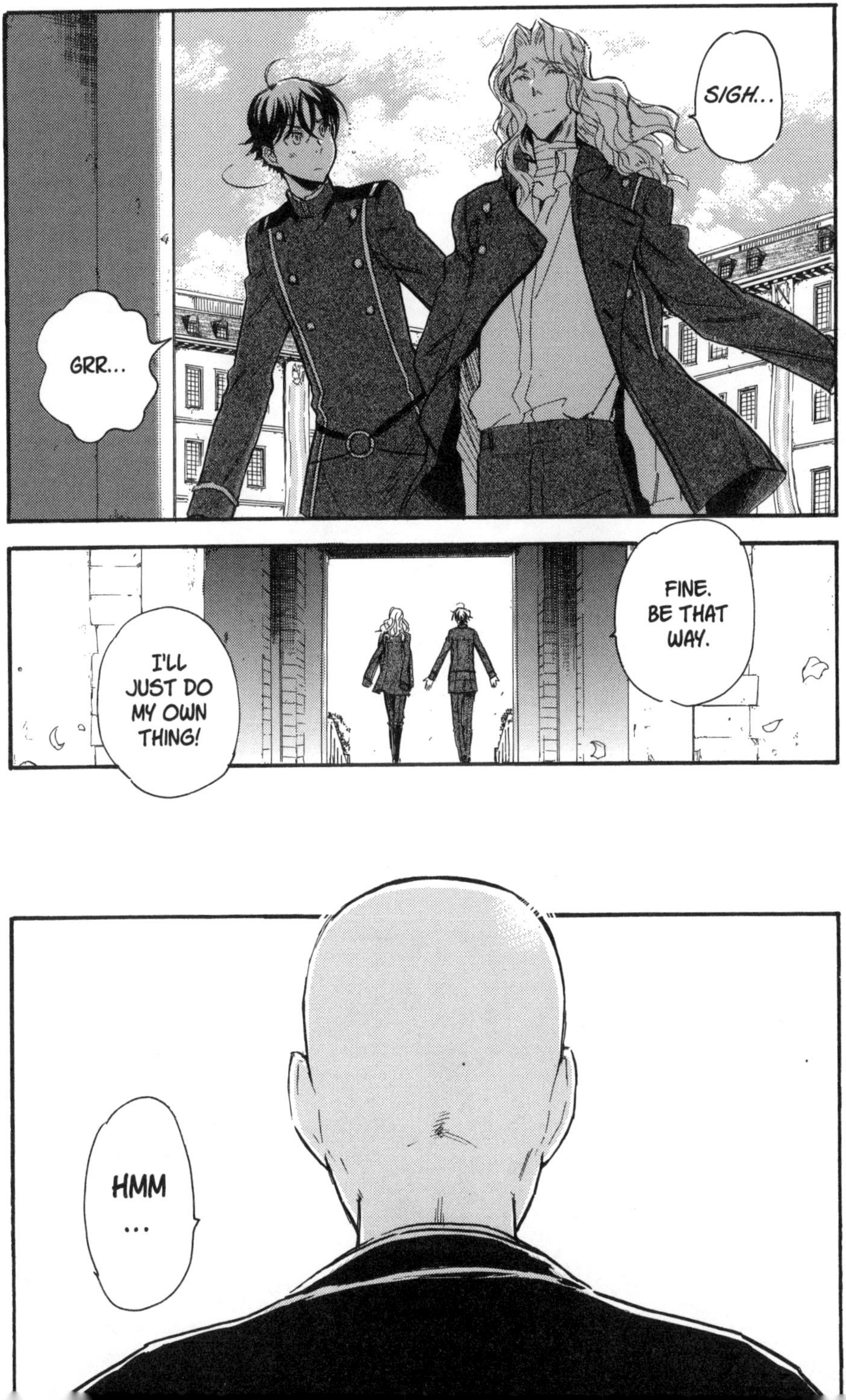
SIGH...
GRR...
FINE. BE THAT WAY.
I'LL JUST DO MY OWN THING!
HMM ...

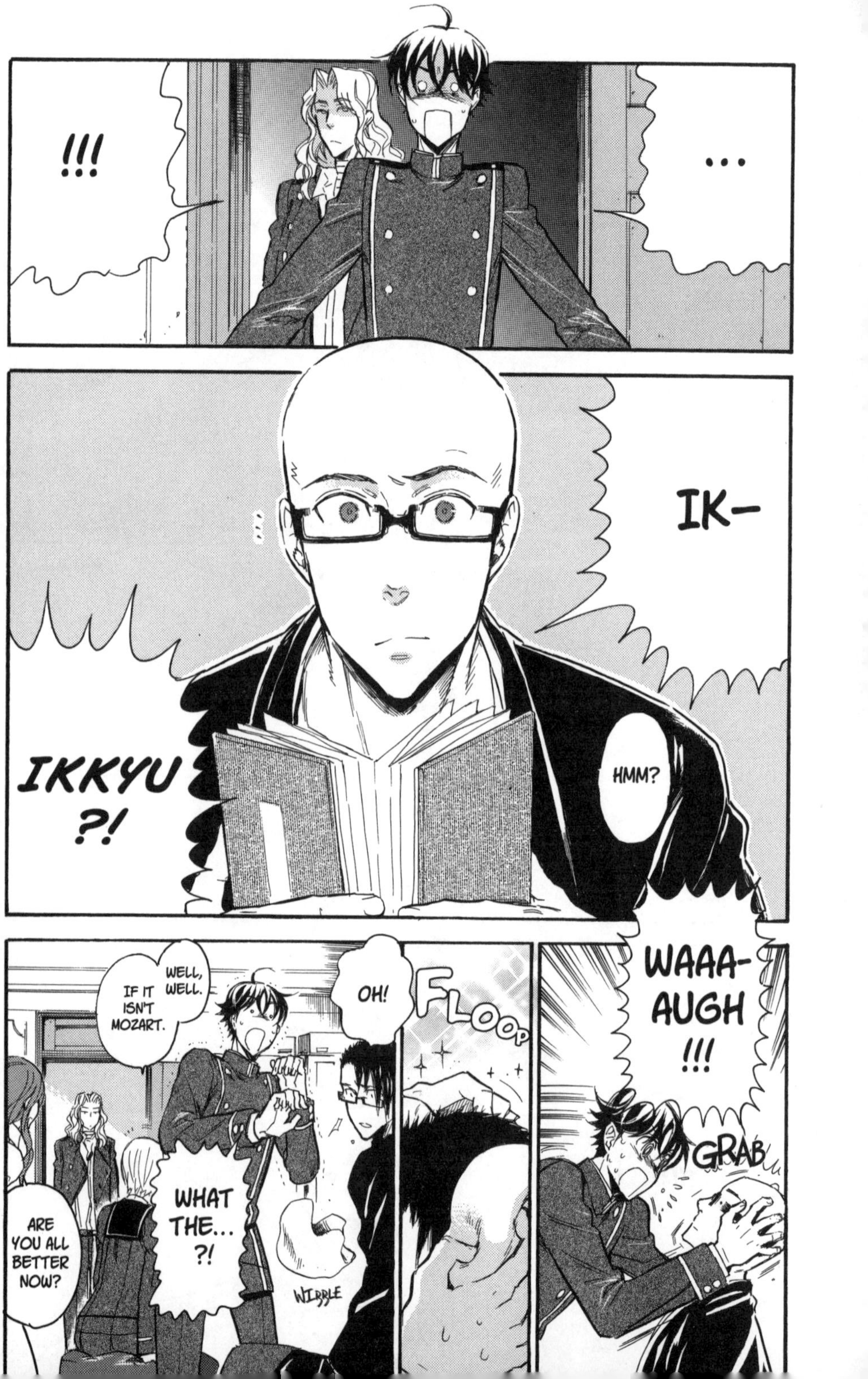
...
!!!
IK-
HMM?
IKKYU ?!
WAAA-AUGH !!!
GRAB
FLOOP
OH!
WIBBLE
WELL, WELL. IF IT ISN'T MOZART.
WHAT THE... ?!
ARE YOU ALL BETTER NOW?

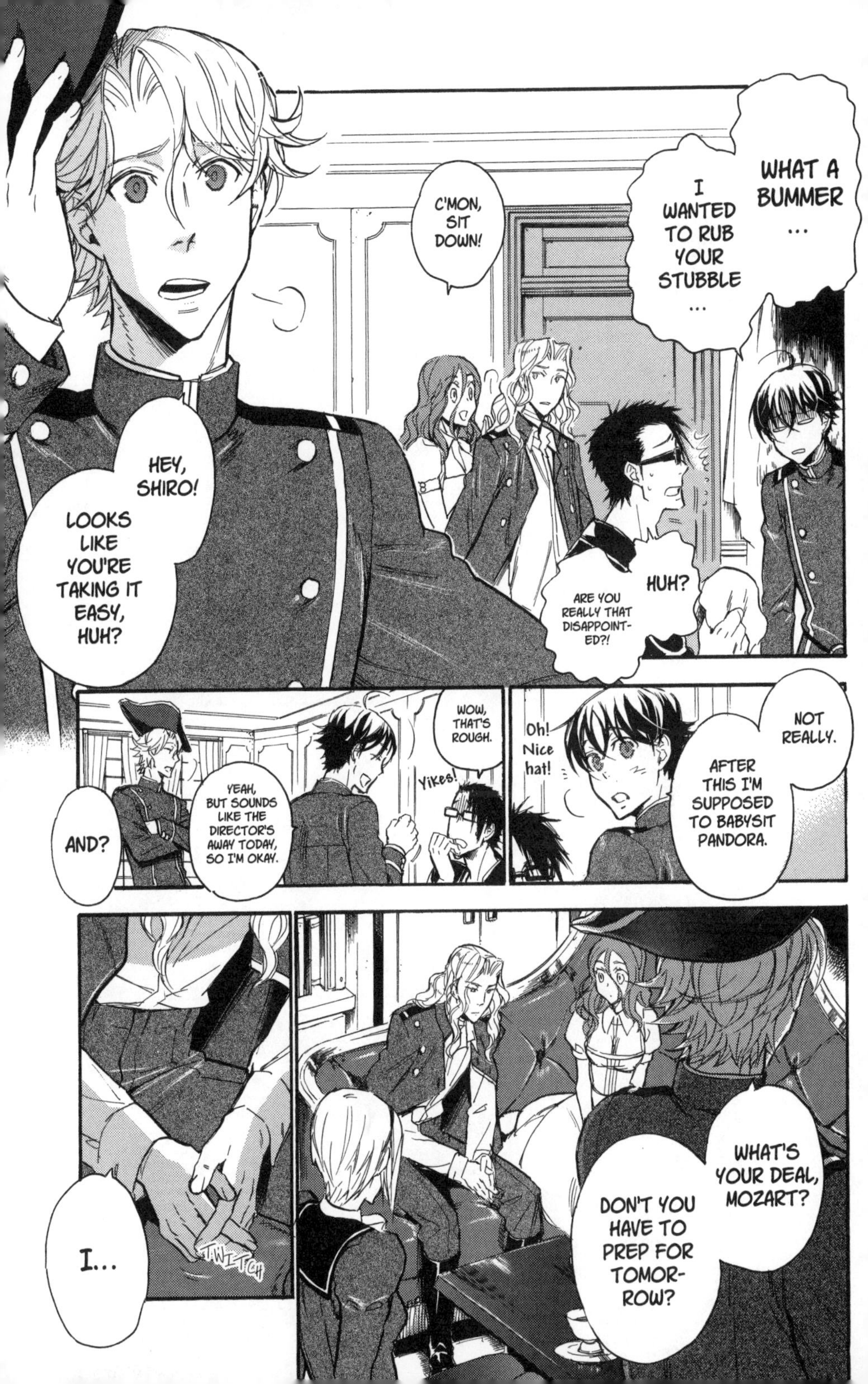
WHAT A BUMMER...
I WANTED TO RUB YOUR STUBBLE...
C'MON, SIT DOWN!
HUH?
ARE YOU REALLY THAT DISAPPOINTED?!
HEY, SHIRO!
LOOKS LIKE YOU'RE TAKING IT EASY, HUH?
NOT REALLY.
AFTER THIS I'M SUPPOSED TO BABYSIT PANDORA.
Oh! Nice hat!
WOW, THAT'S ROUGH.
Yikes!
YEAH, BUT SOUNDS LIKE THE DIRECTOR'S AWAY TODAY, SO I'M OKAY.
AND?
WHAT'S YOUR DEAL, MOZART?
DON'T YOU HAVE TO PREP FOR TOMORROW?
TWITCH
I...

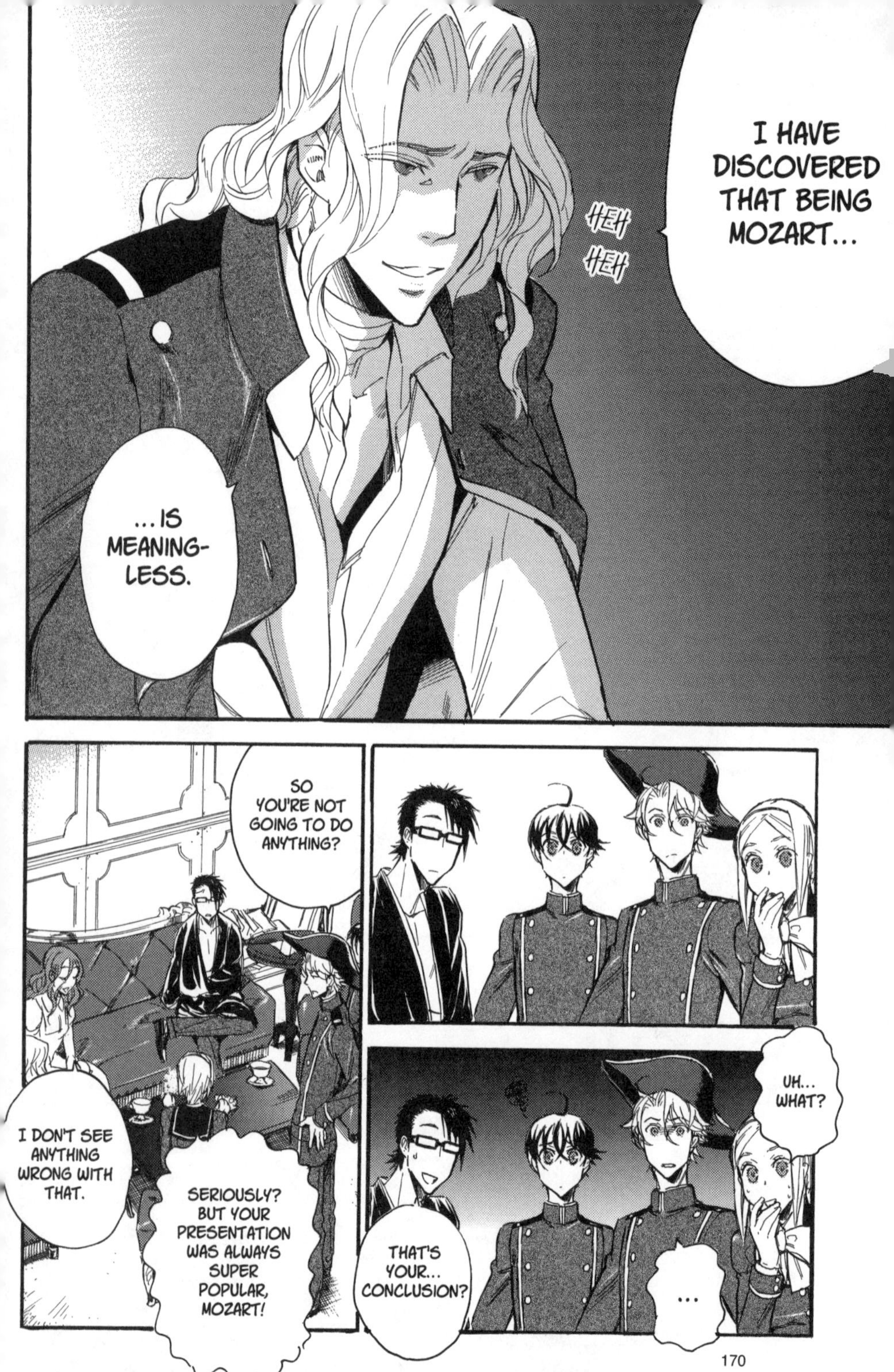
I HAVE DISCOVERED THAT BEING MOZART...
HEH HEH
...IS MEANING-LESS.
UH... WHAT?
...
THAT'S YOUR... CONCLUSION?
SO YOU'RE NOT GOING TO DO ANYTHING?
I DON'T SEE ANYTHING WRONG WITH THAT.
SERIOUSLY? BUT YOUR PRESENTATION WAS ALWAYS SUPER POPULAR, MOZART!

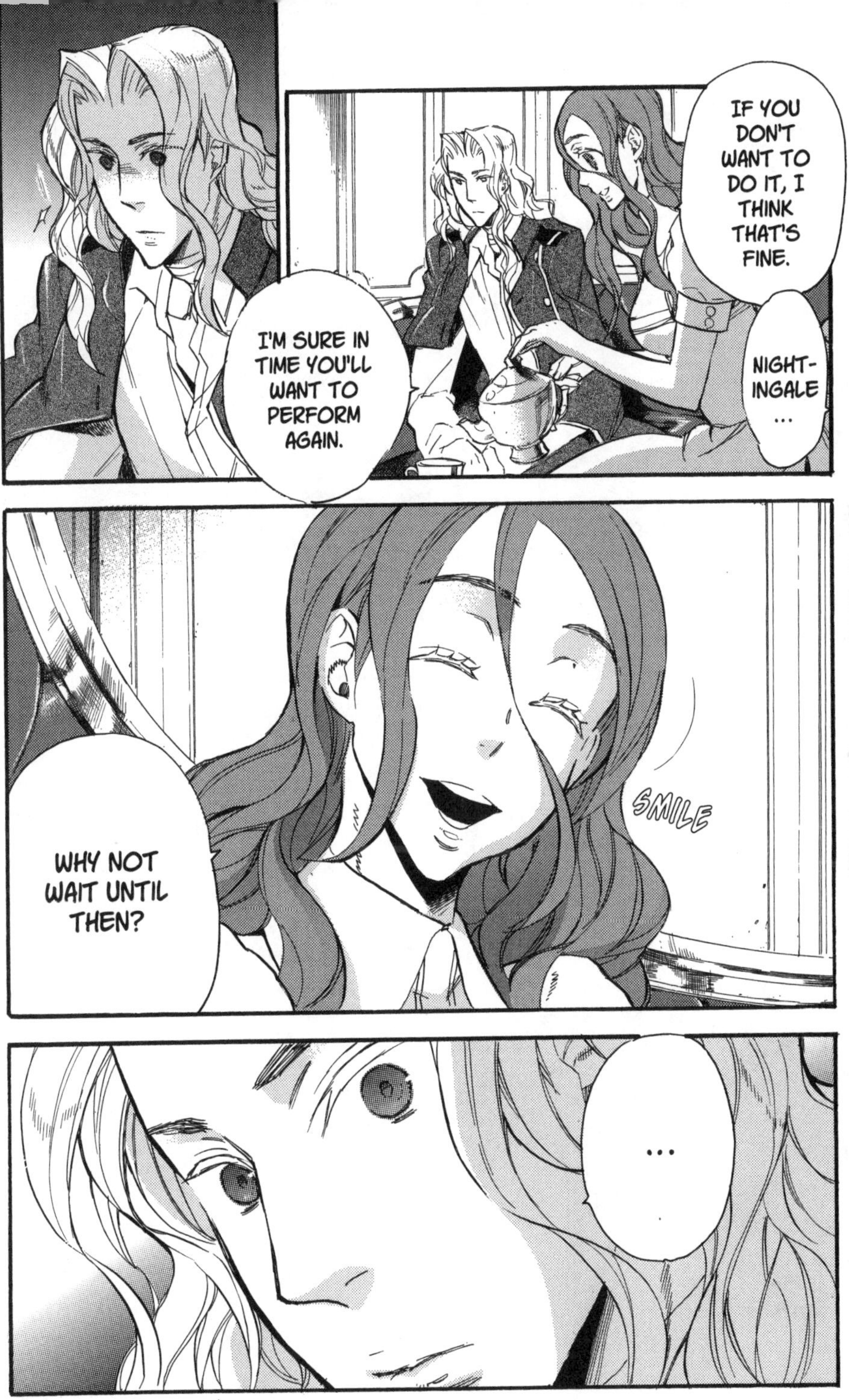
IF YOU DON'T WANT TO DO IT, I THINK THAT'S FINE.
NIGHT-INGALE...
I'M SURE IN TIME YOU'LL WANT TO PERFORM AGAIN.
SMILE
WHY NOT WAIT UNTIL THEN?
...

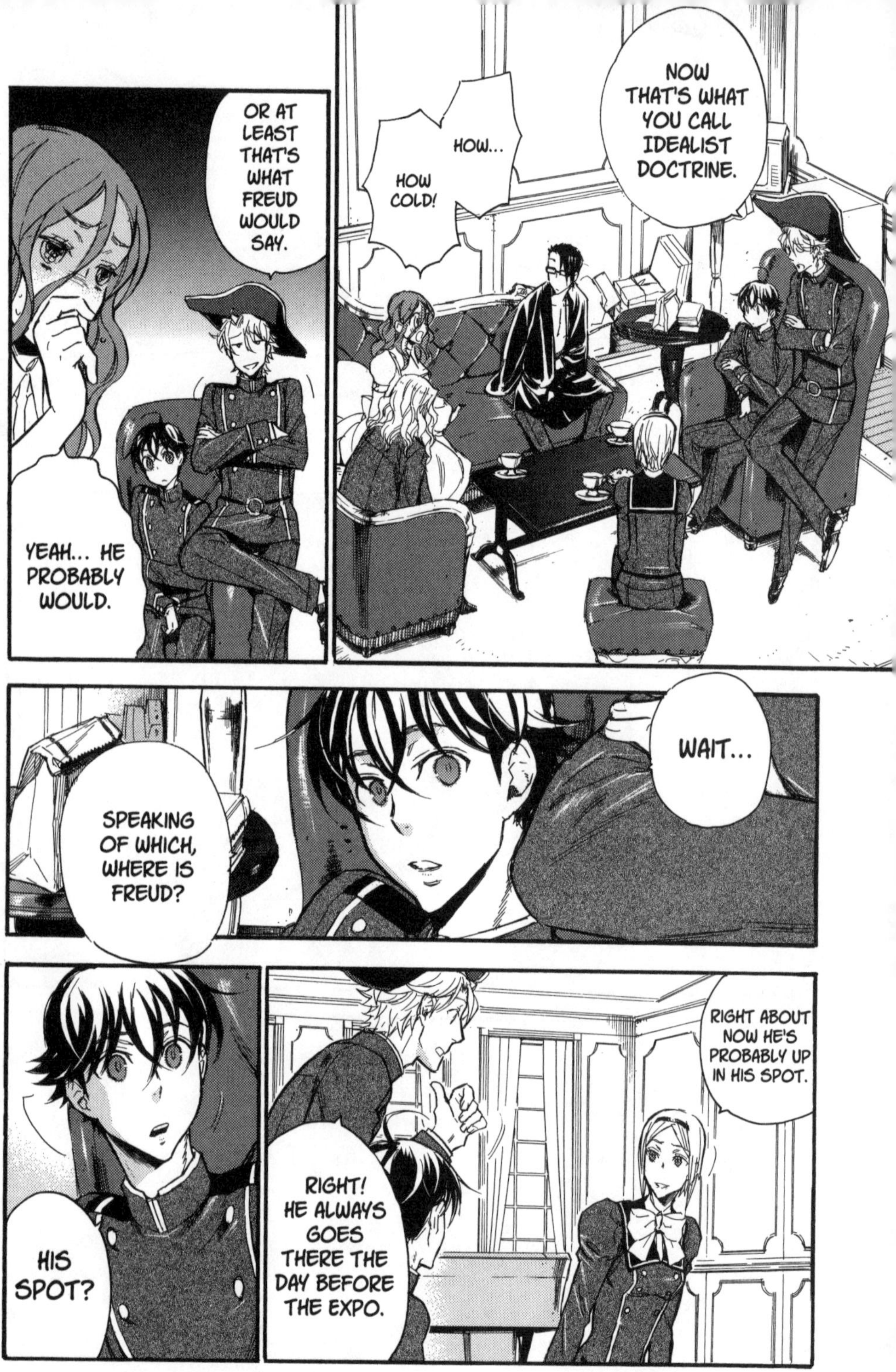
NOW THAT'S WHAT YOU CALL IDEALIST DOCTRINE.
HOW...
HOW COLD!
OR AT LEAST THAT'S WHAT FREUD WOULD SAY.
YEAH... HE PROBABLY WOULD.
WAIT...
SPEAKING OF WHICH, WHERE IS FREUD?
RIGHT ABOUT NOW HE'S PROBABLY UP IN HIS SPOT.
RIGHT! HE ALWAYS GOES THERE THE DAY BEFORE THE EXPO.
HIS SPOT?

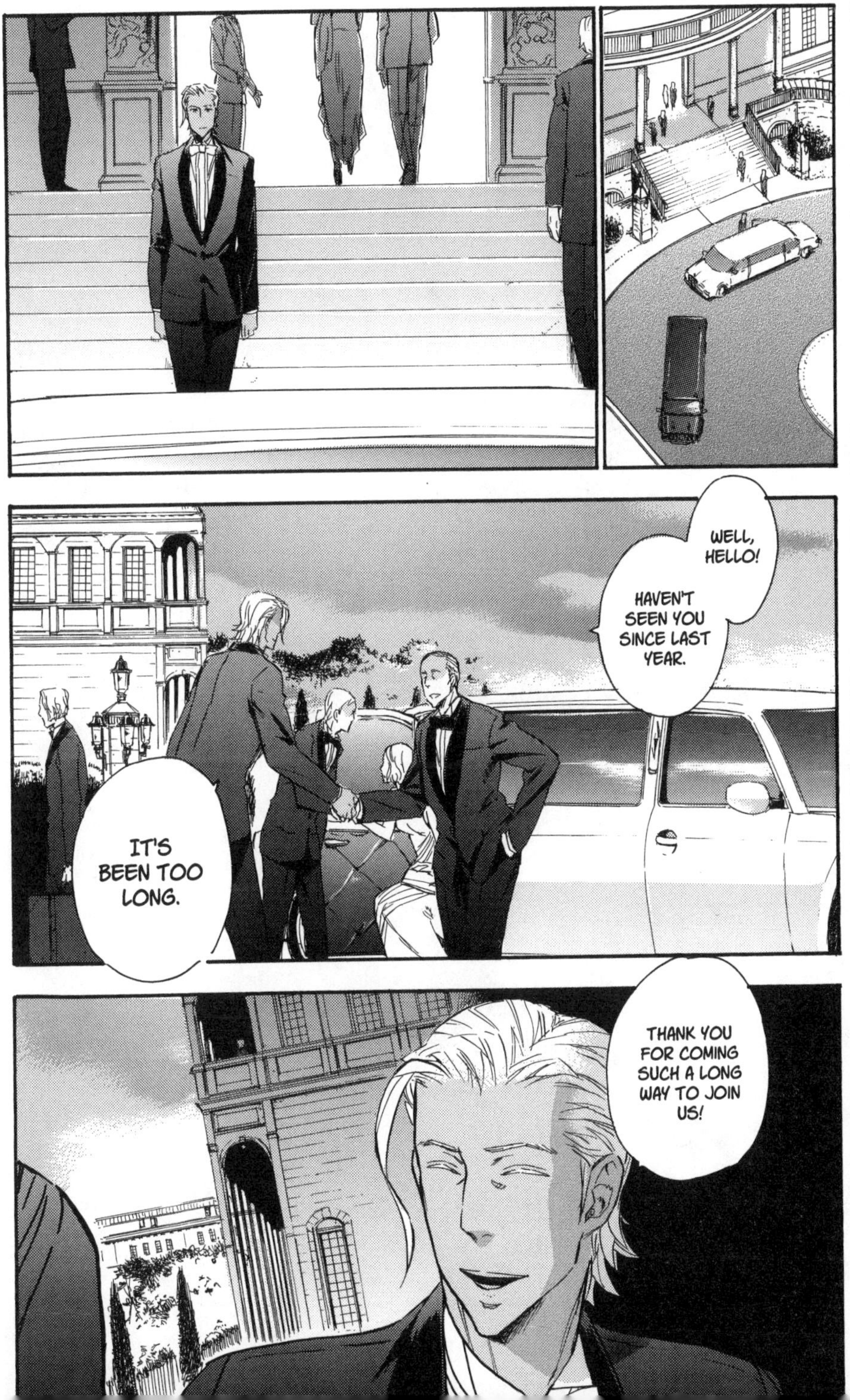
WELL, HELLO!
HAVEN'T SEEN YOU SINCE LAST YEAR.
IT'S BEEN TOO LONG.
THANK YOU FOR COMING SUCH A LONG WAY TO JOIN US!

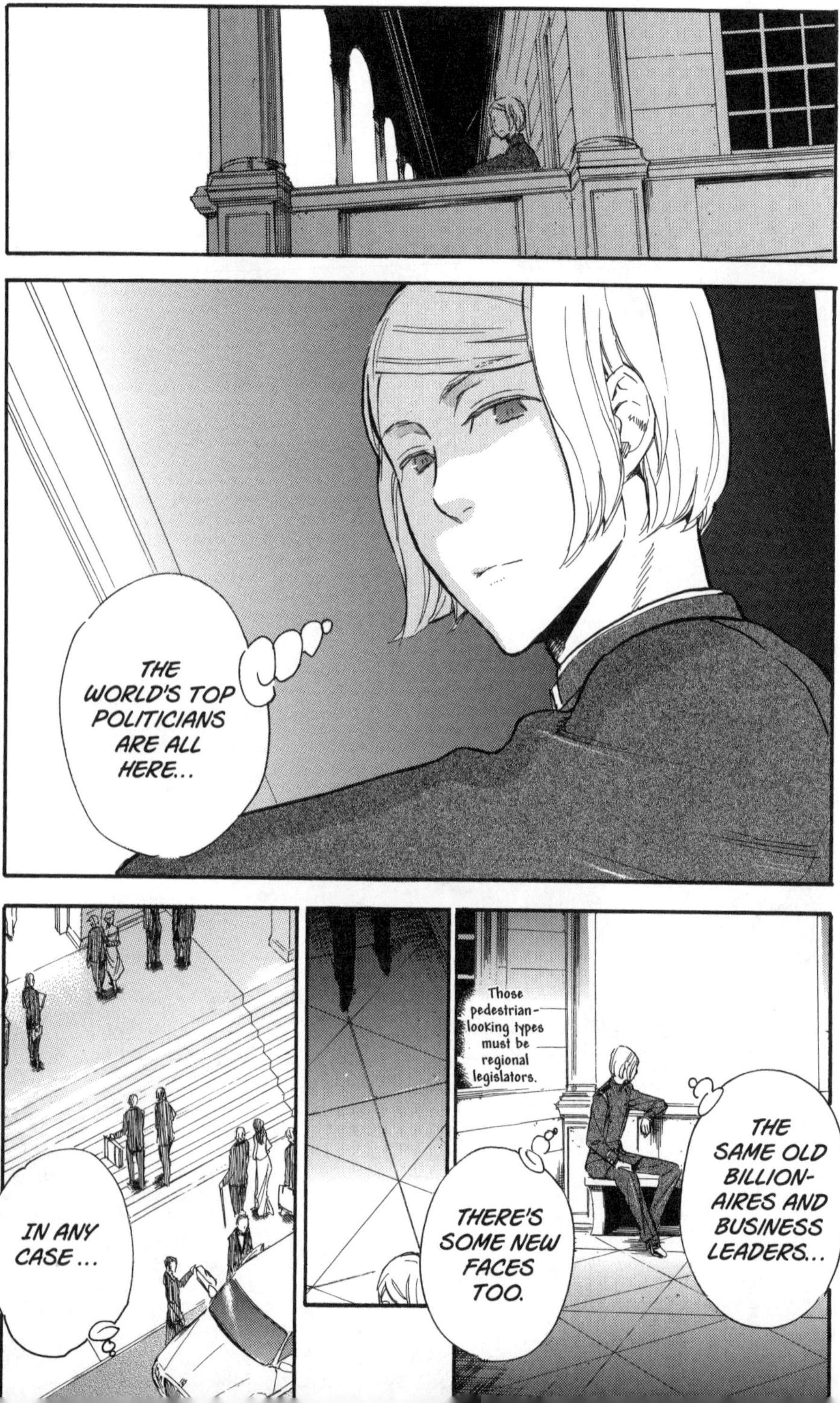
THE WORLD'S TOP POLITICIANS ARE ALL HERE...
THE SAME OLD BILLION-AIRES AND BUSINESS LEADERS...
Those pedestrian-looking types must be regional legislators.
THERE'S SOME NEW FACES TOO.
IN ANY CASE...

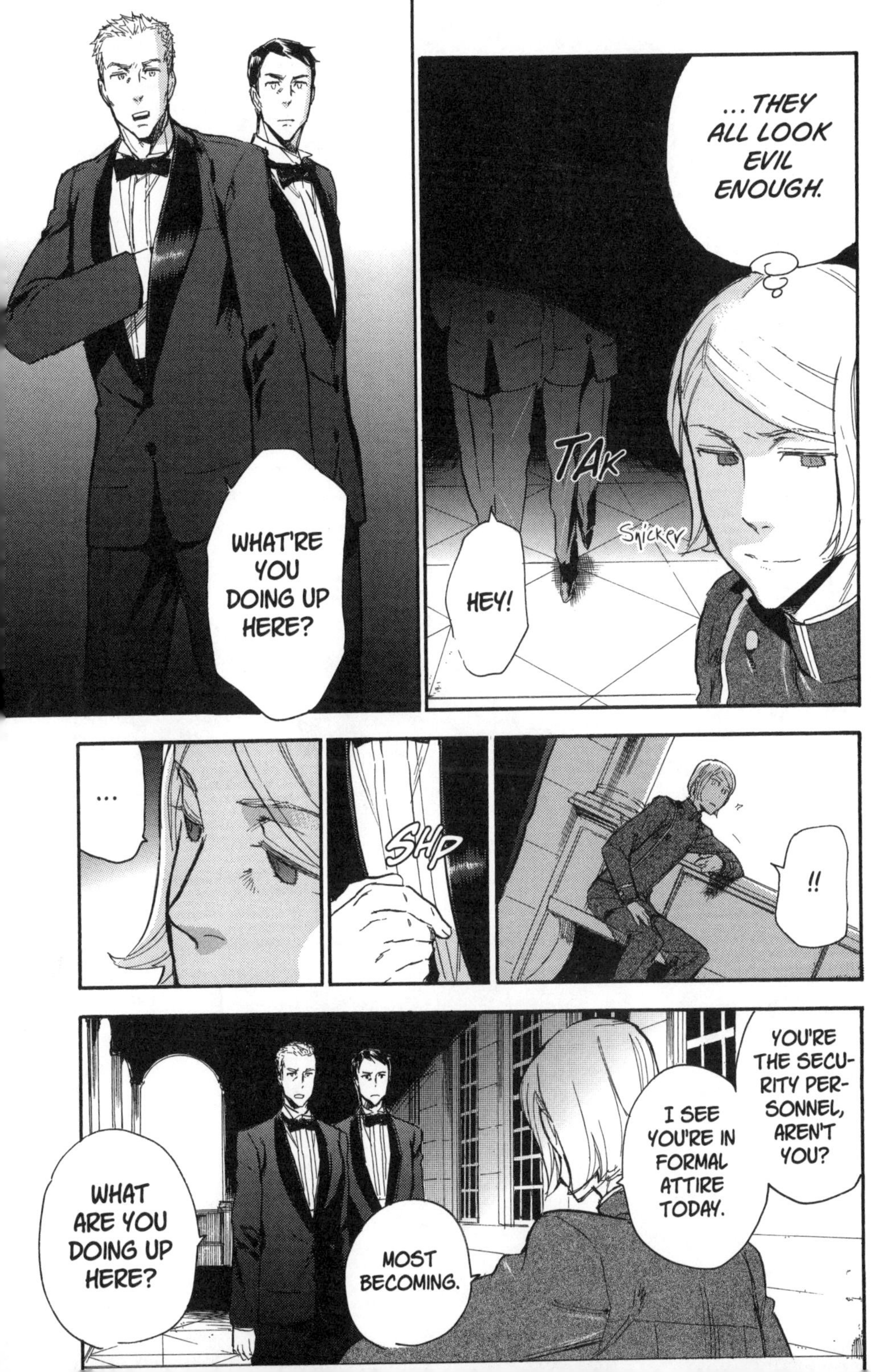
...THEY ALL LOOK EVIL ENOUGH.
TAK
Snicker
HEY!
WHAT'RE YOU DOING UP HERE?
!!
SHP
...
YOU'RE THE SECU-RITY PER-SONNEL, AREN'T YOU?
I SEE YOU'RE IN FORMAL ATTIRE TODAY.
MOST BECOMING.
WHAT ARE YOU DOING UP HERE?

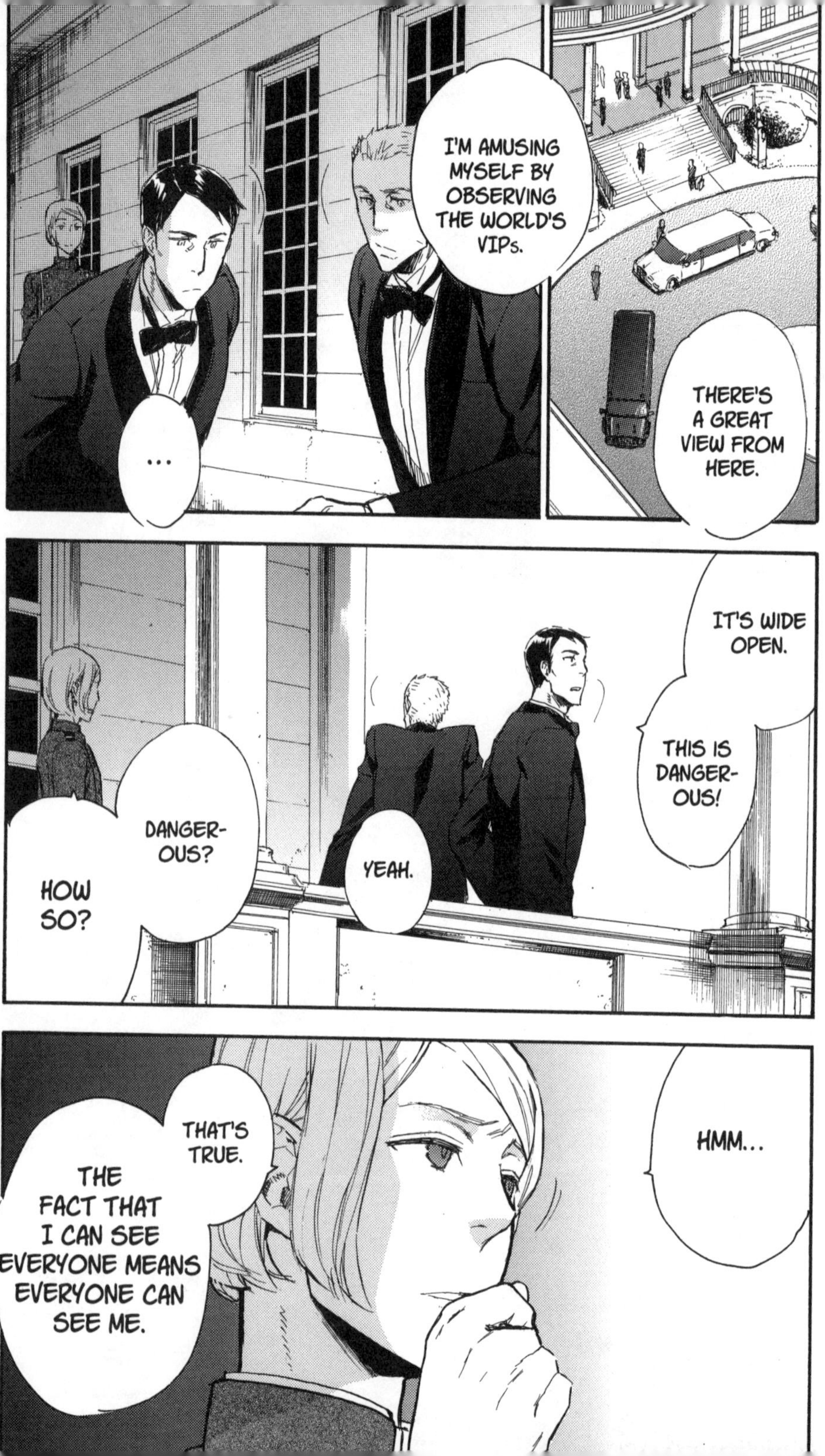
I'M AMUSING MYSELF BY OBSERVING THE WORLD'S VIPs.
THERE'S A GREAT VIEW FROM HERE.
...
IT'S WIDE OPEN.
THIS IS DANGEROUS!
YEAH.
DANGEROUS?
HOW SO?
HMM...
THAT'S TRUE.
THE FACT THAT I CAN SEE EVERYONE MEANS EVERYONE CAN SEE ME.

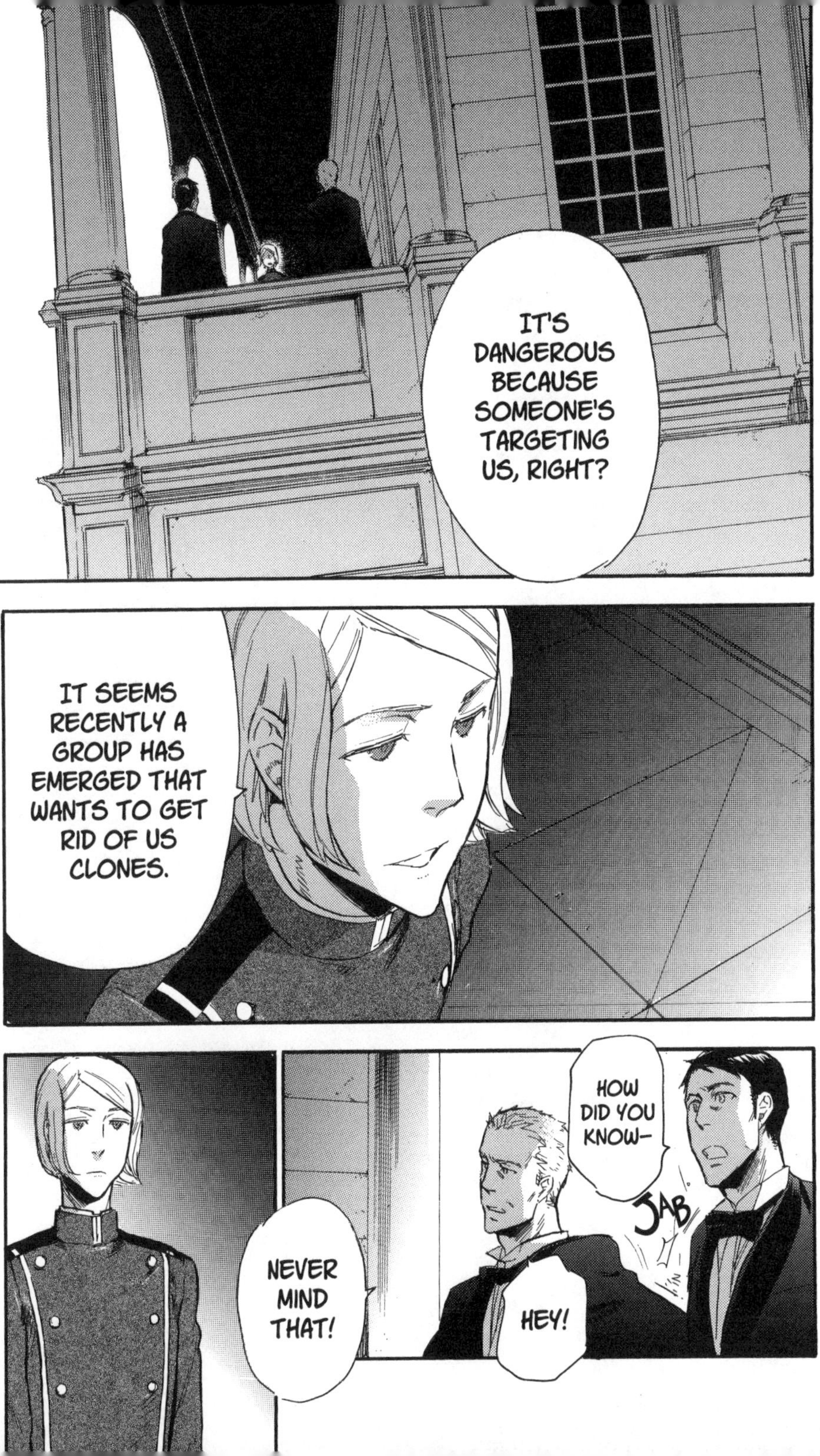
IT'S DANGEROUS BECAUSE SOMEONE'S TARGETING US, RIGHT?
IT SEEMS RECENTLY A GROUP HAS EMERGED THAT WANTS TO GET RID OF US CLONES.
HOW DID YOU KNOW-
JAB
HEY!
NEVER MIND THAT!

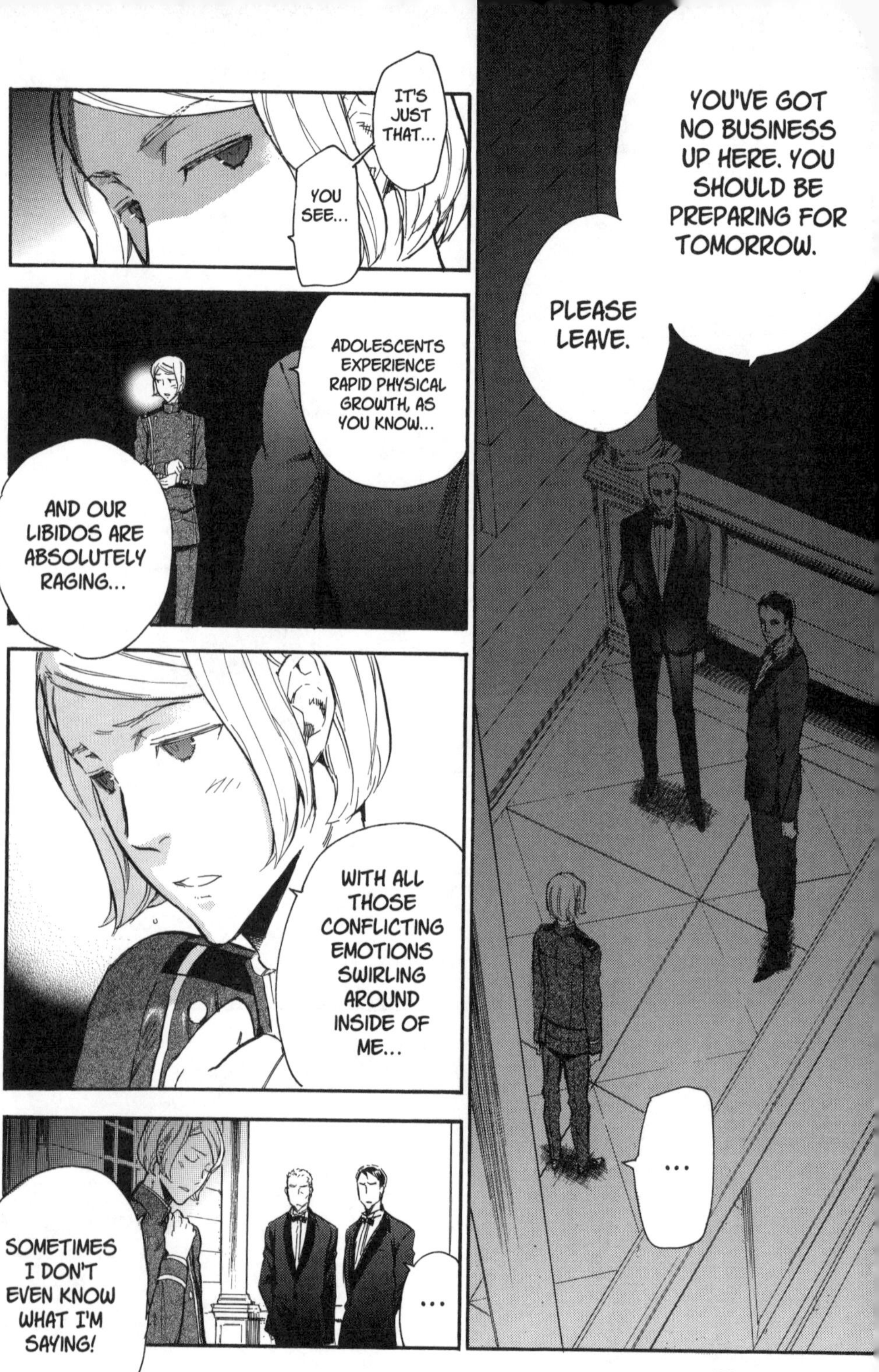
YOU'VE GOT NO BUSINESS UP HERE. YOU SHOULD BE PREPARING FOR TOMORROW.
PLEASE LEAVE.
...
IT'S JUST THAT...
YOU SEE...
ADOLESCENTS EXPERIENCE RAPID PHYSICAL GROWTH, AS YOU KNOW...
AND OUR LIBIDOS ARE ABSOLUTELY RAGING...
WITH ALL THOSE CONFLICTING EMOTIONS SWIRLING AROUND INSIDE OF ME...
...
SOMETIMES I DON'T EVEN KNOW WHAT I'M SAYING!

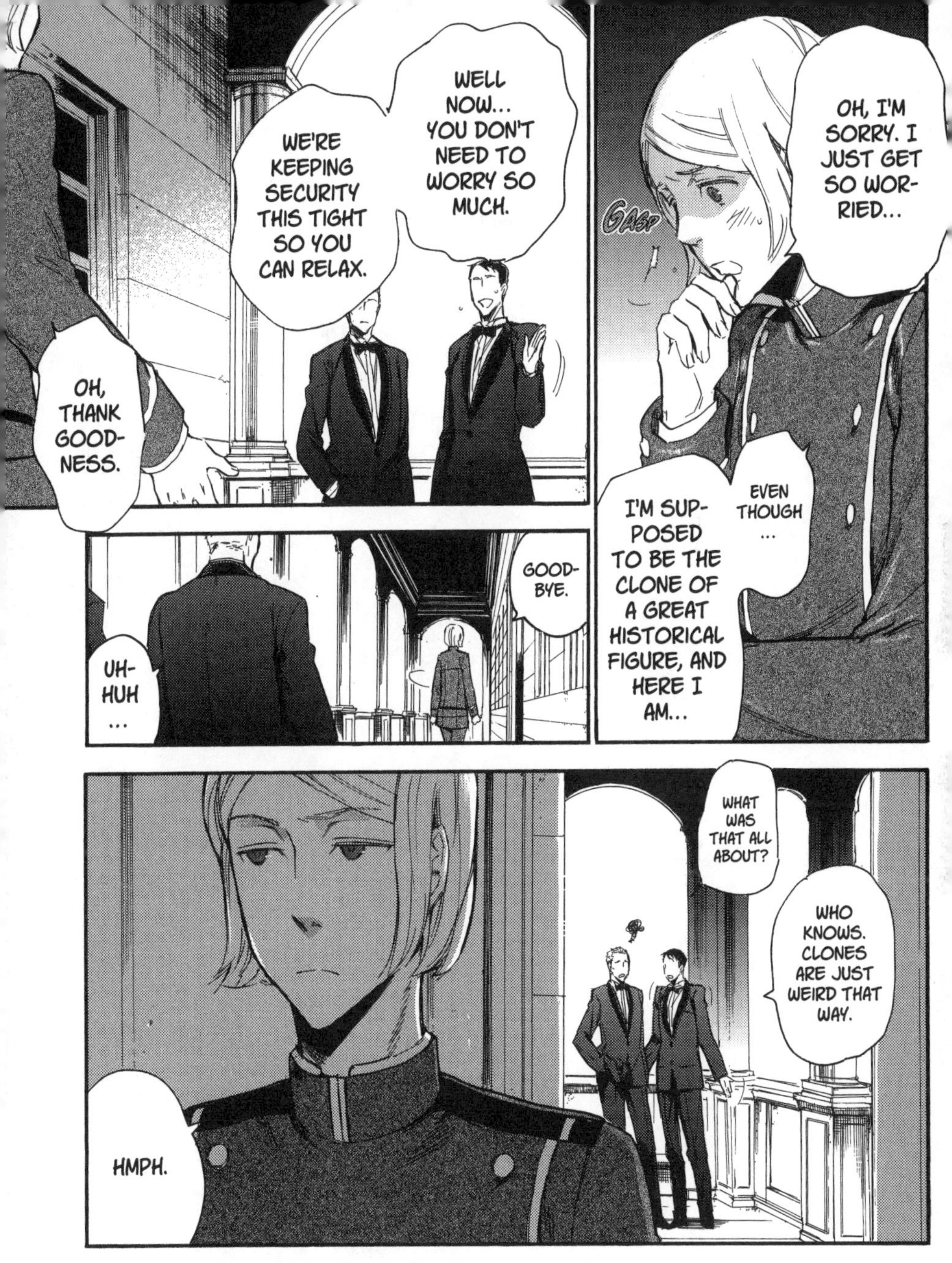

GASP
OH, I'M SORRY. I JUST GET SO WORRIED...
EVEN THOUGH...
I'M SUPPOSED TO BE THE CLONE OF A GREAT HISTORICAL FIGURE, AND HERE I AM...
WELL NOW... YOU DON'T NEED TO WORRY SO MUCH.
WE'RE KEEPING SECURITY THIS TIGHT SO YOU CAN RELAX.
OH, THANK GOODNESS.
GOOD-BYE.
UH-HUH...
WHAT WAS THAT ALL ABOUT?
WHO KNOWS. CLONES ARE JUST WEIRD THAT WAY.
HMPH.

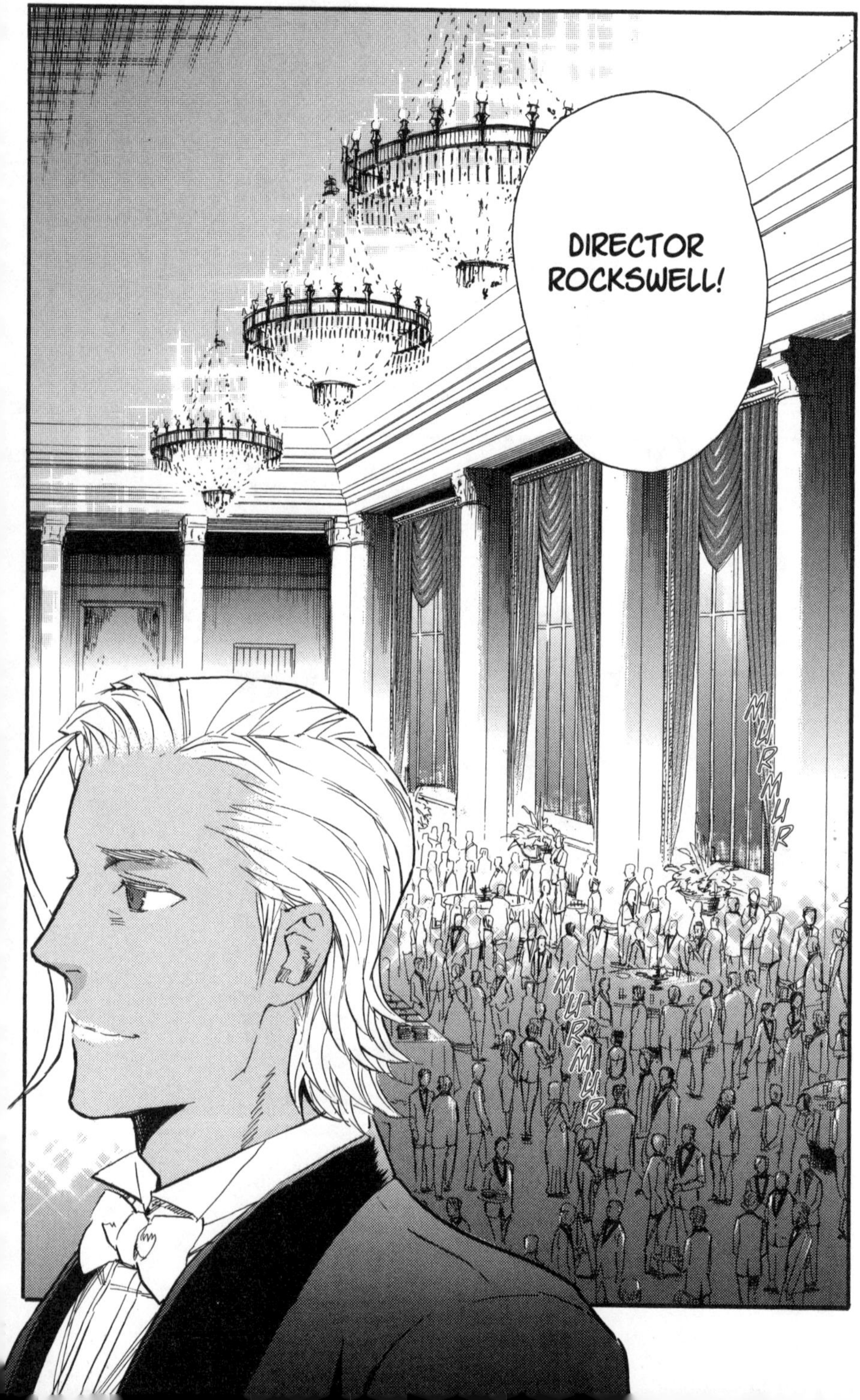
DIRECTOR ROCKSWELL!
MURMUR
MURMUR

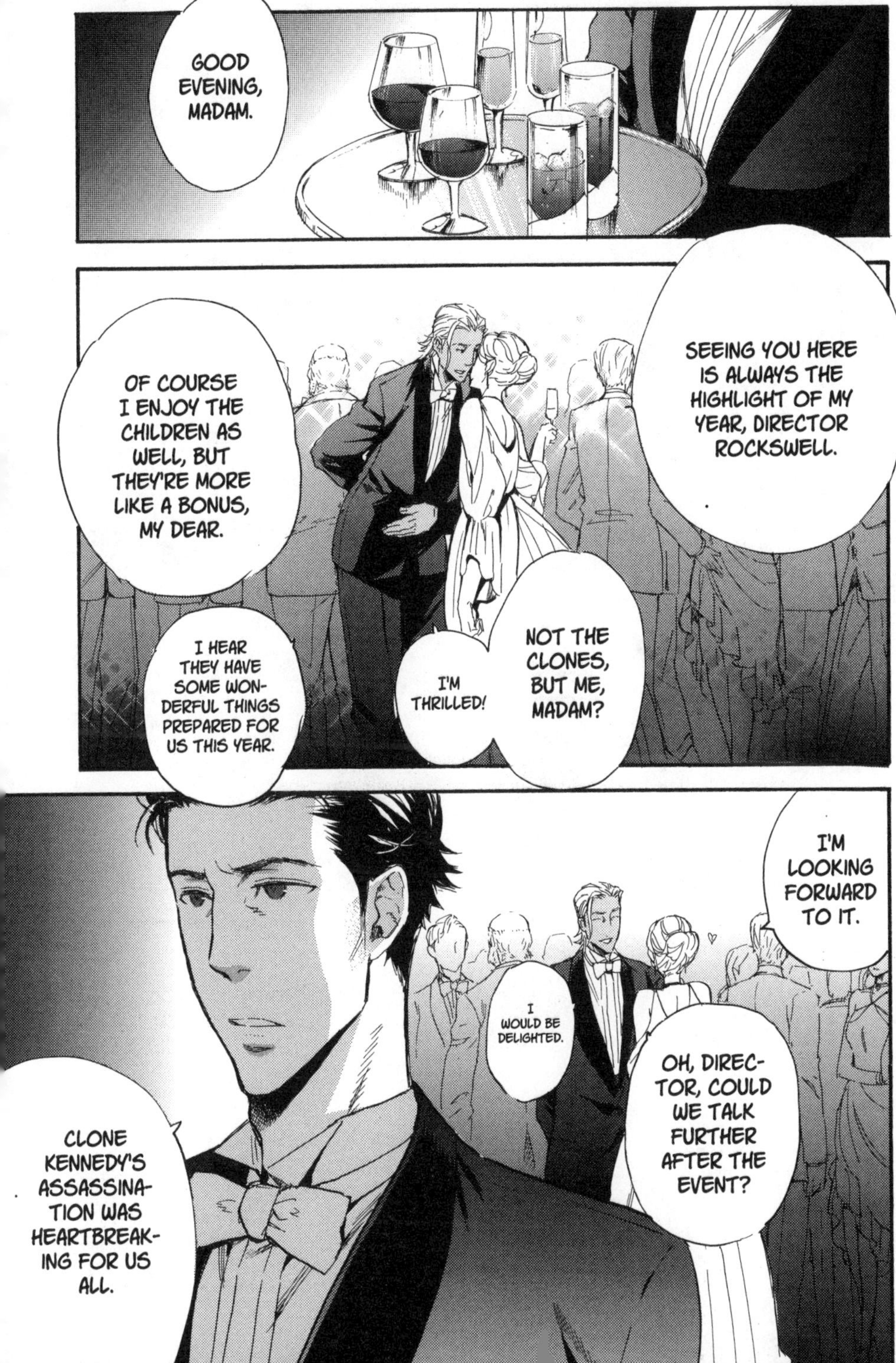
GOOD EVENING, MADAM.
SEEING YOU HERE IS ALWAYS THE HIGHLIGHT OF MY YEAR, DIRECTOR ROCKSWELL.
OF COURSE I ENJOY THE CHILDREN AS WELL, BUT THEY'RE MORE LIKE A BONUS, MY DEAR.
NOT THE CLONES, BUT ME, MADAM?
I'M THRILLED!
I HEAR THEY HAVE SOME WON-DERFUL THINGS PREPARED FOR US THIS YEAR.
I'M LOOKING FORWARD TO IT.
OH, DIREC-TOR, COULD WE TALK FURTHER AFTER THE EVENT?
I WOULD BE DELIGHTED.
CLONE KENNEDY'S ASSASSINA-TION WAS HEARTBREAK-ING FOR US ALL.

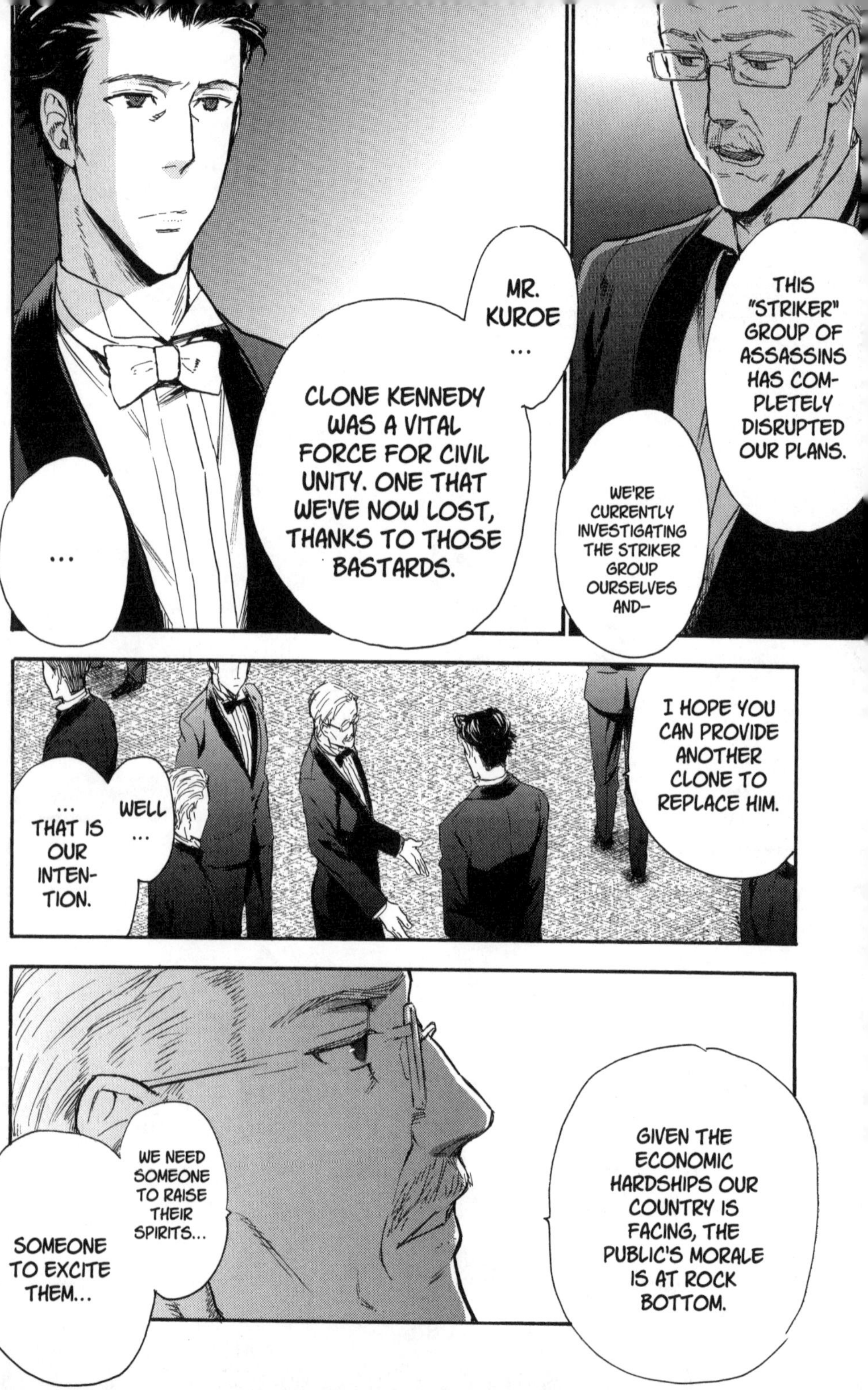

THIS "STRIKER" GROUP OF ASSASSINS HAS COMPLETELY DISRUPTED OUR PLANS.
WE'RE CURRENTLY INVESTIGATING THE STRIKER GROUP OURSELVES AND—
MR. KUROE...
CLONE KENNEDY WAS A VITAL FORCE FOR CIVIL UNITY. ONE THAT WE'VE NOW LOST, THANKS TO THOSE BASTARDS.
...
I HOPE YOU CAN PROVIDE ANOTHER CLONE TO REPLACE HIM.
WELL...
...THAT IS OUR INTENTION.
GIVEN THE ECONOMIC HARDSHIPS OUR COUNTRY IS FACING, THE PUBLIC'S MORALE IS AT ROCK BOTTOM.
WE NEED SOMEONE TO RAISE THEIR SPIRITS...
SOMEONE TO EXCITE THEM...

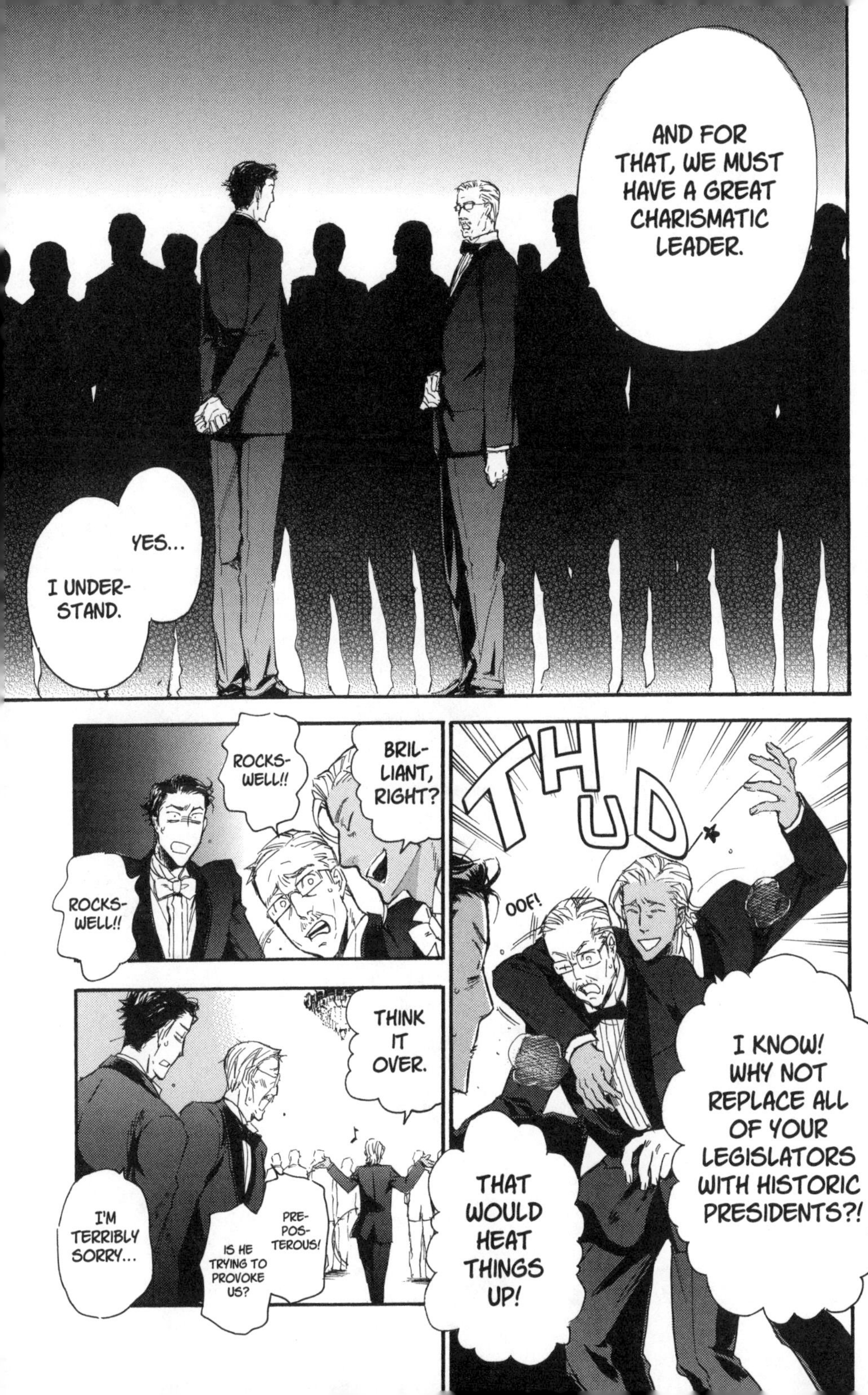
AND FOR THAT, WE MUST HAVE A GREAT CHARISMATIC LEADER.
YES... I UNDER-STAND.
THUD
OOF!
I KNOW! WHY NOT REPLACE ALL OF YOUR LEGISLATORS WITH HISTORIC PRESIDENTS?!
THAT WOULD HEAT THINGS UP!
BRIL-LIANT, RIGHT?
ROCKS-WELL!!
ROCKS-WELL!!
THINK IT OVER.
PRE-POS-TEROUS!
IS HE TRYING TO PROVOKE US?
I'M TERRIBLY SORRY...

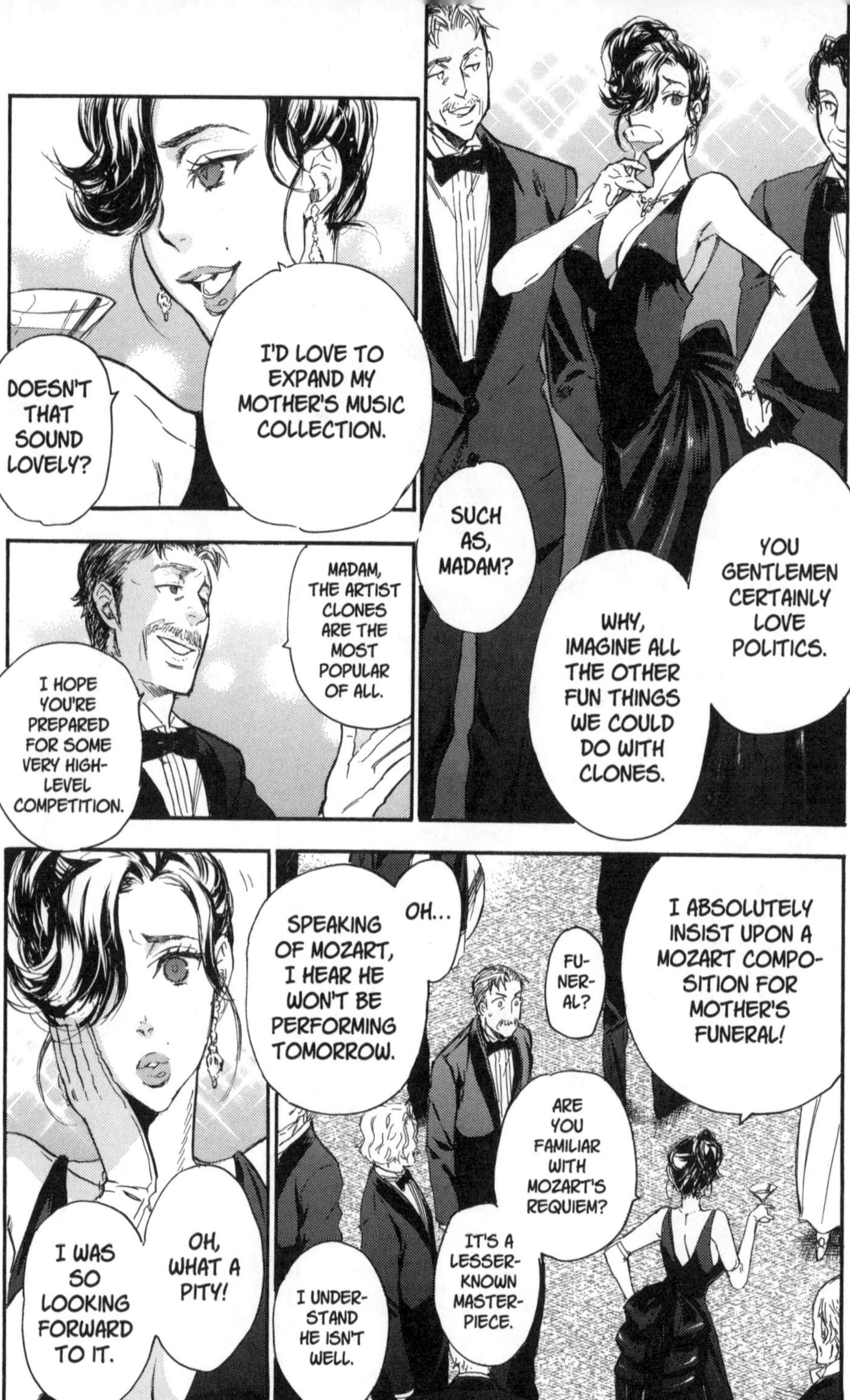

YOU GENTLEMEN CERTAINLY LOVE POLITICS.
WHY, IMAGINE ALL THE OTHER FUN THINGS WE COULD DO WITH CLONES.
SUCH AS, MADAM?
I'D LOVE TO EXPAND MY MOTHER'S MUSIC COLLECTION.
DOESN'T THAT SOUND LOVELY?
MADAM, THE ARTIST CLONES ARE THE MOST POPULAR OF ALL.
I HOPE YOU'RE PREPARED FOR SOME VERY HIGH-LEVEL COMPETITION.
I ABSOLUTELY INSIST UPON A MOZART COMPOSITION FOR MOTHER'S FUNERAL!
FU-NER-AL?
ARE YOU FAMILIAR WITH MOZART'S REQUIEM?
IT'S A LESSER-KNOWN MASTER-PIECE.
OH...
SPEAKING OF MOZART, I HEAR HE WON'T BE PERFORMING TOMORROW.
I UNDER-STAND HE ISN'T WELL.
OH, WHAT A PITY!
I WAS SO LOOKING FORWARD TO IT.

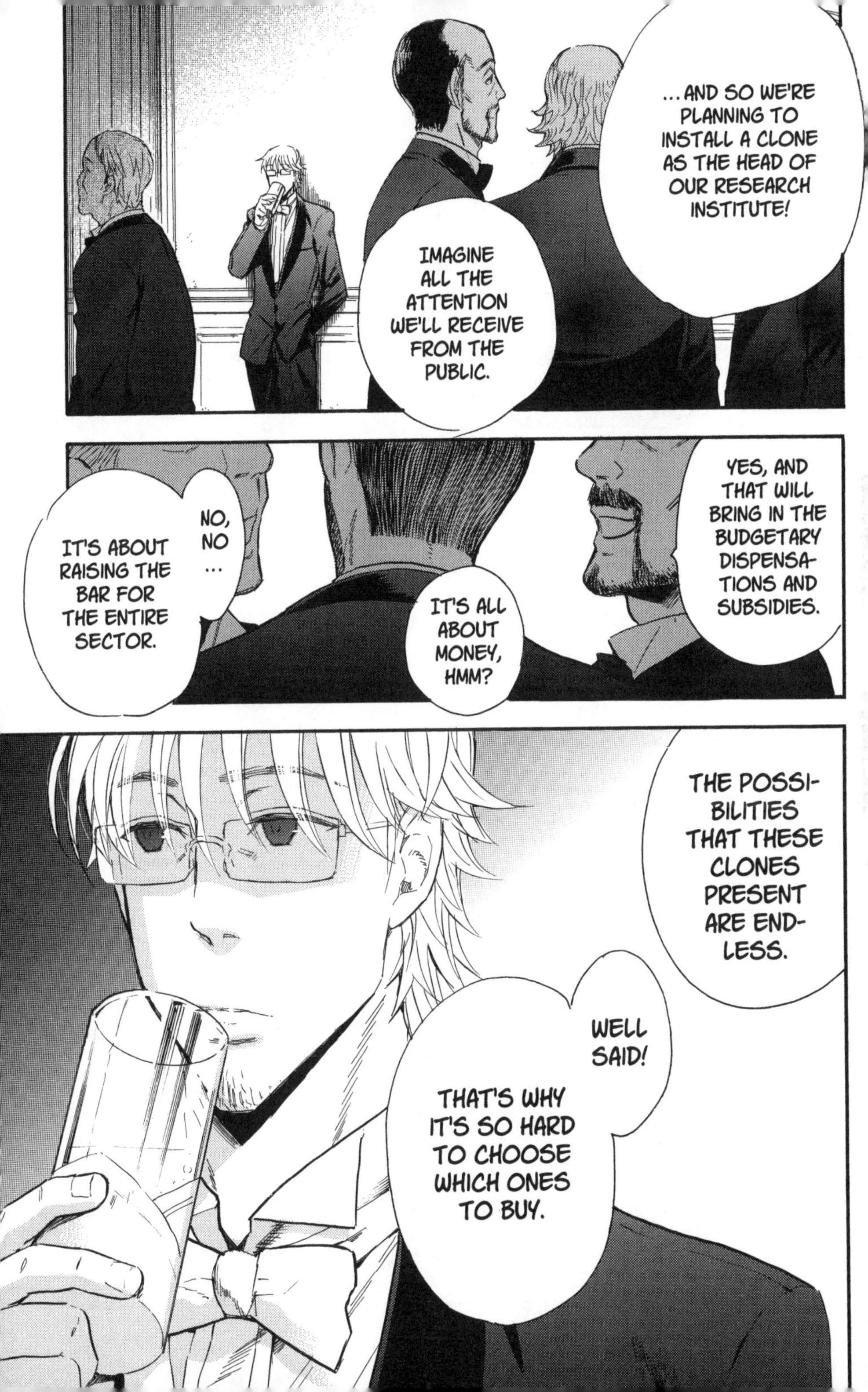
...AND SO WE'RE PLANNING TO INSTALL A CLONE AS THE HEAD OF OUR RESEARCH INSTITUTE!
IMAGINE ALL THE ATTENTION WE'LL RECEIVE FROM THE PUBLIC.
YES, AND THAT WILL BRING IN THE BUDGETARY DISPENSATIONS AND SUBSIDIES.
IT'S ALL ABOUT MONEY, HMM?
NO, NO ...
IT'S ABOUT RAISING THE BAR FOR THE ENTIRE SECTOR.
THE POSSIBILITIES THAT THESE CLONES PRESENT ARE ENDLESS.
WELL SAID!
THAT'S WHY IT'S SO HARD TO CHOOSE WHICH ONES TO BUY.

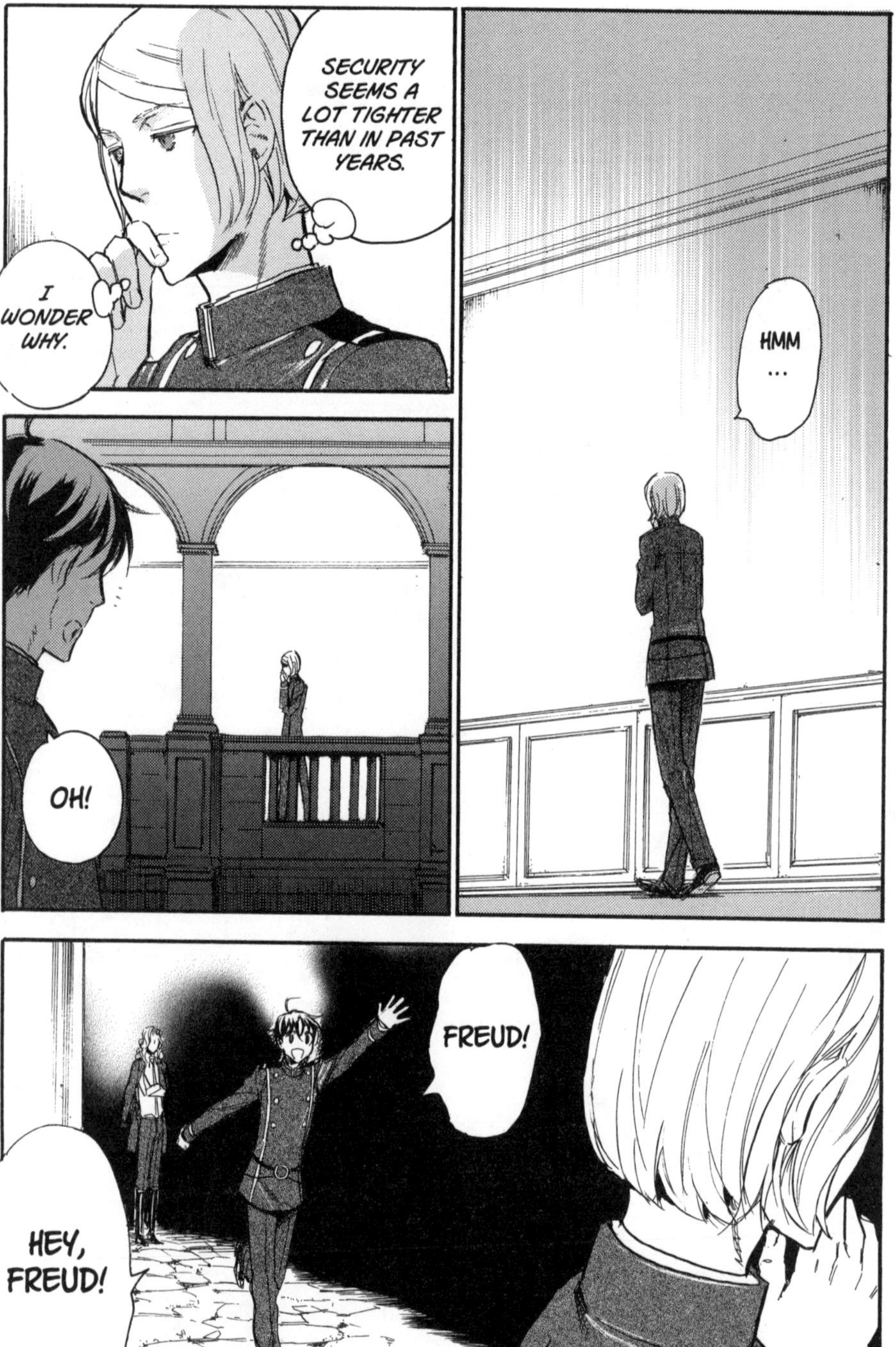
HMM ...
SECURITY SEEMS A LOT TIGHTER THAN IN PAST YEARS.
I WONDER WHY.
OH!
FREUD!
HEY, FREUD!

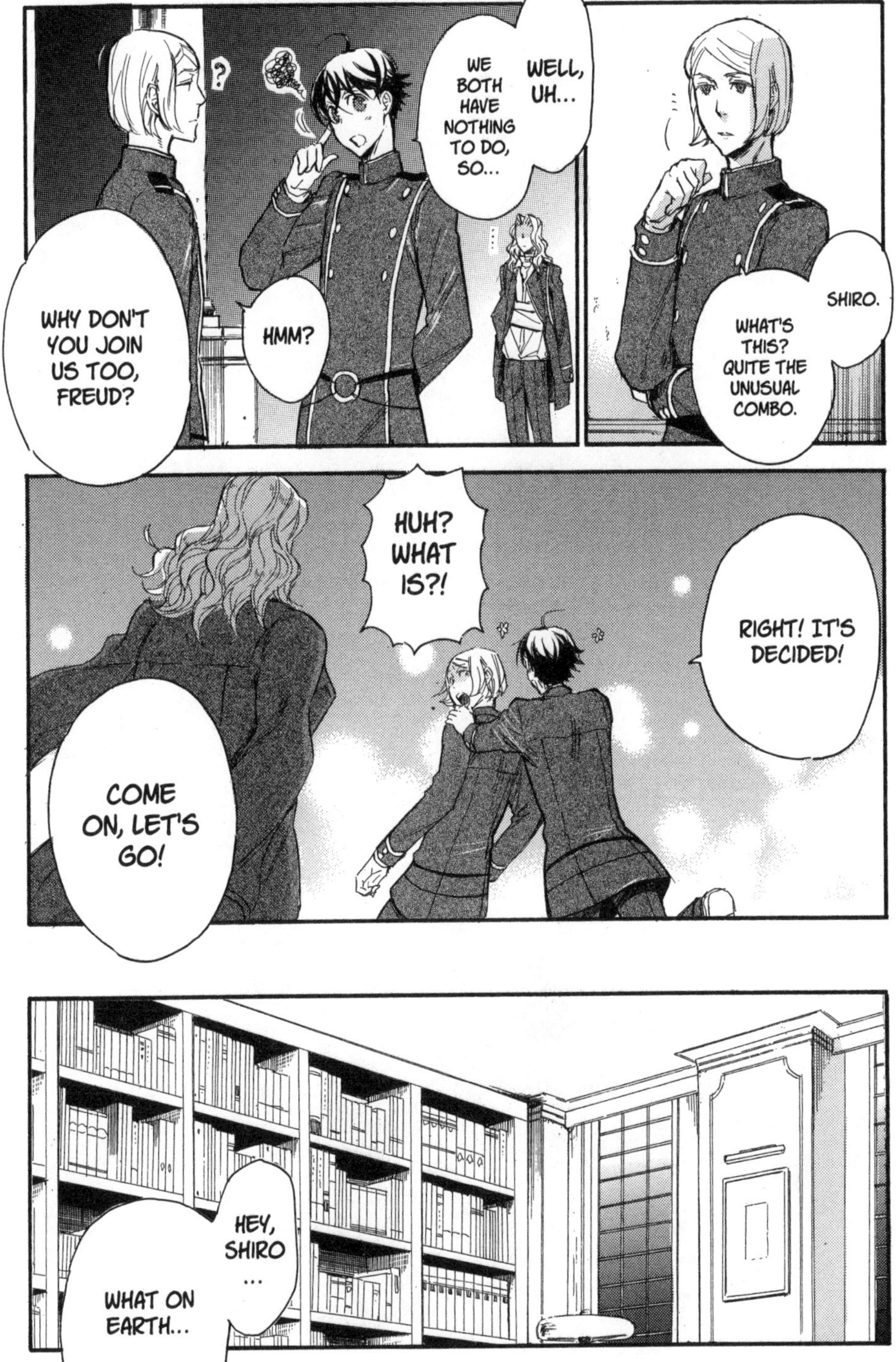
SHIRO.
WHAT'S THIS? QUITE THE UNUSUAL COMBO.
WELL, UH...
WE BOTH HAVE NOTHING TO DO, SO...
HMM?
WHY DON'T YOU JOIN US TOO, FREUD?
RIGHT! IT'S DECIDED!
HUH? WHAT IS?!
COME ON, LET'S GO!
HEY, SHIRO...
WHAT ON EARTH...

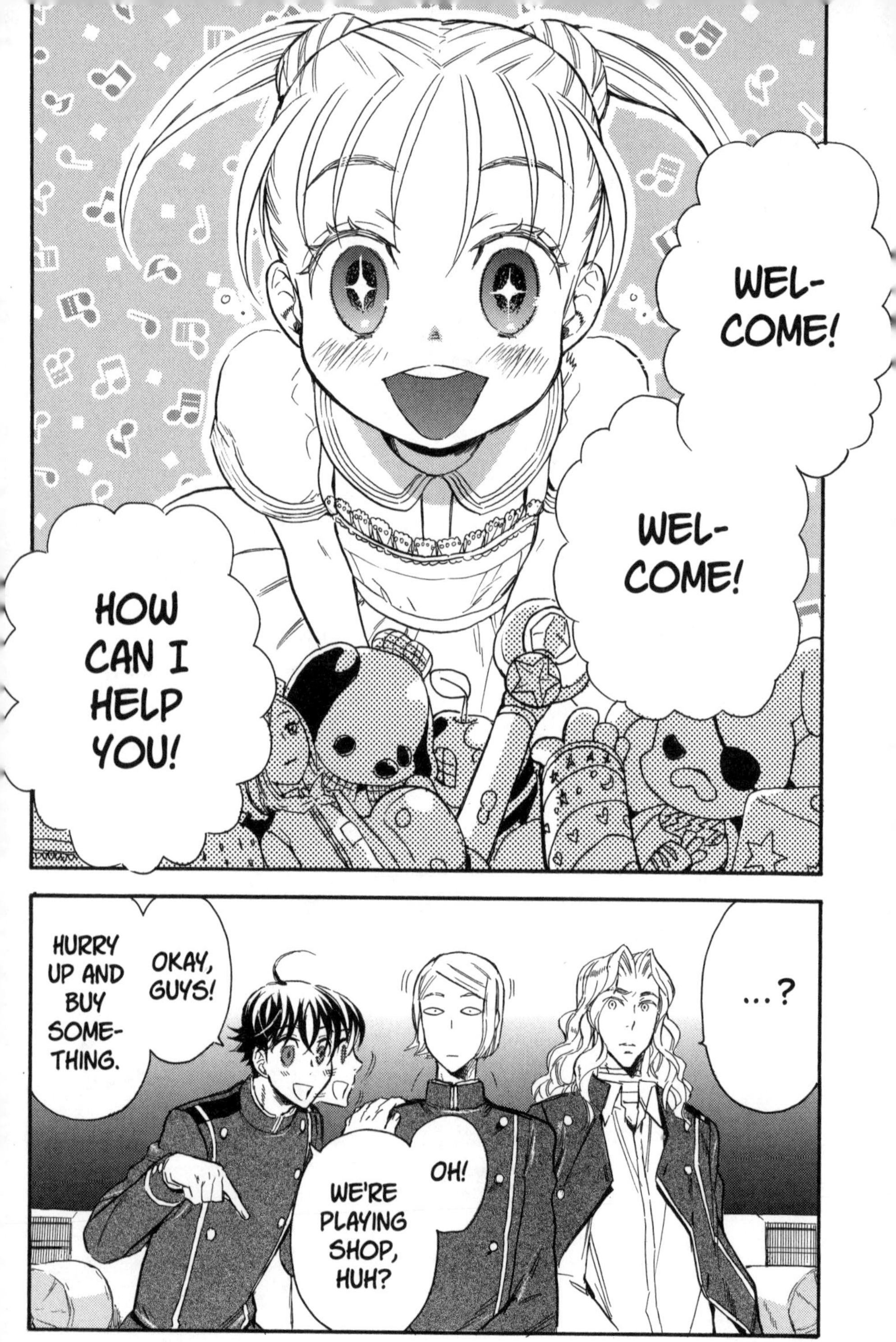
WEL-COME!
WEL-COME!
HOW CAN I HELP YOU!
...?
OKAY, GUYS!
HURRY UP AND BUY SOME-THING.
OH!
WE'RE PLAYING SHOP, HUH?

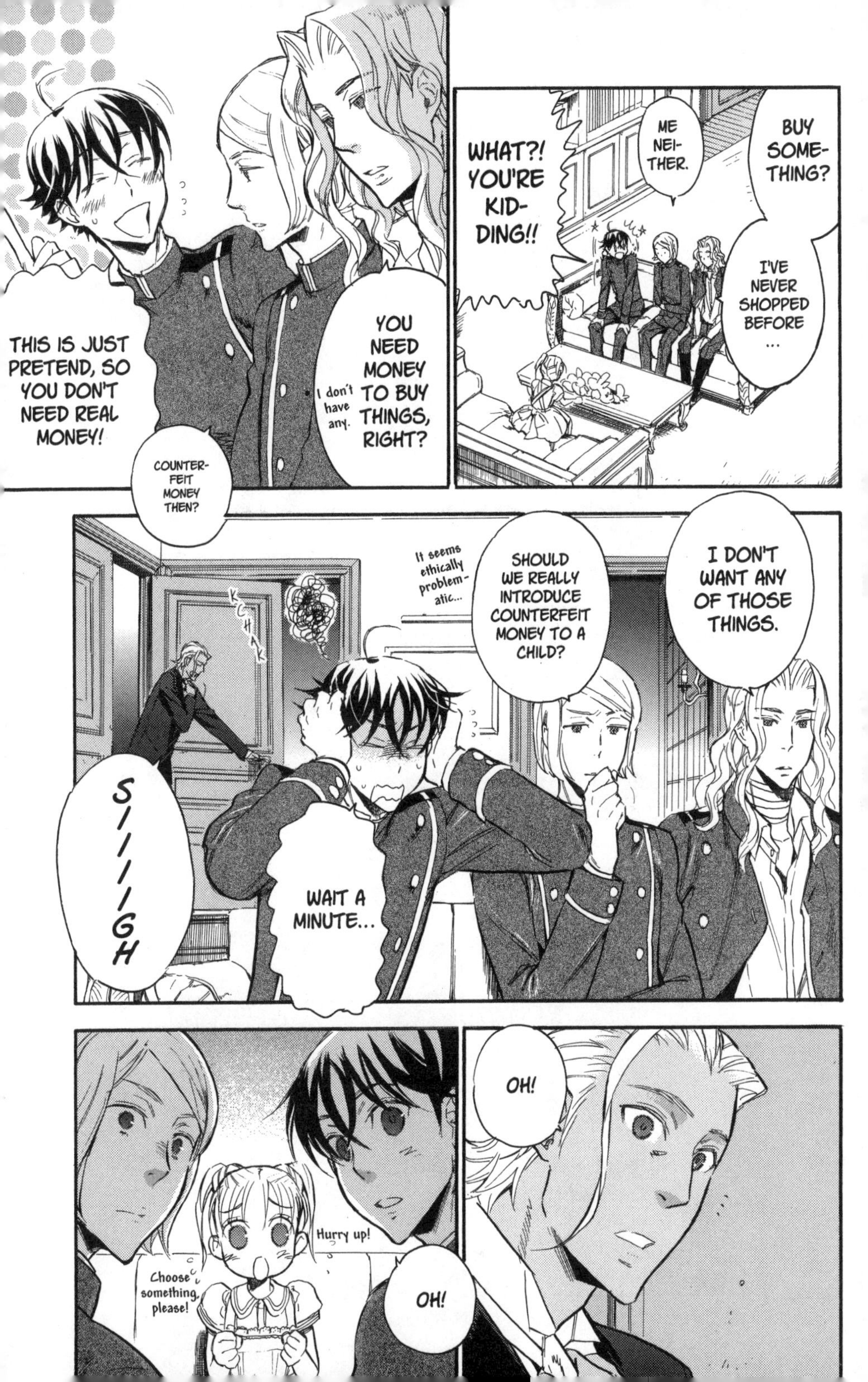
BUY SOME-THING?
I'VE NEVER SHOPPED BEFORE ...
ME NEI-THER.
WHAT?! YOU'RE KID-DING!!
YOU NEED MONEY TO BUY THINGS, RIGHT?
I don't have any.
THIS IS JUST PRETEND, SO YOU DON'T NEED REAL MONEY!
COUNTER-FEIT MONEY THEN?
I DON'T WANT ANY OF THOSE THINGS.
SHOULD WE REALLY INTRODUCE COUNTERFEIT MONEY TO A CHILD?
It seems ethically problem-atic...
KCHAK
WAIT A MINUTE...
SIIIIIGH
OH!
Hurry up!
OH!
Choose something, please!

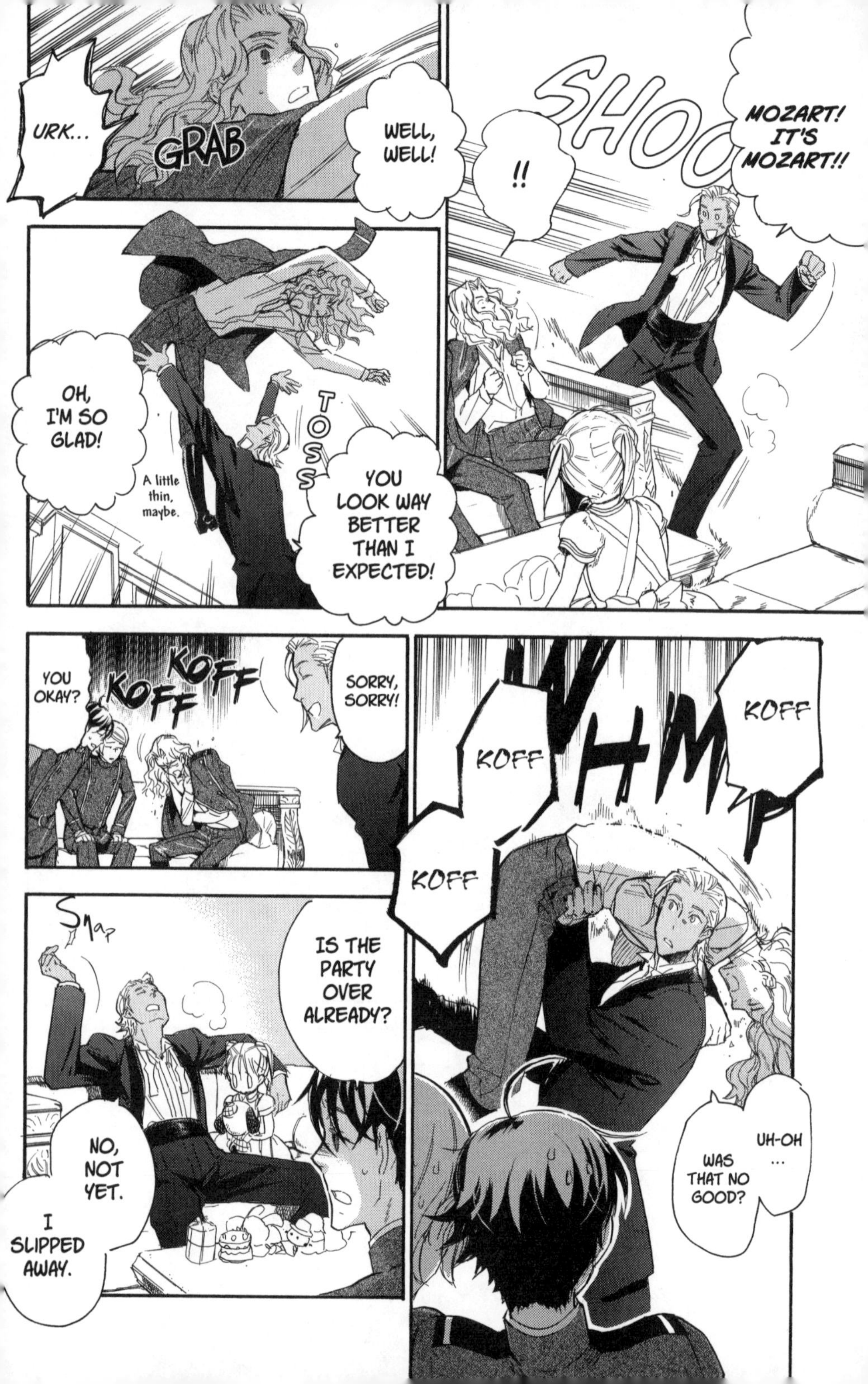
MOZART! IT'S MOZART!!
SHOOO
!!
WELL, WELL!
URK...
GRAB
TOSS
OH, I'M SO GLAD!
YOU LOOK WAY BETTER THAN I EXPECTED!
A little thin, maybe.
WHMP
KOFF
KOFF
KOFF
UH-OH ...
WAS THAT NO GOOD?
SORRY, SORRY!
KOFF KOFF
YOU OKAY?
IS THE PARTY OVER ALREADY?
Snap
NO, NOT YET.
I SLIPPED AWAY.

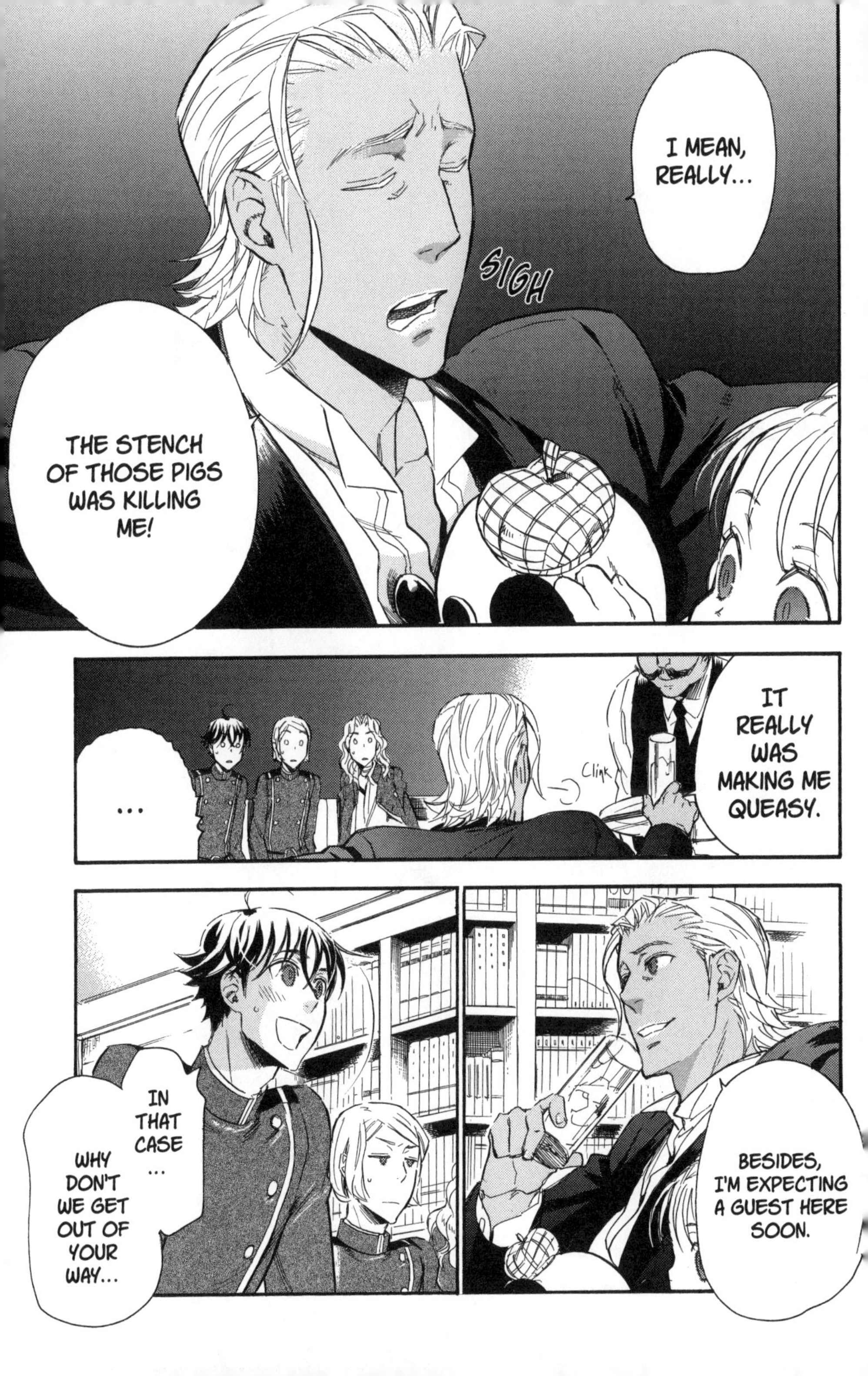
I MEAN, REALLY...
SIGH
THE STENCH OF THOSE PIGS WAS KILLING ME!
IT REALLY WAS MAKING ME QUEASY.
Clink
...
BESIDES, I'M EXPECTING A GUEST HERE SOON.
IN THAT CASE...
WHY DON'T WE GET OUT OF YOUR WAY...

OH NO... IT'S FINE.
I want to go.
BUT ...
STAY!
PLEASE COME IN.
HOORAY! ♡
HOP
PANDO-RA?
DART
HEY THERE!
COME ON OVER HERE.

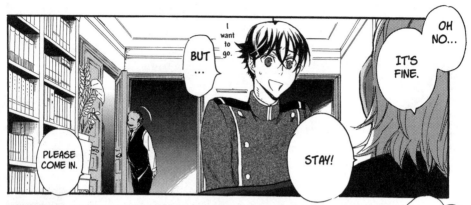

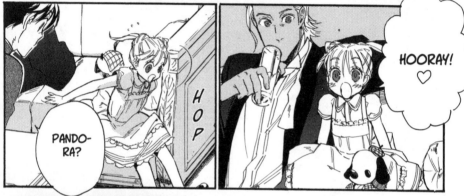

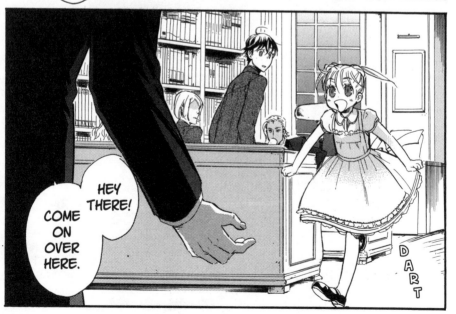

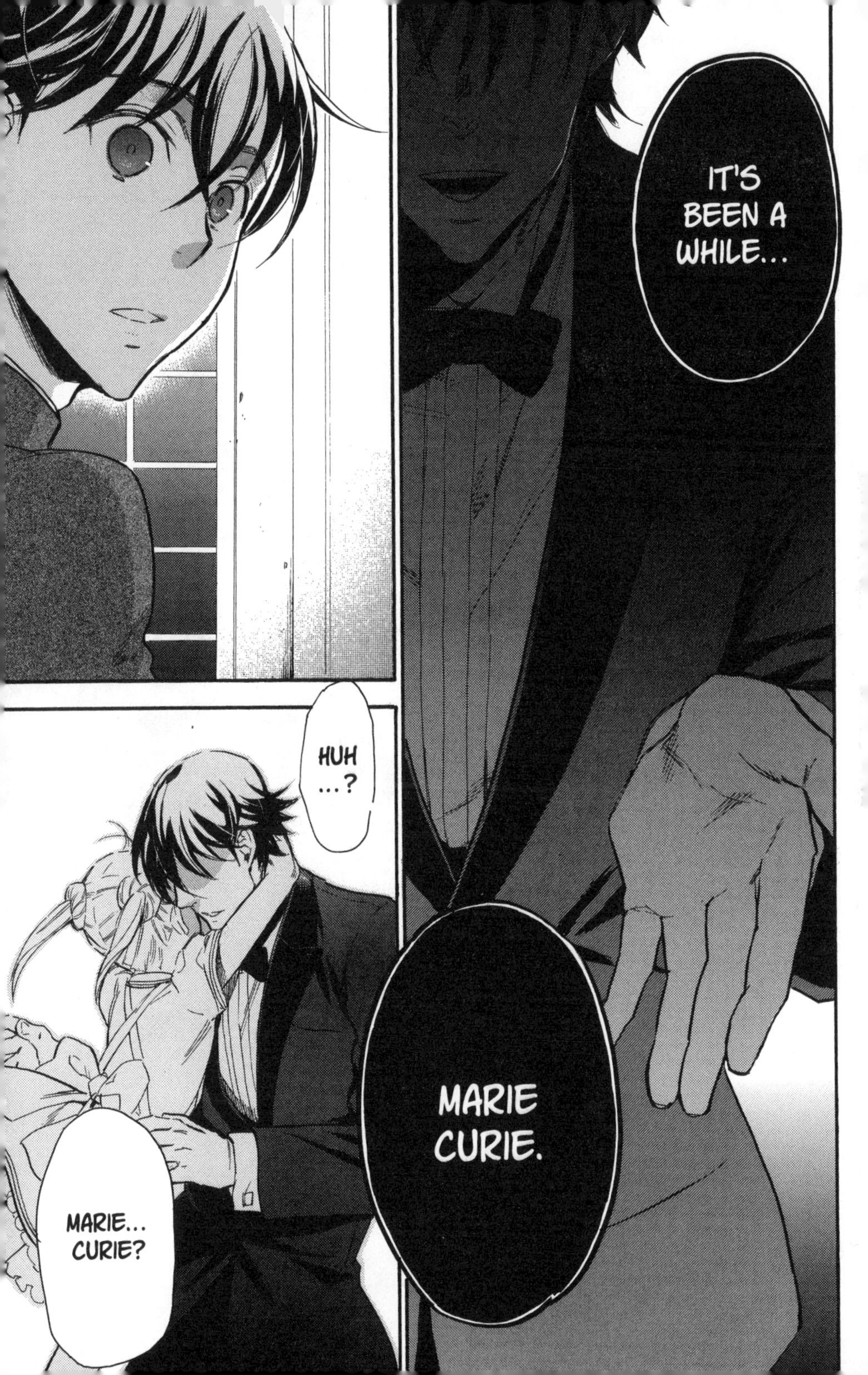
IT'S BEEN A WHILE...
MARIE CURIE.
HUH ...?
MARIE... CURIE?

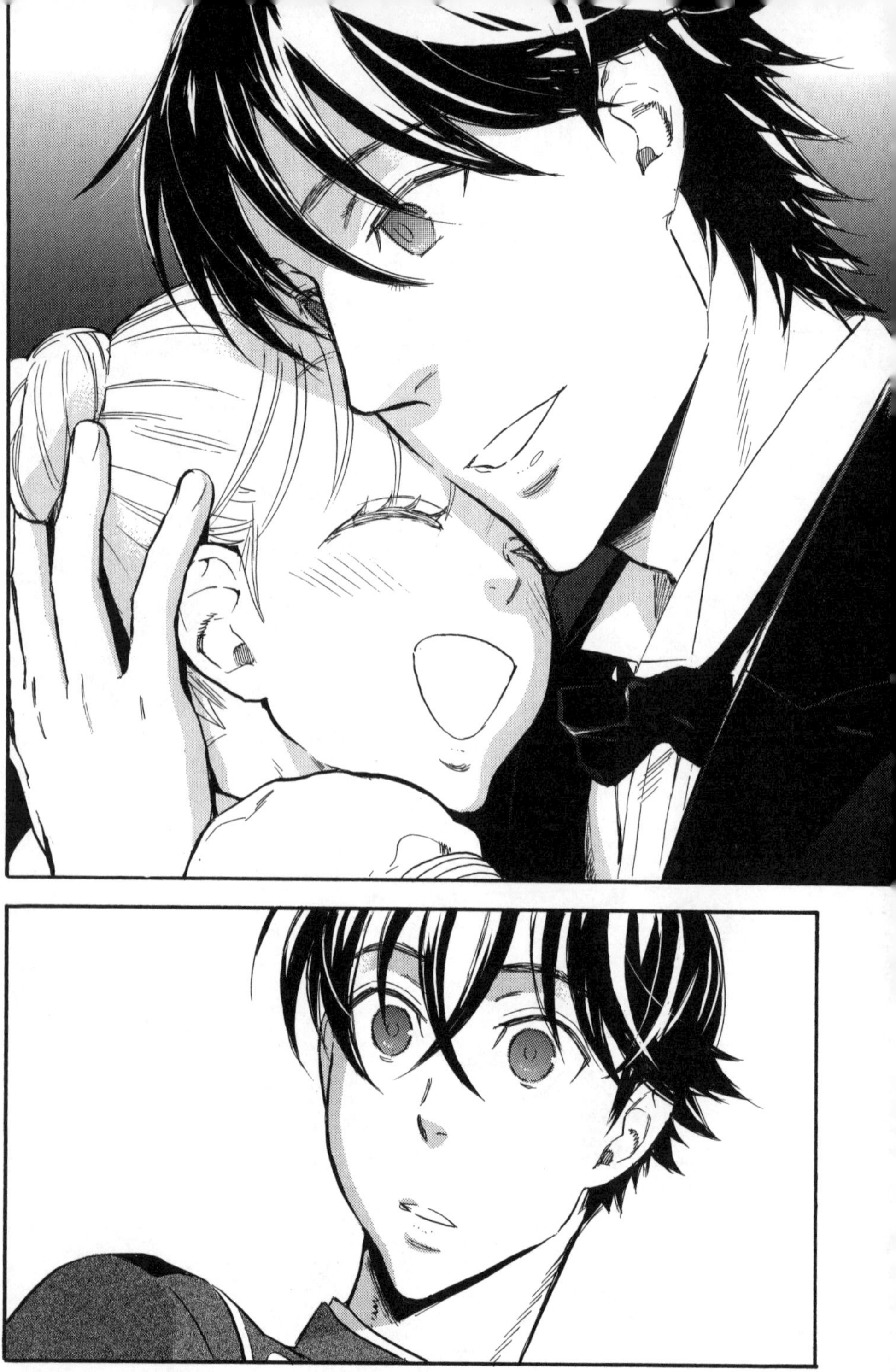

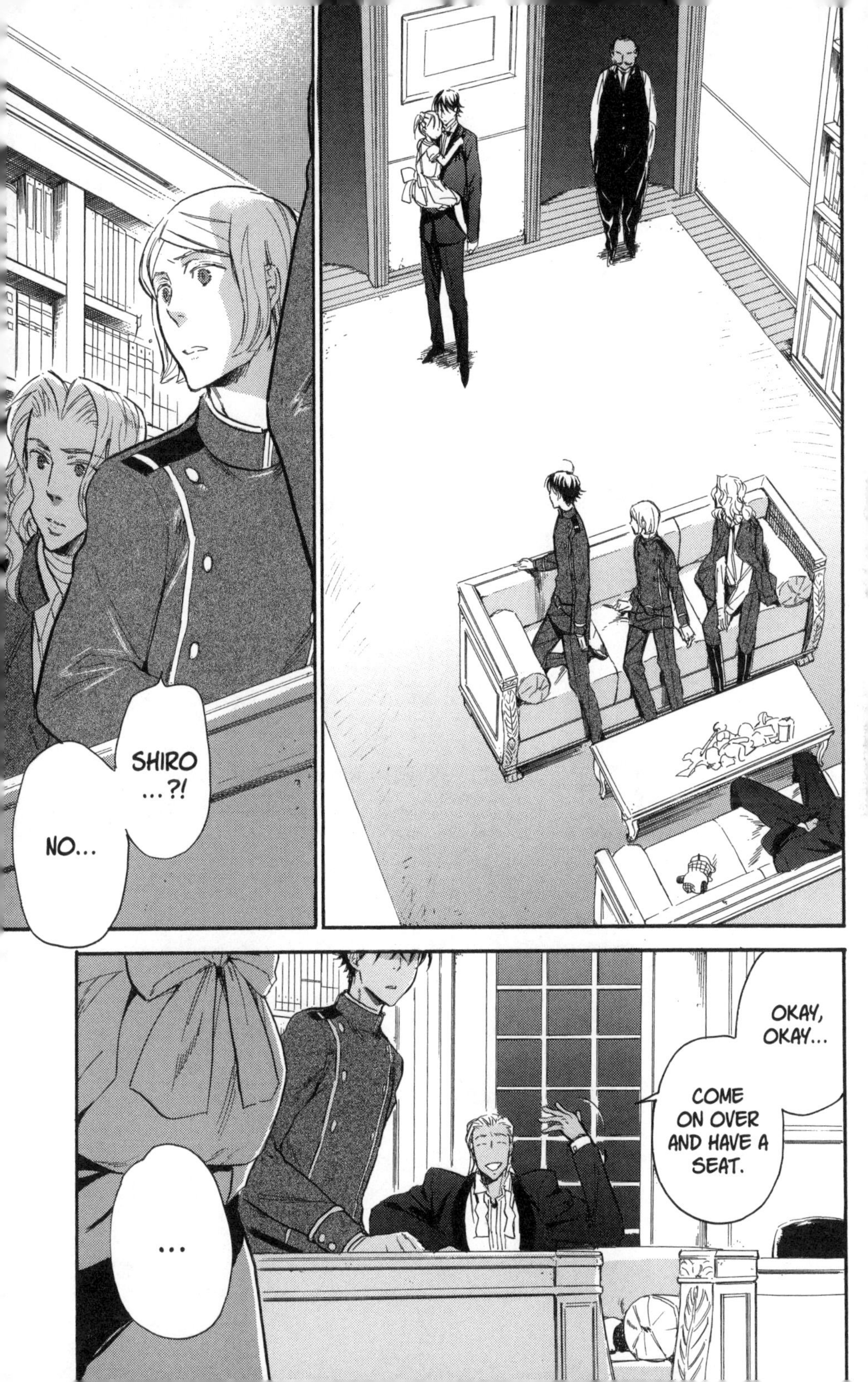
SHIRO ...?!
NO...
OKAY, OKAY...
COME ON OVER AND HAVE A SEAT.
...

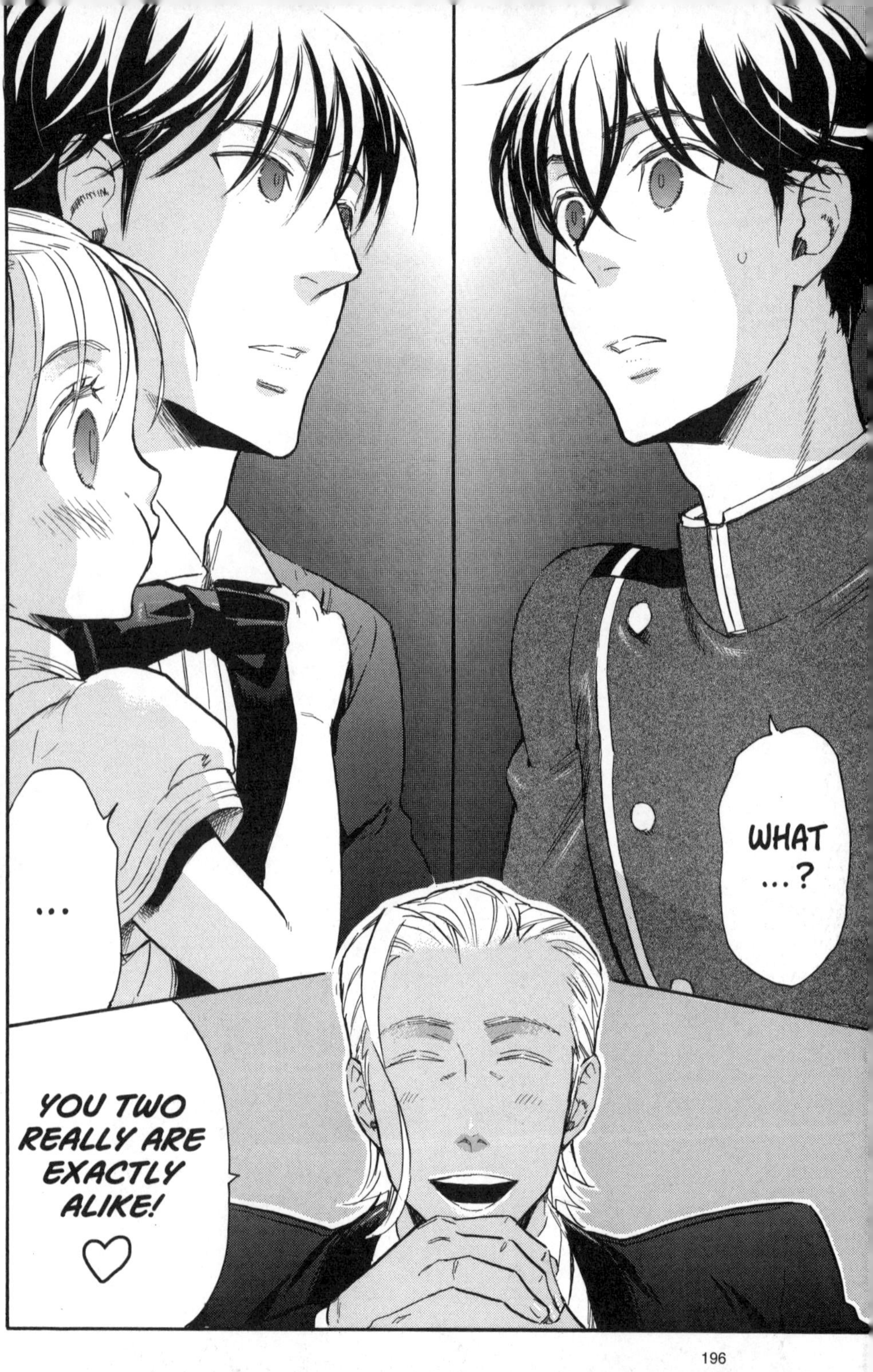
WHAT ...?
...
YOU TWO REALLY ARE EXACTLY ALIKE! ♡

afterschool charisma

VOLUME TWO

end

SHORT COMIC

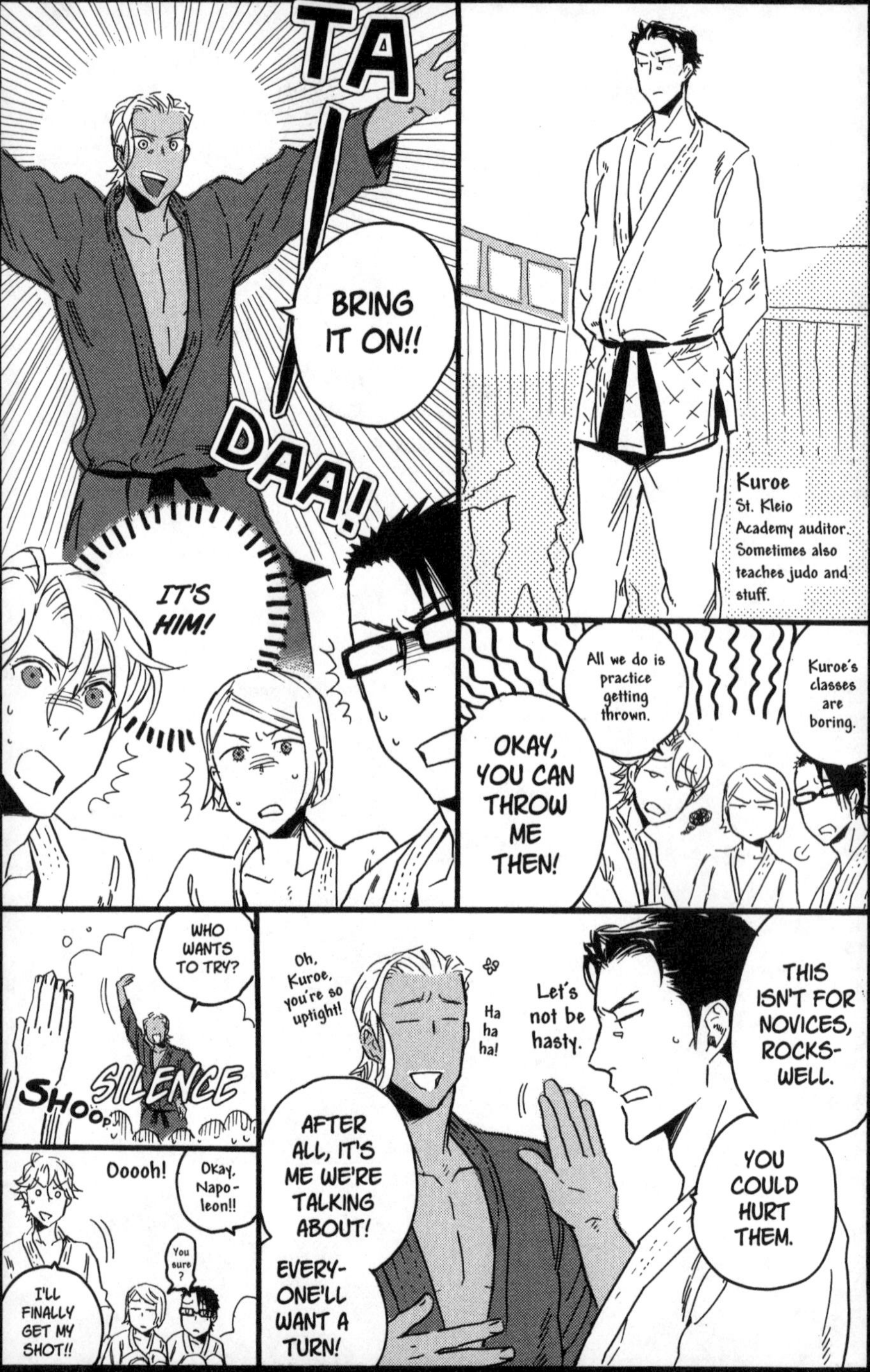

Kuroe
St. Kleio Academy auditor. Sometimes also teaches judo and stuff.
Kuroe's classes are boring.
All we do is practice getting thrown.
OKAY, YOU CAN THROW ME THEN!
TA-DAA!
BRING IT ON!!
IT'S HIM!
THIS ISN'T FOR NOVICES, ROCKSWELL.
Let's not be hasty.
Ha ha ha!
Oh, Kuroe, you're so uptight!
YOU COULD HURT THEM.
AFTER ALL, IT'S ME WE'RE TALKING ABOUT!
EVERYONE'LL WANT A TURN!
WHO WANTS TO TRY?
SILENCE
SHOOP
Okay, Napoleon!!
Ooooh!
You sure?
I'LL FINALLY GET MY SHOT!!

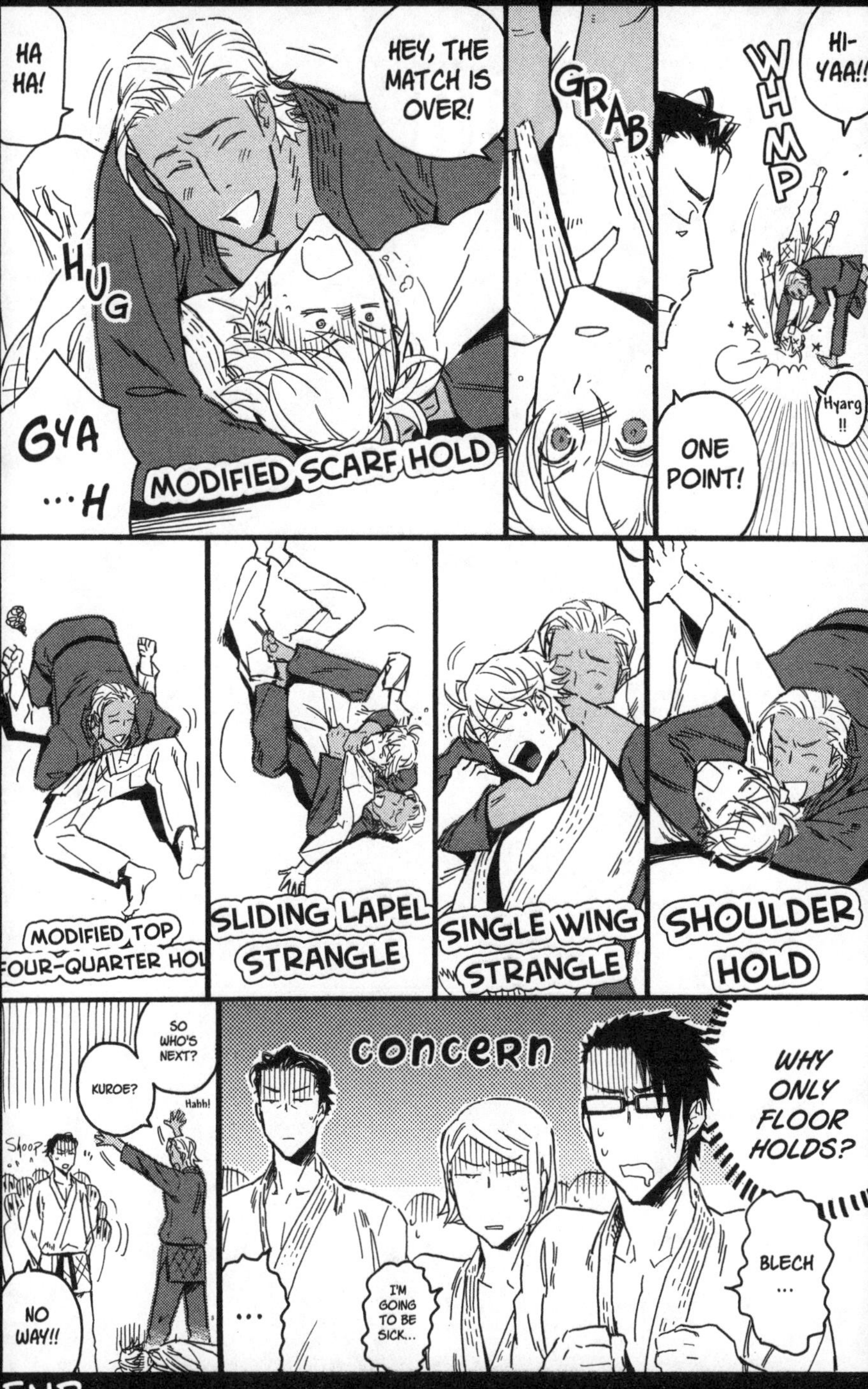
HI-YAA!!
WHMP
Hyarg !!
ONE POINT!
GRAB
HEY, THE MATCH IS OVER!
HA HA!
HUG
GYA …H
MODIFIED SCARF HOLD
SHOULDER HOLD
SINGLE WING STRANGLE
SLIDING LAPEL STRANGLE
MODIFIED TOP FOUR-QUARTER HOL
concern
WHY ONLY FLOOR HOLDS?
BLECH …
I'M GOING TO BE SICK…
…
SO WHO'S NEXT?
KUROE?
Hahh!
Shoop
NO WAY!!

END

Suekane, Kumiko.
Afterschool charisma.
Vol. 2 /
2011.
33305240648000
sa   02/21/18

AFTERSCHOOL CHARISMA
VOLUME 2
VIZ SIGNATURE EDITION

STORY & ART BY **KUMIKO SUEKANE**

© 2009 Kumiko SUEKANE/Shogakukan
All rights reserved.
Original Japanese edition "HOUKAGO NO CARISMA"
published by SHOGAKUKAN Inc.

Original Japanese cover design by Mitsuru KOBAYASHI (GENI A LÒIDE)

TRANSLATION –○– CAMELLIA NIEH
TOUCH UP ART & LETTERING –○– ERIKA TERRIQUEZ
DESIGN –○– FAWN LAU
EDITOR –○– ERIC SEARLEMAN

The stories, characters and incidents mentioned in this publication are
entirely fictional.

No portion of this book may be reproduced or transmitted in any form or by
any means without written permission from the copyright holders.

Printed in Canada

Published by VIZ Media, LLC
P.O. Box 77010
San Francisco, CA 94107

10 9 8 7 6 5 4 3 2 1

First printing, January 2011

PARENTAL ADVISORY
AFTERSCHOOL CHARISMA is rated T+
for Older Teen and is recommended for
ages 16 and up.
ratings.viz.com

www.viz.com

www.sigikki.com